SITTING RINGSIDE
VOLUME 1

BY DAVID PENZER
WITH GUY EVANS

Contact information: guyevanswcwbook@gmail.com

ISBN Information: 979-8-9903205-0-5 (Paperback Edition)
Also available in Hardcover

ALSO BY GUY EVANS

NITRO: The Incredible Rise and Inevitable Collapse of Ted Turner's WCW

Grateful (with Eric Bischoff)

CONTENTS

FOREWORD

Y ou've heard of the most likely to succeed - well, David Penzer was the *least* likely to succeed in the wrestling business.

David wasn't a wrestler, but make no mistake about it - he grew up in the business the hard way. As you will read about in the pages ahead, he was really on the 'outside looking in' for a number of years, working extremely hard just to get a break. Once he got that break, David definitely made the most of his opportunity - and I applaud him for how far he took it.

For a while, David and I used to ride in the same car together, and I always enjoyed those times on the road. You could throw out different ideas to him creatively, and he was really good at seeing details that maybe you didn't see, or helping you get back on track in that department.

He was just very good at his job - a quick learner, reliable, and smart enough to stay away from confrontation. David caught on very quickly to some of the bullshit that goes along with the wrestling business. He didn't fall into the locker room bullshit - the 'he said/she said' type of stuff. He was like Switzerland in that aspect - neutral - knowing not to give a stupid opinion, or to get swayed too easily by the guys.

David was smart - having grown up in a very intelligent family - and after a while, he would kind of direct the younger wrestlers: *Don't fucking do that around this guy*, or *hey, be more professional* - that type of thing. In the wrestling business, you need people like that to have around, and David was a positive model of what an employee should be. He helped us all to weather the storm.

What I really appreciated is that David understood and respected the history of the business. Everybody likes to talk about the "greatest worker of all times," but the great workers of today are built on the great workers of before. David grew up watching myself and Dusty in Florida, and I don't think he ever forgot that. He gave everyone respect - and that's why he excelled from the position that he started at.

So well done, David - you did well, and you're still doing well today.

Congratulations on your book!

Kevin Sullivan
March 2024

PREFACE

As of early 2023, David Penzer and I found ourselves in a similar position. We were each in possession of various rare materials - formats, memos, multimedia and the like - pertaining to the long-defunct (but increasingly still relevant) World Championship Wrestling (WCW). For David, of course, the acquisition of these documents and files came from first-hand experience - he was the ring announcer for WCW during its absolute peak, in addition to filling numerous other roles during his tenure (1991-2001) with the company.

Conversely, I obtained my own 'treasure trove' of documents through a different kind of association with WCW, as in 2018, I first published the book, *NITRO: The Incredible Rise and Inevitable Collapse of Ted Turner's WCW* (an expanded hardcover edition followed in 2021). David had been one of over 120 interviewees for that book, but last year, I reached out to him with the idea of producing a WCW-themed *scrapbook*. It was an effort to find a home, so to speak, for at least the printed materials at long last, and soon, we began work towards that end.

After just a short time working with David, however, I realized that a 'scrapbook' would be selling his story short. As I listened more to his thoughtful remembrances of the WCW days - not to mention the times *before* he got into the wrestling business - it soon became obvious that a different kind of book was needed. Eventually, we decided upon combining our original idea with a full-length autobiographical story - so guess what? You're getting *twice* of what we first envisioned!

Sitting Ringside Vol. 1 is the story of David's personal and professional life, from his early years growing up in South Florida, to the lofty heights of WCW and the 'Monday Night Wars', and eventually, the collapse of the entire company. Our narrative concludes in late 2001, but David's story, quite obviously, didn't stop there. We cover the next chapter of David's life - aided by a similar array of bonus content (relevant to TNA, the XWF, and much more) - in *Sitting Ringside Vol. 2!*

For this volume, we hope that you enjoy both the main narrative, as well as the formats, scripts and notes which are featured in the back of the book. A quick editorial note first: we made the decision to limit, for the most part, discussions of key events and people to a specific time frame (ending in 2001). In other words, events which may have occurred *post-2001* (both positive and negative) will be discussed, at great length, in Volume *2* of this series. That fact is helpful to keep in mind when David remembers Bobby 'The Brain' Heenan, or 'Mean' Gene Okerlund, or 'Rowdy' Roddy Piper - or sadly, a long list of other such legends who have since passed on.

In any event, I consider it a privilege to help write anyone's life story, and for that, I would like to thank David for his trust in making this happen. He showed a level of dedication, enthusiasm and accessibility that is simply a dream for any collaborator. His story is unique, inspiring and captivating - and I was grateful to help him tell it.

I would also like to thank Kevin Sullivan for writing the foreword, and most importantly, you - the reader! Your ongoing support is much appreciated.

And with that, it's time to take you ringside…

Enjoy!

Guy Evans
March 2024

SITTING RINGSIDE
VOLUME 1

1:

INTRODUCING...DAVID PENZER

You know what's funny? I've been talking in front of crowds from the start.

In a galaxy far, far away - long before you ever heard my voice on a professional wrestling broadcast - you could find me *somewhere* addressing people on a microphone. Even back in elementary school, I was already getting started on honing my public speaking skills, although at the time, I probably just thought talking on the mic was *cool*. Believe it or not, I actually did the morning announcements at my school. Typically, I would also recite the pledge of allegiance to start each day. In fact, the more that I think about it, I kinda *ran* things at Tropical Elementary in Plantation, Florida - even as a fourth grader!

I mean, think about it: do you know anyone who organized a 'Presidential Primary' as a ten-year-old? I don't want to date myself here, but this would have been back in 1976 - the year that Carter ran against Ford for President. At the time, please understand that I was very, very (very!) into current events. I'd read the newspaper cover to cover. I'd watch the six o'clock news at home. I pretty much followed everything I could that had to do with politics.

Evidently, *so* fanatical was I about the election that I basically organized - with maybe a little help from a couple of teachers - our own version of it at school. I didn't get anything for doing that, by the way - but then again, I wasn't *expecting* to get anything for it, either. It was just something that I wanted to do. The assignment was to go home - to Mom, or Dad, or to your brother or sister, whoever - and discuss who *you* thought was the best candidate. You had to talk with your family about what each candidate was for - what each candidate was against - and ultimately make a decision (because as ten-year-old

1

kids, we had that kind of insight, apparently) about who was the best option.

Now come on, that's pretty funny. Can you even *imagine* a kid doing that today? Back then, things were a little bit more civil, I guess - but even still, I look back on that now and think, 'If I would've done that years later' - you know, ran my own Presidential Primary at school - 'I could've been on the *Tonight Show*…or *Good Morning America*…or something!'

So you're telling me, responds my son whenever I recount this story, *that you basically peaked in elementary school.*

Very funny, Jarrett.

I guess if I *did* peak back then - given the events which ultimately transpired - I must've made one helluva comeback.

Early school days in Plantation, Florida

Famously, the '76 election ended up as a narrow win for Carter, who often gets talked about as the worst President in the history of our country (probably because he was the *nicest* President we ever had, but that's a different story). In any event, by the time Carter was settling into his new surroundings, I was soon to be enamored with an engrossing new interest: professional wrestling.

I find myself saying this a lot, but it was a totally different world back then. In terms of entertainment options, we only had six TV channels to choose from, and for the most part, no one ever heard of getting another TV set - or even the concept of watching multiple shows in multiple rooms. Therefore, as kids, we pretty much watched whatever Mom and Dad were watching. If that meant Monday Night Baseball, for example (and yes, there *was* a Monday Night Baseball at one time), it was basically either that - or no TV at all.

The exception to that rule, as people who grew up in that era will remember, tended to happen on the weekends. One Saturday around noon, my cousin Jeff and I had the remote in our hands, but we couldn't find anything to watch. Finally, Jeff turned to me and said, 'Hey, let's turn on wrestling.'

Wrestling, I responded quizzically.

What's wrestling?

He turned the dial to Channel 6, and lo and behold, there it was - *Championship Wrestling from Florida (CWF)*. I'm going back 47 years in my memory bank now, but I still remember that very first episode. There was a wild brawl with all the babyfaces and heels coming out. You had two of the most charismatic wrestlers getting involved – 'Superstar' Billy Graham and 'The American Dream' Dusty Rhodes, who were feuding with each other - and they were bleeding all over the place. Let me tell you, if you had even the *slightest* inclination to like professional wrestling, this kind of stuff was going to get you hooked.

And *hooked* I was - seemingly in an instant.

Ever since I watched that first episode with my cousin, there's never been a time when I *wasn't* hooked on this business. Even as I write this, I'm thinking about an amazing piece of business which went down just *yesterday* - the press conference for *WrestleMania 40*. While on Thursday nights, I usually spend some time at my community clubhouse - you know, hang out for a bit, have a couple of drinks, play a little trivia - I was glued to my TV at home instead. I sat there *captivated* by four of the greatest entertainers in the industry ('The Rock' Dwayne Johnson, Cody Rhodes, Roman Reigns and Seth Rollins) as they played out an incredible story of their own - and let the record show that it was a hell of a moment!

At this point, I've been around pro wrestling for decades. I haven't just watched it - I've *lived it*. Nevertheless, it *still* fascinates me - just like that 11-year-old kid who watched CWF on Channel 6, every Saturday from noon-to-one, each and every week without fail.

As wrestling fans will be aware of, Eddie Graham was the owner, promoter and booker of CWF. Eddie had a well-known *shoot* background, and accordingly, he liked to bring in wrestlers of a similar description. Most of the matches on the one-hour CWF TV show were one-sided 'squash' matches (presented as such to build up new talent or occasionally, promote an angle here or there), with a characteristically stiff style of holds and counterholds. Usually, the finishing move to a match would be something like a body slam or an elbow drop - much different than the mainstream style of today.

Eddie's son Mike formed a tag-team with Steve Keirn, and they did about as much of the high-flying stuff as you could see back then. Now let me be clear: when I say 'high-flying', they did spots like a 'dropdown, leapfrog, dropkick' kind of sequence - and *that*, by the way, would pop the crowd tremendously. In comparison to the rest of the show, they would come out and do these crazy matches, and although people would probably yawn at what they did today, it was really quite incredible for the time.

4

Subsequently, provided he was in the main event, Dusty would come out and do *his* style, where he would brawl, bleed, and, of course, go over!

At the time that I started watching, Dusty was absolutely *on fire* as a babyface. He pretty much drove the entire promotion - he was *the* star, *the* man...*the* top guy in the Florida territory. When CWF would do shows from the old Fort Lauderdale National Guard Armory, which I attended, we would get Dusty about twice a year. When they announced he was coming back at the shows, it would be an automatic sellout - either you got tickets during intermission, or you didn't get 'em at all.

People often talk about what Dusty meant to the fans in Florida, but he really transcended the state. He went to Georgia Championship Wrestling - where he became the star of that show - and then he would pop up in the WWF. I remember word spreading about Dusty among hardcore wrestling fans (the ones who would trade tapes, put out newsletters and organize fan clubs), around the time promoters started booking him as a special attraction. There would be times when he'd be gone from Florida for a couple of weeks, but he'd always have a presence on that show regardless. He would tape promos in order to extend whatever feuds were going on, and after a while, you'd start to recognize where he was by the sets used in the videos. He'd tape something in front of the WWF ring, for example - on the floor where Vince used to interview people - and he'd say something like, 'Next week, I'm coming back - and don't forget Joe Leduc, we got unfinished business!'

Sitting at home, you'd say to yourself, 'Okay, he taped that in the WWF, and then he taped *that* in Georgia Championship Wrestling - that's their set.' At the same time, Dusty would also tape a bunch of stuff in Florida to use in those other territories! Consequently, by the time his star started to rise, Dusty was seemingly *everywhere*, enjoying a status that was - outside of maybe Andre the Giant - relatively unique in the wrestling business.

I actually attended one of Dusty's most famous matches - the night in which he wrestled (under the guise of his masked 'Midnight Rider' persona) Ric Flair, for the NWA World Heavyweight Title, at the Miami Beach Convention Center. Prior to the match, Dusty had lost a 'lights out' cage match to Kevin Sullivan, with the stipulation being that the loser had to leave the state of Florida for sixty days. In Miami, however, the 'Rider' showed up to beat Flair for the belt, seemingly avoiding the condition - as agreed to in advance - that he would reveal his identity if defeated (*and* face a one-year suspension as a result).

When us fans left the arena that night, we all thought that the 'Midnight Rider' was the World champion. That was on a Wednesday, but once we turned on the TV come Saturday, the storyline took an unexpected turn. CWF viewers were told that as President of the NWA (the largest governing body for wrestling in the country), Bob Geigel needed to know who was *really* behind the 'Midnight Rider' mask. After all, it was explained, Geigel needed to make travel arrangements for the new champion - and plane tickets couldn't be bought for an anonymous wrestler!

Ultimately, Dusty refused to take off his mask for Geigel - at the risk of triggering that one-year suspension - and therefore, he was forced to relinquish the belt. That was *brilliant* booking, by the way. It established that Dusty could beat Flair for the title, while also raising anticipation for a repeat championship match between them.

Man, I *still* get goosebumps thinking about that stuff.

Once Dusty left the promotion, Championship Wrestling from Florida - in my opinion, at least - never fully recovered. In its heyday, however, its shows were drawing between 3000-5000 people - every Wednesday Night in Miami Beach, mind you - all based upon a one-hour TV show.

Looking back, while CWF's production quality (if I can use that term) was pretty much horrible, that's what sort of made it cool, to be honest with you. Nowadays, I suppose you could say it was the epitome of an old-school wrestling promotion, especially with how it was run, by Eddie Graham primarily, as a truly *professional* organization (*You give the same effort*, Eddie reportedly instructed many of his talent, *whether you wrestle in front of five people - or five thousand*).

In terms of how he represented Florida wrestling, Eddie (previously a huge draw himself as a wrestler) developed an incredible amount of credibility statewide. His untimely death in 1985 was a front-page story on the local sport pages, and numerous editorials were written on his impact both in and out of the ring. "Eddie Graham...real name Eddie Gossett," reported the *Tampa Tribune*, "...had the image of a man in a relentless and often brutal pursuit of victory in the ring... [but he] was also known for his compassion and benevolence beyond it.

"...In 1980, Senator Richard Stone awarded to Graham - [for his civic contributions] - an American flag which flew over the White House."

Similarly, as the iconic voice for each and every broadcast, Gordon Solie legitimized the entire promotion. We probably took Gordon for granted back then, but he was absolutely amazing in his ability to tell a story with words (and sometimes, his mere inflections alone). If you didn't know any better, you might have thought Gordon wasn't excited about the action, but when you go back and watch those old shows, you can see that he *was* - he just wasn't over-the-top about it. He treated wrestling the way it should be treated by an announcer - he called it like a sport.

My favorite aspect of CWF used to happen twice every hour. Gordon would have something pre-taped for every town in the territory that week: *Ladies and gentlemen, Championship Wrestling from Florida is coming to Fort Lauderdale and the Fort Lauderdale*

7

National Guard Armory, this coming Friday night. Match time is eight o'clock - tickets on sale at the box office.

Now keep in mind, you didn't know what the card was until Gordon told you what it was. Neither did you know what the feuds were - you had no frickin' idea. You couldn't predict when the big angles were going to happen; in fact, you didn't even know what 'angles' were!

But if you tuned in, Gordon would run down the card, which in those days, may have only been four matches or so. *For the Florida Tag Team titles,* he'd say, *Mike Graham and Steve Keirn will defend against Mr. Saito and Mr. Sato with Masao Hattori in their corner. Also, the Polish Power Ivan Putski will take on Big, Bad Bobby Duncum...*

And so on. As simple as it sounds, the way he did *that* was a thing of beauty.

Then, during one of the commercial breaks – and this was my favorite part - they'd have all the heels talking about the upcoming matches in pre-taped interviews, and in the other commercial break, all the babyfaces would do the same. It was just one of the elements that made me obsessed with professional wrestling, the larger-than-life characters, and how it was all put together.

Obsessed is definitely the right word. I made my parents get cable just to see Georgia Championship Wrestling. I read every wrestling newsletter there was. I got every wrestling magazine. I would actually sit on the floor of the store reading those magazines - to the point where if I bought ten of them, the owner would let me take the rest for free. I used to cut out ads in the paper for wrestling shows, look at them and say to myself, '*This* is the one I'm gonna go to!'

Before long, I started to daydream a little.

Was it possible - as far-fetched though it seemed - that someday, *I* could be a part of this?

8

2:
MIND GAMES

For the longest time, the wrestling business was a mystery to me. This might sound ridiculous in hindsight, but if you were only *reading* about a wrestler in another part of the country, you probably didn't even know how to pronounce their name (case in point: Ole Anderson was *Ol' Anderson*, as far as I knew, and Verne Gagne was pronounced *Verne Gange*).

Throughout my early years of being a fan, my dad (better known to others as Dr. Bill Penzer, PhD, a clinical and organizational psychologist) would usually take me to the matches. When I think about those memories now, it's hard not to crack up a little, mostly because Dad would sit there calmly in all of the chaos! Irrespective of the fans jumping up and down, he would relax and enjoy some reading material - something like a *Time Magazine*, a *Newsweek* or a *Psychology Today*. It was just a little bit different than the type of literature that I loved - *Inside Wrestling, The Wrestler, Apter mags...*

My dad was born in the Bronx, as was I, on May 21st, 1966, and we lived in New York until I was six (my mom, also a Bronx native, didn't work, but she raised my brother Michael and I at home). On the surface, it may have seemed like a fairly conventional arrangement for the time, but in fact, we had a pretty unique family dynamic. I actually grew up with another sibling - and she was born in Korea.

Back then, a lot of babies had sadly been abandoned in Vietnam and Korea. A campaign was started for American parents to adopt some of those children, and while it never became as well-known as *USA for Africa*, for example, the program helped a lot of Asian kids find new homes in the States. Both of my parents were very involved in that effort, and they ended up adopting Jodi when my brother and I were still young.

9

Jodi had been abandoned on the streets of Taegu, and subsequently, she spent time in a foster home before my parents adopted her. Without going into too many details - she's a very private person and would rather I didn't - her story has a very happy ending. Jodi went on to have a wonderful life, and we all count adopting her as the best thing to ever happen to our family.

Given what I ended up doing with my life, one of the few memories I have of New York is pretty ironic in hindsight. We lived in an apartment in Yonkers, and often my Grandma Sadie would take me outside in my carriage. What's funny is that she had this way of introducing *me*, in this very kind of formal manner, to the people we encountered on our travels. *Hello, Mister Policeman*, she would say. *Meet David.*

Hello, Mister Trashman - meet David!

In 1972, we left New York and moved to South Florida, following my dad getting hired as an organizational psychologist at Eastern Airlines (the original incarnation of the airline - "number one in the sun" was their tagline). Unfortunately, my dad quickly became miserable in the job, and although he had hardly any money in his pocket, he decided to develop his own practice - *Center for Counseling Services* - based out of Plantation, Florida.

An ad which ran in the October 3rd, 1976 edition of the Fort Lauderdale News

At the time, the society-wide stigma around mental health was *just* starting to go away. There's no comparison to today, obviously, but at least in our area (and the Jewish middle-class communities we knew in South Florida), there was kind of an understanding that, *hey, you can talk things out, and it helps.*

Once my dad started helping people, word soon got around, and in time, he ended up having 40 people working for him. He had this big facility with maybe 15 or 20 offices inside, and as the one who started it all, he'd get a piece of the action, so to speak, of what everybody else was making.

That entire industry was *rolling* in cash back then. This was before insurance stepped in and changed things - back then, believe it or not, they were still paying 100% of the fee. Towards the end of my dad's active therapy career, he would be lucky to get 30% or 40%, but when he started, it was *100%*.

Well, back in the '70s and '80s, if you were charging $100 an hour, multiplied by 40 hours a week...*you* do the math, I guess. For a kid from the Bronx, I guess you could say that my dad did pretty well - and before long, he became a sought-after speaker at various professional conferences. He was asked to comment on stories about pertinent mental health topics, and ultimately, he authored three influential books about cancer (specifically, how to deal emotionally with the cancer diagnosis of a loved one). For these reasons, among many others, I admired my father greatly.

Sure, I may have idolized the stars of professional wrestling, but from the start, Dad was *truly* my hero.

"Success in life is not complicated," he once wrote, "but it demands effort and discipline. Whether it be school, work, a significant relationship, playing a sport or taking up a hobby, it demands showing up, taking action, [and] trying your very best."

While only at the start of my journey, I was determined to carry his advice with me.

11

Probably because of my dad, there's been one consistent factor throughout my life: if I was ever interested in something, I'd usually find a way of making it happen.

I never put these pieces together until later, but I definitely got a certain entrepreneurial streak from him, too. It started real early with me: as a 16-year-old, for instance, I set up a mobile DJ company with my best friend Lenny Horowitz - *D & L Sound Productions* is what we called it. Before I knew it, I was out DJing every weekend, to the extent that I didn't really go to any of my school events. I didn't go to the dances, nor did I show up at the football games. Instead, I was out there *working* on the weekends, which actually was a lot of fun for me. It wasn't that my parents said, 'Hey, you gotta go to work' - no, I enjoyed doing it. On a good night, Lenny and I could make up to $300 per gig, and soon, with a bunch of weddings and 'sweet 16' parties under my belt, I found myself getting more and more comfortable on the microphone.

As a Senior, I then hit the radio airwaves (using the alias 'Dave Lawrence') on Piper High School's student station, WKPX-FM - the *first* of its kind in the Southeastern United States. Although I was officially enrolled at J.P. Taravella High, Piper offered a two-hour radio class to students across the Broward County district - provided you met certain requirements first. In my case, because I already had my accreditations as a Senior, I only needed to show up to two classes a day, meaning I could do my radio deal from nine-to-noon each morning.

A local reporter observed life at the station in February 1984:

Dave Penzer, or Dave Lawrence as he's known to listeners, talks fast. Real fast.

In 16 seconds, Dave, 17, can tell you the record that just played, what the next tune will be and then report a weather update.

12

"When I first was on the air, I would step on some records [talk while the music was playing] because I didn't have my timing down," said the clean-cut teen, as he reached for a pre-recorded cassette, flipped a few electronic buttons and pulled the microphone so close to his lips that he almost kissed it.

Then the white light blinked on in Studio A at WKPX. This means 20 seconds remain before the currently playing song is over.

Twenty seconds is all Dave has to make sure his fingers are going to hit the correct switches and that he isn't going to flub his lines.

"That's all for Dave Lawrence. Tracy Marlo will strut her stuff next on WKPX, South Florida's best music."

Tracy winced at Dave's ad-lib remark.

That summer of 1984, I did the night shift on-air - eight-to-eleven. At the time, I was a big *General Hospital* fan, and Jack Wagner, the star of the show, had a song out called *All I Need*, originally made as the 'love theme' for Frisco, his character, and Felicia (his co-star played by Kristina Malandro, who would later marry Wagner in real-life). In essence, it was just a backing song for their on-screen romance, and I don't even know if they intended it for release or not.

Anyway, I called up ABC, the network which broadcast *General Hospital*, and got in touch with someone from the show. After telling them that I was a Senior in high school - and more importantly, a DJ who kept fielding requests for the song - I convinced *somebody* (and God knows who it is) to send the song to me. Now, to the best that anybody has ever been able to prove (let's put it this way: no one has ever proved *otherwise*), I was the first person to play that song on the radio, and it eventually hit No. 2 on the *Billboard 100* - just for the record. If I'm being totally honest, probably four people listened to my 'breaking' of the song, but hey - a first is a first.

After finishing up with the radio station at Piper, I got a call one day from Tramonte Watts, the evening DJ on Y100 - the number one pop radio station in the Miami/Fort Lauderdale area. I used to listen to Tramonte every night, so just imagine my reaction - the phone rings, and it's, 'Hey, David Penzer, this is Tramonte Watts from Y100.'

13

Yeah, right, I thought. *Hey Lenny - you need a little work on those impressions, bud.*

But it was Tramonte, alright - and he was calling to offer me an internship, potentially with the chance to move up at Y100 over time. As I had just enrolled at the University of Florida, I ended up saying 'no' to the opportunity - and for a while, part of me regretted that. After all, the dream of the wrestling business seemed like a remote possibility, and I always figured I'd do *something* on a mic.

Everything seemed to be heading in that same direction, whether it was the mobile DJ business that I ran, or the high school radio gig I had just wrapped up. But regardless of what I was doing, my dad remained firmly in my corner:

David, you can do anything you want to do.

He really believed that. He really thought that I could do whatever I put my mind to - even if, as I was about to find out, he sometimes had to do it for me.

On that note: this story makes me so sad to think about, but it's the reality of life - it happened.

On December 31st, 1986, I was supposed to be DJing solo at a New Year's event. There was just one problem: I had a massive anxiety attack before the gig started, to the point where - and I'm not kidding you - I literally had to push myself to do *anything*. I basically became a spectator standing in the corner, helplessly looking over at the makeshift DJ.

And who was the makeshift DJ, you ask?

"David!" yelled my dad across the room.

"Just tell me what fucking record to play!"

14

That's what my dad would do for me.

College is where I first developed issues with anxiety. As I was part of a fraternity, I'd gotten into smoking weed, which was somewhat of a bigger deal than it is today (now that it's legal, I don't touch the stuff, ironically). I guess that inadvertently, marijuana had the opposite effect on me than advertised, especially after I was given a bad joint and went into a full-blown panic. It was only the first episode, unfortunately, of many to come thereafter.

If you know me, you'll know that I'm an open book when it comes to the topic of mental health - and particularly, the battle that I have fought (and continue to fight) in that same arena. Quite frankly, it's a struggle that continues to this very day - to this very *minute*, as a matter of fact. If you have some knowledge about anxiety and panic attacks, it might make sense to think about potential triggers, but in my case, nearly anything could set it off. Even the simple act of going to the movies, for example - specifically exiting a dark theater and going into the light outside - could be enough, I learned over time, to be an inciting incident. Some mornings, I would wake up in bed and feel wonderful, but other times, the anxiety would hit, and it'd be full-on panic mode.

We've all heard stories of successful people, at the height of their notoriety, unexpectedly quitting what they're doing - and often, mental health is the culprit. I may not have been where they've been, in terms of their specific career choice or occupation, but I've been *there* - if that makes sense to you. The mind is a very powerful thing, and when you're in the middle of a battle 'upstairs', it wants to *win*.

In my opinion, there's a lot of merit to the idea of anxiety having a genetic basis. Before me, my dad had his own challenges – and he was pretty open about what he experienced. "Back in the '70s," he told *The Sun Sentinel*, "I went through five years of agoraphobia [an

15

anxiety disorder]. So I understand what [people] are talking about. I lived the nightmare."

As I got older, Dad shared some of those struggles with me. *Do you remember*, he asked me, *when I took you and your brother to the Dolphins game?*

Yeah, I said, curious as to why he brought it up.

We had to leave in the third quarter, he said.

Right, I replied, *you had an emergency that needed tending to*.

No, David, he revealed, *I was having a panic attack that day*.

I just couldn't stay there, he said.

One time, I witnessed a case like that for myself. During a visit to Boston College, we all thought Dad was having a heart attack in the hotel room. They called an ambulance to come get him – and he went to the hospital as I recall - but it turned out, in the end, that he had suffered another panic attack.

Dad used these experiences to propel the writing of *Getting Back Up From An Emotional Down*, a book I know he was very proud of. "I was the helpless victim," he wrote in the introduction, "of a very serious and debilitating emotional upheaval. Darkness covered my soul. It was then that I was simultaneously patient and doctor and, strangely enough, doing better treating others than my therapist and I were doing treating me."

Now that I think about it, my dad's own mental health journey was - at least in part - probably what made him so great as a psychologist (and, in helping him provide guidance to me). I know that every time I'd have an attack of my own, I could pick up the phone and call him. He would sit on the phone with me for hours - or however long it took to talk me down.

16

It's hard to understate my dad's impact on me, and candidly, he saved my life on many occasions.

There was a time in which I had a massive onset of anxiety while driving home from college with all my stuff - to the point where I couldn't even get behind the wheel. I reached out to my dad, and he had a bunch of appointments on his schedule, so it wasn't like he didn't have a ton of stuff to do or anything. Nonetheless, he dropped it all, flew up to Gainesville and drove me back home.

Another regretful episode happened in 1987, when I actually had tickets to go to *WrestleMania III* with Lenny. I had my plane ticket booked, the hotel reservation ready, but two days in advance, I got horrible anxiety and ended up not going. As my parents didn't have pay-per-view at the time, I watched the historic Hogan-Andre match at a friend's house instead.

To coin a phrase from the wrestling business, the anxiety definitely went *over* on me that night.

When it comes to my time at the University of Florida, I often joke - as the former social chair in my fraternity - that I basically majored in partying. I guess I didn't realize you also had to go to class to get good grades, and I lasted about a year-and-a-half before seeing the writing on the wall.

To this day, I probably couldn't pass an algebra class if my life depended on it. You know those scenarios where you have to work out how fast Train A is moving, or at what point it meets Train B? Believe me, *my tutors would need tutors* to help me understand that.

Curiously, I once had a brief vision of being a meteorologist. Working as a weather man seemed like a form of communication that I could excel in, but all that stopped after taking a single oceanography class. I didn't realize you actually need to know the science behind what you're talking about – as opposed to just reading something off a teleprompter, pointing to a board and rambling on about the cold front coming in.

I figured some nerd at the National Hurricane Center took care of all that. Oh, but how wrong I was! You need to know a ton about atmospheric pressures, tides, marine life, ecosystems, and a *whole* lot more, buddy. My head was spinning after about six weeks.

Not to steal his gimmick or anything, but realizing that I didn't know anything about math and science left me, for lack of a better word, in something of an *abyss*. Someone recently pointed out that I'm listed as an alumnus at the University of Florida, and that's a pretty hysterical fact to me. In reality, I dropped out of there in unceremonious fashion, and although my dad continued to provide his encouragement, things had definitely hit a snag at this point.

Of the few hazy memories that stand out from college, I do remember watching 'Tuesday Night Titans' - the short-lived, bizarre, zany wrestling-talk show produced by the WWF - and daydreaming aloud with my roommate.

Man, we would say to each other.

If we could just go and have a drink with Bobby 'The Brain' Heenan and 'Mean' Gene Okerlund, that would be the coolest thing in the world. If we ever make it in life, maybe there could be an auction or something - you know, with the chance to meet them as a prize. Maybe that chance will come to us one day.

Yeah, I'd say while the TV screen flickered.

Imagine that.

3:
BOB'S PROMISE

After dropping out of college, there was a period where I really couldn't manage. Between a shrink that my dad found for me - and the time he devoted personally to the cause - I was in a massive amount of therapy. All I wanted was to start to find my way in life, but unfortunately, I didn't really know how.

As far as I was concerned, I had lost my way, once and for all - and I was *never* going to be okay again. I was truly convinced of it, and I had dozens of conversations - many of them ridiculous, in hindsight - with my dad on the same subject.

I'm just never gonna feel better, I would tell him.

You say that every time, David, he would counter.

After a while, I would sort of laugh whenever my dad would say that, because part of me - somewhere deep down - *knew* that kind of talk was ridiculous.

Nonetheless, for the moment, my motivation was at an all-time low. I had the anxiety attacks to contend with. Pot was out of the window due to it being an apparent trigger of all those problems. I didn't drink at the time, and I had precious little in terms of a social life. Overall, it was quite the contrast from being the social chair in a fraternity - and I didn't quite see a way out.

All of a sudden, I viewed myself as a miserable person - and someone badly in need of regrouping. For about six months or so, I would even say that I was non-functional, to be honest with you - unless I absolutely *had* to go and do something. Even in those situations, I would basically have to fake it to get through things, and

19

consequently, any grand plans, future goals or lofty ambitions were totally off the table. Wrestling was a distant memory - I didn't think it was achievable, anyway - and I had enough to worry about on a day-to-day basis.

Finally, I started to think about my predicament and ponder the obvious question: *What the hell am I doing?*

In the interim, my dad became a 50% partner in his friend's limousine rental business. His friend had been looking to expand the company for a while, which originally had only one limo in its inventory. My dad stepped in to buy another one - getting half of the company as a result - and I went to work driving the old vehicle.

Oh, the stories I could tell you about that job. How about two 300lb people having sex in downtown Fort Lauderdale - during lunch hour, I might add - with the limo rocking back and forth. Did I paint a good enough picture for you? *I'll* never forget it, that's for sure…and not in a good way.

Outside of those - shall we say, interesting experiences - the driving gig went pretty well. Things were at least starting to head in a positive direction, and gradually, I started finding some ways to cope.

What happened next is a coincidence almost too good to be true.

In kind of a freak situation, we discovered that my dad worked with someone who was connected to the wrestling business. Now, remember - even as late as the 1980s, wrestling was still very much considered a closed industry. There were no internships - that's a laughable concept - and you couldn't go work in the mail room of a wrestling company or something. As time progressed, it eventually became easier to establish a foot in the door, but back then, you really needed someone to say, 'Here, I'll unlock this door and let you into a world that nobody's supposed to see.'

That person, for me, became Dr. Red Roberts (shoot name: Dr. Michael Brannon, a legit psychologist who still practices in South Florida). It turned out that a guy who worked for my dad's counseling center was friends with Red, who had portrayed a villainous doctor gimmick locally for over a decade. Essentially, Red's schtick involved him trying to outwit opponents with his psychological expertise - I believe he once had a wrestler *Baker Acted*, for example, in order to avoid an upcoming match! Red later formed a tag-team with Rusty Brooks, who had made some appearances on WWF television and consequently, was a pretty big deal on the Florida indy scene.

"Doc was a genius," remarked one local wrestler of Red, in comments given to the *Miami New Times*. "He really worked the crowd. He used the...I'm-smarter-than-you, I'm smarter-than-everybody-in-the-room [thing to great effect]."

According to legend, Red first got started in the business after working in a youth rehab facility, where many of the occupants were wrestling fans. After completing his undergraduate and postgraduate studies in counseling psychology, he later claimed that becoming a wrestler had helped offset the cost of his medical training. "Wrestling paid my way through my master's program and doctoral program," he affirmed to one reporter at the *Sun Sentinel*.

Beginning in 1987, Red then got involved with an upstart company called the Global Wrestling Alliance (GWA), which had its operations based out of Hollywood, Florida. The GWA took a unique method of raising capital for its new venture: they put the company up on the penny stock market, and an initial public offering raised more than $500,000. Through his contacts in the psychology world, my dad managed to get a message through to Red, and in doing so, he basically let him know: *Hey, my son loves wrestling, and he can talk on a mic. If you ever need someone, he'll be there for you.*

The booker for the new promotion was Bob Roop, a pretty big name in regional wrestling during the '70s. Joining Bob (and Red) in the endeavor was Larry Malenko - aka 'The Great Malenko', and

21

father of Joe and Dean Malenko – who ran the GWA training school in Davie, Florida. Dave Heath, who later went on to achieve fame in the WWF as Gangrel, happened to be one of the students at the school, as was Norman Smiley, ultimately one of the more respected workers in the entire business. At a price tag of $1,500, aspiring wrestlers got 30 lessons at the facility - the equivalent of paying $4,050 in inflation-adjusted dollars today.

The *Orlando Sentinel* covered the GWA training school story in tongue-in-cheek fashion:

Those who say that Florida is lagging behind the rest of the nation in providing quality education should take note of the Sunshine State's lead in one key field of study. Florida now has three professional schools designed to fill the pressing need for more trained professional wrestlers.

Apparently, the sustained increase in popularity that professional wrestling has enjoyed over the last few years has created a considerable number of job openings for those skilled in the arts of grunting, grimacing and, of course, body slamming. As a result, the business of training wrestlers has become almost as lucrative as wrestling itself.

One school, Global Wrestling Alliance of Fort Lauderdale, went public last April…applicants are not required to provide the school with SAT scores.

At first, Red, Bob, and Larry offered to have me come by the initial GWA taping at the Diplomat Hotel. I think they were just trying to be nice, more than anything. *Just hang around*, they collectively shrugged, and that's exactly what I did - hang around! I didn't really go there to do anything, and unsurprisingly, nothing really came of it.

Soon after, though, I began showing up to the GWA training school, which also functioned as the main company offices. I showed up there during the day. I showed up there during the night. I showed up whenever I could, basically, hoping that something might come of it. Finally - and amazingly - Larry Malenko started asking me some questions: *So, why are you here exactly? What are hoping to get out of this? What do you want to do here?*

Larry showed a willingness to impart some of his knowledge - and to take me under his wing. I look at that situation now and think, *Man - what are the chances that a colleague of my dad's could have helped open this door for me?* Talk about good fortune. Not only had I been lucky enough to have a reason for being there - simply in the first place - but now a guy like Larry Malenko was showing an interest in *me*.

I think a lot of it had to do with how I presented myself. In the beginning, my attitude was basically like, *how can I help you guys? I'll do anything I can to help. I'll take out the frickin' garbage. I'll pass out flyers. I'll do anything I can to make your life easier, and I'll start at the absolute bottom. I just want to be here, and I just want to be a part of it - wherever that may lead.*

At the time, I was thinking to myself, 'Whatever happens with this, at least I can say that I *tried* to live my dream.'

Luckily, the guys really embraced my approach - and in some ways, who's *not* going to embrace that kind of mindset? I don't want to put myself over here, but from their standpoint, you had a decently intelligent guy (college notwithstanding!) who wanted to come in and help. He didn't want to get paid. He didn't have an expectation of getting *any* money, actually. He wasn't acting like a mark or taking pictures, or asking people for autographs. He just wanted to be around it because he loved it.

I think if I *would* have been a mark - if I had started taking pictures and shit - they would have told me, *hey, don't come around here anymore*. It would have been easy for someone like Larry Malenko to blow me off, and he probably should have at the time. I really *was* just a mark, and Larry was as old-school as they come. On the other hand, he was a super nice guy who loved the business, and fortunately, he loved to help others who did, too.

For a time, they had me work with Alex Marvez, who many wrestling fans will be familiar with, as the GWA 'street team'. Alex and I would go out to promote the shows, boost attendance at the live events, and spread the word about the promotion at-large. I actually promoted the biggest house that the GWA ever did - a combination show/fundraiser which my dad put on for the Broward County Mental Health Association. Now granted, as part of doing that, we reached out to people on the board of the Association, and other therapists who were making good money. We would say, 'If you buy two tickets to the show, or four tickets for 50 bucks each…you can either go - or, if you don't wanna go - we'll have somebody from the inner city that wouldn't normally have that opportunity go instead.' It was kind of a tax-write off for those people - but it had a good outcome for everyone involved.

GWA television eventually aired around the world - including in the UK - but its tapings acted, primarily, as a means of selling the house shows. Philosophically, the TV was made so people would want to see the blow-off to angles in-person, but to become a truly *global* entity, the company needed to expand - and to penetrate as many markets as possible. *The Tampa Tribune* picked up the story in a January 18th, 1988 article:

Forgive professional wrestlers Bob Roop and Red Roberts if they feel as though they've been caught up in the political spirit of things. As presidential candidates crisscross the country in search of support, Roop and Roberts are canvassing the state - in search of television markets.

…GWA has been around about a year, Roop and Roberts have been involved for about five months. The organization has been working in the Caribbean and points south, but now is turning its attention to Florida. They have big plans and are undertaking them with a no holds-barred attitude.

"We are the only publicly owned alliance," said Roop, who with Roberts was in town Wednesday attempting to sell the product to local television stations. "We sold penny stocks and made $1 million. That's a lot of capital behind us."

The working capital is important, of course, but now, television is the highest priority.

"Television markets are the key," said Roop, who explained that GWA intends to shoot matches around the state.

When it came to what role I might play in the promotion, I was realistic - in other words, I knew I had no athletic ability. The guys weren't going to put me in the ring to do anything - but I *could* talk on the microphone. By this point, I knew I could entertain a crowd if needed.

Ring announcing was always going to be my 'in', and I expressed that desire to Larry whenever we talked in his office. The only problem was that Bob and Red already had a ring announcer for television - some Elvis-impersonator guy whose involvement predated mine - but I kept hanging around regardless. Finally, they came up to me and said, *Alright, here's the deal. We're gonna run a house show in Clewiston, Florida. This is your chance, kid - you can ring announce this show for us.*

Almost in disbelief, I drove over to Clewiston for the show and realized something: I still wasn't totally *smart* to the business. I obviously knew that the people on the show weren't going to be hurting each other, but I wasn't sure about how it all went down in practice.

Now granted, I had seen them going over stuff at the GWA tapings. I knew it was *essentially* a work, and I knew there was a booker who put together the stories. It wasn't like I was 11 years old again - when I bought the business as a shoot - but still, I just wasn't...*sure*.

Look, we're talking about 1988 here - a time before most of the exposés, documentaries and books came out on the wrestling business. It was right around the time when people were *starting* to get smart - a little bit - and certainly, I had a subscription to all the wrestling newsletters. In other words, I knew what I knew - but what I didn't know was a whole lot more.

When I got to the Clewiston show, they gave me the card and my eyes went straight to the main event: Iron Sheik against Corporal

25

Kirchner. In the back of my mind, I thought, 'Okay. They're not gonna try and hurt each other - they're gonna try and entertain the crowd.' At the same time, I thought to myself, 'But do they like each other? Do they interact with each other? Are they in, like, *separate* dressing rooms?'

I just didn't know.

Before the event got underway, I found myself in the dressing room when Iron Sheik walked in. He went around the room greeting everybody: *How are you, sir? How are you, sir? How are you…*

He then turned to look at me: *How are you, sir?*

Now, think about the mark in me for a second. Outwardly, I was just like, 'Good, thank you, sir. How are you?' But inside, I wanted to scream from the earth above: *I JUST MET THE IRON SHEIK - AND HE ASKED ME HOW I WAS!*

Next, Corporal Kirchner came in and he and Sheik - remember, they were booked against each other in the main event - joined together in a huge embrace: *How have you been? It's so great to see you…so what happened with Vince?*

Dude - lightbulb.

Done.

I get it now, I thought. *This is a total fucking work.*

They're all friends.

I can't say I was surprised, necessarily, but again, I didn't know for *sure* - nobody in my position did. I had never been in a dressing room where two guys on a national level - who had previously been involved in a major feud together - happened to be around each other.

26

Now, you might point to the fact that a year earlier, the Iron Sheik (ironically) had been caught in a car with Jim Duggan, despite each of them being on opposite ends of the face/heel spectrum. It became big news on a national level, with various outlets, including the *Orlando Sentinel*, making note of it in their sport pages:

Perhaps you missed the news, but two professional wrestlers -- Hacksaw and the Iron Sheik -- were arrested this week when a New Jersey state trooper found marijuana and cocaine in their car.

Correct me if I'm wrong, wrestling fans, but aren't Hacksaw and the Iron Sheik bitter enemies in the ring?

While that incident had been well-publicized, I still didn't know the extent of wrestling being a *total* show to the fans. I didn't know that the guys gave each other hugs and caught up on their families before the matches. I didn't know that rather than hate each other, they truly had a lot of affection for each other. I didn't know they basically shared the same fraternity - the fraternity of wrestling.

Now that I *did* know, it didn't change my mind about what I thought of the business - if anything, it made me respect the guys more. It didn't all come as a big shock, but like I said before - *lightbulb*.

In a way, there were no more questions to be answered - other than this one, of course: *So how far, exactly, am I gonna be able to take this wild ride?*

I don't even know if I got paid for that first show. Maybe I got 20 bucks or something - I can't remember. All I know is that the experience, in and of itself, had been priceless.

A lot of memories flash back as I'm writing this. I'll never forget 'Exotic' Adrian Street, for example, proudly showing me his merch stand on display. Adrian was so far ahead of his time in that part of

27

the business - and in many other areas - partially because he had gone through the Memphis territory (and unless you were Jerry Lawler or the person wrestling him in the main event, it wasn't great money in Memphis. You needed to learn how to adapt and sell those gimmicks). In Clewiston, Adrian had a '45' single that he sang on which he used as his entrance music, and he would go ahead and sell those to the fans. Then he had a book on display that he wrote - sort of like an autobiography, but not exactly - with these pink pages on it, which fit along perfectly with his gimmick. Adrian was so proud of those pink fucking pages, and he sold a bunch of those that day, too. I remember him saying to me, *look, do you like this? The pink pages! The pink pages!*

Across the board, there was no shortage of talent involved in the GWA. Gordon Solie signed on as a Vice President for the company, and rumors swirled that Integrated Business Corporation (the holding company which controlled the GWA) had plans to expand the roster further - specifically, by targeting one of the WWF's biggest stars. In his book *Swimming with Piranhas: Surviving the Politics of Professional Wrestling*, Howard Brody - formerly the President of the NWA - recalled the circumstances surrounding this audacious plan:

Incorporated in May '86, the GWA was put up for public sale in late April 1987, with seven million shares of over-the-counter penny stock selling at 40 cents per share. The holding company that controlled the GWA penny stock was a Boca Raton group called Integrated Business Corp. Penny stocks are securities that sell for less than one dollar per share.

...Not long after the group's first set of television tapings, the board of directors at GWA replaced [promoter Patrick] Schaefer because he was supposedly going through money like it was water; $50,000 for their first two hours of television. Red [Roberts] replaced him, but neither Red nor Schaefer actually managed the company's finances. That job belonged to Scott Sherman, one of Integrated Business's managing partners, and George Edison, their corporate attorney.

...At one point, [Scott and George] tried to negotiate with Randy "Macho Man" Savage through his father, Angelo Poffo, to get him to jump from the WWF to the GWA by offering him one million dollars in stock.

28

In its first 19 months of operation, the GWA had managed to lose $147,000. In short order, Red Roberts told the local media, the group expected to start making a profit, but such a turnaround never came.

External factors were at least as much to blame as anything else. While originally, the GWA had been authorized to issue 75 million common shares of stock (at $0.0001 par value), the already-troubled penny stock industry (i.e. the financial vehicle for the entire enterprise) faced an unprecedented regulatory backlash soon after. Over a 12-month period, the Securities and Exchange Commission (SEC) initiated a well-publicized crackdown against a variety of penny-stock firms (most notably, F.D. Roberts Securities, Inc., a New Jersey-based firm with offices in Boca Raton), and eventually, trading was halted on more than 100 penny stocks. Concurrently, the GWA began the process of losing its television coverage, and before long, it started to cease operations entirely.

As far as I could tell, the rapid decline of the GWA offered a pretty good indication of something: this whole wrestling thing probably wasn't going to work out for me. I had used my 'in' – and the company I was involved with soon fell apart. That kind of seemed like a bad omen.

In the end, I walked away from that situation with only a couple of shows under my belt (they kept that Elvis-impersonator as their TV ring announcer, in case you were wondering), and therefore, I needed to figure something else out. I wouldn't say that I erased wrestling totally from my mind - I had learned a great deal at the GWA school, after all - but I needed a fresh start regardless.

Fortunately, I soon learned about a job which promised a chance to practice what I was already good at. *They're hiring for a social host on a cruise ship*, someone told me. *You get a percentage of the sales on board - plus you get to live on the ship!*

I quickly took the job, got myself on board, and it was there that something awesome happened.

It was there that I met Lisa.

Like myself, Lisa was looking to find her way in the world. She had come from rural Nova Scotia in Canada to join the ship as a bartender, and from the second she stepped on board - about two weeks after I did - I noticed her *immediately*.

Lisa always jokes that I like the 'Plain Janes', but she wasn't like that to me - not at all (it's just that the no-makeup-and-ponytail thing looks pretty great to my eyes, if I'm being honest). We sort of started dating on the cruise ship, but neither one of us wanted to commit to anything. I will say that Lisa changed her mind about that a little faster than I did!

Funnily enough, Lisa had a grandfather who used to go to the wrestling matches at *Grand Prix Wrestling*. He would sit in the front row every week with a cane (that much better to hit the heels with), and supposedly, he would react to everything going on as if it were legit.

Lisa was attractive, a nice girl, and a little bit different than the 'hustle and bustle' of South Florida, Boca Raton, that kind of stuff - but in a *good* way. She kind of grounded me - she still does, as a matter of fact - and we quickly fell in love together.

Several years later, Lisa ultimately became my wife, but who knows - in an alternate universe - we could have stayed on that cruise ship forever. Maybe I would have become cruise director one day - but as fate would have it, a new cruise director came in and wanted to hire all of her own people. I gave my notice - Lisa followed me a couple of weeks later - and we've been together ever since.

To this day, Lisa is still my best friend, and she's still gorgeous too. I'm the luckiest man in the world, if I could use that cliché -

mainly because I'm not the easiest guy to live with. Why she puts up with me…I'll never really know.

Now don't get me wrong, I'm not a *total* asshole, but I like to be a wise ass, in a playful way. I'm 'ADD' out the *ying-yang* - and lazy as hell about certain responsibilities. As a wife, that means you have to bother your husband 14 times before he does what you're asking him to do.

Nevertheless, we have stayed in love - and knock on wood, I hope she keeps me around a little longer.

Okay, okay - guys, I hear you. Let's get back to our little *rasslin'* story, shall we?

As I fire back up the DeLorean, I remember my parents being proud of me after I got off that ship. Obviously, the circumstances had not been the greatest beforehand, but I persevered through it anyhow – only to outkick my coverage by meeting a pretty Canadian girl!

Another sign of progress occurred in April of that year, when my dad and I went to *WrestleMania IV* in Atlantic City (we actually attended the following year's event as well). There were no anxiety attacks as in the previous year, and it ended up being one of the best father-son trips that we ever had.

On the weekend of *WrestleMania IV*, I figured that all the wrestlers had to come in through the same hotel entrance. Therefore, I waited diligently at the front desk for a glimpse of Hulk Hogan, 'Macho Man' Randy Savage or Ted DiBiase - and that turned out to be the most fun part of being there. Some fans would try to get a picture or an autograph, but I just wanted to get a *look* at the wrestlers up close. I wanted to see who they were riding with, how they traveled to the shows together. Even after ring announcing those couple of shows, these kinds of things still fascinated me.

You know what? I'll be honest. *Everything* about wrestling still did.

I started getting curious again about the GWA situation. As it had been run as a public company, it couldn't exactly close down in a day, and therefore, I figured Bob Roop would know how long the process would take. Once I called Bob to catch up on things, it soon became pretty obvious, unfortunately, that it was all over, *kaputz* - a done deal.

Somehow, we got around to talking about what Bob was going to do next. As he pondered his future over the phone to me, I realized that I needed a hook to continue our conversation – and to continue our relationship, quite frankly. At one point, Bob mentioned something about the training school and what was left there - and in response, I said probably one of the smartest things that ever came out of my mouth.

Bob, I asked, *do you want to buy the ring and promote indy shows together?*

If I owned half of that ring, I figured, that meant being on *all* the shows that Bob and I could promote together. If I was featured on all those shows, that meant driving down the road with Bob - a famous booker in the wrestling business and a well-known figure from the territories. It meant still being *connected* to the business in some form or fashion. Was it as cool as ring announcing The Iron Sheik versus Corporal Kirchner? Probably not. But maybe, I thought - *just maybe* - it might end up being better.

I want to talk about Bob for a second. He's a very, very intelligent guy - more than he gets credit for, actually. Similar to a certain 'Taskmaster' that we'll hear later on about, Bob is a certified history buff, with a curiosity about a wide variety of things. At this time, he was sort of lost, I thought - a feeling that I could certainly relate to. He was depressed, drinking a lot, and he had a wife and child to support at home. The territories were basically a thing of the past, and Bob was *way* out of shape with zero income coming in. I would love to tell you that he thought my idea was revolutionary - just an unbelievable spark of creativity - but in truth, I think he was kind of desperate.

In a sense, Bob was as desperate as I was - and I don't mean that in a negative way. I guess it was two different kinds of desperation, really. I was desperate to keep my dream going, but Bob was desperate to pay the bills - a very *different* desperate. Ironically enough, Bob was also involved in the process of writing a book, the publication of which, he believed, was sure to solve all of his problems. I don't know if it ever came out.

In any event, Bob agreed to my spontaneous proposal, and according to my best recollection - which could be wrong on this particular detail - we came up with $500 each to purchase the ring. I'm sure that I borrowed the money from my dad - although if I did, I would have paid him back later!

Together, Bob and I started driving up and down the roads, as far north as Fort Pierce - and all the way south as Key West - promoting our indy shows. A lot of times, we would put up the ring for the shows ourselves - and that was a pretty interesting sight in and of itself. On one hand, you had an overweight, broken-down ex-wrestler - and on the other, you had a non-athletic, 5-foot-6 guy who couldn't lift ten pounds. If that visual had a name, it would be something like this: *Abbott and Costello put up a wrestling ring.*

Even still, it felt like a whole new world was opening up for me. As we drove around from show to show, Bob proceeded to teach me everything he had learned about the wrestling business. So many light bulbs would go off in my head, particularly as he explained things about the wrestling I grew up watching - things I had never realized before.

Bob was friendly with a guy named Danny Miller, who was the event coordinator for Championship Wrestling from Florida. As part of his job, Danny would go to the various live events, make sure everybody got paid, ensure the building was set up right and

33

ultimately, that the event actually took place. Danny would settle up with the box office, write down the receipts and send a portion of the money back to Eddie Graham. When Jim Crockett, Jr. bought the Florida territory, Danny ended up doing the same thing for their business, too.

Anyway, Bob and Danny were talking one day, in advance of a *Clash of the Champions* which was being broadcast from the Knight Center in Miami. Danny had access to the building and consequently, Bob thought maybe I could tag along: *Hey, for that Clash of Champions show, is it okay if Penzer comes by?*

Sure, responded Danny. *That's fine by me.*

This was a big freaking deal for me. On June 8th, 1988, I went to the backstage area at the Knight Center, which was a strange building attached to a hotel. I checked in with Danny at about three o'clock, and while looking around, I asked him: *Hey, is there anything I can do to help?*

I can't think of anything, Danny said. *But you probably know some of the local guys you've been booking on the indies here. They're down in the dressing room - why don't you go down there, say, 'Hello?'*

I went down to the dressing room and sure enough, I did know a bunch of the guys - just like Danny said. For the next hour, I sat back, shot the shit a little bit, and kind of just reflected on the whole experience: *Wow, here I am at a 'Clash of Champions' - the big time. Maybe I do belong in this business after all...*

Boy, was my bubble about to get popped.

Who the hell are you, and what the fuck are you doing in my locker room?

The voice - unmistakable.

34

The tone – pissed off.

The wrestler?

Ric. Fucking. Flair.

The Nature Boy was *hot* – and he was staring right at me.

Uh, I said nervously, *Danny Miller told me to come down here...I'm helping him out tonight. Bob Roop organized it...*

I don't give a shit about Bob, interrupted Flair.

I don't give a shit about Danny Miller, he continued.

I stood there in silence.

Are you a wrestler? he asked.

No, sir, I said, *but I've ring announced before...*

Well, Flair shot back, *are you ring announcing tonight?*

No, I conceded.

Well then, Flair thundered, *get the fuck outta my dressing room - and don't ever come back! You're not supposed to be here, and I don't give a fuck what anybody else says. This is my fucking dressing room...I'm fucking Ric Flair!*

What choice did I have? I got out of there quick – and I'll never forget how dejected I was.

Despite that disappointment, Bob and I continued for a couple of years going up and down those roads - until one day, he called me unexpectedly with some news: *Hey, you might want to sell the ring,* he told me, *or at least put it in storage.*

Ole Anderson's booking WCW now, Bob said, *and I'm gonna go 'agent' up there for him.*

Shit, I thought as Bob continued to talk. *So this is it for me.*

In the heyday of Georgia wrestling, Bob had been sort of a henchman for Ole. Back then, Bob would go on the road, get the finishes for guys, make sure nobody was late, and generally keep Ole informed about what was going on. Given their history, it wasn't a surprise to me that Ole ended up bringing Bob into WCW.

They actually had an interesting relationship. In his autobiography, Ole recalled a story of he and Bob dissuading a mark who wanted in the business:

I remember Bob Roop wrestling a heavy-set kid who worked at the hospital as an orderly. Bob had him trapped in the 'sugar'. The kid was crying and begging to be turned loose, so I told Bob, "Bob, don't let the guy go. Break a finger or something, but don't just turn him loose."

Bob was really a nice guy. He absolutely hated to do that kind of thing, but I loved it. I loved it. I told Bob, "Do it! If you don't, this guy is gonna come back one day and tell everybody that he can beat your fat ass."

"I don't think he needs it," Bob argued.

The guy was crying. "Oh, no! I don't need to have my finger broke. I won't tell nobody!"

I egged Bob on. "Look at him, Bob. He's a big kid. He's gonna tell everybody in town that he kicked your big, fat ass all over the ring. You'd better do something."

"Oh, no, Mr. Anderson! I don't have to have my finger broke."

"I think we can just let him go," Bob repeated.

"Oh, yes, Mr. Roop. I won't say nothin'…"

Hey, listen, I eventually said over the phone to Bob. *Look - I'm happy for you. Obviously, I'm disappointed at the same time. Let's stay in touch, and if there's any way you could help get my foot in the door...please let me know.*

Realistically, I never really thought - not in a million years - that anything was going to come of that. It was my stubbornness talking, really, and honestly, I could have thrown in the towel at this stage. The idea that Bob Roop - as the new agent in town - would go up to WCW and pull a favor for a *non-wrestler*...well, that simply didn't happen in the world of 1990.

Nonetheless, Bob promised me that he would pass on my name, and son-of-a-bitch - *he actually did it.*

I don't know, man - somebody up there *must* have been on my side.

4:
Enter The Walkin' Man

*A*lright, said the voice on the other end of the phone, *Bob Roop said you're a good guy. He said that we can trust you.*

So here's what you're gonna do: we're gonna rent you a van, and we're gonna pay for the gas – but we're not gonna pay you. You're gonna find five guys that are good enough to put our guys over on TV. You're gonna drive them up to Gainesville, Georgia, and they're gonna give you 25 dollars each.

The voice belonged to Jody Hamilton (aka 'The Assassin'), whose renown in the business, famously, went back to 1958 – and when he headlined Madison Square Garden at the age of 19. As of the early 1990s, Jody was now working behind the scenes at WCW, and he eventually became a mentor to many of the company's biggest stars. In the WWF, the area just behind the curtain was known as the Gorilla position (in recognition of Gorilla Monsoon), but in WCW, with no disrespect to the late, great Gorilla, it was the *Jody* position to me.

I'd have to say that Jody was my favorite wrestler of all-time. There was an angle he did with Dusty that to this day, probably ranks as my favorite angle ever. It was in the Florida territory, of course! Jody got dressed up as El Santo, one of the most famous *luchadores* in Mexican wrestling history, under the pretense of presenting Dusty with some memorabilia from Mexico.

In setting up the angle, Gordon Solie explained that in Mexico, there existed much admiration for CWF and "*the tremendous amount of good work that Dusty [had] done for children...all over the years.*" It all built to the presentation of an honorary plaque for Dusty, which in an incredible swerve, then got used as a weapon against him!

38

As 'El Santo' viciously laid out Dusty on the floor, his real identity soon became clear: The Assassin!

Jody delivered a memorable promo that day, and that was typical for any time he got behind a microphone. I always liked the way that his interviews were intelligently spoken, as he used big words at a time when most guys were fairly simple talkers. Jody was just so different in that area, and it made him stand out on a completely different level.

As part of his role for WCW, Jody oversaw the booking of enhancement talent for TV (i.e. the 'job guys', or the wrestlers brought in to lose on television). To manage the process, he had a number of enhancement bookers overseeing different regions of the country - he had 'The Italian Stallion' and George South in Georgia and the Carolinas, for example; Rip Rogers took the Indiana/Kentucky/Ohio area; Mike Jackson was in charge of Alabama, and so on - but there was no one based in Florida.

That person became me. The route called for me to start in Fort Lauderdale, then drive across Alligator Alley - going across the whole state in the process - before driving up the West Coast of Florida to pick up more of the job guys (a task easier said than done, by the way, because if they looked bad on TV, *I* would look bad for booking them). Next, I'd go across I4, and then up from Orlando to the Atlanta, Georgia area - and cities like Marietta and Columbus, where the WCW TV tapings usually happened. It was about an 11-hour drive each way - and for that, as per the deal I made with Jody, I'd get $25 from each of the wrestlers. If I booked five guys, that equated to a total of $125 for my efforts.

You might be wondering why Jody called me in the first place - good question! If I had to put the pieces together, here's what I *think* happened. I think that Bob said to Ole Anderson - probably in passing - *Hey, Ole, I've got a friend I've been promoting shows with. He's not a wrestler, and he's not even a referee...but he can talk on a mic a little bit. Any opportunities for him?*

With Ole being Ole, I can imagine him shrugging and basically saying: *No.*

I can also imagine Ole saying something else to appease Bob: *I don't know, why don't you talk to Jody or something?*

It's unlikely to me that Bob believed anything was going to come out of it, but that's beside the point. He fulfilled his promise to me, and that is exceedingly rare in life, as it is in the wrestling business.

Moreover, it's important to remember the predominant mindset in the business back then. If you think about the reception I received at the Knight Center - getting chewed out of the locker room by Ric Flair - that was kind of what you got as an outsider. There may have been *some* people who were friendly with fans - Jim Cornette and Eddie Gilbert come to mind - and the early fan associations were starting to become more prevalent. But that wasn't the norm - not at all - and the subset of fans with access to 'the boys' was almost nonexistent.

Essentially, the mentality was: *If you're not a wrestler here, and you're not a referee here - get the fuck out.*

If you happen to be invited here by someone else, don't go backstage.

That's what made it so crazy when Bob told me out of the blue one day – prior to Jody calling me – that I was going to get a phone call.

It didn't quite sink in at first: *What? Really?*

Yeah, Bob said. *I can't promise anything else for you, but I did what you asked me to do.*

In reality, how could I have expected anything else from Bob? If bringing me in, regardless of what I would be doing, ended up going badly in some way, it could easily have cost him his job. That's how seriously they took *kayfabe* and the ethics of the business back then.

Before I showed up to a WCW building for the first time, I needed to know something from Bob: *You're gonna be there before I arrive, right?*

Yeah, he replied. *Why?*

Well, I said, *If Ric Flair sees me again and fucking throws me out...that's it. That's the end of me in the wrestling business!*

Oh, okay, Bob said. *I'll be there - you don't need to worry about it.*

As fate would have it, Bob's car broke down before the tapings, and as a result, he was late to the building! That left me in a position where I was hiding from Ric Flair.

Yes, I know what I just wrote: I was *literally* hiding from Ric Flair.

In my mind, I thought I was going to have the quickest career in WCW history. *If Ric Flair throws me out again,* I worried, *this whole experiment is over!*

Realistically, Ric wasn't going to recognize me anyway – especially a few years after the fact. Knowing what I know now – and particularly with the way those guys were running back then - he wouldn't have remembered me if I had gone up and asked him for an autograph. In retrospect, he was just in a mood that time at the Knight Center, and he was looking for someone to pick on; I saw him do it to other people as time went on. Ric is a nice guy normally, but if he gets a stick up his ass, he can be a dick and take it out on other people.

Anyway, as far as I was concerned, my mindset that day was simple: *hide from Ric Flair until Bob Roop comes as backup!*

Fortunately, the wrath of Flair never materialized - at least in my direction - but as those first tapings wrapped up, I expected that my WCW story was over: *Alright, favor done to Bob*, I imagined them saying, *see ya later now*.

And you know what? If that's all I ever did, I'd probably still have a helluva story to tell you. I was involved in the wrestling business, at some level anyway, and I promoted independent shows with Bob Roop. I did some ring announcing for a while. I was part of helping a WCW TV taping take place.

At the same time, it never hurt to ask.

Excuse me, Mr. Hamilton, I said to Jody before leaving.

You want me up next week?

Jody looked at me.

Yeah, he said.

Wait, I thought.

Really?

At the time that Bob and I ran indies, I had still been driving the limousine for my dad's friend. Once I started bringing the enhancement guys up to WCW, I had to stop doing that - and Dad sold his share of the business back. Lisa was busy working for my dad as a receptionist at the Counseling Center (off-the-books, I might add. I figure it's been long enough, right?), while my new schedule called for a pretty hectic workweek: I would leave on Sunday night, pick the guys up and arrive in time for WCW's Monday (and Tuesday) tapings. I'd then leave the Atlanta area on Tuesday night, arrive back home

Wednesday morning, and then work Thursday, Friday and Saturday as a waiter at Ruby Tuesdays.

Looking back, I think I was insane.

The whole situation was kind of crazy, in fact, especially considering that Bob - almost as soon as I started, actually - lost his own gig at WCW.

Ole lost the book, and subsequently - as often happens in the wrestling business - his buddies were the collateral damage. Already, Bob was considered a guy who you either loved or hated - there was no in-between with him. You were either a 'Bob Roop guy', so to speak - or you wanted to pick up a fork and stab him in the ankle.

Bob moved away to Michigan in the aftermath, and interestingly, we never really stayed in touch. Our friendship - which had been based in *business* from the start - never endured past that point, almost as if it had served its purpose for each of us. Over the years, I occasionally wondered why we both let the relationship elapse.

Now that I'm revisiting the subject, something important just occurred to me. I guess just like a good therapy session, the act of writing this book is revealing things that deep down, I probably knew already! The fact is that both Bob and I had our reasons for not maintaining contact with each other. On his end, I'm sure that Bob was thinking, *This motherfucker. I got his ass 'in'. He's involved with WCW now, and I'm sitting at fucking home!*

On my end, I can see now that more than anything, I was probably embarrassed about what had transpired. It was an awkward situation to be in - I mean, what was I going to say to the guy? *Hey Bob, I know you're sitting at home - but let me tell you about everything going on with WCW...*

Whichever way you slice it, my mentor was gone - and in order to move forward, I would have to forge a path without him.

43

In some ways, it's a shame that Bob and I didn't work together longer. All in all, he did so much for me - and no matter what, I'll never, ever forget it. Without Bob taking a chance on me - and subsequently, teaching me everything he could about wrestling - you never would have heard the name David Penzer. People can have their different opinions about Bob, but that right there is a *fact*.

So great was Bob's influence on me that at first - in my efforts to locate suitable enhancement talent - I relied mostly on guys that we had both booked over the previous two years. Once he left, however, I had no choice but to take ownership of the process myself. I took trips to Tampa to look at potential new recruits. I went to Orlando for the same reason. I had business cards printed to explain to guys what I was doing.

For the boys packed in the van each week, 'doing a job' - and the subsequent national TV exposure that came with it - offered the chance of becoming a bigger star in one's local area. Just being in the ring with the Four Horsemen, Dusty Rhodes, or Nikita Koloff, for example - especially if it looked like you could hold your own for a couple of minutes - instantly improved your viability (and credibility) in a local market. If you were losing to Ric Flair on worldwide television, well - now *you're* the main event in a place like New Port Richey, Florida.

In some *very* rare cases, entire careers could be made out of the opportunity – such as with Marc Mero, who starred in WCW and the WWF after I first booked him to do a job for us. If I recall correctly, Marc didn't want to travel up in the van, nor did he want to pay me the $25. I think he gave me $10 and met me at the building! Soon after, Dusty (then a member of the WCW booking committee) practically fell in love with Marc, gave him that little Richard gimmick, and the rest, as they say, is history.

That's not to say that life as an enhancement talent was easy, though, especially if you were a heat magnet like Chris Sullivan. Chris was one of the guys that I brought up regularly from Florida, but he seemed to get off on the attention that came with pissing off some of the biggest stars in the locker room. One time in Chattanooga, Tennessee, we happened to be running a show at a university campus, and the boys' dressing room for the night was the college's wrestling room. There were mats all over the place, but more pertinently, a rope hanging from the ceiling, like you'd see in any gymnasium. As a result of Chris' antics, the boys decided to tape him to that rope and leave him hanging for all to see. *The person who lets him down*, went the clear instructions to the rest of the room, *is going back up there*. Chris must have been up there for an hour before Janie Engle from the WCW office let him down.

Yes sir, my new vantage point allowed access to a completely different side of the business - and it was *wild*. How about we start with the bar at the Ramada Inn near Atlanta Airport, or as we called it, *The Dungeon?* The General Manager of that hotel was a wrestling fan, and she would give the boys a rate of $35 per night (a good deal to begin with, sweetened by free shuttle rides to the airport). Pretty much everyone stayed there except for Ric, who opted for the Marriott hotel down the road. As per its moniker, after all, *The Dungeon* wasn't the nicest hotel.

It was just insanity after the TV tapings - a huge party with all the boys and their girlfriends, or wives, or whoever they were (I didn't take a survey at the time). People would go behind the bar and pour themselves a drink, and I'm sure only some of that stuff got paid for. The bar staff tried to keep track of everything, but as you can imagine, it quickly got to be ridiculous.

One night, everybody was already three sheets to the wind when Sid Vicious - all 6-foot-9 of him - walked into the bar. Sid was working for the WWF at the time - and I'm not even sure why he was in Atlanta - but he came in and started bragging about his success up North. *I'm gonna headline WrestleMania*, he gloated. *WCW sucks - it's a country promotion!*

45

In response, two people that you probably wouldn't expect to intervene - because they were two of the smallest people in the business back then - started arguing with Sid. Mike Graham and Brian Pillman came right back at him, and Mike in particular didn't need much encouragement. Mike was especially notorious for not backing down to anyone - he'd pick a fight with a giant in a heartbeat - and *look out* if he had a pint of vodka in him.

It wasn't like Mike was just being silly, either - he was a legit shooter with the ability to take people down. At first, he asked Sid the obvious question: *Why are you here in this bar?*

You guys suck, taunted Sid, continuing his tirade.

You're a fucking steroid freak, hammered Mike right back. *You can't work worth shit. You'll never draw a fucking dime. Go home, take your money and go play fucking softball.*

Like everyone else, I was sort of paying attention out of the corner of my eye at first. It wasn't like the entire place had gone silent, or that everyone was preoccupied listening to all this. All of a sudden, though, things got more heated.

I'll show you guys, menaced Sid.

I'm going to my car.

Now fuck - in 2024, I'm going to run to my room in this situation, because I'd be *sure* that the guy is going to start shooting everybody. In this case, however, I don't even think it occurred to us that something like that could happen, which shows you how much the world has changed. Now granted, we *had* all been drinking - but I don't think one person stopped and said, *Wait - what if he brings a gun?*

46

Meanwhile, with Sid out of the room, Mike was busy holding court. *What, is he gonna bring a tire iron? What, a baseball bat? I'll still kick his ass, that motherfucker. No fucking talent motherfucker...*

I can still see Mike ranting on like it was yesterday, mostly because he'd get so animated when he got pissed off (and when he was inebriated - or both).

Dramatically, Sid Vicious then returned...holding a fucking *squeegee* in his hand.

That's right - a squeegee.

Come on, motherfuckers! he yelled.

I'll kick your asses!

I kid you not, the *entire* bar paused for a beat - and then the place *erupted* in laughter. Sid was left standing there - in a half-confused silence - holding his fucking squeegee.

He couldn't get out of there fast enough.

Like I said, the Dungeon environment was *nuts*. The Iron Sheik would stop by and snort coke on the bar tables. Multiple people would end up in the pool. Harley Race - who was legitimately one of the best shooters in the world and had one of the strongest set of hands that I've ever seen - used to walk around the place and take people out with this stun-gun like device (like he couldn't already kick your ass). Harley would target people by buzzing the thing right on their ass, and the electronic jolt would be enough to take you off your feet. It sent me flying over two bar tables on one occasion!

Another time, Harley was busy fucking with Butch Reed, and Butch got *hot* about what was going on. The entire place emptied out, the boys moved aside all the tables and chairs, and everyone formed a big circle in front of the bar. If Butch got the best of Harley, even though Race was 50-something at the time, it would have been a legendary feat - but once they both got to shooting, Butch eventually tapped out.

Backstage with Harley

It was like a big fraternity party at the Dungeon. Everybody that didn't live in Atlanta would go there after the tapings - the job guys, the announcers, everybody. Nothing was off-limits, other than capital murder, I *think* - and I wouldn't be surprised if that happened every once in a while.

I remember once when Kevin Sullivan's daughter, Shannon, brought her boyfriend along to the bar, and I guess the boyfriend decided to challenge the Nasty Boys to a drinking contest.

I'm gonna cut off your eyebrows, promised Brian Knobbs of the Nasties.

No, I'm gonna cut off your eyebrows - you fat motherfucker, came the response.

Shannon's boyfriend was not a big guy, but he continued to engage with them anyway. Meanwhile, Kevin was laughing at the boyfriend - Shannon was laughing at him, too - and the rest of us were laughing at *everything* in the background...like all of this was normal!

Obviously, the Nasty Boys were *gimmicking* the boyfriend the entire time - I mean, that's what they did - and the boyfriend totally passed out. They ended up cutting off his eyebrows, putting him on a luggage cart and pushing the cart into his hotel room. He woke up the next morning with a massive hangover - and without those eyebrows.

No one ever saw *him* around the wrestling business again.

Shit like that was common. You know what, let me rephrase that - I don't want to say it was common, but it wasn't *unexpected* for these things to happen, if you follow me. There was always going to be some shenanigans going on, because the last couple of people at the bar were usually shit-faced, and it would soon turn into, 'Let's see who can take the other guy down.'

I don't know if any story will go down in infamy more than Sid and his squeegee, though. He'll never live it down, although at this point, a lot of people who witnessed it have either forgotten about it, died, or just don't talk about it anymore. For the longest time, however, some of the smart fans in the business would show up to the arena with squeegees - and hold them up whenever Sid came out.

Come on, motherfuckers!

For several months, I kept bringing guys up to TV and hanging around backstage, but after a while, I got put in charge of *all* the enhancement guys - regardless of who brought them in - getting them to sign releases, taking care of the necessary paperwork, and that sort of thing. All the guys had to sign a standard piece of paper which basically said, 'If you get hurt, we don't have to cover you!'

The release wasn't worth the paper it was printed on, quite frankly, but it gave us the right to put those guys on television (it also determined whether or not the guys got paid. No signature = no pay).

One time, Al Snow had come in for a tryout match, and I went up to him to introduce myself. As I remember it, I basically told Al that I needed him to fill out the form - no big deal.

Well, said Al, *what exactly is it?*

It's just a standard release, I said.

Okay, Al responded. *Could I at least read it over?*

Sure, I shrugged, *but like I said, it's just a standard release - everybody signs them. If you don't sign it, they won't be able to use you...but sure, take as much time as you want.*

Now, it wasn't the first time that something like that happened (one time, I remember a guy wanting to call his lawyer), but on this occasion, Terry Taylor - one of the WCW agents backstage - happened to be watching us. I think Terry sensed there was tension going on, and when he approached me about it, I told him all that I knew: *He just wants to read the release.*

Terry went back to talk to Al, who interpreted the situation as me having 'stooged him off' to Terry! As is typical in the wrestling business, I ended up getting heat with Al as a result. At the time, it all got way overblown - although we've since conceded it was much to do about nothing.

After a period handling just those releases, Jim Ross asked if I would shepherd some of the contracted talent to do interviews, and soon I was doing that, plus running off copies of the formats - anything to help. Slowly but surely, they were starting to trust me a little more.

I next got the responsibility of ringing the bell, up by the hard camera, which only brought me closer to the action. The best match I ever saw was from that vantage point, as a matter of fact: Sting's Squadron versus The Dangerous Alliance at *WrestleWar* '92 in Jacksonville, Florida. If you go back and watch that match, you'll notice there's a little delay at the finish. That's because I was so into

50

the match that I forgot to ring the bell! I kind of snapped out of it when Keith Mitchell, our director, started yelling in my ear from the production truck: *Ring the fucking bell!*

I kept all that in mind several months later - on August 2nd, 1992 - when Ron Simmons won the World Heavyweight title, becoming the first African American to achieve that distinction. It was again my job to ring that *fucking* bell, and I made sure not to mess it up this time. During that weekend in Baltimore, I technically should have been on my honeymoon (Lisa and I tied the knot exactly one week earlier), but I couldn't give anyone an excuse to get rid of me. *Ah, Penzer's not here*, I could imagine them saying. *Something about a honeymoon. You know what...do we even need him around anymore?*

Considering my ongoing dedication, work ethic and paranoid feelings that it could all soon end, I basically operated as what they call a *stooge* in the wrestling business. Better yet, you could have called me *Stooge of the Year* - and no one would have accused you of hyperbole.

(Fun fact: we gave serious consideration to that title - 'Stooge of the Year' - being the name of this book!)

All I did was walk around all day, whether it was with a sign-in sheet in hand, getting guys to show up for their interviews, or doing a thousand other errands to help. Evidently, my activity backstage was so constant that Junkyard Dog gave me a fitting nickname: *The Walkin' Man.*

(Many of the old-timers in the business still call me that to this day, as a matter of fact).

Look at the Walkin' Man, Junkyard Dog would say. *Walkin' here - walkin' there - walkin' all over. All day and all night, he walks!*

I did this stuff every week (if you're keeping score, that's driving the guys up, plus doing all those errands with my Walkin' Man routine) for more than *two years*. I even got to sit in on the production

51

meetings - which for the fan in me, was a pretty cool experience - although the extent of my involvement evolved over time. At the very beginning, Jody would come out of the meetings and say to me, *Here's the sheet - go run it off.* Once they got more comfortable with me, however, they started to say, *Hey, Penzer, why aren't you at the meetings?*

Incrementally, I had steadily been living my dream at an ever-increasing level. I wasn't always *seeing* how the sausage was made – because I wasn't regularly at ringside or anything - but I was certainly *hearing* about it now in those meetings. All along, my compensation - if you can call it that - remained the same: $25 from each guy that I booked.

It stayed that way until I met Scott D'Amore, who had just started Border City Wrestling in Ontario, Canada. Although he was based in Windsor, Scott had a significant presence in Michigan - just over the border - and he was looking to book guys on TV. He came up to me at a wrestling convention and asked if I could help.

When I took it back to WCW, Jody said, *Sure - have him come down. We need some new faces anyway.*

A couple of those faces went on to become big names in the business - the one-time 'Terry Richards', for example, who later starred as Rhino in ECW, and Adam Copeland - Edge - who wrestled as 'Damon Striker' on an episode of *WCW Pro* ("My name was [supposed to be] Damien Striker," Edge later revealed, "[but] WCW got the caption wrong!").

Similar to my deal, D'Amore received $25 from each of the guys he brought to the tapings. As I facilitated the whole thing, we worked out an arrangement where he gave me $10 per head. I eventually worked out a similar system with Bobby Starr, who began taking enhancement talent to the tapings from Baltimore. Now, keep in mind - when we did the Disney tapings for our syndicated programming, those events would sometimes go on for a week. For that entire week, I would be getting $25 from each of my guys, $10 from Scott's guys, and $10 from Bobby's guys on a daily basis (did I mention that entrepreneurial streak that I got from my dad?).

Jody didn't care about who was getting a piece of who's action. All he wanted was guys who could work, who didn't have big egos, and ideally, guys who had a little bit of size on them (they didn't have to be huge, *per se*, but you wouldn't want to show up with someone 5-5, 150 either). Nobody gave a shit about what it took to get the job guys up to TV - or what money was changing hands with whom - as long as we made sure to get them there in the first place.

Nobody had a problem with it - that is, until Sid Vicious, recently returned to WCW after being that 'big star' in the WWF, randomly made an issue out of it (like Sid didn't have his own shit to worry about). Because they were Sid's guys, Harlem Heat (Booker T and Stevie Ray) got a stick up their asses about it, too: *Why are you taking a piece of another guy's action? You're not doing anything!*

To hell I'm not, I said.

After I told Booker and Stevie about everything I had been doing to help - and for how long I had been doing it for - things kind of settled into a half-work, half-shoot joke between us. They were still pissed off about parts of it, but they weren't really going to push the issue too much. Eventually, they settled on calling me by a nickname: *Kickback.*

Guys had to kill time a lot back then, and we didn't have as many options of amusing ourselves. Something that might start as a shoot could easily turn into something just to fuck with someone about - and that was definitely the case with me. Once in a while, Booker and Stevie would come up to me and say, *Why are you taking all those kickbacks, man? Come on 'Kickback', why are you doing this to all those guys?*

Before it became such a gag, though, I was truly worried that the whole thing was going to blow up in my face. Thankfully, Jody soon reassured me: *Don't worry*, he told me once the matter reached his ears. *I got your back, Penzer.*

If Sid fucking Vicious thinks he's gonna come back, Jody said, *and change the way I've been doing things for years - a way of doing business that everybody knows about - he has another fucking thing coming.*

That's just the kind of guy Jody was. I'll never forget sitting behind the curtain with him and just soaking up his knowledge. His wife, Rosemary, would cook these incredible meals for him - usually something Italian - and she'd make these unbelievable salads to-go. As Jody was a big guy, it might take him 30 or 40 minutes to get through lunch, but I would just sit there - and he would just *tell me shit*.

You couldn't pay for that kind of education.

I distinctly remember Jody talking about his time booking the old Central States territory, which was pretty much on its last legs when he got there. The story goes that Jody started to get the territory moving in the right direction, under the assumption that he would receive a commensurate raise from promoter Bob Geigel. According to Jody, Bob then reneged on their deal, causing Jody to say, 'Fuck you' and head back to Georgia.

After listening to the story, I asked Jody why he put himself in that position; in other words, why he would want to associate himself with a dying territory. His answer was simple: *'cos I knew I could get that fucking territory back.*

That one statement - *I knew I could get it back* - is indicative of the mindset of guys from Jody's era. If you were good and confident about what you were doing, you actually *wanted* to go into a 'down' territory. You relished the challenge of being able to prove people wrong and *draw money*, which as Jody would tell you, happens to be the entire point of pro wrestling.

54

I wasn't the only one who benefited from Jody's tutelage - far from it, in fact. Scott D'Amore was there for a lot of those lessons, too - and in time, Jody became a hugely influential mentor for him. Scott would even send in tapes of him wrestling up in Canada to the WCW Power Plant - our training facility - so that Jody could discuss, in real-time, Scott's performance over the telephone.

Even today, Scott still credits those talks with Jody as being instrumental in his career - but while Scott and I seemingly had a lot in common, there was one key difference between us.

Unlike myself, Scott was just *brimming* with confidence. I think he felt like, 'You know what? If this WCW experience doesn't work out, I've got my Border City Wrestling thing back home.'

For me, on the other hand, I was always afraid. I was worried that at any given time, my dream could be pulled out from under me.

I had come this far already, and I didn't want it to end.

On a couple of occasions, I went up to Jim Ross to tell him - because I don't think anyone really knew about it - that I could do some ring announcing, too: *If there's ever an opening, Mr. Ross, please let me know.*

We never had that conversation again, as in early 1993, Jim left to go to the WWF after Eric Bischoff got a promotion to become WCW's new executive producer. Consequently, Tony Schiavone took over a lot of Jim's off-camera duties, particularly as it related to production and keeping everything organized backstage. Right around the time he started in the role, Tony pulled me aside one day and asked me: *Hey, you're the guy that drives people up from Florida, right?*

Yeah, I replied.

Well, he said, *you know we have a ring announcer position open right now.*

The saliva started forming in my mouth. Recently, the company had moved Tony Gillum from his backup ring announcing position to play-by-play, but he totally screwed up in the job and got fired. That left an opportunity for someone new to work under Gary Michael Cappetta, who had long occupied the lead ring announcer role.

Alright, I thought to myself as Tony continued, *here's my chance.*

I was chomping at the bit to accept Tony's big offer, but before I could say anything...

So, there's this guy from Tampa we'd like to give a tryout to, Tony said. *His name is Dino Puglia. I used to work with him in the WWF - will you bring him up next week?*

Man, oh man – talk about a letdown.

Okay, I answered solemnly - before Tony nodded, finished the conversation and walked away.

Penzer, I said to myself, *if you don't say it now...it's never gonna happen for you.*

5:
STEP UP TIME

It was now or never.

Uh, Mr. Schiavone, I finally muttered out, stopping Tony in his tracks. *I don't know if you know this or not, but I talked to Jim Ross about ring announcing before. I've ring announced some indy shows, and I'd like an opportunity for this job as well.*

Oh, said Tony. *I didn't know that.*

I'll tell you what, he said. *You bring this guy Dino up next week for a tryout, and we'll give you a tryout the week after that.*

Whoever does the better job will get it.

Wow - there was about to be a lot on the line for me. It's one thing to say, almost in passing, 'Hey, I can ring announce, too – in case you ever need anyone', and another thing to actually do it under pressure. I knew that if I didn't perform well in my tryout, this whole wrestling experiment thing, for all intents and purposes, was *done*.

I worried about it, and the pressure reminded me of something my dad had talked about over the years: his concept of an emotional 'dam'. Dad believed that over time, anxiety and stress can build up to the point of spilling over – assuming strategies aren't used to keep it all at bay. Evidently, I had kept it together long enough to create a *hell* of an opportunity for myself, but there were practical considerations to think about, too. I mean, put yourself in my shoes for a second: if they gave the job to Dino, why would I still be driving guys up in the van? Why would I keep doing that 11-hour journey each way?

57

This was the shot I'd be waiting for. Would there be a better opportunity? I doubted it.

In preparation for my tryout, I realized that I *did* have a couple of things going for me. First, I had been watching Gary up close over the previous two years. Therefore, I knew the way that the WCW production worked, including what the ring announcer heard in his IFB (*interruptible foldback* device), which is how the production truck communicates with on-air talent. Secondly, I was hoping that my time as the Walkin' Man may have helped to serve my cause: *Well, Penzer already drives up anyway*, I imagined them saying. *Why not make him the backup ring announcer?*

When it came time for Dino's tryout, he actually screwed up pretty bad, introducing a couple of guys in the wrong order. Dino had a great voice, but unlike myself, he didn't know what to expect in terms of the IFB, or anything else on the production side. In essence, he got totally lost out there.

That's not to say that I did great in comparison, by the way - I didn't. I was a nervous wreck before hitting the ring; petrified, really. I was so concerned about messing up that I wrote down *every* freaking word that I ended up saying (that includes 'and', 'to', and 'the', in case you were wondering). I wrote down the name of each city that the wrestlers were from. I wrote down everything that could be said in between the matches, too. I guess you can say that it worked, but in hindsight, I ended up 'winning', if you can call it that, basically by default.

But hey, like Al Davis used to say – *Just win, baby.*

My dream had been extended - and I could hardly believe it myself.

58

Getting that job was a huge stepping stone for me. My new schedule called for me to do house shows over the weekend, and then the 'B' TV shows (syndicated tapings like *WCW Pro*) on Mondays and Tuesdays. Meanwhile, Gary handled the 'A' TV shows - and some of the house shows in larger markets.

From a financial standpoint, I was now getting paid $150 per night - plus I got to keep my gig driving the enhancement guys. Not only that, but I continued getting those precious 'kickbacks' (much to the chagrin of Sid, I'm sure) from the guys like Scott D'Amore. It wasn't a bad arrangement, honestly.

Nonetheless, now being on the road for the first time, I had a lot to figure out. Sure, I had been 'Stooge of the Year' for quite a while, but let's be honest - I was still green as gooseshit about the business overall. I had a lot of questions which lacked obvious answers - including, for the time being, this little doozy: *Why is this guy being so nice to me?*

I mean, really: why was Randy 'Pee Wee' Anderson - part of the WCW refereeing crew - being so freaking nice to me?

Hey, Penzer, he said to me one day, *Why don't I show you the ropes a little bit?*

At the time, I figured that Pee Wee was just being a nice guy – but we soon developed a genuine friendship. We started traveling together constantly on the road, and in the process, I learned a lot about his background, including the fact that he grew up poor in Rome, Georgia - and that he happened to be a legit *badass*. Pee Wee showed that rep for the world to see one night on TV; some jackass jumped into the ring while DDP cut a promo, and Pee Wee responded by stretching the fuck out of him. He had been taught the same as all the refs back then: *If you jump over them rails, you're fair game to get crushed!*

(If you check out footage of that incident, you'll also see my finest moment, by the way - dragging a fan off the canvas to the floor!)

59

Pee Wee first broke into the business with Arn Anderson, one of his closest childhood friends. He spent some time in Louisiana, where Bill Watts had him drive Junkyard Dog around, and he even trained to be a wrestler briefly. As Pee Wee was small in stature (hence the nickname), I think he realized that refereeing was going to be his calling, but don't get it confused - he was a tough motherfucker. Pee Wee Anderson could fucking *go*.

Eventually, Pee Wee found his way into the NWA, and later WCW, remaining close with Arn throughout it all. It wasn't until a long time later that I realized what provoked our friendship in the first place.

Oh, I finally realized, *now I get it. Once I went on the road, WCW started paying for my hotel and rental car. By buddying up with me, Pee Wee got a free room to share - plus a free ride!*

You know what? I think we were both using *each other*. Initially, I needed someone to teach me the ropes - just like Pee Wee said - and Pee Wee needed...well, somebody to cover those expenses!

Having said that, a few months into traveling together, Pee Wee stepped up for me in a major way. Some context: it was in the latter part of 1993 when Ole Anderson (who had retained influence over the years) decided he wanted the ring announcers off the road. In our place, Ole envisioned hiring a local DJ in each town that WCW was running, thus saving the company a few bucks in the process.

Therefore, it appeared that the arrangement I had just been getting comfortable with had flipped on a dime. Looking for answers, I approached Gary Juster, WCW's head of live events, to see what could be done.

Gary, I said, *I can't get off the road. This is how I'm learning.*

I know, Juster said. *But what am I supposed to do? You try telling Ole Anderson.*

My suggestion to Gary was that if WCW no longer wanted to cover my hotel and rental car, I would find a way - in exchange for an additional $50 fee - to get to the shows myself. Essentially, for the cost of $200 per show (my usual $150 payment plus a new $50 travel stipend), WCW would have me show up at no additional expense to the company.

Juster went to bat for me with Ole and got it approved - even though to this day, I have no idea what would have happened if Ole said, 'No.' I was desperate to keep doing what I was doing.

For the next four months, my work life became kind of like that movie - *Planes, Trains and Automobiles*. I had to do whatever I could to make the shows on time - including taking Greyhound buses, if necessary.

That was an interesting time in my life, man - riding on a Greyhound bus, and drinking vodka to put myself to sleep on the way home. Fortunately, most of WCW's shows ran in the Southeast, but obviously, there were times when that wasn't the case. One time, I took a bus all the way back to Florida from *Chicago*. Other times, I would try to link up with different guys, or piece my travel together by committee.

Occasionally, things got pretty hairy in trying to make it all work.

Remember when I told you about how Pee Wee stepped up? Well, during this time of uncertainty, he was so good to me. Whenever possible, he would let me ride with him - even though his car wasn't covered by the company – despite it being easy to say: *You're on your own now, kid.*

Pee Wee went as far as to give me airline miles if I couldn't get a Greyhound bus in time. Back then, the big gimmick in WCW was that if you got a full fare ticket - which in those days, functioned as good as cash on an airplane - the wrestlers would choose to drive to the next town instead. Even if it were a six- or seven-hour journey by car, they were then able to pocket the full fare ticket - or, more accurately, the cash equivalent of same. There were a lot of those tickets flying around, but nonetheless, Pee Wee stopped me one day and said: *Penzer, I know that you're busting your ass. Take this.*

It was over a thousand dollars in airline money - or a thousand dollars in cash, essentially - which was a big fucking deal in 1993.

Eventually, I got my free car and hotel benefits reinstated - but I never forgot that Pee Wee did that for me. From that point onwards, he could ride with me anytime that he liked.

Looking back, this specific period of my life - the time after I was appointed as the backup ring announcer - seemed to go by so quickly. I was mostly focused on riding the wave, trying to see how far I could go with it all, and apparently willing to endure anything in order to find out.

Once I had a few months under my belt, I realized how lucky I was to sit under the 'learning tree', so to speak, of WCW's *lead* ring announcer - Gary Cappetta.

I always regarded Gary's delivery as impeccable. A great example of his work could be seen on July 3rd, 1991, when on the first night of WCW's *Great American Bash* tour, he announced that Ric Flair - recently fired after a contractual dispute with then-Executive Vice President Jim Herd - had been stripped of the World Heavyweight Championship.

Due to Flair's popularity among WCW fans, it was an immensely challenging situation for Gary to be put in. In advance of the announcement, I remember Dusty and some other people on the booking team scrambling to come up with a new main event, with the next pay-per-view less than two weeks away. At that time, it was extremely rare for me to have that kind of access to the booking room, but because of the nature of the situation, it all sort of played out in front of everyone.

Dusty and company put a lot of thought into how Gary should present the bad news, fearing that the crowd would instantly turn against the show - and the promotion in general. They knew that Gary was sure to get booed out of the building, and consequently, it was a 'sell out' to see it all unfold at the *Jody* position. To Gary's credit, he managed to take the sting of his message by giving the fans something to look forward to. He built anticipation towards revealing that Barry Windham, a certified fan favorite, would be getting a shot at the title in Flair's absence. Gary didn't completely mitigate the disastrous effects of Flair's departure - no one could do that - but he made the absolute best of a horrible situation. From the outside looking in, that might look like an easy task, but trust me - in front of a crowd of angry people, it is *anything* but.

When things like the Jim Herd-Flair debacle went down, fans often made note of the differences between WCW and our competitor, the WWF. There were many differences in fact - including, interestingly, the way each promotion treated their ring announcers.

The psychology of ring announcing in WCW contrasted with what our peers did in the WWF. For most of WCW's history, we didn't have a Hulk Hogan in the main events to keep the crowd present, and consequently, it was a constant sell job in between the matches: *Tell 'em who's coming up,* we'd hear from the producers. *Tell 'em they're gonna be on TV...tell 'em to yell and scream!*

In other words, it required a little more inventiveness to involve the crowd, and in that respect, Gary would do this routine which amazed me with its effectiveness. He would start to set it up about a quarter of the way through the show. *Ladies and gentlemen,* he would say, *we have applause meters in the production truck. They're telling me that so far, this is the fifth hottest crowd we've had in 1994!*

People would go *nuts* over that. *Number four on the list*, he'd continue, *was Philadelphia, Pennsylvania earlier this year. Let's see if y'all can make a lot of noise and beat Philadelphia!*

Cleverly, he liked to set up a North vs. South dynamic. *Macon, Georgia*, he'd announce a couple of matches later, *they're telling me - based on the applause meter backstage - that you have now beat Philadelphia! You've now moved up to number four!*

This went on the whole night until at the end, Gary would make another announcement to a raucous reaction. *Macon, Georgia - I just got word that you are the number one audience this year!*

The people would react like they had just won the lottery. If I was in the crowd, I probably would have rolled my eyes at it - it was pretty corny, really - but what did I know? It *worked*. It worked amazingly well, as a matter of fact - and seemingly every time.

Like I said, Gary and I never had a Hulk Hogan to hook people into staying at the WCW shows - that is, until the company signed the man himself in June 1994.

While a lot of our audience, having been raised on a different style of wrestling, didn't care much for 'The Hulkster' at first, it was definitely a risk worth taking. After all, WCW had yet to make a profit since being created by Turner Broadcasting, and the company had been mediocre for so long. If you have a chance to grab some mainstream attention, you take it - in my opinion - and signing Hulk Hogan helped.

In recent years, Hulk has come under fire for making some terrible comments, at a moment of weakness and at the worst time of his life, which I'm sure he regrets every day. There are people who will want to 'cancel' Hulk forever, I guess - but in my view, that's simply not what he's really like. From my position, I had plenty of time to witness the real person, such as before a WCW pay-per-view at the Bayfront Center in St. Petersburg, Florida (incidentally, being at the Bayfront Center was a real thrill for me. The building had been part of the old CWF territory, and I can still hear Gordon promoting the monthly events there).

Anyway, it was just before show time when I was running off some formats upstairs. Usually, the copy machines would be located in the offices of whatever building we were in, but for some reason, I had to go into this strange little room which had a couch for guests to sit down on. I was busy observing all this when I noticed a family, including a kid in a wheelchair, slowly start to enter the room.

It was one of the saddest things that I've ever seen. The child was as disfigured and sick as you could possibly imagine. When I asked if the family needed some help, the mother simply said, 'No, we were just told to come to this room and stay here.'

All of a sudden, Jimmy Hart brought Hulk into the room, and the faces of that entire family *lit up* - including that of the child, for whatever understanding he had of what was going on (unfortunately, it didn't seem like a lot). I witnessed Hulk spend at least 20 minutes with the family, taking pictures with them and answering their questions, and there wasn't a reporter in sight. Other than Jimmy, Hulk and the family, the only other person in there was me - and not because I was told to be there, but only because I was running off the formats.

You can say a lot of shit about people, but what goes on when *nobody* is watching says a lot, too. Hulk didn't have to do that - he could have easily said when they asked him, 'That doesn't work for me, brother' (because we all know he said that a lot!). I don't know how long the child lived for - his condition was just horrible - but I do know his family has that memory. Their son got to meet Hulk Hogan - and for a little while, at least, Hulk put a smile on all their faces.

On television, unfortunately, Hulk wasn't having the same positive effect on our audience. Pretty quickly, his good-guy schtick had turned passé, and some kind of change - even a drastic one - seemed to be necessary.

Towards the end of 1994, Gary pulled me aside to let me know the unfathomable: he was leaving.

At first, I thought he was just fucking with me, but as the weeks wore on, Gary maintained that come May 1995 - the expiration of his WCW contract - he would no longer be associated with the company.

My understanding was that Gary was getting about six figures to do the job, but in my opinion, he viewed that compensation in a different light once Michael Buffer - he of 'Ready to Rumble' fame - came into WCW.

Primarily a ring announcer from the world of boxing, Buffer had been brought in to provide more of a 'big fight' feel, relative to WCW's main events on pay-per-view. I never received confirmation of this, but the rumor was that he received anywhere between $6-10,000 for each WCW appearance that he made. I don't think that became the only issue for Gary, but without question, he was greatly aggravated by the whole thing. Not to tell his story or anything, but he basically left out of principle, I thought.

People have often asked for my opinion about Michael Buffer coming into WCW, and my response has always been the same.

Look, this is America. We live in the land of the American Dream, where anyone can be a millionaire; anyone can be famous. The guy came up with an amazing catchphrase in *"Let's Get Ready to Rumble!"* (interestingly, Buffer initially brainstormed "Man Your Battle Stations" as the original slogan - look that one up), and he delivered the line flawlessly. As we say in the wrestling business, he got that thing *over*.

66

Now did Michael deserve the money that he was getting, based on the fact that he only came out to introduce one match? I don't know. If it got a pop out of the crowd - which it always did, by the way - God bless the man, as far as I'm concerned.

I mean, listen - I could have tried to come up with a line. I could have gone to Eric and auditioned something out - but I didn't. Why would I get mad about that?

People have become rich for much less in this world. I don't want to date myself here, but once upon a time, somebody came up with a pet rock idea and it ended up taking off. I guess I just can't look at people and try to pick apart their success, because that success is what makes this country great. I look at Michael Buffer and say, *Bravo, my friend*. He was able to come up with *one line*, and that's all he needed to amass - if you believe some reports - a net worth approaching $400 million (and believe me, he defends the copyright on that shit like a motherfucker).

Personally, Michael was always very kind to me, and I'll leave you with a story about him. My brother once ran into him at a boxing show, hosted at the *Hard Rock Hotel & Casino* in Hollywood, Florida, several years after we worked together.

I don't know if you remember my brother, he said. *The ring announcer for WCW…back when you did the main events there?*

Of course, Buffer said, *I remember your brother very well - please tell him I said hello.*

He then added a comment which I've remembered ever since.

I just got lucky, Buffer said, *but your brother had talent.*

I thought that was very gracious on his part - and a hell of a compliment too.

67

6:
NEW BEGINNINGS

For many reasons, it's difficult to compare the wrestling business to any other. When Gary revealed that he was leaving WCW, no one really talked to me about the position he was vacating - or even what his departure could imply for my future. There were no formal 'sit-downs' or meetings about the lead ring announcer role, nor was there an application process to sort through candidates. I probably could have asked for a meeting to discuss it at different times, but mostly out of fear and paranoia, I didn't.

It was *intimated* that I might be taking over, and certainly, Gary prepared me (extremely well) for that possibility. Nonetheless, I didn't want to tempt fate by bringing up the issue to the wrong person. I didn't want to run the risk of them putting a larger microscope on the whole deal: *Yeah, you know what, maybe we should take a closer look at this, what with Gary leaving and all...*

Sometimes, you can ask too many questions and get an answer you don't like - especially in this business. I figured I would just shut my mouth, continue to learn under Gary, and hope that my number eventually got called.

It would have been nice to have some reassurance, though - especially once Lisa and I welcomed our first son, Jarrett, into the world on February 3rd, 1995.

Earlier that day, Lisa's water broke while she was at work, but after doing an examination, the doctor sent her home.

It could be a day 'til this baby comes, the doctor explained, *or it could be a week from today.*

68

Things didn't sound too urgent, so I headed for Disney (and the *WCW Worldwide* tapings) that afternoon. Before I arrived there, Lisa gave me my marching orders: *Do NOT drink tonight*, she said.

Eh - the doctor said it could be next week, I shrugged.

Now, if you know anything about those WCW Disney tapings, you'll know that everybody stayed at the same hotel, and consequently, when the day was over, you basically went poolside and started drinking. As usual, the party was in full swing that night when around eight o'clock, I got an unexpected phone call.

I'm giving birth, Lisa said.

Needless to say, I had to sober my ass up real quick! Lisa insisted that I get a rental car with a phone - so we could talk to each other the whole way - and eventually, I arrived at Westside Regional Medical Center. Soon after, Jarrett was born, and as any parent will tell you, it suddenly all became *real*. You can prepare all you want for it, but nothing prepares you – absolutely *nothing* - for what it feels like when that baby comes.

I hugged my new son, spent the night in Lisa's room, and then got my ass back up to Disney - and back to wrestling.

On June 18th, 1995, WCW held its *Great American Bash* pay-per-view at the Hara Arena in Dayton, Ohio. It was the first major event since Gary left the company, and personally, I still didn't know where I stood. I wasn't sure if I would be taking over – at least on anything more than a temporary basis - or, alternatively, if the company had somebody in mind.

Prior to this event, I had never worked a pay-per-view as a ring announcer before, a fact enough, all by itself, to cause some measure of apprehension. At some point during the day, I then learned that

Michael Buffer couldn't make it to introduce the main event match. That marquee bout happened to involve a couple of guys with just a *little* bit of respect in our business: Randy Savage and Ric Flair.

For most of that day, I was *sure* that someone else was going to come out of the woodwork. Were they really going to let me introduce Savage and Flair? Yes, it appeared - they really were, and much to my amazement, I eventually went out there and did it.

Okay, I thought to myself, *even if they do bring someone in to replace Gary, I got to introduce Savage and Flair on a pay-per-view.*

Evidently, I must have done a good enough job, because soon after, Gary Juster approached me with an update: *Penzer, we're moving you up to Atlanta, and we're making you full-time.*

So there it was.

For the time being, at least, I was their guy!

After four years of hard work, I could finally call myself an employee of Turner Broadcasting, with a title, salary, and all the benefits it implied. For people already with a child and another soon on the way (my second son, Dillon, was born in February 1997), the promotion provided Lisa and I with some degree of comfort.

No matter what happened now, I was *in*.

Furthermore, I perceived the company's decision at the *Bash* pay-per-view – i.e. letting me introduce the Savage-Flair main event - as something close to a vote of confidence. It wasn't until many years later that I learned of the *true* circumstances around that decision. Had I known all of the information at that time, I probably would have been horrified.

It turns out that WCW were informed about Buffer's non-appearance a couple of days in advance. In response, they immediately reached out to the guy who had just walked out of the company: Gary Michael Cappetta!

From what I understand, Gary had a simple request when they asked him to do the main event: *Alright, sure - just pay me what you pay Buffer.*

You knew I was leaving, Gary told them, *and you didn't do anything to keep me on board. Now you wanna bring me back for this show? What is it, you don't have confidence in your current ring announcer?*

They tried to make some excuses about it being a special, one-off kind of thing, but Gary repeated his request anyway: *Whatever, just pay me what Buffer gets.*

Obviously, WCW wasn't going to do that, and ultimately - as kind of happened when I became Gary's backup - I sort of got the shot by default! If I knew all of that then, I would have interpreted the attempt to get Gary as the higher-ups lacking faith in me: *Oh, here comes Gary already back for a 'one-off' appearance. It's just a matter of time before he comes back, period. They obviously don't see anything in me...*

Ringside with Michael Buffer

Looking back, I let my head get in the way of enjoying a lot of those early experiences. To continue moving forward, however, I

71

needed to work on overcoming that - especially with responsibilities of my own to think about. After all, getting hired as a Turner employee meant moving to Georgia, taking my growing family with me, and learning to lessen my dependency on Dad (who I had so often needed when in a vulnerable state).

Sure, at 29 years old, it was maybe a little later than most to be doing that, but look - it is what it is. I had a legit job at this point, health insurance, benefits, and a new family to provide for. Dad was still going to be there for me - that part would never change - but certainly, on account of my leaving the state, it wouldn't quite be in the same way as before. Unconsciously, I'm sure that probably affected me, but at the end of the day, I needed to carve out a lane that was separate from him.

Doing that had always been a desire of mine, sure - but it was never the *plan*, if that makes sense. Back then, I don't know if I ever thought to myself: *Okay, here's how I'm gonna stand on my own two feet - I gotta make it in the wrestling business.* No - it was always a leap of faith for me - or, more accurately, one leap of faith after another.

Now that I think about it, I was never *consciously* trying to get anywhere - I was just looking to extend this adventure for as long as I could.

Nonetheless, here I now was - sitting ringside at the point of no return.

Once I became a Turner employee, my focus quickly changed. No longer did I have to consume myself with just getting *in*; now, I was officially on payroll, and I wanted to demonstrate my value however I could. It's one of the reasons why I decided, fairly early on, to get more familiar with the WCW production process. I started helping out Tony Schiavone in that area - with no expectation of additional compensation – just to secure my position a little more. With time, I began getting a little bit more comfortable in my surroundings, but at no point did I get cocky about it.

To no small degree, a lot of that had to do with Eric Bischoff.

As of 1995, Eric was now the Executive Vice President of WCW - and as such, he was responsible for signing off on my new role. Clearly, I was immensely grateful for that opportunity, but I came to see working under Eric as a challenging situation. Quite frankly, he wasn't really a people person, and because I was always so paranoid about my dream coming to an end, I guess that fact was significant to me. Looking back, I must have resembled a child being desperate for attention, or something - because apparently, no matter what I did, I just couldn't get that attention from Eric.

In fairness, Eric's disposition hadn't much changed since he first entered WCW as a third-string announcer. But once he became the boss, I would often be looking for feedback like, 'Hey, you did a really good job tonight', or even a, 'Thanks a lot, Penzer – nice work' - or maybe a pat on the back or something - but with Eric, it was simply this: *none of the above*. He would just kind of walk past you, seemingly lost in thought, and probably dealing with a thousand other issues at the time. In hindsight, now that I know more about the stress that Eric was under - especially as time went on - I can only imagine what he must have been going through.

Back then, however, it wasn't exactly the greatest feeling on earth that my boss wouldn't look me in the eye - let alone even talk to me when I walked past him in the hallway. I was already on edge at the best of times, and that lack of reassurance kind of did a number on my mental health. It made for frequent conversation between Lisa and I, and it's partially the reason why I did everything with an unrelenting attitude: *You gotta keep showing up, Penzer,* I thought. *You gotta do your job. You gotta work hard. You gotta do extra shit. Help out in production - just do anything to keep this dream alive.*

73

Over the years, people have often observed that you didn't hear my voice much on the actual WCW broadcasts, as our main announce team would usually be heard as a wrestler entered the ring. My voice, conversely, was typically muted on the master audio track (except for certain occasions, like the first match on a pay-per-view) - and this was an intentional decision by Eric.

For the record, I personally had no problem with it.

Previously, I think it had annoyed Eric - not on a personal level, but strictly through the lens of *business* - that Gary Cappetta received so much attention. Gary enjoyed a lot of camera time, but that was a consequence, I would argue, of his coming up in a different era. Gary had successfully followed in the footsteps of Howard Finkel - the greatest ring announcer of all-time, in my opinion - *en route* to becoming the second person, as far as I can remember, to develop a *personality* in that role.

Historically, such as in the territorial days of wrestling, there existed no such thing as an *official* ring announcer. It was basically just somebody's brother-in-law in each town that a promotion was running in, and even in Jim Crockett Promotions, they didn't have a permanent person in that spot - until Gary. Both he and Howard Finkel changed the game for all of us - and thank God they did!

Nevertheless, as far as Eric was concerned, he perceived ring announcers to be more transactional - with less of a need for personalities. I know that Eric believed that our airtime was too valuable for a ring announcer to monopolize. He thought we could better use that time to promote things to our audience - the merchandise, live events, pay-per-views and so on - and that made perfect sense to me.

If you think about the average ring introduction, you might be talking about 60 to 90 seconds of a guy walking to the ring. Over the course of an entire show, those instances add up, to the point where conceivably, you might have 10 to 15 minutes devoted for that purpose. For the audience at home, why give them nothing but the ring announcer during those intros? You're basically giving them a reason to change the channel - in addition to leaving serious money on the table.

Eric explained all this to me, and I got it completely. *This is your show*, I shrugged, matter-of-factly.

I will do whatever you tell me to do, I continued. *This is not about my ego*.

That particular comment is kind of funny looking back, and I'll tell you the reason why. I once heard Eric say that he had no respect for people without an ego, and you know what? That basically sounds about right. It may have been one of the reasons why I didn't get much time with the boss.

I do want to make this abundantly clear though: I have come to think the world of Eric Bischoff. I respect the fuck out of him and admire him in many different ways. Sure, I may have been like a child yearning for attention - just like I said - but that wasn't Eric's responsibility to take care of. He gave me an opportunity - he gave me a job - and at the end of the day, that's all that fucking matters.

Furthermore, Eric deserves credit for being an extremely hard worker, an extremely confident person, and extremely *driven* towards making WCW successful. Prior to his tenure, the company had seemingly tried everything it could to legitimately compete with the WWF, but nothing ever seemed to click. I remember when Bill Watts was brought in by WCW in 1992, for example, during a period in which the company was floundering. Based on his historical success in Mid-South, everybody thought Bill was going to be the savior - until he started to implement his ideas. Famously, he eliminated jumping off the top rope, as well as the mats surrounding the ring below. He made a series of questionable acquisitions, slashed the payroll like crazy, and ended up getting fired in controversial fashion.

Watts' dismissal came after a racially charged interview he gave with the *Pro Wrestling Torch* reached the desk of Hank Aaron, the former Atlanta Braves right fielder and at that time, a Vice President in the Turner organization. It ended up becoming a big controversy, but soon after, WCW had Robert Fuller, dressed in his getup as Colonel Parker, lead Booker T and Stevie Ray out to the ring in *chains* - while wearing prison outfits. They billed the future 'Harlem Heat' tag-team as *The Posse* in a match taped for *WCW Saturday Night*, but thankfully, it never made air. Word got back to someone at Turner and from what I remember, the entire segment was *burned*.

Such embarrassing incidents only further cemented the idea of WCW as the 'red-headed stepchild' of Turner Broadcasting, but our trajectory changed, in my opinion, once Eric got in a position to make his moves.

One of those moves was hiring Zane Bresloff - a certified marketing genius who had long promoted arenas for the WWF. As far as I could tell, Eric and Zane made up *the* team - *the* duo that our company needed to be successful. They maintained a constant dialog over the phone - almost a never-ending brainstorming session, in essence - always talking about new markets, new buildings, or new strategies to take us forward. It was abundantly clear that Zane, to use an expression common in the wrestling business, "had Eric's ear," and I thought they worked tremendously well together.

Known affectionately as 'Insane Zane', Bresloff could be a bit of a bullshitter at times - I mean, who *isn't* in the world of marketing - but certainly, he was a very unique character. That character was explored at great length, incidentally, in a section of the book, *NITRO: The Incredible Rise and Inevitable Collapse of Ted Turner's WCW*:

As a diminutive, red-headed Jewish man with a curious dislike for large crowds, [Bresloff] could hardly have been considered a likely candidate to become the most revered events promoter in wrestling. But in 1985, after several years working as an executive for *Select-A-Seat* - the precursor to *Ticketmaster* - Bresloff single-handedly enabled Vince McMahon to gain a foothold in the Denver, CO market.

76

Before long, Bresloff was booking and promoting arenas for the WWF nationwide, highlighted by his instrumental role in hyping the seminal *WrestleMania III*.

...[But] for all of Bresloff's status and affluence, he cared little about materialistic pursuits, usually sporting a trademark t-shirt-and-shorts combination at home or in public. His quirks, like refusing to wear socks and leaving shows as soon as they started, all became part of the charm. But ultimately, and perhaps in a manner reminiscent of Don Draper's smooth self-assuredness in *Mad Men*, Bresloff's most successful sales act was to sell himself. While physically he more resembled a character from an earlier age (unfortunately, the principal in *Ferris Bueller's Day Off*, as evidenced by the relatively frequent requests for his autograph), Zane's sheer competency garnered universal respect amongst his peers.

I remember Zane for being high-strung, always 'on the go', and perpetually positive - even when there was nothing to be positive about. He also seemed to be a genuine supporter of mine, perhaps even a mentor at times. He saw potential in me that I don't think I even realized, mostly about what I could do away from the ring. At house shows, he ended up pushing for me to 'settle the houses', something that required the approval of Gary Juster (who as I mentioned earlier, was WCW's *internal* head of live events). It involved dealing with an important matter at each venue - the *money* - and clearly, that task came with significant consequences. When Juster explained to me what I would be doing, he gave me the explanation for it: *Penzer, you are 'over' huge with Zane Bresloff!*

There remained ample reasons to be paranoid about my job, but little by little, I was getting more ingrained in the WCW system. More importantly, it would soon become apparent that the timing of everything couldn't have been better.

In the summer of 1995, TNT announced that it was launching a new prime-time show - *WCW Monday Nitro* - putting us in *direct* competition with the WWF.

We all thought the idea was *nuts*. Everybody recognized it would take an insane effort to grab the WWF's audience away from them -

and I include Eric in that category, too. He's told the story many times about how the decision was made - and the nature of his meeting which preceded it all with Ted Turner. I think that tells you, pretty clearly, that Eric never even *dreamed* we would get such a high-profile time slot. He was as surprised as everyone else.

It wasn't until September 4th, 1995 - the date of the first *Nitro* at the Mall of America - that I realized we had a shot. The production set-up looked major league. The energy was palpable. The card was impressive. You had Brian Pillman and Jushin Liger in an exciting first match, Sting versus Flair (which always did well in the ratings) to anchor the middle of the show, and Hulk wrestling on 'free' TV in the main event. It was a very different look, feel and format than what we typically did on *WCW Saturday Night*.

At the beginning of the Sting-Flair match, Lex Luger famously walked down the aisle - despite his wrestling at a WWF house show some 24 hours earlier. I had no idea Lex was going to show up (realistically, I think that including Lex and Eric, probably only five people did), and I got goosebumps when he went 'nose-to-nose' with Hulk. *You know what*, I thought to myself, *I think Eric might just have something here.*

The show blew away everyone's expectations to record a 2.9 cable rating, translating to just under 3 million viewers. Critics pointed to the fact, however, that *Nitro* had been launched on a night when *Raw* was preempted, meaning that the true test would come the following week - when both shows aired at the same time.

Originally, the title sequence for *Nitro* featured multiple shots of Leon White - aka Vader - who was booked to face Hogan, provisionally, in the main event of week two (Lex coming in allowed WCW to change those plans). In the end, Leon didn't make a single appearance on our new show, and instead, he left the company soon after, following an infamous backstage altercation with the former

'Mr. Wonderful', Paul Orndorff, who was now an agent for WCW behind the scenes.

We were doing a taping at Center Stage when it all went down. As was typical back then, Terry Taylor, Tony Schiavone, Paul and I were responsible for rounding up guys for their interview slots. At the end of the night, we only had one promo left to tape - Vader - and because he was headlining the next pay-per-view, it was kind of a big deal.

Generally, Leon was a nice guy, but on this occasion, he was just in a *horrible* mood. When I initially went to go get him for the promo, he basically told me - in no uncertain terms - that it wasn't gonna happen.

Uh, I don't think he's coming any time soon, I said to the rest of the group.

He's in a pretty bad mood.

Terry Taylor then went with me to talk to Leon - only to suffer the same fate. By now, Paul was getting really pissed off: *This guy's a Prima donna*, he said, speaking of Leon. *This is wrestling. We've got a show to do...I don't care what's going on, he needs to do the interview!*

Paul decided to take those thoughts to Leon directly, and unsurprisingly, they started to get into it. Soon, they moved their 'discussion' into another office - just the two of them - and there was a lot of back-and-forth going on. There are different versions of what happened next, but all I know is this: when Leon White came out of that room, his face looked like it *exploded*.

If you've ever seen any backstage photos from the '90s, you'll know that the agents back then didn't dress like the 'producers' of today. With this in mind, the fact that Paul wore *flip-flops* during the confrontation - during the fight, no less - is what elevated this story to legendary status!

79

Leon probably spent 15 minutes trying to get the swelling down, mostly by dumping his face into a nearby ice bucket. I'm not saying that Leon wasn't a tough guy, and I'm not saying he didn't get a shot or two in either. But while people may argue over the details, his face basically told you everything.

I once heard Paul recount the entire incident at a wrestling convention. He admitted that at one point, Leon *did* throw a blow which sent him to the ground - a 'sucker punch' as he called it - but he was sure to blame the flip-flops for that.

Leon then made a mistake, Paul said.

...He let me get up.

As we approached the first head-to-head match-up between *Nitro* and *Raw* - September 11th, 1995 - I felt cautiously optimistic. At the same time, I truly didn't expect that night's result in the Nielsen ratings: a 2.5 to 2.2 ratings win in our favor.

Just by itself, winning the 'real' week one had been a huge achievement for our company, but subsequently, we went on to do what few thought was possible. We split the remaining contests for 1995 - seven wins for *Nitro*, and seven wins for *Raw* - which had to be considered a major success, according to any reasonable metric.

In the process, I noticed something that had never been the case before - at least in my time around WCW. For years, there had never been anything resembling a team atmosphere (probably because historically, we couldn't draw 800 fans to a house show with all of our stars), but now, the tide seemed to be turning.

Holy shit, everyone collectively realized.

This could fucking work.

80

SITTING RINGSIDE VOLUME 1

FAMILY

7:
LESSONS FROM THE TASKMASTER

Ah - life is good, I thought.

Talk about living the dream, man.

This is the life.

So picture this: I was flying back home after a show in the Chicago area - in first class, I might add – and salivating over the in-flight menu. *Let's see*, I thought, *should I get the steak? Hmmm. How about a filet mignon? Oh - make-your-own sundaes. I like the sound of that…*

Eventually, I settled on the filet mignon, helping myself to a cocktail for good measure. After devouring the meal in short order, I lay back in my seat, closed my eyes, and pictured everyone else back in Orlando. Guys like Pee Wee were on their way to that night's event - a major house show, incidentally, with Hulk Hogan headlining - while I relaxed comfortably at 30,000 feet. I had already done my job, after all - just like they asked me. I had given Pee Wee the various wrestler's entrance music - a series of theme songs recorded on *cassette tapes* (am I dating myself yet?) - so that task was taken care of. If Pee Wee didn't have the case with the cassette tapes inside - for those not familiar with the medium - he literally wouldn't have *any* of the wrestler's music, but there was no risk of that. He had the tapes - I gave him the case - and there was nothing more to worry about.

Would you like another cocktail, sir?

Oh, yes, I would - thank you so much.

I laid back a little more.

86

Yep, this really is the dream, I said to myself.

I got a cocktail, and I'm eating filet mignon. I got an ice cream sundae coming up...

And to top it all off, look at me - I did it!

I'm in the wrestling business!

I mean, really - life is pretty...damn...

Shit!

Suddenly, my stomach dropped - all the way from the plane and back down to earth.

I never gave Pee Wee the fucking music, I realized.

I'm gonna get fired.

I'm gonna get fired!!!

At the drop of a dime, my mindset totally changed - just like that. I was soon in a state of panic, because having that entrance music - especially for someone like Hogan - was a big fucking deal. *What an idiot.* Here I was, practically jerking myself off like a jackass - while traveling in the complete opposite direction - having fucked up my one and only job.

I grabbed the first flight attendant that I could find and told her what was happening. Believe it or not - and maybe this is a commentary on how standards have changed over the years - the flight attendant had the pilot send down a message. Before the plane landed in Atlanta, the airline had me booked on a flight to Orlando, and once I got there, they hustled me off the plane as quickly as possible. To top it all off, they actually went underneath the plane, got my suitcase (with the cassette tapes inside) and handed it to me - before anyone else left their seats!

I ran through the Orlando International airport, got myself in a cab, and headed straight to the arena. I didn't get there in time for the opening match - and some of the guys, *sans* entrance music, were certainly pissed about that - but ample time remained before Hogan, and some of the other big stars, were going to feature in the main event. That was a huge relief in itself, because if Hulk didn't have his music, it would have been a fucking nightmare.

Finally, I had a second to catch my breath - that is, before Kevin Sullivan pulled me aside.

Kevin looked at me and had only one thing to say: *What the fuck?*

Sorry, Kevin, I responded. *Pee Wee was supposed to remind me.*

Kevin stared at me in silence.

What? I said sheepishly. *I'm just telling you the truth!*

Kevin looked like he wanted to explode.

Everybody fucks up, he said - *everybody. Nobody's perfect. There's not one perfect person on this earth. But when you try to blame other people for fucking up, that makes you look a hundred times worse.*

Just take responsibility for it, he continued, now berating me. *Just cough it up - you did it! Say you're sorry, and never let it happen again, because when you screw up like that twice...that's when it's more than a mistake. Then it's an ongoing issue.*

That day, Kevin taught me one of the best lessons that I ever learned. When I screwed up, I *did* kind of have a habit of putting the heat on somebody else - or at least I tried to. There had been a similar situation on a trip to San Francisco, for example - prior to the Orlando house show incident - when Kevin remembers me again making excuses for something. As Kevin tells it, he eventually had enough of my whining and opened the car door.

Get out, he said.

(Interestingly, I don't recall *that* incident as vividly as Kevin does – but maybe it's because I blocked it out of my mind!)

In any case, Kevin was absolutely right, and I found myself teaching similar lessons (well, not the whole getting-out-of-the-car thing) to my very own kids: *Everybody screws up - everybody.*

But you take responsibility for it - and you learn from it.

At the beginning of *Nitro*, Kevin was indispensable, I thought, as the matchmaker for Eric. He had an amazing wrestling mind, with an uncanny ability of convincing people to do things that usually, he had a vision for well in advance. The boys appreciated being able to give their input - and Kevin was great at listening to their comments - but most of the time, they were going to do what Kevin had planned out anyway. He would frame it in these kinds of terms to some of the bigger stars: *This is what I wanna do, but what do you think?*

Sometimes, those same stars didn't quite see the vision, but Kevin - or 'The Taskmaster' as he was known - usually found a way to make it happen. It's funny in hindsight, because if you look at the *character* that Kevin Sullivan played in the wrestling business, he tended to be sort of a manipulator - and it was kind of like that in real life, too. I'm not saying that in a derogatory way - Kevin was a huge positive for us. By cutting through the egos in the locker room, he had a way of influencing people; of *bringing them into his web*.

Just like he taught me a lesson or two, Kevin sort of took everybody under his wing. In his own unique way, he was an

89

incredible teacher to a lot of our guys, and I think that's why the angle with him and Brian Pillman (the famous worked shoot 'Booker Man' storyline) was so effective. At the time, nobody except a handful of people - maybe Kevin, Brian and Eric, I would imagine - actually knew what was going on. I remember a talent meeting in Orlando, for instance, where Kevin and Brian shot an angle - totally for 'the boys' - even though there were no cameras around (Eric happened to be in on it too). In other words, they had a confrontation just for the talent - purely to sell their dispute as a *shoot*. They must have had a blast with it. I know it put me in the position of being a mark again - even though I was working with them in the same company!

For a couple of months, Pee Wee and I had the privilege of driving to shows with Kevin and Nancy Sullivan, and during those rides, Kevin would write the 'TVs' - i.e. what he wanted to book on each episode of *Nitro* - as we went from town to town. Sometimes, he would even ask me to write down his ideas.

Penzer, he would say, handing me a notepad, *jot this stuff down that I say*. Kevin would proceed to dictate what our fans ended up seeing on the shows each week, so for the record, anybody who says that he wasn't directly responsible - as much as anyone else - for the early success of *Monday Nitro*, doesn't know what they're talking about.

At the time, I was a student of the game, and I wanted to learn as much as I could. It ended up being one of the coolest times of my life, because at the age of 16, I had been *that* fan who was booking his own storylines - his own promotion, actually (!) - planning out my fictional shows on a yellow legal pad. Now, here I was - all of these years later - being part of the number one show on cable television, and writing down Kevin Sullivan's concepts. I didn't have much of a say in anything, but occasionally, Kevin would stop and ask me: *So, what do you think, Penzer? Do you think this match would be any good?*

To be totally, abundantly clear, I had absolutely *nothing* to do with putting together those shows. I was just kind of being Kevin's stooge, quite frankly. For Kevin, there was probably some fun in making the

90

ring announcer write his ideas down - as opposed to him writing it all down. That's kind of how we entertained ourselves before the Internet or before cell phones and all that stuff. Even though it might sound like a small thing, a running joke like that - *Oh, Penzer - you're just my stooge* - is how we made the time go by. Nobody took that type of stuff personally, and if you did take it personally, you didn't last long in the business.

In essence, Kevin already had his creative ideas in mind, and by the time he handed me that notepad, he was mostly formulating matches at that point. He had a lot of the angles planned out in advance - it was more just the matches that needed to be finalized. *This guy is gonna wrestle the TV champion*, he would say, *so we need to start getting him over. Who do you think he could have a good match with?*

Alternatively, he might say something like, *Disco can get Jericho over - go ahead and write that down. Disco Inferno and Chris Jericho - that'll be entertaining.*

Kevin is a genius in a lot of ways - and not just with respect to wrestling. He's one of the smartest people that I've ever met, and he is so knowledgeable - about so many different things - that it truly blows my mind. When you're involved in the wrestling business, you tend to grasp on to (and remember) the negatives, and to some extent, maybe that's natural. When you're on the road, you might get into an argument, or get mad because you got yelled at, and you might take that experience with you for the entire next week. It wasn't always roses - that's for sure - but with Kevin, I can see now how great he was in dealing with people.

Unfortunately, my time riding with 'The Taskmaster' didn't last very long. The reason was pretty simple, and Kevin would be the first to say it, too - he ended up booking his own divorce.

It all started when Kevin - still active as a wrestler in addition to his booking duties - came up with an angle for Nancy, his real-life wife and a manager on WCW television. According to the storyline, Nancy was scripted to leave Kevin for Chris Benoit, and to sell its legitimacy, Kevin had them travel together, share hotel rooms and hold hands in public. They even tried to kayfabe *me* on the whole deal, but ultimately, in an example of life imitating art, Nancy and Chris got together for real.

I'm not sure exactly when it stopped being kayfabe and when it first became real, but it led to a number of uncomfortable situations for me. Things got a little crazy on that front, and for a while, I thought it was better to keep some distance from everybody.

During the early years of *Nitro*, it was my understanding that Kevin came up with the angles and storylines - and Eric had to sign off on everything. If Eric had a different vision for something, he might enhance one of Kevin's concepts or make it a little better, but they were still Kevin's ideas to start with. Of course, Eric could have always tossed out Kevin's ideas, but I don't recall that happening a lot. I always thought that Eric's goal - unless he absolutely fucking hated what Kevin came up with - was to make Kevin's ideas as good as they could possibly be.

When it comes to Kevin and Eric's relationship, I think people sometimes forget that this is a business. It's like working for UPS or something - I don't know, you pick the employer. Sometimes you roll your eyes at your supervisor when he does certain things, but at the end of the day, he's your supervisor - like it or not. Whether you agree with him being in charge, it's not your call, ultimately - so you work there, and to keep your job and your benefits, you kind of just roll with it. That's sort of how it was with Kevin and Eric, in my opinion. Kevin was the wrestling mind - with Eric having more of a sales background - but in the end, there was only one boss.

I'm not saying that a lot of Kevin's stuff didn't get *tweaked* by Eric, because only one person had the final say. I will say this, however: in general, Kevin created it - and Eric approved it.

92

Crucially, and as is well documented, Hulk Hogan - by virtue of the creative control clause in his contract - had a significant say in creative. Nonetheless, Hulk and Kevin had a great rapport and relationship, and I distinctly remember Kevin being very proud of that. He was proud of it, in large part, because that's a hell of a tough situation to be in. Here you have Kevin as the booker, but then you have Hulk Hogan with the power to veto his ideas. At first, you got the impression that Hulk - while still a major coup for our company - didn't really want to do it in WCW, if that makes sense.

Backstage with the Hulkster

I think Hulk had been worried coming into WCW. He was concerned about not drawing in the main events and consequently, damaging his reputation in the process. I'm sure it's one of the reasons why he had creative control in the first place, and Kevin had no choice but to work around it. In time, however, Hulk grew to appreciate that Kevin cared about what he thought. I also think that Kevin knew - in both the back and the front of his mind - that eventually, Hulk *had* to turn heel. It was just about making him comfortable to get there.

That's basically the reason why the 'Dungeon of Doom' storyline happened. I mean, straight up - Kevin will tell you that he thought it was *horrible* - but he did it, at that time, because Hulk didn't trust him yet. Hulk was used to character-based wrestling with big guys - you

93

know, gigantic monsters for him to vanquish - and so what did Kevin do? He brought in Kamala. He brought in John Tenta as 'The Shark'. He brought in Zeus. He brought in all these crazy characters to form an equally crazy cult called the Dungeon of Doom.

It was so, *so* over the top, but it was meant to be - again, it's what Hogan was used to. Kevin felt like if he just said, *Look, Hulk - I wanna turn you heel next week*, the response would have been, *What the fuck are you doing to me, brother?*

Alternatively, by Kevin developing that angle - and booking Hulk against guys like 'The Shark' - he was able to develop the trust necessary for creative co-existence (and eventually, Hogan came to trust Kevin implicitly). If you remember, Kevin even added Jimmy Hart into the 'Dungeon of Doom' mess, as Jimmy was Hulk's buddy who migrated with him to WCW. Paul Wight, in a debuting role as 'The Giant', emerged as yet another opponent for Hogan, and because Hulk saw money in him, Paul featured in the main events immediately.

To summarize, whenever anyone says, 'The Dungeon of Doom sucked,' Kevin will say, *Yeah - it did, but there was a reason for it...and it ultimately worked for that reason.*

Without that Dungeon of Doom angle - and admittedly, it *did* suck - we wouldn't have had what happened next.

In early 1996, you got the sense that something was building. First, our house shows started drawing really well, mostly due to a hot program between Randy Savage and Ric Flair (a fact, incidentally, that often gets lost to history). Savage and Flair started the fire, so to speak, but soon, two defectors from 'Up North' were about to set it ablaze.

Initially, I knew that Scott Hall, formerly Razor Ramon in the WWF (and previously, 'The Diamond Studd' in our company) had been signed to a WCW contract. That said, I had no idea *how* they were going to handle his debut on television. One way of doing it, as was often the case historically, would have been to bring him out for a backstage interview. He could have recorded a promo on a set somewhere, or maybe featured in a hype video previewing his arrival: *Coming soon!*

In the end, none of those conventional methods were used, and consequently, the debut of Scott Hall became far more groundbreaking than anyone could have imagined. On May 27th, 1996, *Nitro* returned from commercial break with a seemingly pedestrian match in progress: Steve Doll versus 'The Mauler' Mike Enos. *"Welcome back, live, to the first hour of this edition of WCW Monday Nitro on TNT,"* said Tony Schiavone on commentary. *"We are taking a look at 'The Mauler' completely maul his opponent, Steve Doll..."*

Suddenly, an unmistakable figure made his way through the crowd. He soon made his way to ringside - the crowd at the Macon Coliseum completely dumbfounded - before stopping to grab *my* microphone: *Hey, gimme a mic!*

Seemingly consistent with his Razor Ramon character, Scott then entered the ring, faced the hard camera, and powerfully delivered a prophetic promo:

Hey - you people, you know who I am. But you don't know why I'm here.

Where is 'Billionaire Ted?' Where is the 'Nacho Man?' That punk can't even get in the building. Me? I go wherever I want, *whenever* I want. And where, oh where, is 'Scheme Gene?'

... 'cos I got a scoop for you. When that Ken Doll look-a-like, when that weatherman wannabe comes out here later tonight, I got a challenge for him - for Billionaire Ted, for the Nacho Man, and for anybody else in uh... 'dubya-dee-dubya'.

At this point, a lightbulb went off in my head. The WWF had previously run a series of skits mocking some of our older talent - Hulk and Randy in particular - with Ted Turner (as 'Billionaire Ted') even failing to escape parody. As soon as that 'Billionaire Ted' phrase came out of Scott's mouth, I saw clearly what we were doing - *I got it.*

I already knew that Kevin Nash (the former 'Diesel') was coming in behind Scott - his own WWF contract similarly expired - but no one could have foreseen *this* as a creative idea. It was designed to look like Vince McMahon had ordered an invasion of our own little *rasslin* company, setting the scene, apparently, for an interpromotional angle like no other: WCW versus the WWF!

Scott drove this point home as he closed his promo:

You wanna go to war?

You want a war?

You're gonna get one.

Only one thing occurred to me as Scott left the ring: *this is too good to fuck up.*

This is how it was all laid out in the production format:

TNT 117 Page #3 (Rvd. 5/27/96 5pm)
Macon, GA/Airs: Monday, May 27, 1996   Air Time & Program Length: 8:00pm-9:59:50pm eastern

RING: (2:30)   1-M   2-M
                      STEVE DOLL   vs.   MIKE ENOS w/Col. Parker

Match Note: Match Continues & Ends In This Segment...Tony Pitch To Gene
                   (2:30) Includes A :45 Interruption....
                   Ring Interruption @ 8:37:04...
            Note: Break to interruption (8:33:45- 8:34:10)
            Break to bell (8:33:45 - 8:34:10)
            8:34:00 - Large man spotted in audience makes his way to the ring - he requests a microphone
            8:34:26 - Col. in ring w/ Enos - Doll leaves - large man in ring - he makes references to "Billionaire Ted/Nacho Man, etc." It is apparent
he   is (was) a wrestler from WWF. He declares war w/ WCW/WWF - ref gets him to leave. Announcers are speechless - match is
completely   interrupted - go to break.
            Result of match: No winner!
            Break @ 8:36:40   8:36:04

"He declares war w/ WCW/WWF..."

96

At the end of the show, Scott unexpectedly returned on camera, this time at the announce table, teasing that another surprise would be coming:

Hey, looky here. Ken Doll - you got such a big mouth…and we…are sick of it.

This is where the 'Big Boys' play? What a joke. I tell you what - you go tell 'Billionaire Ted': you go tell him…get three of his very, very best.

…We are coming down here, and like it or not - we are taking over.

After Kevin Nash subsequently made his own debut - on the June 10th, 1996 edition of *Nitro* - it soon became clear that as a duo, both Scott and Kevin brought a swagger that we never had before. There were so many layers to the 'invasion' storyline, including the fact that both guys had been discarded, essentially, as midcarders in WCW some years earlier - before going on to achieve success in 'New York'. Triumphantly and defiantly, they had now returned to challenge 'our' guys (Sting, Lex Luger and Randy Savage) to a 3-on-3 match in the process, with one important detail left on the table: *Who was the third man?*

It all led to one historic night: *Bash at the Beach* in Daytona Beach, Florida, on July 7th, 1996. Towards the end of the main event match, Hulk came down the aisle - ostensibly in an attempt to help the babyfaces - before siding with Scott and Kevin instead! To the shock of everyone in attendance, Hulk attacked Randy, took out the referee (Pee Wee Anderson, incidentally), and soon, the entire match was thrown out!

"He's the third man!" bellowed Bobby Heenan on commentary. *"Hulk Hogan has betrayed WCW! He is the third man in this picture!"*

I do want to clear something up that has become part of the narrative in recent years. It has been said that within WCW, 'nobody knew' - including the announcers - that Hogan was going to turn.

97

A more accurate representation would be that nobody knew for *sure* - in other words, none of us *really* knew if Hogan would actually do it. On the day of the event, a lot of chatter was going on backstage, and in general, the feeling was something like, 'Wow - if they can actually convince him to do this, *holy shit.*'

That is where the shock factor came from for those of us working in the company. To be totally honest, we weren't blindsided in the same way that the fans were, because interestingly, *Bash at the Beach* wasn't like some of the other surprises that came later (Roddy Piper's debut was a good example of that, because very few people had forewarning about it, and therefore, most of us were legitimately stunned). On this occasion, however, I personally knew that Hulk had stayed at Kevin Sullivan's beach house the night before (a measure taken to ensure that Hogan's agent wouldn't talk him out of it), so I understood - based on my relationship with Kevin - that Hulk turning heel was definitely 'Plan A'.

That said, Hulk was nowhere to be found when we started the show, and therefore, it wasn't until he came through the curtain that we knew it was a definite. When he finally did come out, drop the leg on Randy, and join forces with Scott and Kevin, I'll be transparent about my initial reaction. I thought it was a cool angle, but I didn't think it was going to be historic or anything. I didn't think it was going to be *that* big of a deal; that is, until the people reacted in the way that they did, specifically in response to his promo. In an amazing visual, debris littered the entire ring as Hulk unloaded on the Daytona Beach audience:

Well, the first thing you've got to realize, brother...is this right here is the future of wrestling. You can call this...the New World Order of Wrestling, brother. These two men right here came from a great big organization up north...and everybody was wondering who the third man was. Well...who knows more about that organization than me, brother?

Well, let me tell you something - I made that organization a monster! I made people rich up there. I made the people that run that organization rich up there, brother. When it all came to pass, the name Hulk Hogan, the man Hulk Hogan, got bigger than the whole organization, brother! And then Billionaire Ted, amigo...he wanted to 'talk turkey' with Hulk Hogan. Billionaire Ted promised me movies, brother...Billionaire Ted promised me millions of dollars...and Billionaire Ted promised me world caliber matches. As far as Billionaire Ted, Eric Bischoff, and the whole WCW goes - I'm bored, brother!

That's why these two guys here, the so-called Outsiders...these are the men I want as my friends. They're the new blood of professional wrestling, brother - and not only are we going to take over the whole wrestling business, with Hulk Hogan and the new blood...the monsters with me, we will destroy everything in our path...Mean Gene!

As only he could, Gene made reference to the garbage all around Hulk and the Outsiders, setting up Hulk for a grand finale:

Look at all of this crap in this ring. This is what's in the future for you, if you wanna hang around the likes of this man Hall, and this man Nash.

Hulk took Gene's interjection and raised his promo to another level:

As far as I'm concerned, all this crap in the ring represents these fans out here. For two years, brother...for two years, I held my head high...I did everything for the charities...I did everything for the kids...and the reception I got when I came out here...you fans can stick it, brother!

Because if it wasn't for Hulk Hogan, you people wouldn't be here. If it wasn't for Hulk Hogan, Eric Bischoff would be still selling meat from a truck in Minneapolis, and if it wasn't for Hulk Hogan, all these Johnny-Come-Lately's that you see out here wrestling...wouldn't be here. I was selling out the world, brother, while they were bumming gas to put in their car to get to high school. So the way that it is now, brother, with Hulk Hogan and the New World Organization of Wrestling, brother, me and the new blood by my side....whatcha gonna do, when the New World Organization runs wild on you? Whatcha gonna do?

Even though Hulk butchered the 'New World Order' phrase (*"New World Organization"*) at the conclusion of his promo, I thought it was a *fantastic* interview. Already, you could see that turning heel had given him a new lease of life, because up until this point - as fans back then will remember - Hulk Hogan hadn't exactly set the world on fire in WCW. I would even go as far as to say that without turning heel, I don't really know what would have happened to him, or how WCW might have utilized him going forward.

99

A large portion of the credit, in my view, goes to Kevin Sullivan, who was instrumental in getting Hulk to turn. As time went on, Eric really took ownership over the nWo storyline - it was really his pet project, from my perspective - and consequently, Kevin's role often gets overlooked. But make no mistake about it - the Taskmaster taught us another lesson that night.

Even the great Hulk Hogan couldn't escape his web.

8:
IT'S ONLY TUPELO

As the nWo storyline took off, we started to create real distance between ourselves and the WWF. What had been a back-and-forth competition was becoming one-sided, and as we continued to win in the ratings war, I thought that the WWF appeared very wounded. At this point, Eric - in my opinion, at least - started to smell blood in the water.

At the beginning, I think Eric had the goal of *beating* the WWF - and making WCW the number one promotion - but not necessarily putting them out of business. This is my interpretation, of course, but I think as time went on, he became *obsessed* with putting them away. Personally, I wouldn't have gotten any satisfaction from that happening, and I definitely wasn't rooting for it - but Eric was.

He might have gotten a little full of himself. Famously, we would have these 'rah-rah' meetings where he talked about the WWF being on the verge of shutting down. Again, this is my personal interpretation, but I think he thought he was close to pulling it off - and consequently, he wanted to *tell* everybody that he was close. He wanted to brag about it; it wasn't like, 'Let's all work together and finish the job.' It was, 'This motherfucker' - speaking of Vince McMahon - 'is going out of business.'

What fired Eric up was not so much the 'rah-rah' in itself, it was more like, 'We're gonna put these motherfuckers out of business, and we're gonna win this fucking war.' But everybody had friends that worked in the WWF, and naturally, a lot of people thought, 'But wait a minute - we don't want our friends to be out of a job. We'd just like to continue to win, and still be the biggest company in the world.'

Eric has since explained that it was the 'company line' to talk in those terms, but that's his story to tell - and not mine. In any event, some of the 'rah-rah' meetings were effective, but some of them - well, they didn't go so well.

I remember one meeting that happened after a house show in Tupelo, Mississippi. A little back story first: I was in charge of overseeing the music for the show, and as we previously established, it was all triggered via cassette tapes. A lot of times, the cassette machine was up in the sound booth - near where the suites were located - and as a result, I didn't always have full control over it. Nonetheless, we typically had individual tapes cued up with individual entrance themes, so Sting's song would be on one tape, while another would have Randy's Savage theme - you get the idea. As long as the tapes were rewound correctly, the sound guy just had to press 'play' and the song went off without a hitch.

Well, on this night, Kevin Nash and Scott Hall wanted to come out to the Fugees song, 'Ready or Not'. As WCW didn't have an official license to use the music, we didn't have a tape with that specific song prepared. Instead, we had to purchase the actual retail album that 'Ready or Not' was featured on - *The Score* - and have the tape cued it up the right position. It was the third song on Side A - I'll never forget it.

Unfortunately, while I was in the ring to introduce Kevin and Scott's match, the sound guy put the tape in *the wrong way*. If you know anything about cassette tapes, that obviously meant that we were now playing Side B - the wrong side! Once you start doing that, it's not so easy to get your cue point back, especially in a live environment, and the sound guy had no idea where the song was located.

Meanwhile, Kevin and Scott were still backstage, refusing to come out until the error was resolved. In turn, that led to five of the most uncomfortable minutes of my life, as I tried in vain to stall in the ring for time (while simultaneously getting on a headset and attempting to fix it). At some point, I guess Sting finally turned to those guys and said, *Dudes, just go out there - how long are we gonna wait?*

We need our music, Kevin and Scott shot back.

It's only Tupelo, responded Sting.

Shortly after the show, Kevin and Scott took this story to Eric. *This is the reason why WCW has been where it's been*, they said. *You don't value a town like Tupelo, Mississippi.*

Before the next *Nitro* on Monday, Eric called a meeting with all the boys. *I want you to know*, he began, *that I brought Kevin and Scott in for more than just their talent. We've not had a history of being successful in this company, and for the most part, if we drew a thousand fans, that was considered a good house.*

That can't be, he continued. *These guys have sold out Madison Square Garden, and they come from a machine that knows how to do it right.*

I don't have all the answers, he said, *but we've gotta take from their knowledge to grow as a company. What we did in the past just didn't work.*

In essence, what Eric told us had some validity - Kevin and Scott really did add a lot to our company. They helped in areas people wouldn't even think of, such as public relations, or helping Zane Bresloff with first-day ticket sales. They provided a lot of assistance, and in that sense, Eric was right.

But then, of course - with Eric being Eric - he had to add a parting shot.

And by the way, he said, *if I ever hear, 'It's Only Tupelo' again...I'll fire that person on the spot.*

103

Although he was usually a very laid-back guy, you could see the steam coming out of Sting's ears. I don't even think he meant the initial comment in the way it was received - he was basically saying, 'What, are we gonna sit here all day while they flip a cassette tape back and forth?' At some point, as they say, the show must go on, but when Eric made that statement - *I'll fire that person on the spot* - Sting got *hot*. He left the room and I can only assume there was a conversation or two thereafter.

More than anything, the incident underscored the fact that it was a new day in WCW. The mainstays of the company, like Sting, Lex Luger, or Ric Flair and the Four Horsemen, had been used to doing business in a certain way, but now Kevin and Scott had returned from 'Up North' saying, 'Yeah, there's some things that could be improved down here.'

At the time, I think some feelings were definitely hurt, and the incident may have started some of the tension between the various factions backstage (adding fuel to the fire was the fact that the nWo were getting cheered as if they were babyfaces). In the meantime, though, it only served as fodder for a popular joke at the bar.

Hey, someone would say if a guy was looking down.

It's only Tupelo.

Today, Eric would probably say that the 'Tupelo' incident could have been handled better, but that's the kind of stuff he did - for better or for worse. At times, you felt yourself kind of believing his rhetoric about the WWF: *They're not even having water delivered to the building...they only have a month left...they're desperate...*

If you look at the history books, there was probably some truth to it - the WWF really was struggling at one point. In time, I think they got to a stage where they had to just throw everything out there - and thus the 'Attitude Era' (eventually) was born. I'll never forget watching some of the stuff they did with Dustin Rhodes as 'Goldust', for example, mainly because I knew Dustin pretty well (he was good friends with Pee Wee, and when Dustin was still with us in WCW, we loved to all meet at the same bar). To see Dustin portray that 'Goldust' gimmick - and knowing his father as such a 'Man's Man' - well, it blew my mind that Dustin pulled that off.

As of the fall of 1996, however, while you could see pieces of the 'Attitude Era' to come, the WWF still trailed us in every aspect. At the time, one of the advantages that we had - an advantage which often gets overlooked, I might add - is the impact that the cruiserweights had on our programming. Sitting at ringside, I was able to witness some of the most revolutionary matches in the history of the business, and the cruiserweights, supporting the star power of the guys 'on top', were a huge part of that.

I'll always remember the backstage chatter when Rey Mysterio, Jr. showed up for the first time. The talk started as soon as he came to the building, and you could already hear the murmurs in catering. Quite frankly, Rey was a lot smaller than people expected him to be, especially when you saw him standing next to someone like a Kevin or a Hulk. He was shorter than I was, for crying out loud, and I'm 5-foot-6 - on a good day.

Back then, a guy that size was *unheard of* - you didn't even have enhancement talent that small. The thought process in the business was, 'Well, if we put someone like that on TV, who is the other guy beating? He's beating a midget.'

Some people had been indoctrinated, by virtue of their experience in the industry, towards developing a certain mindset - one which dictated what wrestling *should* be (and conversely, what it shouldn't be). A lot of the old timers in the back - the agents, for example - were sitting there questioning it, too: *We're gonna put this motherfucker over? That's just fucking acrobatics. He's a fucking gymnast - it doesn't make any sense, and it gives away the business.*

105

Out of respect for Konnan, who was influential in introducing many of the *lucha libre* talent, it wasn't said too much in the open - but you knew that the feeling was there. There was resistance towards the business changing, because in the '60s and '70s, it had been typical to go out there, grab an arm, and work that arm for ten minutes - but by the '90s, things were evolving in the other direction - and fast.

I'll tell you this though: 60 seconds into Rey Mysterio Jr.'s first match, nobody ever murmured *shit* again.

He was a fucking *star*. He shut down the entire locker room within a minute, and eventually, I'd argue that he (along with guys like Juventud Guerrera and Psychosis) changed the entire business - and for the better.

I always want to acknowledge that story, because the next time somebody walks in the dressing room, how about this for a rule?

Before you say anything, wait to see the fucking guy *work*.

With the cruiserweights tearing up the undercard, guys like Chris Benoit and Eddie Guerrero starring in the midcard, and an endless supply of top guys in the main events, we developed an unbelievable wave of momentum. *Nitro* featured a perfect storm of action, storylines and star power, and quickly, the nWo storyline was establishing itself as revolutionary in the business. Almost every week, an apparently infinite number of ex-WWF wrestlers were jumping ship to wear the 'black-and-white', and even as the ring announcer, I found myself hooked on the suspense too - just like everyone else!

Nitro became must-watch television, especially when there was a surprise planned for the audience. On those occasions, aside from a select few (including Eric, Kevin, Keith Mitchell in the truck, and Janie Engle, who was Eric's assistant and responsible for the logistics, such as hiding a debuting wrestler), the contents of the final segment would be a closely guarded secret. In the show format, you might know who was wrestling in the main event, but under the section, 'Match Notes', you would see only the following: *TBD*.

At Halloween Havoc '96 - like I said before - I had no freaking idea that Roddy Piper was going to come out to close the show. I felt like I was a kid again, watching CWF on Channel 6, unable to predict what would happen next. When those bagpipes started playing, I 'popped' (internally) as much as the fans did!

There had been a time when wrestling fans had to make a decision: *do you tape Nitro and watch Raw, or do you watch Raw and tape Nitro?*

At this point, there was no real decision to be made. Seemingly *anything* could happen on our show, and therefore, you *had* to watch Nitro - live.

You may recall that earlier in our story, I discussed becoming a full-time employee at Turner Broadcasting. There was just one thing I left out of my explanation - the $35 per day in 'per diem' money! That came in pretty handy with regard to food *and* beverage on the road…if you catch my drift.

Oh, there's one other thing I forgot to mention, too - as far as working at Turner goes. It's about my salary.

Okay, I hear you say, *so what are you going to tell us now, Penzer? You sweet talked your way into a six-figure deal?*

Yeah - try 20 grand.

That's right. Once I got promoted to lead ring announcer, they had me on salary for 20 thousand dollars a year.

Well, that's a little misleading, I hear you retort. *You were probably making double that just in kickbacks, Penzer. Don't go playing the 'woe is me' card now. You had the Scott D'Amores of the world driving from here to Timbuktu to make you a quick buck.*

That's pretty funny, dear reader. In fact, I had to give up on those kickbacks once I went full-time - and Scott took over a lot of it in my absence (you're welcome, buddy).

Believe it or not, I actually took a pay *cut* in taking over from Gary.

Well, that was then, I hear you reply. *By the time Nitro was rockin-n-rollin', you were making well into the six figures - surely. So how much are we talking here, Penzer? 120 grand? 150? 200 grand, Penzer??*

Yeah - how about 28 grand.

Let me explain. Originally, I had been told by Gary Juster that if I took the 20 grand, did a good job and lasted a year, I was sure to get a significant raise. I did get a couple of incremental, cost-of-living type increases - getting me up to that 28 grand figure - but basically, I was *just* getting by.

My total 'employee package' - according to Turner corporate - amounted to 50 thousand dollars a year in value. As such, they would point to the fact that I was getting health insurance and retirement contributions, but who can think about retirement on 20 grand a year? Now don't get me wrong, that money went a lot further back then, but even still, I thought, *In that case, why don't you just pay me 40 grand and not make me an employee?*

Yes, I'm doing this on a dream, I told Juster one day, *but my wife doesn't work, and we have a young son. I'm doing this because I love it - but I can't be at this level forever.*

Once Craig Leathers became the person I reported to, I revisited the conversation with him.

Craig, I said, *I was told that if I lasted a year, I would get a significant increase. You know what I make, and you know what raising a family is like.*

Okay, he responded - *I'll take care of it.*

A couple of weeks went by before Craig gave me an update: *They turned you down*, he said matter-of-factly.

Sorry, Penzer.

In my wildest dreams, I *never* would have imagined that.

What do you mean they turned me down? I asked.

Who's 'they'?

Nick Lambros, said Craig, referring to one of the WCW Vice-Presidents.

Okay, I said. *So...could I talk to Nick Lambros?*

Yeah, he said, *but I wouldn't suggest it.*

Craig, I said. *What do I got to lose here? I can't live on 28 grand for the rest of my life. If they fire me, I'll be crushed from a personal standpoint - but I got a family now. I gotta at least fight - if anything, they'll probably respect me for it.*

Soon after, I scheduled a meeting with Nick Lambros, at which I explained everything I had done (and was currently doing) since joining the company. *This is how often I'm on the road...my wife doesn't work as she stays home with our son...A while back, I was promised a significant raise...*

Nick stopped me mid-stream with an interjection: *You're no 'Mean Gene' Okerlund*, he said.

You're no Bobby Heenan, he continued.

Nick then closed the conversation in unequivocal fashion: *You're not getting a raise.*

Okay, so Nick didn't fire me, but that...

That was a kick in the balls.

See, joked Craig when I told him.

I told ya, Penzer.

Yeah, I conceded. *You were fuckin' right, Craig.*

I truly didn't know what I was going to do next, because keep in mind - I was a ring announcer. There were only two places to work - and one of them had Howard Finkel. If you understand anything about Howard's significance in that company - and to our business - I don't really have to say any more.

We could go to Eric, offered Craig.

But then again, he continued - seemingly in the next breath - *I don't know if Eric's gonna listen to me.*

You know how much he has going on.

Craig ultimately decided he would go to Eric, but in the meantime, I didn't get my hopes up.

You know it's funny - the world was such a different place in 1996. There was no texting, and cell phones weren't ubiquitous yet. You couldn't call your wife on a 250-mile drive from town to town, and as such, you often spent long stretches out of touch with the people closest to you. For me to call home, I had to sit on my hotel bed with a prepaid card - hoping my hotel wouldn't charge me for a long-distance call - just to get a few minutes with Lisa.

I checked in with my dad whenever possible. Curiously, while he certainly kept an interest in *me*, he had hardly noticed the explosion in wrestling's popularity. If I had to describe his eagerness towards the business, it remained where it had been when he first started taking me to the matches, sitting there obliviously with his copy of *Time Magazine*. I think in his mind, his son was going around the country and living his dream, but I'm not sure he realized exactly what that entailed.

Hey, Dad, I would say, *I'm working with Ric Flair now.*

Cool, he'd reply, the enthusiasm palpable.

Hey, Dad - I'm working with Kevin Sullivan now.

Nice, he'd respond.

None of that really meant anything to my dad, but his interest soon piqued when I told him this: *Hey, Dad - I just went to a barbecue at Harley Race's house.*

What? Harley Race's house?

Harley had been the World Champion during the times when my dad took me to the shows, and therefore, *that* story was over with him. It was kind of a seminal moment in my dad realizing, I thought, how cool his son's life had become.

111

It also told me something else - if I could put *my* psychologist's hat on for a second.

Maybe - *just maybe* - he had paid a *little* more attention at those shows than perhaps he let on.

One night, I was sitting backstage before *Nitro* when Eric walked into the room.

To this point, I think the only time Eric had spoken to me was that conversation - the details of which I shared earlier - regarding my presence on TV. If you remember correctly, I think he had been bothered by all the 'TV time' that Gary Cappetta received, and he wanted to use me in a different way moving forward.

Therefore, when Eric showed up, I assumed he was there to speak with Tony Schiavone, who I happened to be shooting the shit with.

Hey, Eric said, looking in my direction.

I just want you to know that I doubled your salary.

Wow - talk about a swerve.

Oh - thank you very much, Eric, I said. *I really, really appreciate that.*

And that, my friends, was the end of our *second* interaction - save for one thing. Eric, evidently, had something to add before leaving the room - and I've never forgotten it since. I almost braced myself - as if to expect one of his famous parting shots - only to be pleasantly surprised instead.

You work hard, Eric said to me.

112

At first, I thought it was an odd thing for Eric to say, but Tony soon snapped me out of it: *Do you know how much of a compliment that is?*

It's kind of an off-hand compliment, I said. *I would prefer he say, 'You do a great job', or something.*

Tony shook his head.

Eric doesn't worry about who does a great job, he said. *Eric looks at work ethic. For him to say that you work hard...that's the best compliment that Eric knows how to give people.*

Tony really shifted my perspective with that one.

With that said, it's *possible* there may have been another factor at play. Before all this happened, Eric and Nick Lambros had something of a falling out. *Rumor has it* that Eric gave me the raise - at least in part - as a way of shoving it up Nick's ass.

Eric had a history of doing stuff like that. One time at Disney, the Public Enemy stole a production van, drove it around Orlando and ended up getting arrested for DWI. The word was that Eric was going to fire them, but when David Crockett, WCW's executive producer, *insisted* on that very thing happening, Eric decided to change course. At that point, Eric and David had never gotten along, so when David said, *I demand that you fire them,* Eric let the Public Enemy keep their jobs - just to piss off David.

Either way, I think once Eric went to bat for me, I was probably due for *some* kind of raise. To get double the salary, though...well, that was more than just appreciated.

At this point - with one child here and another on the way - it was *life-changing* for me.

9:
BACK TO THE FUTURE

S*tarrcade '96* is when I first noticed we were *really* on fire. A red-hot Nashville crowd ate up the December 29 pay-per-view, which featured, on the undercard, an array of incredible matches: Ultimo Dragon vs. Dean Malenko, Jushin Liger vs. Rey Mysterio, Jr., and Jeff Jarrett vs. Chris Benoit, just to name a few.

In the main event, 'Rowdy' Roddy Piper beat Hollywood Hogan in a *non-title* match, a curious stipulation given its initial build-up on television. Nonetheless, after Piper and Hogan's historic rivalry in the '80s, it was fun to see them feud again - albeit this time, with the roles reversed! With those guys on top, *Starrcade '96* became the most purchased WCW pay-per-view, to that point, in company history.

Roddy was always one of my favorites. I remember him doing commentary in Georgia Championship Wrestling, where he was extremely charismatic, with a habit of saying stuff that nobody else was at the time. Everything from the lines that Roddy came up with to the critiques he gave the wrestlers were just so different. Like many fans, I then remember his babyface turn in Georgia - after he defended Gordon Solie from Don Muraco - and then his introduction to the WWF in 1984. I was a huge mark for *Piper's Pit*, and I give Roddy credit for getting me hooked on the WWF - just like Dusty did with Championship Wrestling from Florida.

Back then, I honestly never could have imagined that someday, I'd get to know the real guy: Roderick Toombs. I think he was the most complicated guy that I ever met in the wrestling business - and that's saying a lot.

114

On a personal level, Roddy was hard to get to know - mostly because of some of the things that happened in his early life. Without going into too many details (because that's not my place), I know that he had a *horrible* childhood. I personally had many conversations with Roddy (more on that in Volume 2 of *Sitting Ringside*), but in all those conversations, he *never* talked about anything that happened before turning 15 (the year in which he entered the wrestling business). As a matter of fact, I never heard him talk about those early years with *anybody* - although he did, to the best of my knowledge, eventually confide in a few people.

It's amazing, quite frankly, that Roddy didn't decide to jump off a building, given everything that he experienced. Equally amazing is the fact that he became ultra-successful, one of the best talkers in the history of the business, a great worker, and a transcendent wrestler as well. He starred in movies. He had a wife and four children. He did all that - despite battling a lot of demons in the process.

My interpretation is that Roddy kind of 'blacked out' the first 15 years of his life - a task much easier said than done (you can black stuff out, in my opinion, but you can't ever forget it). He was a very, very complex person, and as a result, some people perceived him as distant. In reality, he was one of the kindest people you could ever meet. Whenever he saw you, he'd give you a hug, bring you in close and put his arm around you: *Hey - how are you doing? How's the family?*

He was the warmest person in those situations. Right now, I can see it in my mind's eye - the way he stood up to greet people and shake their hand. When he met a fan, he would put both of his hands around their one hand, and he'd pat them on the back while listening intently. *Roddy,* they'd say, *you're my hero. I'll never forget the angle with Jimmy Snuka...*

Thank you so much, he would respond. *If you don't mind me asking, what did you like about it?*

Believe it or not, Piper actually showed a very sweet personality in those moments.

When it came to business, on the other hand, he didn't fuck around.

There was an angle on *Nitro* - it aired on November 18th, 1996 to be exact - where about ten police officers tried to hold Roddy back from getting to the nWo (Eric Bischoff had just been revealed, in storyline, as being aligned with the group). If you go back and look at that footage, you'll see that the cops in the ring couldn't hold Piper back.

Well...*that's* Roddy. Whether he was scripted to act like that or not, he would have done it anyway.

Roddy legitimately viewed everything that happened *as if* it were a shoot. Part of that was based on his self-perception; he saw himself as a tough guy, a street fighter, and that's what he wanted his reputation to be. Therefore, if you put him in a situation where he was being held back by ten cops, he was going to fight like mad to get through them. Knowing him, I know that's exactly what he would have done in the same, real-life situation.

I'll say it again - in Roddy's mind, pro wrestling was a *shoot*. Okay, he wasn't really hurting anybody (although from what I heard, he was stiff as fuck), but there was a reason why he used the word 'fights' instead of 'matches' in his promos. From his perspective, he would think, *Okay, the finish is predetermined - but everything else is a fucking shoot*. He lived his entire life that way.

It might have been almost a defense mechanism for him. I think Roddy believed, as a result of his background, fame and fortune, that people would try and take advantage of him. He was wary about being exploited, and maybe, although this is speculation on my part, that's partly why he treated things the way he did.

116

Roddy was a conundrum in many ways. He was so unbelievably talented - and confident - but at the same time, he was painfully insecure. Having learned a little bit about psychology, it seemed like Roddy felt he could never achieve *enough*, like he could never *be* enough. You could say that everybody has insecurities (mine arose, during my time in WCW, because I was so afraid of losing my dream), but Roddy's were especially fundamental.

For him, it all went back to those early years.

Behind the curtain, I perceived Roddy's relationship with Hulk as similar to the dynamic between Hulk and Randy Savage. It was hard to know how much was a shoot, how much was a work, and how exactly they were going to get to where they needed to go. While there would have been an outline in place for their program, I think Hulk wanted to get to a certain place with the storyline, and Roddy wanted to get somewhere else - if you follow me. That makes for an interesting back-and-forth that doesn't always get talked about, because to work together, guys have to meet in the middle sometimes. If you're looking at it on paper, you might say, 'This is easy - Piper comes out at *Halloween Havo*c, they have a match at *Starrcade*, do the return at *SuperBrawl* in San Francisco' - and that all happened, sure - but it would have been a tug-of-war all the way.

As much as Roddy liked and wanted to make money for his family - and to continue supporting his lifestyle - he did *not* want to put Hogan over. In his mind, Piper would have equated losing to Hogan as an admission that he was *second* to Hogan, and even though Hogan was now a heel - and typically 'won' after some kind of shenanigans - Piper still didn't want to do it anyway. Similarly, once Hogan found out about Roddy not wanting to do the job, he didn't particularly want to put Piper over either (although, in fairness, there are stories about Hulk being ecstatic after the *Starrcade* finish, following the crowd's reaction to Piper's win).

117

Knowing Piper, I doubt that he ever would have agreed, when first coming into WCW, to lose to Hogan in any fashion - irrespective of whether he got the 'thumbs up' first. Piper was a very smart businessman, and rather than show his hand, he probably would have said something like this: *Let's talk about it when we get there.*

When it did come time for their rematch at *SuperBrawl,* I don't think Hulk trusted Piper to put him over, particularly in San Francisco, a city with which Piper had history. Ultimately, I think it all came down to Hulk's creative control, and he came out on top - this time with the belt on the line - aided by the interference of Randy (which also gave Piper somewhat of an 'out'). I know one thing for sure - behind the scenes, it couldn't have been easy to get there.

In their promos building up the matches, Roddy and Hulk argued about who was the *true* icon of the business; who was the bigger draw, who made wrestling, and who was the reason why everybody was watching. They probably could have taken it further than they did, to be perfectly honest with you, but it didn't affect my enjoyment of it at the time. I was *enthralled* by it, from a fan's perspective, and their interviews, in particular, were brilliant.

Away from the cameras, I know that both guys truly believed their own promos, but there was one key distinction between them. The difference was that Hulk, in my opinion, didn't *care* all that much about the 'icon' label (his motivation was elsewhere), whereas Piper, conversely, really did care about it - a *lot.* From his standpoint, Piper would argue that the heel usually gets an angle over; therefore, he would have thought of himself as the reason why *WrestleMania* (and the Piper-Hogan rivalry in the '80s) worked in the first place.

Now, don't get me wrong - there was certainly a respect between each of them, and even a mutual admiration at times. Both guys started the entire dance of where wrestling is today, and I think they recognized that fact, albeit to differing degrees. There was just no trust there.

118

As 1997 progressed, the Piper-Hogan program - other than a brief resumption around *Halloween Havoc* - mostly took a backseat creatively. In its place, a thrilling saga developed between Sting and the nWo, leading to some of the most memorable moments in *Nitro* history.

Seemingly on a weekly basis - and usually at the most opportune time - Sting would descend from the rafters to thwart the villainous nWo, promising an eventual pay-per-view clash to come against Hogan. The genesis of the storyline went back to September 1996, when Sting declared himself a "free agent" - neither affiliated with WCW nor its renegade invaders. Once he finally demonstrated his loyalty to WCW, Sting amazed fans with his willingness to stand up to the nWo - although crucially, he remained officially inactive as a wrestler.

At first, it appeared that Sting might wrestle earlier in the year, but ultimately, the booking team delayed his return until *Starrcade* - the end of the year. Therefore, it might be tempting to believe that it was all mapped out in advance; that waiting to deliver Sting vs. Hogan had been a deliberate decision. On the surface, it certainly appears that way - but that's not how I remember it.

My perception is that we kind of lucked into the whole deal. Originally, Sting had been put in the rafters because we were trying to tease if he was with the nWo or WCW. After a period of several months, the gimmick then got him so over that it took on a life of its own. If you look back at some of that Sting-nWo stuff, it almost doesn't make sense - even for a wrestling program - but for whatever reason, the people really got with it.

I could easily be wrong, but I'm pretty perceptive about this shit - and I had a pretty good view of things at ringside. I certainly don't think WCW envisioned the entire 15-month build from the very start, or even that Sting-Hogan would be the money match eventually. It speaks to my long-held belief that in wrestling, the best stuff is often organic.

That's not to take anything away from how the storyline *developed*, however. It was *beyond* cool to witness some of the entrances, escapes and exploits of Sting, and our fans always went nuts over it. You could have written out some of those same scenarios, given them to other people, and it wouldn't have received anything near the same reaction. That speaks to the ability of Steve Borden and everyone else involved to pull it all off.

On that note, Steve - the real guy - was always very nice to me. He wasn't overly friendly, but compared to the rest of his clique (and especially Buff Bagwell and Lex Luger), he presented himself quite differently. Lex in particular was a total dick, and he didn't give many people the time of day back then. If you asked Lex if he could do something, maybe production-wise, he would just make a bunch of jokes about you, and soon get the locker room laughing in hysterics. Lex was pretty much unbearable at the best of times, but I never found Steve to be like that.

Therefore, once the storyline took off, Steve was very deserving, I thought - especially considering his long tenure at WCW - to receive that kind of attention. I also think that once everyone realized there was something special going on, they managed the situation extremely well. Let's just be honest - they pretty much hit a home run every single week. Nobody had ever done anything like what was happening on our program, and Sting looked like a fucking superhero.

Famously - or shall we say, *infamously* - it all crescendoed at *Starrcade '97*. In the main event spectacle, Hogan and Sting finally locked up together, with much controversy surrounding the finish of their match in particular. It appeared that fans were supposed to believe that Sting had been screwed - the victim of an apparent 'fast' three-count from referee Nick Patrick - but Nick's three-count was anything but. Effectively, Hogan simply pinned Sting before the match was restarted (by virtue of Bret Hart's involvement), and although Sting officially won the belt that night, things definitely didn't come off as intended. The impact of the entire debacle has been discussed, dissected and debated ever since.

People *still* talk about what happened that night - but let the record show that I got the scoop from referee Nick Patrick! Several years ago, Nick broke his silence on the subject during an interview with me:

What happened was two people - Sting and Hulk - they were the two franchise guys...and the two franchise guys were butting heads at that point in time.

One guy came up to me and told me to fast count it - to get some heat and give him an out.

The other guy said, 'Don't fast count it. Keep it nice and slow.'

The person that was in charge evidently didn't want to make a call, didn't want to pick a side, and made themselves scarce all night long...to where I couldn't find them to ask them, 'Hey, what do you want me to do?'

In other words, it was a good old-fashioned *clusterfuck*, but I'll tell you something else that might surprise you. At the time, I don't know if I actually realized that anything went wrong - because no one in WCW really talked about it afterwards. For the longest time, I don't know if it even occurred to me that Nick was supposed to count fast on that three-count. I don't know that I even *thought* about it until many years later.

Bret Hart joined an already-stacked WCW roster in late 1997

121

Obviously, we were trying to play off the Montreal Screwjob, which had just happened a month earlier in the WWF. Logically, Bret Hart and Hulk would figure to be the next big program, giving Sting a run with the WCW belt (and allowing Bret to claim he was also an undefeated World champion). That all makes total sense and sounds like the right direction to go, but clearly, the execution left a lot to be desired.

You look back now, and there's all this controversy about Sting's readiness for the match (and the jokes about him not being tanned enough!), but none of that really registered at the time. I just figured that what we saw is what they wanted to do, and with a never-ending slate of shows coming up, we were simply on to the next one.

In essence, 1997 had been the year of the nWo. The storyline enveloped everything that happened on our show, and in the moment, it was hard to argue against that strategy. We had beat the WWF every single Monday - for the entire year - extending, overall, to an 18-month winning streak.

Eric featured heavily as the heel leader of the nWo. To be blunt, it worked with Eric because, well - he was kind of being himself in the role.

With all due respect to Eric, I'm not sure that anyone else was as natural as a heel. He *oozed* asshole - and I mean that in a positive way. Since he signed off on every creative idea, I thought it was smart to have him as the spokesman for the group. In that role, he could do certain things to advance the storyline - as opposed to the talent who liked to put themselves over.

One of Eric's most incendiary on-screen acts was his 'firing' of Pee Wee, a segment which allegedly caused Pee Wee's church group - having bought the termination as legit - to start a fundraiser for his family. When an angle hits that close to home, it can do strange things

122

to people - and Pee Wee, as a matter of fact, happened to be no exception.

After he was featured in the angle, we noticed a bit of a change in Pee Wee's personality. Now, I want to first make clear that Pee Wee had just beaten testicular cancer - following an initial diagnosis of the disease in January 1996. He had undergone the removal of his left testicle and a series of grueling radiation treatments.

That is obviously a very serious thing, and I know that first-hand - my sister was diagnosed with breast cancer at the age of 31, and, as I mentioned earlier, my dad authored a series of books on the subject of dealing with a cancer diagnosis. Even today, people still use the terminology that my dad introduced, relative to the emotional place that one travels in such situations: *Cancerville*.

Pee Wee was living in *Cancerville*, and naturally, he feared that the cancer might one day return. Although I understood all of that, Pee Wee did start treating people differently after getting more airtime. He got a little bit too big for his britches at that point.

Like everyone else, he was also doing drugs, and I'm sure that clouded his judgment more than a little bit. At the time, no one thought too much about it - we just wanted the old Pee Wee back.

Hey, remember my explanation in chapter five - the one about the emotional 'dam'?

Well, around this time, my dam finally broke.

It was truly one of the worst episodes that I ever went through, and it lasted for about six months. You wouldn't know that if you saw me at a show, but I was right back in that vulnerable, scared and petrified place that I had been as a college student. Suddenly, it was painfully hard just to get on a plane, or even to put on my tux before a live show.

So many times, I looked in the mirror and asked myself: *How am I gonna be able to go out there and do this?*

As I said before, we're talking about a very different time. In 2024, I could have gone to Turner HR and said, *Hey, I'm having some mental health issues*, but it was a completely different story back then. It's just not the way that things worked.

Furthermore, I was in the wrestling business - not the most forgiving of businesses in any sense of the word. Therefore, I basically had to *pretend* I was okay to get through it. I'm not trying to put myself over in saying that - and there's some truth to pretending as a coping mechanism, actually. When you do something long enough, you can get by on pretending - at least for a while.

Eventually, I confided in Pee Wee that I was going through some problems, mostly because I quit drinking during those six months. Previously, I had done what everyone else did - you know, drink after each and every show. At the end of the night, you drank a ton of booze, ate at a Waffle House (you were lucky if you could get a Whataburger or something) and finally stumbled on into bed. Obviously, I wasn't doing all that anymore, and I guess Pee Wee and some other guys got curious.

I even quit drinking soda at the bar, opting to drink an orange juice instead - just anything I could think of to make the panic go away. It was a horrible feeling to be so lost again, and I was back to calling my dad every night - lost-distance charges be damned.

Once again, Dad was there to be my guide, to talk me down, to remind me that *this too shall pass* - even though I would have bet my life that it wouldn't.

David, he would say, *You don't want to throw away what you worked so hard for.*

You're right, I'd eventually concede, and Dad was right, actually - because *nothing* could stop me from showing up.

124

For example, you may have noticed that little mention has been made to the *backup* ring announcer spot after I took over from Gary. The reason for that is simple: we didn't have one.

Intentionally, I never brought it up with anyone. Instead, I was proud to be the only ring announcer that WCW had, and also that I did *all* the shows - not to mention travel with the same guys I had grown up watching on TV.

Nonetheless, I learned a lot during this down period, and that helped when going through the cycle *again* - to varying degrees of intensity – numerous times in the years ahead. No matter how hard it is, how uncomfortable it is, or how hurtful it is, you just have to try and move past a mental health battle. I won't say that the mind will let you win if it knows you can push past it - it'll still try and pick other battles with you - but you have to recognize, inside your heart, that there *is* a way to move forward.

Let's just be real about it: you really have no other choice. Or think about it in this way - there's two choices at hand, really. Either you can *not* go out and *don't* do what you love, or, alternatively, you can try and push through the panic when it hits. Eventually, I can tell you that it does go away, whether that process takes five minutes, an hour, or even longer.

To be clear, I've been on medication for a long time - there's one pill I use to take the edge off called Klonopin - but you *still* have to make a conscious decision. It's a hard decision, and it's hard every time.

For me, I just made the decision that if I was going to live my dream, I wasn't going to let frickin' anxiety and panic get in the way of it. I was just gonna push through it: *fuck off, go away, and let me do what I love to do.*

125

After two-plus years on the air, *Nitro* had proven itself to be a revolutionary program in the history of wrestling television. There were so many innovations that the series introduced, and, in fact, many of those elements still affect the business today.

When *Nitro* started, we had a really great formula: surprises, nostalgia, lucha libre high-flying action, star power, storylines and promos. That nostalgia element was achieved, I thought, by presenting the stars of the '80s (Hogan, Piper and Savage, for instance) with a 'new coat of paint'. In doing so, we were able to bring back a lot of the so-called 'lapsed fans' - and, concurrently, get a new generation of stars over to the audience.

Personally, I had always been a fan of storylines and promos, dating back to my days as a loyal CWF viewer. Back then, the matches were one-way 'squash matches' anyhow, with the idea being that people would have to pay - at the arenas - to see the big stars wrestle each other. The format for wrestling TV remained similar over the years (although I do remember the NWA experimenting a little in that regard), but it decisively changed with *Nitro*, where the incentive became more about drawing ratings than drawing a house. That's a pretty big shift in the psychology of the business, and to be competitive again in the ratings war, the WWF had to adapt to it.

In WCW, our main events never had the best 'work rate' - if I can use that term - but that didn't matter to me (or, evidently, the millions of other people who tuned in every Monday). The match to me was always secondary, and I was always the guy who liked to fast forward to whatever the *post-match* angle was. That's where a lot of the best stuff on *Nitro* happened too.

For the longest time - right before we went off the air - we would have this crazy, chaotic in-ring brawl, with the fans littering the ring with trash and debris. Kevin Sullivan was a master at building *heat*, and no matter what city we were in, the audience reacted accordingly. I spent years getting accustomed to ducking beer bottles from my

126

ringside seat, and therefore, I can tell you this - any notion that we *planted* fans for that purpose is patently absurd!

A little down time during a live edition of 'Nitro'

If you think about it, we probably should have *discouraged* that behavior - purely for safety reasons - but it made for such a great visual that no one stepped in to stop it. It all grew out of the organic reaction that came out of Hulk's turn in Daytona Beach, and soon, it took on a whole life of its own.

Even though I was ducking those bottles, it was a pretty cool sight (if you ask me) - and just another reminder of a familiar message: WCW was the 'cool' wrestling promotion, and we didn't plan on that changing anytime soon.

10:
FANTASY CAMP

Another underrated element of WCW's success, in my opinion, was our incredible announce team. I think we had the most varied, charismatic and talented group of announcers ever - a 'Murderers Row', if you will - including (albeit in different combinations, and at different times) Tony Schiavone, Dusty Rhodes, Mike Tenay, Larry Zbyszko, Scott Hudson, Mark Madden, Bobby 'The Brain' Heenan *and* 'Mean' Gene Okerlund.

I mean, come on - think about some of those names!

Previously, there had never been such a fusion of announce team talent, and consequently - at least in my mind - we covered all possible bases on commentary. Even Eric - the play-by-play man for *Nitro* when it first came on the air (in addition to everything else he was doing) - offered a lot with his own particular style. You could feel Eric's passion for the product, quite naturally, because he was the one running the thing!

Prior to show time, all the announcers on the show - including myself - gathered together in our own little trailer, usually sometime between the production meeting, lunch and whenever *Nitro* went live. Let me tell you: that was an *amazing* group of people to sit back and listen to - and that's pretty much what I did, by the way. I just sat there and laughed for the most part, because really - who wouldn't? Here you had Gene telling a bunch of stories in that signature voice of his. Larry Zbyszko would chime in with tales about the Gagne family and his tenure in the AWA. Lee Marshall would generate laughs just because he was so over-the-top. Bobby Heenan was one of the funniest guys in the history of the business, and Tony Schiavone had a great sense of humor as well. Dusty could basically breathe and it was entertaining. Oh, and before I forget, Mike Tenay was extremely funny, too - believe it or not. Mike had one of the most dry senses of humor that I've ever seen in my life.

I had so many good times in that trailer and in some ways, I wish I would've cherished it even more. There was an abundance of knowledge in that room; so many different personalities gelling together, enjoying each other's company. It was an honor and a privilege for me to be a part of it.

I've often thought that fans would probably pay good money to sit there - like I did - for two or three hours and just listen, if only to witness it all. It kind of felt like one of those 'Fantasy Camp' experiences that you read about - you know, 'pay X amount of dollars and play basketball with Michael Jordan.' The difference was, in this case, I was actually getting paid to be there!

Let me tell you more about our star-studded announce team:

Dusty Rhodes
Other than Hulk Hogan, Dusty was the biggest *star* - to my mind - in the history of the wrestling business. He was an unbelievable promo (better than Hogan in that regard), one of the best at working a crowd, insanely charismatic, and he was a great booker, too (as a booker, I think the best thing Dusty could have done is take three months off every year, but that's easier said than done in this business). When I look back on everything, just the fact that I got to meet Dusty - let alone work with him - still blows my mind, to be honest with you. That was a dream come true in and of itself.

People talk about the well-known 'Hard Times' promo that Dusty cut, but to me, his best promo aired on the July 2nd, 1994 edition of *WCW Saturday Night*. In storyline, Dusty's son, Dustin, had been betrayed by Arn Anderson and was feuding with Bunkhouse Buck and Terry Funk. Subsequently, Dusty offered to team up with his son in a tag-team match against Buck and Funk, and in doing so, he used his real-life issues with Dustin as the basis for the promo:

129

Come here, Dustin. I want everybody to bear with me just for a minute...I want to talk to my son in front of the whole world. When you were born, when you were a baby...I went off to seek my fame and fortune. I neglected you! Then later on, when I became World's Heavyweight Champion, I neglected you. Then lately I became this corporate cowboy, if you will...in public with a suit and tie on. And I neglected you! And when it came down to choose a partner, I was off in Hollywood...and I neglected you.

Let me tell you something. Bunkhouse Buck...let me tell you, Colonel Parker... they all nothing but chicken feeds - that's all they are, brother. Let me tell you something else...Terry Funk is nothing but a lowlife, watermelon-thief, egg-sucking dog!

And let me tell you about Arn Anderson. Arn Anderson - my son offered up his innocence, and you paid him back in scorn! The hell with you, Arn Anderson! Arn Anderson has never been nothing but a walk-behinder. And when you walk behind, and you're not a leader, then the view never changes, baby! The view never changes, baby! The view never changes!

You have the ability to be the World's Heavyweight Wrestling Champion. There is not a greater athlete at your age in this sport. But I want to ask you a favor. I want to ask you a favor in front of...in front of God and the whole world. I know that the *Clash of Champions* on August the 24th, you put your name on the dotted line. I don't want you to look for another partner! I don't want you to go and find another man! I don't want you to go out and get on your knees and beg another scum-sucking pig to be your partner! I'm asking you if you can carry this old out-of-shape, old bent-out, old spindly-legged man...I want to be your partner!

I don't need no handshake. Because out there, right now tonight, there's people with their brothers, their sisters and their wives. They are blood! The Kennedy's were blood! The Earp's were blood! The Rhodes are blood! I don't need a handshake! What I need now from you, is just a hug and a kiss, to seal the deal, baby!

I love that promo so much. I was honored to be at ringside for it, and let me tell you, it was truly authentic. What Dusty said truly hit me in the heart, and I wasn't the only one - he grabbed everybody in attendance that day.

In a general sense, everyone can understand and relate to the 'Hard Times' promo, but this truly took you into the family dynamic. It doesn't matter if it was planned or not, because it was *real* - that I can assure you. It was Dusty's way of trying to make things right with Dustin - while trying to do a wrestling angle that would sell tickets.

130

Dusty was always very kind to me, and…well, let me rephrase that. That's not *exactly* true. When I was just a stooge, he paid absolutely zero attention to me. He wasn't nasty, rude or anything like that, but it was basically like I didn't exist. Once I established myself, however, he started talking a little about *me* going into play-by-play - sort of tongue-in-cheek style - once Tony had been "put to pasture," in Dusty's words. I don't know how serious Dusty really was about it, but I think there might have been something to it.

It might sound outlandish at first, but maybe you don't know - because only the most hardcore fans are probably aware of this - that I *did* have a turn at the announce table. We had a syndicated version of *Monday Nitro* for the international markets (labeled in those markets as *WCW Worldwide*), and I actually worked with Larry Zbyszko as the play-by-play announcer on that show. I had to use the 'Dave Lawrence' pseudonym (a call back to my High School DJ days – for those of you keeping track), in order to avoid a pretty awkward situation – me 'pitching' to myself when announcing over the footage of our shows!

In any event, I think that Dusty thought I did a good enough job on the international stuff that maybe an idea got in the back of his mind. I don't know that he necessarily thought, 'Hey, in ten years, Penzer is going to be our number one play-by-play guy,' but he wouldn't have kept alluding to it for no reason. There must have been something to it, but for obvious reasons, I'll never really know.

Tony Schiavone
Tony was a mentor to me, and he was another person who really embraced me – when he didn't have to, quite frankly. Tony basically taught me the ropes, so to speak, especially when it came to different aspects of production. I think it really impressed him that I offered to work in that area – even though I wasn't getting paid anything extra – just to learn about the business from another angle. I think Tony's

mindset was, *Okay, this guy Penzer really wants it. He's not looking for more money – he's just looking to learn.*

In general, Tony was great to work with - and Tony was *hilarious*. Most people are familiar with the infamous 'Shockmaster' debut at *Clash of the Champions XXIV*, for example, when Fred Ottman fell through a prop wall on live television. I distinctly remember that Tony laughed so hard about that, I didn't even think he could continue the broadcast!

On a professional level, Tony was the person who I first reported to, and in turn, he reported to Craig Leathers, with regard to production matters, and ultimately Eric with respect to announcing. People often talk about the 'sports-like' feel that a lot of our shows used to have, and I think Tony deserves credit for much of that. He used his background as a baseball announcer to skillfully sell the legitimacy of whatever we were doing, and in that sense, he made it feel *real* to the fans at home.

Things changed a little bit later on, but I'll save all that for when we get there.

Mike Tenay

Mike was often referred to as 'The Professor' - and that's how I got to know him as well. He seemingly knew every fact there was to know about every wrestler, including, most notably, the luchas coming in from Mexico, in addition to the performers we brought in from all over the world (he also gets major props for hatching the idea for Goldberg's undefeated streak). By virtue of his professionalism, knowledge and insight, Mike added a lot of credibility to our program.

Goldberg (pictured here with me and Rickey Medlocke) caught fire with an undefeated streak – and Mike Tenay came up with it

When you first meet Mike, he comes off as a really nice guy – and he is, truly – but he's *really* a wise ass.

A *big-time* wise ass.

Mike liked to stir the shit - in a major way - but in a funny way at the same time. It was never meant to be mean or anything, and, in fact, Mike usually delivered his zingers with a smile on his face. That's just how it was with Mike, but you'd never think that from the outside looking in. He didn't grow up in the business - unlike some of the other guys in the announcer's trailer - but he could hang with those guys (and the comedic timing of someone like Bobby) without any problem.

Mike basically came to WCW in his forties, and therefore, I always wondered if he picked up the wrestling-style of humor really fucking quick – or, alternatively, whether it had secretly always been there, lurking under the shadows. I know this for sure, though: once you saw the *real* Mike Tenay, it was a *totally* different person than what you would see on television.

None of what I just said should be construed as a negative, as for the record, there's not one bad thing I could say about Mike. It's just funny because sometimes you see someone on television, and you develop an idea of what they would be like in real life. Sometimes your idea of that person is accurate, and sometimes it isn't – at all. Mike Tenay was in the latter category.

That man was *devious*.

You know what? Do yourself a favor and pull up Mike's interview with Stacy Keibler. It aired on the September 20th, 2000 edition of *WCW Thunder*, and the clip tends to make the rounds every now and again on social media. In storyline, Stacy was pregnant at the time, and there was a mystery surrounding who the father was. From the outset of the interview, Mike went off on Stacy in ruthless fashion:

Stacy, we've seen you on WCW 'TV', dressed in the shortest mini skirt that I've ever seen. The way that you provocatively climb into the ring and dance. Hell, you even come down to the broadcast position and climb up on the broadcast table – while we're trying to announce a match.

You know, if it wasn't for the fact that I'm a married man – and that I have some morals – I probably would have taken a shot!

Stacy, we need to know who the father is. Is the father Ric Flair? You know, I asked Ric…and he didn't deny it.

Stacy, how many have there been? Can we count them on one hand? Two hands? What's the over/under, Stacy?

…Stacy, I see you're starting to 'show' a little bit. I guess you've probably taken yourself out of the WCW swimsuit competition, next Monday on *Nitro*, when we crown a new 'Miss WCW'. I guess the upside for you though is…you're probably gonna be the most popular person in your Lamaze class – even if you're there all alone.

After Stacy eventually walked out – and Mike responded by saying, "*Save those tears for somebody who gives a damn!*" the Professor turned to address the camera directly:

Boy, she's gonna make a terrific mother.

Now, don't get it confused - Mike was never that malicious in reality! Nevertheless, when it comes to that tone…that delivery…

That was the real Mike Tenay.

Just with a smile on his face.

Larry Zbyszko

Similar to Mike, I thought Larry added a lot to our product, albeit in a different way. He was really effective at taking his background as a wrestler and translating it into the color commentary position, and he made people believe in the in-ring action. Essentially, he was the ex-wrestler who took it all seriously – that was his role.

If you notice, Larry always went back to the idea that this was a legitimate contest; for example, when a guy would choose to taunt the crowd instead of making a cover, Larry was great at pointing out that error. For a while, he even became a huge babyface on our show, mostly because he was one of the few people standing up to the nWo.

Personality wise, Larry was sort of a different kind of guy, almost reminiscent of Lee Marshall - who we'll get to in a second. Larry was friendly, but mostly, he tried to keep to himself, and for the most part, he kept everyone else at arm's length. If myself, Mike, Tony, Gene and Bobby were laughing about something, Larry was *there* – but he wasn't exactly jumping in the middle of it, if that makes sense.

Larry was more mellow, relaxed and laid-back than the rest of us, but he was a super smart guy – and very talented. Famously, he loved to golf, and trust me – if he could golf every day and never do anything else, he would have done that for the rest of his life.

As I alluded to earlier, Larry loved to tell stories about the AWA, and particularly, the Gagne family. At one time, Larry had been married to the daughter of Verne Gagne, and he kind of lit up, so to speak, when talking about that whole experience - especially some of the strange things that Greg Gagne might have been doing back then.

135

I have nothing against Greg, by the way, but he was sort of like another Mike Graham to me. Similar to Mike, after all, Greg was the son of a famous promoter, a shooter, and a little bit on the small side. He probably had somewhat of a small man's complex, and that provided a lot of fodder for some of Larry's best stories.

Larry got a kick out of telling us about it, I think, because it was part of his life we could all relate to. The guys all understood what Larry was getting at when he recounted some of those stories, because he was talking about *the business* – a language that everyone was familiar with.

We all listened intently to the Verne and Greg tales, and for his part, Larry enjoyed being able to vent his emotions a little bit. It was mostly kind of tongue-in-cheek stuff – not overly negative or anything – but it was illuminating regardless. It's hard enough for someone to deal with a father-in-law (or a brother-in-law) once a marriage breaks down.

Let alone in the wrestling business.

Lee Marshall
With all due respect, Lee Marshall was a very strange guy. He was known for (literally) phoning in his 1-800-COLLECT 'Road Reports', a segment which became a recurring element on our show. Essentially, his 'reports' were presented as if he was calling live from a 'Nitro party' – typically being hosted in the next city we were visiting – but in reality, 'Stagger Lee' recorded the audio elsewhere in the arena.

He had an odd sense of humor, and you might have been able to sense that in watching our shows. Without fail, Lee would always include a "weasel" reference to conclude his road reports – and he was so, *so* proud of that. It was done as a way of playing off one of Bobby Heenan's nicknames, but everyone kind of rolled their eyes at it. One time, I remember they pitched back to the announce table after one of Lee's segments, and Bobby came out with a classic one-liner: *"I hate this guy!"*

Now don't get me wrong, Lee was a nice person, but I don't think he offered as much as he thought he did. He came to us after being a big deal in Los Angeles, because – for those who don't know – he had once been the voice of 'Tony the Tiger'. I don't want to speak ill of him too much, and certainly, he remained a much bigger deal than I was. By the WCW days, however, Lee's career was kind of winding down.

More than anything, though – and not to be redundant – I can't help but remember how proud he was of that "weasel" thing. He was really, *really* proud of it – he truly thought it was *that* hilarious. It cracked him up like you wouldn't believe, but nobody else really got it.

I think he may have done it once and everyone kind of chuckled politely. Lee must have taken that as, 'Okay, we've really got something here. We gotta keep doing this.'

The strange thing is that nobody laughed after the second or third time, but Lee kept on doing it – and he never, *ever* stopped.

Scott Hudson

Before he joined WCW, Scott Hudson was an announcer on a local indy show with television, and those broadcasts were popular with our Atlanta-based talent. At the time, Scott was working with Steve Prazak, and both guys were huge fans who - within a certain radius at least - turned their fandom into a degree of notoriety. Through this experience, Scott became tight with several guys who became real players for our company, including Diamond Dallas Page, Kanyon, Glacier and Disco Inferno.

Funnily enough, I used to joke with Scott that he got Disco his WCW contract. There had been a time when Disco had a tryout at Center Stage, and seemingly, Scott and Steve brought their *whole* crew down to watch. They took up about a third of the seating, and throughout the entire match, they were all chanting: *Disco sucks! Disco sucks!*

Now understand something: in real life, Disco is a certifiable heat *magnet* (I can be pretty annoying, too - but Disco makes me look like a loser in that regard), but Disco never got *that* much heat - like he did at the tryout - for the rest of his life! Because of Scott, Steve and the gang, Disco looked like the greatest heel on earth!

On a personal basis, I love Scott Hudson - he was the nicest guy in the world. He was someone that *never* got down, regardless of whatever product we were putting out on TV. It was like he carried a positive light that never got dark, and one of the reasons for that - maybe the main reason - is actually pretty interesting. Scott was extremely successful in his 'shoot' career as a criminal investigator (in the U.S. Northern District of Georgia), so he didn't really *need* wrestling, in my opinion. No one else in the announcer's trailer could say the same, regardless of what they were making, and that caused some friction between Scott and the other guys.

I think Scott is on record as saying he was paid $1,500 a week at WCW. Bobby and Gene seemed to have a particular issue with that, and it all spilled out one day in the trailer. Mark Madden witnessed the altercation and discussed it in an interview years later:

Scott was kind of the jack-of-all-trades, and because his job let him come and go - despite his responsibility - he was, you know, *available.*

One day in the trailer, Okerlund starts bitching at Hudson 'cos he doesn't make any money [in WCW]. We think he's kind of kidding, right? But Okerlund's voice starts rising and rising, and he goes, 'God damn it! You don't make hardly any money, [and] that keeps the money for the rest of us down. You're cheating all of us!'

I'm thinking, '[Gene]'s not kidding - he's really mad.'

138

Then Bobby chimes in and starts yelling at [Scott] for the same thing. Before you know it, you didn't have to get between them…but [myself and some others] are going, 'Guys, calm down.'

It was *really* heated, [and] those guys were really hot. It was [really] a tense situation.

No doubt, Bobby and Gene were hilarious people in general, but let me tell you something: they were damn serious about their money.

Bobby Heenan
It's often been claimed that Bobby sort of looked down on WCW, a product of the success he had reached in the WWF previously. I think there's probably some truth to that, and Gene sometimes displayed hints of that attitude as well.

That's not what I want to talk about here. I want to talk about the fact - if you remember, dear reader - that I had once *daydreamed* about hanging out, if only for a few minutes or so, with the great Bobby 'The Brain' Heenan and 'Mean' Gene Okerlund. In my wildest dreams, I never could have imagined that one day, I would find myself working alongside them!

So many things had to fall in place for me to live that dream - so many twists and turns that were unlikely to land in my favor. For instance, what if my dad never had a pipeline to Red Roberts? What if Larry Malenko didn't give me the time of day? What if Bob Roop never called up Jody Hamilton? What if Jody never bothered to give me a call? What if the opportunity to be a *backup* ring announcer never came about? What if I succumbed to anxiety and fucked up my tryout?

It's amazing how life works sometimes, and I would often reflect on that when seeing Bobby in action. He ended up being extremely nice to me, and sort of took me under his wing - a dream come true for the adolescent fan in me.

139

Man, how lucky was I?

Of course, Bobby had an extremely quick wit, the fastest that I've ever seen (he also had a heart of gold, too - just for the record). I'll never forget the time when one year, my wife organized a birthday party at our house and Bobby was invited. There was a guy who WCW fans might remember named Joe Gomez, a Tampa native who got the nickname of 'The Mayor' because he seemingly knew everyone in the city. Anyway, Joe saw Bobby at this birthday party and said something pretty innocuous to him: *Hey, Bobby, we need to meet for dinner sometime.*

Without missing a freaking beat, Bobby turned around and said to Joe: *Why don't you just give me 50 bucks, and we'll call it even?*

When I say he didn't miss a beat, I mean it - Bobby didn't even *pause*, and it wasn't like he had it pre-planned or anything. He was just that good.

Oh, and another thing. You might be wondering what Bobby Heenan might have brought to a birthday party for David Penzer. Well, he decided to bring me a plant.

Yes, I said a plant - it's called the *wandering jew*.

Now *that's* pretty funny.

If you look up his background, Bobby grew up as a poor kid and got his start in this business - which he truly loved, by the way - at the absolute bottom. He used to talk about cleaning up the garbage after the fans left the arena, just because he would get to go in there for free. I guess he was sort of like me in that way - willing to do anything it took to get his foot in the door.

Once he did get that foot in the door, Bobby was very underrated as a *wrestler* (i.e. before he was a manager), and he was especially adept at putting over babyfaces in that role. In his heyday, Bobby was able to take some incredible bumps to pop the crowd - something you wouldn't necessarily know if you only watched him later in his career.

More than anything, though - it was his wit that made him a legend. Even I didn't escape his wrath on-air, such as the time I announced - during a 'War Games' match - that two minutes were left before another wrestler entered. Bobby noted that the timer on the screen said differently, and he responded as only he could: *Three minutes, dummy!*

Another time, Tony observed on commentary that Randy Savage was becoming unglued in my vicinity: "*Savage has David Penzer's chair - and David Penzer!*"

"*I think I'd rather have the chair*," quipped Bobby under his breath.

An ongoing gag for Bobby was to call the cell phones of various people at WCW production meetings. He was always known for doing *something* to make people laugh, and those kinds of stories are too numerous to count. One of the best ones actually comes from Scott Hudson, who tells a tale about one of his first times on the road with WCW:

We were coming to the hotel after a *Nitro*, and it was a group of us [announcers traveling together]. We would [usually] come back to the hotel at 11:30 or midnight. The only people there were [generally] the people working - and maybe some other drunks stumbling out of the lobby bar or whatever.

But we walk in…and Bobby just goes - he just whispers to us, 'I got something'.

That was it. That's all we knew, like, 'Oh my God. What is this gonna be?'

It was a nice hotel, and there was a janitor guy buffing the floor. It's midnight - he's not getting in anybody's way - but [the buffer] is plugged in *way* ass over there.

Bobby comes up to this thing right near the check in - the registration desk. Bobby wraps his foot around the cord, and we see it - we're already dying. Of course, Bobby takes the bump, pulls the buffer out of the guy's hand like a shot…and the guy's just standing there like he's still holding it.

141

The janitor watches the buffer fly across the lobby, and Bobby grabs it, takes another bump, rolls around the hotel lobby with the buffer, and by this time he's unplugged it from the wall. He's got the cord going in 14 different directions and he's yelling: *What the hell? Get this thing offa me!*

The janitor guy is now running over there, trying to do what he can, not knowing there's no way he's gonna stop Bobby from doing his bit. We're of course up against the pillars of the lobby, deader than 4 o'clock laughing - until Bobby finally got himself 'free' of it.

He did this thing you would see him do where he dusted off his arms - even though there was nothing there to dust off. He dusted himself off, pointed at the buffer, looked at the janitor and goes: *Get that fixed.*

Then he went up and checked in!

As long as I live, I'll just never forget that. I had never experienced [something like] that before. [On the other hand], Tony was like, 'Oh yeah, he does that every now and then. That's just Bobby.'

[Meanwhile], I couldn't breathe, and my stomach hurt from my muscles tightening up from laughing. But that was Bobby. He was always on.

It was midnight after the show was over, and he was still putting on a show - just for us.

Gene Okerlund

There's probably a better comparison someone could make, but to me, 'Mean' Gene Okerlund was like the *Robin* to Bobby 'The Brain' Heenan's *Batman*, or maybe vice versa. They were both very similar in terms of their personalities, sense of humor and the way that they viewed the business. Both guys were exactly what you would expect them to be - hilarious, friendly, and extremely giving of their time and knowledge. From my standpoint, they were simply a joy to be around.

A lot of kids grew up wanting to be Hulk Hogan or Dusty Rhodes, but for me, I wanted to be just like 'Mean' Gene. There's the old adage about never meeting your heroes, but Gene never let me down in that regard. I think about the little things, now - such as when WCW was

142

doing a *Nitro* episode in South Florida, and I decided to bring my family backstage. I had Lisa and both of the kids with me - but I also took my mom and Dad as well. My sister Jodi also came along - and Randy Savage, as I remember it, took quite the liking to her.

...But I digress!

Anyway, back to the story: I thought it would be nice if my dad got to say "Hello" to Gene, and therefore, I introduced them to one another before the show. Now, let's be honest - in general, no one getting ready for a live television program wants to meet someone's Dad. In this case, however, Gene showed a genuine interest in my father: *So, Mr. Penzer - what is it that you do?*

Once my dad replied that he was a psychologist, Gene appeared *fascinated* by that. They each went away, sat down together and had their own separate conversation for about 20 minutes, sharing different observations they had about their respective careers. I'm sure they shared a couple of observations about a certain ring announcer too!

More importantly, from that day forward, my dad (formerly "Mr. Penzer") became "Dr. Penzer" to Gene: *Hey, how's Dr. Penzer doing? Tell him I said hello.*

That's just Gene in a nutshell - a genuinely nice person, as well as a giver (rather than a taker) in so many ways. Gene was also one of the *smartest* people in the history of the wrestling business, and now that I think about it, that intelligence is probably what he most had in common with my dad. When it came to booking, for example, don't think for a second that Gene didn't know what was going on! He chose to bite his tongue about some of the on-air decisions, mostly because it wasn't his 'lane' - although quite easily, it could have been.

With an impeccable degree of accuracy, Gene simply *knew* what the fans wanted. From interviewing the guys - and listening to the people - Gene understood what was working, who was and wasn't over, and which of the wrestlers were connecting with the audience.

143

He never went in the direction of creative or anything like that, but let me tell you something - it would have been interesting.

One funny story that comes to mind about Gene: he used to refer to me as *The Lantzman,* and for the longest time, I had no idea what the hell he was talking about. It's basically a name for a Jewish gentleman, I later realized - but that's how Gene used to pitch to me: *Hey, where is The Lantzman?*

He was one of the funniest, most entertaining and talented people in this world. I tend to get goosebumps whenever I talk about Gene - he was *that* good (and *that* knowledgeable) that I really can't put it into words. I mean, go back and watch some of those old WCW and WWF shows. Look at Gene's timing, the way that he led guys through their interviews. Even if the guy was bland as hell - or basically had nothing to say - Gene found a way of making it entertaining. He was an absolute master on the microphone - the very best at what he did.

As far as I'm concerned - and regardless of who comes along - no one will ever touch him.

'Mean' Gene Okerlund was one of a kind

The sheer gravitas, respect and trust that Gene held among the talent was captured in a *Sarasota Herald-Tribune* article of the time:

144

The taxi door swings open and the show begins. It's 4:15 p.m. on a Monday in Chattanooga, Tenn., and Gene Okerlund again finds himself in the center ring.

"I've seen that face before," the cabbie says.

Okerlund immediately goes with it. He might cruise around Sarasota in his Mercedes convertible without being recognized, or eat dinner at a local restaurant without being asked for an autograph, but anonymity doesn't follow him on the road.

...Suddenly, it clicks with the cabbie. Ray Craze - "Call me Crazy Ray," he says - looks hard in the rear-view mirror. A piece of American pop culture looks back.

"You're an announcer of some kind, ain't ya?"

Silence.

"Is it the rasslin' thing?"

Okerlund nods.

"I knew it!" Crazy Ray says, slapping the dashboard and reaching a hand toward the backseat.

"How ya doin' Mean Gene!"

He's the voice of World Championship Wrestling, and he's revered by fans and wrestlers alike.

...Bill Goldberg, the current WCW champion, used the word indebted. 'Lone Wolf' Scott Hall called him the WCW's biggest star. 'Nature Boy' Ric Flair said he's the best announcer in sports, network or cable. The Giant, Lex Luger, Kevin 'Big Sexy' Nash, [and] Stevie Ray, all attested to Okerlund's impact.

"He works with your character," Hall said. "You're standing there, scared to death, looking out at millions of people, and he helps you get through it. His talent won't be denied."

Said Goldberg: "He has the real power."

Okerlund has the stage, too, every week on WCW's *Monday Nitro*, where he arbitrates between WCW's ever-shifting protagonists and antagonists, often steering them into head-on collisions. It's perhaps the last live theater left on television - "soap operas for males 18-34," as Okerlund puts it - starring 'Mean' Gene as Master of Ceremonies.

145

…Like any opera worth its soap, there's plenty of beef and cheesecake. Take away the pyrotechnics and flying head butts, though, and *WCW Monday Nitro* could easily be an episode of *Melrose Place*. At key junctures, Okerlund's narration hatches Machiavellian schemes, some that play out in the next three hours, others that are planted for coming weeks.

As always, 'Mean' Gene will wear a coat-and-tie to lend some dignity to the proceedings.

Okerlund stands to leave. The taxi waits outside.

"You ready to rock'n roll?"

It's hard to believe that such mayhem will soon break out.

Backstage, the cast assembles as though the bell for study hall just rang. Goldberg and The Giant are joined in a poker game by Bam Bam Bigelow and Brian Adams. A line forms at the buffet. Others read magazines and newspapers or talk quietly among themselves. Nobody's in character yet, except the Nitro Girls, who constantly stretch and work on their steamy routines in agonizingly slow motion.

'Mean' Gene walks in, and it's as though The Godfather just called a meeting of the families. Everybody, from Goldberg to the gaffers, greets him. Okerlund eschews the star treatment, and returns every handshake and hug in royal fashion.

"Gene has a genuine interest in what he does, whether it be as an announcer or human being," said referee Brian Hildebrand, a 12-year veteran whose fight with cancer has brought perspective to the WCW's traveling show. "He's always quick to make you smile. He's got that wicked sense of humor. He's able to make people laugh and feel good about themselves."

Nitro's rattle and hum grows louder as 8 p.m. approaches. Okerlund eventually works his way to a sound stage disguised as a dungeon with metal lockers. He ducks inside and flawlessly rips through several taped segments.

These are shameless promotions. The kind that fill seats and wrestlers' bank accounts.

Before cameras roll, he gauges the mood of each interview. Former tag-team partners Scott Hall and Big Sexy Kevin Nash have broken up, and Hall doesn't want to get back together because Nash hurt his feelings by sucker-punching him while shaking hands. That, and Hall wants to try out a new character.

…Mean Gene quickly jumps on it.

"Why don't you want to be Kevin Nash's friend?" he booms.

146

Hall: "That's kind of a sensitive thing to talk about on national television."

Mean Gene: "Just lay it on me, brother."

Hall: "Gene, I'm just doing this because it's with you. Hey, I'm trying to get the 'Lone Wolf' thing going, and it's better if it comes from you. You plant the seed, and I'll go with it."

Mean Gene needs only one take.

"He could stand out there with a mannequin and get an interview out of them," said ring announcer David Penzer.

Twenty minutes before air-time, everybody gets pumped. Bare-chested wrestlers oil up and flex in front of full-length mirrors. Producers flip on headsets. Crew members check equipment as fans file into seats. There are no second chances on *Nitro Live*. Tony Schiavone, WCW's lead play-by-play announcer, approaches Okerlund.

"You're going to see Gene at his best tonight," Schiavone says. "He's presiding over a contract signing."

Gene looks up from his notes.

"I am?"

As a person, Gene Okerlund was a wonderful guy who loved to laugh, tell a few stories and have a couple of drinks after the show. If you've ever watched any of his outtakes - a lot of that stuff can be found on Twitter nowadays - you can see all of that on full display. Much of the best content actually came out of the customized, tailored promos that Gene would oversee for every city that the WWF was going to - you know, *Ladies and gentlemen, this coming Friday night, the World Wrestling Federation will be in Miami at the James L. Knight Center.* Gene would run down the card, bring on a wrestler to discuss an upcoming match on the show, and they would send out all those different promos to the relevant syndicated markets.

The process of recording those promos didn't just take an hour. It took six or seven hours - and that was at *every* TV taping. The promos were known as local-market, or market-specific interviews - 'market specs' is what we usually called them - and they were very important in the syndicated era. I got to know this first-hand once Gene did the same thing for us at WCW.

In fact, from 1996 onwards, I ended up producing a lot of these interviews, which typically were recorded in this gray box (outfitted with AC and a generic backdrop), situated in the parking lot of wherever we were running TV. Inside the box, we had a basic green screen set up, a teleprompter and just enough room for a producer and cameraman! My job was to find guys to work with Gene, keep a schedule of everything we were doing, and then hand it all off to a producer once we were done. That producer was then responsible for inserting the promos into the various versions of our syndicated shows around the country - a totally foreign model to viewers of wrestling today.

Later on down the line, I ultimately got to host the interviews myself, but in general, they weren't the most high-profile opportunities. Obviously, the tapes were airing only in one market, and therefore, some of the bigger names seemingly didn't have time for it.

Nonetheless, we would typically be in that box from about two to six o'clock at a minimum - but regardless of how long it took, there was one young wrestler who would stand there during every taping that we had. Whether he was booked on the show or not, it didn't matter to him. He would be there waiting for us before we got there, as a matter of fact, just to get another shot at working with Gene - of working with the master.

He used to practically *beg* us to cut promos in that box.

And who was the wrestler, I hear you ask?

I suspect you may have heard of him.

148

11:
ONE OF THE BOYS

That young wrestler was Chris Jericho.

Charisma was never an issue for Jericho, but when he first started in WCW, he found interview situations to be challenging. To his credit, he didn't need to be told that his promos needed work, and by his own intuition, he started turning his weakness into a strength. At every television taping, Chris would stand in that box for three, four, even five hours at a time, and if we couldn't find someone for an interview, he would *volunteer* to do a promo instead.

This is the best practice, Chris told me one day, *that I could ever possibly get.*

He's literally guiding me through this, Chris said, speaking of Gene, *and he's making me feel comfortable on the mic.*

Ultimately, Chris became much more than comfortable - he ended up as one of the most entertaining talkers in the entire business. A lot of it came through sheer repetition, as over the course of one afternoon in that box, he might have cut 20 or 30 promos! At the beginning, Gene would sort of feed Chris stuff to help put him at ease, but then - because Gene was so smart and good at what he did - he would throw out a 'jab' or two, seemingly out of nowhere.

Gene would do that just to see how Chris would react. He was teaching him, really: *If I throw this out at you, what are you gonna come back with?*

It was a fascinating thing to watch.

Slowly but surely, Chris kept getting better at thinking on his feet, and he even would come back with stuff to keep Gene off-balance. Chris would get Gene to crack up at times - a badge of honor all by itself - because Gene didn't lose his composure very often (if at all). One of Chris' ongoing gags (and he was amazing at these subtle details) was referring to 'Mean' Gene as "Gene Mean." Similarly, Tony Schiavone became – according to Chris – none other than "Tony Skee-a-vone!"

Ultimately, Gene helped bring out a side in Chris that already existed off-camera. Jericho could be as entertaining in those moments as he eventually was on television - although it didn't always seem that way at the time! I remember once when we were hustling to get to a show, somewhere outside the suburban Washington D.C. area. As I was opening that show on the mic (and had responsibility over the music), I had to be there *early* - at least by an hour - unlike some of the other guys I was riding with.

With this in mind, Jericho kept making excuses for us to stop: *I need my hair products…I need this…I need that…*

Meanwhile, in the backseat, I was busy freaking out: *Guys, we really gotta get to the show - come on!*

Of course, the more that Jericho saw me freaking out, the more he felt inclined to keep it up: *Oh, wait a minute - I just remembered. We gotta make a quick stop here, too…*

I guess for Chris, it was just payback for all the times that I irritated him - one of which actually made the news, believe it or not. I don't remember the exact specifics of how it happened (that part is a blur), but I remember it was enough to get this warning at the hotel bar: *Penzer, You've got a minute to get outta here.*

Now that I think about it, the phrase *hockey fight* may have also been mentioned, but whatever Chris was saying, I wasn't going to go anywhere - why stop the fun now?

150

As Chris got more infuriated (*You got ten seconds now, Penzer. Nine, eight, seven...*), I ended up getting chased through the hotel lobby. I got tackled to the floor, stripped of my clothes, and to top it all off, I had to get on the elevator in only my underwear! I'm sure the guests at the Philadelphia Hilton appreciated that visual.

A couple of months later, I took my wife out to see *Miss Saigon* at the Fox Theater in Atlanta, about 45 minutes away from where we lived in Peachtree City (guys: my mom bought us tickets for a date night - I can assure you that I was bored stiff). At one point, we called the babysitter - who happened to be the daughter of a family friend, by the way - looking to check in on the kids: *Hey, everything okay over there?*

Yeah, said the babysitter, *but I just saw you on 'Hardcopy'.*

I was confused to say the least: *What are you talking about?*

Um...so Chris Jericho, she began, *stripped you to your underwear...in a hotel lobby...*

Oh my God, I thought. *This is really it this time.*

I'm fired.

Apparently, the TV show *Hardcopy* had been working on an 'exposé' of the wrestling business - and WCW in particular. In an effort to get footage for their 'special feature', they sent an undercover journalist to film us, at the bar, without our consent or knowledge.

Just my luck.

I worried about it all weekend, nervously awaiting my fate come Monday. Once I knew that the office people were back at work, I placed an urgent phone call to Alan Sharp, WCW's Head of Public Relations.

Alan, I said, apologetically, *I saw the thing on 'Hardcopy'...*

Look, I'm so sorry. We were just a bunch of guys messing around. It was just a hockey fight...please tell me I'm not fired.

Alan laughed so hard.

We were told it was going to be an exposé, he roared. *An exposé on all the crazy things the wrestlers did! We were thinking it was gonna be a lot worse than you getting stripped down to your underwear in a hotel.*

Penzer, you took one for the team, Alan said. *Don't even think twice about it.*

Phew – now *that* was a relief.

But just imagine I had got fired over something that Jericho did. What a travesty that would have been. After all, *I* was the one who practically got him started in his second career - the one he excels at to this day! That's right - *I* was the one who spotted Chris Jericho's musical talent!

(It's not surprising, really. I'm a legit music junkie who has attended over 1000 concerts in my life.)

I'm just kidding – *mostly* - but like every joke, there could be a little truth to it. It happened while we were at a bar in West Virginia one night, after Jericho had just got done doing karaoke.

Holy crap, I told Chris when he got off stage. *You can frickin' sing, dude - you should start a band or something!*

Look - I'm not saying I'm the reason why *Fozzy* was founded, but I don't know - maybe I put something in the back of his mind.

In early 1998, Jericho's character really took off when he turned heel for the first time - and partially, it came at my expense.

It was Terry Taylor's idea initially. Jericho was booked to go on a losing streak, leading to him becoming increasingly frustrated, and eventually, throwing temper tantrums after each loss. After one such defeat to Curt Hennig, he walked over to my ringside seat, threw me straight out of it, and started going insane: *"I can't take it anymore!"*

The pattern repeated in the weeks ahead, with Jericho even tearing up my ring jacket! It built to him making a 'heartfelt' apology on January 8th, 1998 - the debut episode of *WCW Thunder*:

Ladies and gentlemen, I stand before you an embarrassed man. I stand before you an ashamed man. I stand before you a changed man. The reason I say that is my behavior over the last couple of weeks has been atrocious. The real Chris Jericho is not the sniveling, whiny baby that you've been watching each and every week. The real Chris Jericho is the man you tune in to watch every single week on your TVs. The real Chris Jericho is the man you place on a pedestal. The real Chris Jericho is a role model that's influenced each and every one of your lives in a positive way. And the real Chris Jericho is sorry.

Dave Penzer, I am sorry - I apologize. I'd like to present you with this suit jacket. I apologize to all you screaming, adoring fans in this arena tonight…and to all you people at home - mark my words. It will never, ever happen again - and you can trust me when I say that. Thank you!

You can guess what happened next. Jericho quickly lost his next match - this time against Ric Flair - and the tantrums continued unabated. *"Wait a minute,"* observed Lee Marshall on commentary. *"What about the whiny, spoiled kid we weren't supposed to see anymore? Off goes Penzer's jacket one more time!"*

"I can tell you right now," added Tony Schiavone, *"as great of an athlete as this young man is, there's no way we're gonna believe him again!"*

Chris Jericho presents me with a new tuxedo on WCW Thunder!

Week after week, our interactions continued, serving to build the foundation for Jericho's new, 'crybaby' heel persona (for the record: I probably had about 5% input in the storyline, with Terry Taylor having 10%, and the rest going to Jericho). One episode, after yet another post-match meltdown where Jericho smashed my chair against the ring post, he came out to present me with - wait for it - a brand *new* chair (as if I couldn't have found one myself)!

It was those kinds of funny, subtle creative nuances that made Chris an incredible performer - and by that spring, he was already on his way to superstardom.

For most of its history, WCW had been known for having a relatively light schedule, a fact which enticed numerous ex-WWF wrestlers to join our roster. However, by the time *WCW Thunder* debuted on TBS, the situation had changed dramatically. In producing *another* weekly prime-time series, we were suddenly on the road more than ever, and, in a business with no real off-season, it looked to stay that way for the foreseeable future.

Being on the road also meant an increased amount of downtime, and in wrestling, more downtime meant more of something else: *hijinks*.

First, you might recall that I was an *employee* of Turner Broadcasting (as opposed to being an 'independent contractor', as is typically common for the wrestlers), and therefore, the company covered my road expenses - the cost of my hotel and rental car specifically. As had happened in the past when I received such benefits, word quickly spread about 'Penzer's perks', and consequently, I started traveling (although in different combinations and at different times) with a whole laundry list of guys, including Jericho, Arn Anderson, Ric Flair, Chris Benoit, Dean Malenko, Eddie Guerrero, Chavo Guerrero, Jr., Hugh Morrus and Billy Kidman. The experiences which followed became, in some ways, the biggest perk of them all.

Becoming part of the fraternity of wrestling

I had never experienced the camaraderie that came with being on the road, with the possible exception of my short-lived fraternity stint at the University of Florida. In WCW, our week basically started on Friday mornings, when we landed in whatever city we had a house show in. We would rent a car, do the show there, and then we had to make a decision each time: *Do we drive to the next show - and get there around one o'clock in the morning - or do we stay the night, wake up and leave at around noon?*

Usually, most guys wanted to stay overnight, because if I'm being honest, they had a better shot of getting into certain debauchery that way (some of them - the ones who were into that). It also allowed them to wake up and work out in the morning, because after all, everyone had *something* that was needed to get themselves going. For example, Arn wasn't Arn until he could get himself in a steam room, sweat out the booze from the night before, and then go out and get on with his day. I'm not exaggerating anything - that was just typical of the life that we lived.

Driving down those roads, you develop a bond which is difficult to describe. In our case, we were with our 'wrestling family', so to speak, more than we were our actual families, and most of the time, there was nothing to do *but* converse with each other; to joke around, to prank or to *rib* as we say in the business. Those times we spent together are ingrained in my memory, even to this day – perhaps more than the actual shows themselves.

Remember, this was before the smartphone era. This was before the Internet became totally ubiquitous. Guys weren't riding down the road playing video games in the backseat, or sitting there with their AirPods on, scrolling through social media. Driving from town to town, you didn't always get a radio signal, or other times, the only thing on AM radio was Art Bell - the guy who believed in aliens and all that stuff.

I remember one, unforgettable three-day road trip where Dean Malenko, Brian Hildebrand (the referee Mark Curtis), Eddie Guerrero and I traveled together in an SUV. We had a cassette tape player in the car, and to help kill time on the road, I picked up a 'Best of the 1970s' album on tape (we were all roughly the same age, and basically grew up in the '70s for the most part, so I figured it was a good choice). We pressed play on day one of the trip and evidently, the album had every sappy 'Yacht Rock' song imaginable - *Brandy (You're a Fine Girl)* by Looking Glass*, Cats in the Cradle* by Harry Chapin*,* that kind of thing.

At first, I guess nobody wanted to get their 'man card' pulled, so we just kind of sat there, humming along and looking out the window together. By the second day, a couple guys started singing at sort of a low volume, but by the third day - *forget about it!* By that point, we had all heard the album a half-dozen times - and everyone was singing at the top of their lungs!

One of the songs on the tape was *Seasons in the Sun* by Terry Jack. Depending on your age, you may or may not be familiar with the lyrics:

Goodbye to you, my trusted friend
But we've known each other since we were nine or ten
Together, we've climbed hills and trees
Learned of love and ABC's
Skinned our hearts and skinned our knees

Towards the end of the song, there's a section which goes like this:

We had joy, we had fun, we had seasons in the sun
But the wine and the song like the seasons have all gone

We were all raucously singing along to that part - Dean in the front seat, myself in the passenger seat, and Brian Hildebrand in the backseat. Eddie was sitting in the middle seat, although he was silent, and not joining in with the rest of us.

Finally, Eddie broke his silence: *God damn it, I can't take this anymore!*

As Dean continued driving, Eddie leaned out of his seat. *This fucking '70s sap bullshit!* he yelled, furiously pushing the eject button.

To our astonishment - and amusement - Eddie completely ripped the tape out. He picked it up, destroyed it and - to top it all off - threw it out the window!

Eddie was kind of like that, in terms of his temperament. You never knew what was going to set him off, and seemingly, he could just flip on a dime. Now don't get me wrong - Eddie truly didn't have a mean bone in his body. He had a temper, sure - but generally, he was the nicest guy you could ever want to meet. A lot of guys will lose their temper and not feel bad about it, but that wasn't Eddie. Within

157

20 minutes of throwing out the cassette tape, he was already acting a little sheepish: *Sorry guys...*

...I just couldn't take it anymore.

Like all the Guerreros, Eddie was especially quick to explode after having a drink or five in his system. On occasion, this could manifest itself into some legendary arguments, such as the one between Eddie and Arn in a Hampton Inn hotel room. As Jericho and I were staying in the next room over, we ended up hearing the whole thing happen. At one point, we even had our ears pressed to the wall - because we couldn't miss a second of it!

So what happened?

Well, Arn never ate until he was done drinking - no matter if it was midnight, four AM, or whenever. On this night, he wanted to order Burger King after downing all his booze, and therefore, he asked Eddie if he wanted anything: *You want some apple pie?*

I don't want a piece of pie, responded Eddie in terse fashion.

Now don't go asking me for any pie! warned Arn in that Southern accent of his.

I'm happy to get you a piece of pie, Arn continued, *but if you don't get a piece of pie, and then you want my pie, there's gonna be problems here tonight!*

Lo and behold, what do you think ended up happening? The order arrived, and sure enough, Eddie wanted himself some pie.

Eddie started getting pissy about it: *You won't give me a piece of pie?*

Then he got bitter: *Look at you*, he said to Arn. *You think your shit don't stink...*

Eddie, responded Arn, *I asked you if you wanted a piece of pie. You said, 'No!'*

I guess at some point, Arn must have offered Eddie a piece after all, because what followed was straight out of a comedy sketch.

Take the pie, Arn said.

No, replied Eddie. *I don't want the pie.*

Take the pie, repeated Arn.

I don't want the pie.

Take the pie!

They kept going back-and-forth like this while Chris and I listened in absolute hysterics. Finally, Arn just gave up: *You know what - I don't want the fucking pie!*

Eddie had a similar reaction: *Good, I don't want the fucking pie either!*

There was only one way to settle it.

They took that apple pie and threw it in the garbage!

Before we knew it, the hotel manager was coming to their door, responding to complaints that other guests were making about the noise. *If I have to come up here again*, he said, w*e're gonna kick you guys out of the hotel.*

For a moment or two, there was nothing but dead silence. The manager then left, got back on the hotel elevator, and all we heard was the doors closing: *Ding!*

Okay, Chris and I thought, calming ourselves down. *It's all over now.*

All of a sudden, Eddie's voice cut through that silence like a knife through butter: *All I wanted*, he yelled at the top of his lungs, *was a piece of fucking pie!*

And just like that – they were off to the races again.

Stories like that *still* bring a smile to my face, just like the time when Arn, Pee Wee and I were riding to Charlotte – probably talking about a recent show or laughing about the latest rib – when we noticed the Steiner Brothers (Rick and Scott) in hot pursuit behind us. At first, we didn't think much of it, but before we knew it, the Steiners started pummeling our car with eggs!

So now, obviously, there's only one appropriate response, right? We coolly pulled into the local 7-11, loaded up on our own ammunition, and spent the next two hours in a high-speed, high-stakes, egg-tossing battle with the Steiners!

To some people, that might sound a little silly – a little juvenile, perhaps – but to us, it was just how we passed the time. It was how we got from one place to another without getting bored. It's how we had a good time with the people that we worked with.

And I tell you what - when those eggs started flying, I think I realized two things at the exact same time:

1) I was living in a crazy fucking world, and
2) I loved every fucking minute of it.

Wrestlers are a unique breed. In any given locker room, you'll find the wildest cross-section of people you could ever imagine. For example, there was a guy by the name of Hardbody Harrison who made sporadic appearances, mostly on *WCW Saturday Night*, over the course of a few years in our company. He wasn't a difficult person to deal with, but he was certainly unique - and very flamboyant. One time, I remember he got in a fight with Alex Wright - at Disney-MGM of all places - and Alex, incidentally, happened to get the best of him.

Jericho shared some interesting stories about Harrison in his first book:

[Hardbody] was in his own world anyway. He was constantly submitting weird angles and stories to the office, trying to get himself a push.

First he came up with the idea of painting his face and becoming Sting's black nemesis, *Stang*. Then he came up with another beauty that had DDP bringing a special magic diamond crystal to the ring. Hardbody would attack him, steal the crystal, and drop it into a tank of piranhas. This chicanery would force DDP to jump into the piranha tank to retrieve the magic crystal live on PPV.

I would've paid to see that one.

Give yourself a minute to take all that in, will you?

Anyway, this guy Harrison used to brag - in tremendous detail, I might add - about everything he was doing away from the ring: *I got eighteen girls working for me, and this is how much money I'm making…*

We all kind of rolled our eyes at it, because without exception, *everyone* thought he was full of crap. Harrison was an enhancement talent, after all, getting paid 150 bucks to lose on our 'C' television show. If he was this big-time pimp or whatever, why the hell was he doing jobs on our TV?

I still don't know the answer to that one.

Harrison kept telling us about his supposed activities - again and again *and again* - until one day, we all got a wakeup call: he had been telling the truth all along!

He was eventually sentenced to life in prison - with no chance of parole - after being found guilty of running a major prostitution ring. I think the U.S. Department of Justice summed it up pretty well:

161

**Former Wrestler Sentenced on Sex Trafficking
and Forced Labor Charges**

Ring Leader In Human Trafficking Organization Sentenced

WASHINGTON – Former professional wrestler Harrison Norris Jr., 42, a/k/a "Hardbody Harrison," from Cartersville, Ga., was sentenced today to life in prison and lifetime supervised release for committing multiple violations of federal sex trafficking and forced labor statutes in connection with a scheme to force women into prostitution.

"These vulnerable American victims were lured by false promises to train as professional wrestlers and suffered horrific physical, sexual, and psychological abuse," said Grace Chung Becker, Acting Assistant Attorney General for the Justice Department's Civil Rights Division. "I commend these women for coming forward and helping the Department hold accountable those who engaged in this shameful conduct."

U.S. Attorney David E. Nahmias said of the sentencing, "Defendant Norris ran a forced prostitution ring in which women were sexually assaulted, held in debt, and forced to work and perform sex acts against their will. This heinous conduct deserved the severe sentence handed down today."

On a lighter note, let's talk a little more about *ribbing*, which is considered par for the course in the wrestling business. For example: there was a year in which Pee Wee and I drove everywhere with Bobby Eaton. I kid you not, for the first six months of that year, they both managed to convince me that Bobby couldn't read!

We would go to a restaurant and to sell the gimmick, Pee Wee would point at the pictures and ask: *Is this what you want, Bobby?*

Pee Wee got me good with that one - as he did another time when it was just me, him and Arn. It involved a betrayal of the worst kind - the ol' double-cross over a strawberry shortcake. As recounting the story may bring me to tears, I'll tag in Arn on this one, who recently discussed it on his podcast:

162

There is a place in Dalton, Alabama called *Dobbs Barbecue*. [They have] the best strawberry shortcake ever - they're famous for it…it's world renowned…or at least, Southeastern renowned.

So we've been talking about it for a couple of days. Dalton pops up [and] it's an afternoon show. The setting is perfect. It's a Sunday afternoon show and then we got to make a drive somewhere for [a show on] Monday.

Pee Wee goes in [to the barbecue place] and Penzer says, 'Hey guys, I'm buying.' He gives Pee Wee like 20 bucks or something. Pee Wee goes in and Penzer's rubbing his hands together. He's going, 'God, I've been waiting on this for a month. I can't tell you how much I enjoy these shortcakes - they're unbelievable.'

So Pee Wee comes back out - never offers Penzer any change - but [Penzer] is so happy [anyway]. He goes, 'Got any change?' and Pee Wee goes, 'Somewhere.' [Penzer] goes, 'Oh, you know what - never mind, guys. I just want to treat you guys anyway. I've been looking forward to this - I don't give a shit if there's any change.'

We start going down the road and Pee Wee opens the bag a little bit. We've gotten 20 miles down the road where we're out in the country now - we're not in town - so everybody can relax, get a fork…even Penzer who's driving…he's gonna eat it while he's driving.

…All of a sudden, I hear Pee Wee go, 'Oh God, they only gave us *two* shortcakes.' Penzer goes, 'What? Look in the bag again.'

Pee Wee went, 'Man, they shorted us.'

We're 25 miles down the road now, and we're not gonna double *back* 25 miles. Penzer is raising holy hell, [but while] I'm eating mine, and Pee Wee is eating his, Penzer realizes he got screwed. He's not getting any strawberry shortcake, and he's red in the face. He's cussin'…

We get done and didn't offer him a bite of nuthin'…at all. Now we're 50 miles down the road and Penzer is still cutting this promo: 'Guys, you don't understand. You could have gave me half of each one of y'alls. I've been looking forward to this forever.'

All of a sudden, he starts back driving - he ignores us - and I hear a crinkling [sound]. I look in the back and now Pee Wee is eating the *third* shortcake - which is Penzer's. Now Penzer realizes that he paid - lost the 20 bucks…no change…had a cake and got screwed out of it by Pee Wee…and man, he pulled over and cut a promo like you've never heard: *Well, give me what's left!*

Pee Wee [just listened] …and put the last bite in his mouth.

163

I don't know if that was a rib, *per se* - or just pure sadism on Pee Wee's part.

Bobby Eaton, Arn and I at Ric Flair's 50th birthday party

One of my most embarrassing moments happened because of a rib. We were doing a live event in Charlotte, and our hotel happened to be right next to where the show was set up. It had a nice, big pool and everything - just a beautiful property.

About 45 minutes before show time, I had just about got my tuxedo on when a bunch of the guys picked me up, carried me to the edge of the swimming pool, and made it *seem* like they were going to throw me in. They were just pretending, believe it or not, but then the late, great Brian Pillman - who was as unpredictable as they come - came over to push me in the water himself!

I did my job that night (aided by my backup tuxedo) because above all, you don't 'sell' a rib to the other guys; in other words, you don't make it obvious that someone got to you. It was just like that time in San Antonio, when a bunch of us - wrestlers, producers, you name it - were taking in the famous Riverwalk downtown. I guess I must have been getting on Scott Hall's nerves quite a bit, because at one point, he looked at me and said: *Penzer, you say that one more time, and I'm gonna push you in the water.*

You don't got the balls to push me in, I said, knowing what inevitably would happen.

164

You don't have a hair on your ass, Scott, I continued.

Within probably half a second, Scott pushed me straight into the water. I didn't say a word about it - I simply got up, went to take a shower, put on some new clothes, and met everyone else back at the bar. Scott bought me a drink once I got there, and I think I earned his respect that day. It was just the way things were - if you wanted to hang with the guys, you didn't bitch, moan or complain about stuff like that.

Upholding that facade could be challenging at times, especially when Curt Hennig - the unquestioned king in the arena of ribs - found a way to get involved.

There's a well-known story of Curt - knowing that Jim Helwig (Warrior) was doing a gimmick where he came through the canvas - defecating in a bucket and leaving it under the ring (talk about something being *the shits*). I remember Curt telling me how he made that all happen in *painstaking* detail. He said that he ate a bunch of Thai food - "really spicy" is how he described it - before taking a Pepto Bismol and making use of a little piece of toilet paper (rolled up and stuck in his you-know-what, just waiting for the opportune time).

He planned that thing out to the umpteenth degree. That was typical of Curt, as with him, it was never as simple as, 'Hey, let's do this as a rib...', *no, no, no*...he was like a Navy Seal going on a mission. He was meticulous about it, and he loved telling you what he was going to do - almost as much as he actually did doing it.

Much to my chagrin, Curt led an entire conglomerate of people in one of the longest-running ribs of all-time. I know Nick Patrick was one of his co-conspirators, and I *think* Booker T was also involved, but the rest of Curt's collaborators remain a mystery to me. Here was the background: I had a briefcase that I carried around from show to show. As I was constantly at ringside - unlike the wrestlers who only came out for their segment or match - I was away from this briefcase for several hours at a time.

At some point, I guess Curt *et al.* figured this all out, and from then on - every time I came back through the curtain - my briefcase would be padlocked to something. I would come back to the locker room and find it hanging from the ceiling. Other times, it might be attached to the locker. Other times still, it might be stuck to the shower head. The prank went on and on (and on), regardless of whether we were doing 'TV', or even at a house show!

It got to the point where as soon as I arrived at a WCW event, I *immediately* went to find the maintenance guy at whatever building we were playing. That poor guy would need a pair of bolt cutters to rescue my briefcase, but in most cases, he could never get the padlock off - only what it was attached to.

To be honest, I might have played it up a bit, acting like I was really pissed off when at times, I actually found the situation pretty funny. Nonetheless, you should have seen the looks I got when I walked through the airport, a beaten-up briefcase with up to four padlocks in tow. Finally, it all got so out of hand that the maintenance people had enough of it, but with no end to the rib in sight, our ring crew started transporting bolt cutters of their own!

Some of the funniest ribs back then involved Doug Dillinger, formerly a police officer in North Carolina, and, for a long time, the Head of Security at WCW. Due to his prior career and connections, Doug introduced the ability to involve *real* police officers in the game of ribs - most of which had guys thinking they were going to jail!

Dusty was a big part of that too. He was so *over* as a person - with or without Doug's help - that he could get those officers to cooperate, put somebody in handcuffs, and literally read them their rights.

I think they got Barry Windham once with that routine, but undoubtedly, the easiest (and most common) target was Klondike Bill, a former wrestler from the old days-turned WCW ring crew member. Bill has become somewhat infamous in recent years, but he was really just a gullible old guy who loved his job. Back in his day, wrestlers

166

didn't retire with a million dollars in the bank, and there certainly wasn't a lucrative market for personal appearances. When a guy like Bill was done, he was pretty much *done*, and usually, that meant getting a job as a prison guard, or maybe at the sheriff's office - or something to that effect. In Bill's case, however, he was able to get (and keep) a gig putting up the ring, and driving up and down the roads was fun for him. He loved still being part of the business, but at the same time, he was maybe starting to lose it a little bit.

Bill had worked in a similar capacity since the days of Jim Crockett Promotions (i.e. since before Crockett sold the promotion to Turner, a sale which ultimately led to WCW being created). At one point, Bill had also been the head groundskeeper for the then-Charlotte Orioles, a minor league baseball team which the Crockett's also owned. The story goes that one night, the team decided to run a contest and solicited Bill to help. Apparently, the idea was to put $1000 in dollar bills all around the stadium, giving one lucky winner the chance to grab as much money as they could - in a period of 30 or 60 seconds - before time expired. Supposedly, they handed Bill a big basket with the money inside and simply told him, *Go put this money out on the field*.

Obviously, the key would have been to spread that money all over the field, thus limiting how much cash that one "lucky" winner could get. Unfortunately, Bill didn't do that. He poured the entire thing on second base, and the guy who won ended up stuffing about $500 in his pocket. According to legend, the Orioles - a *minor* league team, remember - ultimately lost money, relative to that night's gate, as a result of those shenanigans.

From Bill's standpoint, I guess he was just following orders. They told him to put the money on the field - so he went and put that money on the field!

Maybe now you can see why, especially at his advanced age, Bill was an easy target for ribs. One time, I remember that Dusty and Doug got a police officer to confront Bill about a situation at a strip club - another time, it was something about an underage girl.

167

The police would literally come out and say, *Are you Bill Soloweyko?*

That was his shoot name.

Yes sir, he'd say.

Were you at this establishment last night?

Yes sir.

Could you please put your hands behind your back?

In the meantime, everybody who was in on it would be peeking around the corner, desperately trying not to crack up laughing. Two or three times in particular, I remember that Bill was already in handcuffs - thinking he was going to jail - before Dusty came out of the woodwork.

Ah, Dusty! Bill would exclaim. *You got me again - you son of a bitch!*

After a while, I suspect that Bill may have played along a little bit, similar to how I acted when I really didn't care anymore about my briefcase. You have to do that in the wrestling business; besides, Bill was just happy to be there. He loved his job, didn't want to lose his employment, and always got 'smartened up' in the end. To me, that was the whole *point* of a rib, because at some point, you kind of have to explain that it's just a *joke*.

I remember there was one exception to that rule, and quite frankly - for reasons that are self-evident to wrestling fans - it has stayed with me ever since. It happened when I was out with the Mexicans one night. We had taken two cars to get to the bar, and Juventud Guerrera - for some bizarre reason - happened to be the driver of one of those vehicles. While we were all busy drinking, Juvi left his car keys down

168

on the table, and when he wasn't looking, Chris Benoit took those keys away. That part of the rib was pretty standard.

However, when it came to leave, Juvi started desperately looking for the keys, and fellow *lucha* Psychosis was getting mad at him too. This went on for probably an hour as the bar was trying to close up, before finally, Benoit quietly placed the keys back on the table. Once Juvi 'found' the keys, the Mexicans continued arguing with each other in Spanish, probably about something much more serious at that point. I turned to Chris and said, *Alright - when are we going to smarten 'em up?*

I'll never forget Chris' response: *We don't.*

So infamous is this next story that for 20-plus years, it never reached the ears of the public - only the boys. I don't even think I told my wife about this one! It involved Johnny Grunge (one-half of the 'Public Enemy' tag-team) and a young lady from Sturgis, South Dakota.

First, let me say that Johnny was one of my best friends in WCW. He was part of the 'Peachtree City Gang', i.e. the group of us (including myself, Benoit, Steven Regal, and Fit Finlay) who worked for WCW while living in Peachtree City, Georgia (about 30 miles from downtown Atlanta). If we had a rare Saturday night off, we would all go down to the local Japanese steakhouse, drink some booze, and typically end the night singing karaoke together.

Johnny was the lovable fuckup of the bunch, a super nice guy who just couldn't figure out how to do the right thing. If you go back and watch our old shows, you'll notice that when he waved his arms to the 'Public Enemy' entrance music, he couldn't keep up with the beat! In most cases, his charisma and likability are what kept his fuck ups from hurting him.

169

One time, we were in Sturgis for the annual *Road Wild* pay-per-view, an event which coincided with the yearly motorcycle rally hosted in the city. Johnny and I were sharing a hotel room that weekend, and this time around, he happened to check in before me. After I got to the hotel and checked in, I went to put my key in the door, but no dice - it was bolted. I started knocking on the door, wondering what the hell was going on.

Eventually, Johnny answered the door, but he wouldn't let me in. He was laughing so hard that I thought he was on the verge of tears, or about to throw up - maybe both, to be honest with you. He was trying his best to explain to me what happened, but due to laughing so much, he literally couldn't get it out. Eventually, I got inside and I saw it for myself.

It looked like a sprinkler going off. Jim Duggan described the scene as the walls being spray painted. Here's what Bill Demott wrote about the incident:

Several times during my run with WCW, we went to Sturgis, South Dakota, for the Road Wild pay-per-view. These days were filled with motorcycles, naked women, alcohol, drunken men, more naked women, and great food.

During one trip to Sturgis, someone in the company arranged for several of us to be backstage guests at a Lynyrd Skynyrd concert. Teddy, Johnny, Meng and I got so drunk that we never made it to the concert. Instead, we decided to go to a local strip club. As usual, while the rest of us got to know the local dancers, Johnny [Grunge] began to wander. Johnny was never much for staying in one place too long, so we got used to him wandering and meeting up with us later. We didn't know where he went, but we knew he would find his way back to the hotel.

When Teddy and I got back to our hotel in the wee hours of the morning, we saw Dave Penzer walking down the hallway with a mop and bucket. What we saw when we walked into the room was our bed linens and personal items covered with shit!

That's right. I said 'shit'.

I was so stunned that I couldn't say a word, but Teddy was so pissed that he launched into an outburst of obscenities. And the fact that Johnny was nowhere to be found was somewhat suspicious.

We later learned that while we were in the bar, Johnny had brought a lady friend back to our room for a certain sex act...

Needless to say, I got a new room, folks.

That was Johnny Grunge.

Recall that in 1988 - back when I could only hope to be involved in the wrestling business - Ric Flair had cussed me out in front of the locker room at the Knight Center. With this in mind, it was more than symbolic when ten years later, I recounted the story to Flair backstage.

When I told Ric what happened, he was beyond apologetic: *Oh my God*, he said. *I'm so sorry, David.*

We laughed about it together, but Ric was kind of mortified, almost *humiliated* about his behavior.

Our conversation told me a lot about Ric's character, but it also said something about me, too. Simply put, I had come a long freaking way, baby.

I may have still been the butt of a few jokes, but overall - by virtue of my hard work and perseverance, not to mention a little luck - I was now being treated as an equal. To the guys in the locker room, I was no longer *just* a fan, or someone on the outside, or someone just trying to get in the business. For years, on the contrary, I had been firmly on the *inside*, and in the process, I had become one of them.

One of the boys.

I guess I was thinking about that when I encountered Perry Saturn at the bar one night. We were having fun drinking together, but at one point - and for whatever reason - I referred to myself with that very same phrase: *One of the boys.*

171

Penzer, Perry said in response. *You're not one of the boys.*

That fucking pissed me off. In a split second, I had to make a calculation. If I was really 'one of the boys', Perry wouldn't mind me saying something back.

I made my decision, looked at Perry and left no doubt about my feelings: *Fuck you, Perry.*

At first, Perry was stunned: *What the fuck did you say to me?*

Fuck you, I repeated.

Perry leaned forward and looked me dead in the eye.

Why is it 'fuck me?'

Look, I said. *I don't take bumps in the ring, but I travel the roads...I take all the flights you guys do...I make all the shows.*

Since I got this ring announcer gig, I haven't missed one show - Nitro, Thunder, Saturday Night, pay-per-views. No one else can fucking say that.

(Incidentally, my streak of appearances would continue until...well, it couldn't anymore.)

I've taken fucking greyhound buses to make shows, I continued. *I've paid for my own travel to make these towns. I've busted my ass for seven fucking years. If that doesn't make me 'one of the boys'...*

You know what, said Perry.

You're right - you are one of the boys.

172

It's a good thing that Perry Saturn agreed with me. Looking back, it was probably one of the greatest things anyone ever said to me in the business, but I think I had a different reaction in the moment.

All of that 'Fuck You' stuff? Man...

I'm just lucky he didn't kick my ass.

12:
LIFE IN THE FAST LANE

It had taken the best part of a decade, but I had *earned* my respect the hard way. When I say that, you have to remember that I wasn't a wrestler - and that matters in this business for a number of reasons. If you're in the ring taking bumps - or, alternatively, if you have a history of being in the ring and taking bumps - you're in the fraternity of wrestling, so to speak, from jump street. When somebody doesn't have that background in the business themselves, you're not afforded the same level of respect within that circle - and rightfully so, if you think about it.

So often in this business, I've seen guys come into the locker room environment and conduct themselves, quite frankly, like total marks. They go around asking for pictures or for autographs, and naturally, the guys start to feel leery around them. That's not a commentary on wrestlers, by the way - most of them are great guys - but like I said, it's a *fraternity*. If you're not welcome in that fraternity, and especially if you act like you want to be there really, *really* bad, it makes you stand out - and not in a good way.

When I was first establishing myself in the business, I consciously tried *not* to look like a mark. When WCW did a special *Clash of the Champions* for the 20-year anniversary of wrestling on TBS, for example, Andre The Giant was there - and although I desperately wanted to get a picture with Andre, I didn't want to pick up that 'mark' label in the process.

On that note: when the guys used to mess around with my briefcase, I was afraid of them finding something out about me. I was afraid they would discover a secret that other than my closest family members, no one ever had a clue about. Now don't get me wrong -

174

you should know (especially by now) that I'm an open book. It's just that some things aren't always for public knowledge or consumption.

You know what though? Maybe it's time to come clean.

So here goes nothing: I, David Penzer, have been a subscriber to the *Wrestling Observer* newsletter for over 35 years!

There, I said it, okay - it's out in the open!

I'm being dramatic, of course, but back in the day, nobody wanted people to know they were reading the 'kayfabe sheets', or the *dirtsheets* as they are commonly known. Nobody would dare read them in sight of anybody else you were working with. When I drove down the road, I'd have the sheets in my briefcase - and they would be hidden! I wouldn't take them out anywhere in front of people. I wouldn't even *say* that I had them with me.

The funny thing is, it was like the worst kept secret that almost *everybody* was reading the dirtsheets. Probably 80% of the talent and 90% of the office were avid readers behind closed doors. Like me, they wouldn't admit to it - nor would they be caught reading them in public - but they were *definitely* reading them. It's pretty hilarious to say that now, given that everything is so open - and everyone freely talks about it.

Back then, the boys didn't want to be known for reading the sheets, because that would get you major heat with the office. Of course, as I mentioned, the office was reading the same stuff themselves, usually getting their wife or secretary to subscribe to the *Observer* in their name. People did that dance for a lot of years - until the Internet came along, and all the 'scoops' seemed to end up there.

I was always terrified that somehow, my newsletters would spill out onto the floor and I'd be called a mark in front of everyone. Worse yet, someone could have accused me of 'stooging off' information to the Dave Meltzer's of the world. For the record, I never spoke to Meltzer or any of the dirtsheet writers during my time in WCW - but you could read their stuff and figure out the source for a lot of it. Meltzer was very close with Zane Bresloff, for instance, and that's where a lot of his WCW information came from. Zane was a genius, in my opinion, but he also loved to talk. Interestingly, Zane was powerful enough that he didn't have to hide what he was doing - that's how I know this as a fact - and Eric for sure knew about it. Some of Zane's comments were based on what he *wanted* Meltzer to know (guys in the business often provided what they *wanted* to be reported), but some of it, evidently, was just Zane stooging around.

'Logging on' with state-of-the-art technology, circa 1996

It's worth talking about how the prevalence of inside information changed the mentality of the wrestling fan - and the psychology of the business overall. When I first got into wrestling, we were still in the territory days, and most of what went on was a mystery. The newsletters weren't around yet, and personally, I wouldn't discover them until around '86 or '87. In the pre-dirtsheet era, some people still believed that pro wrestling was real – well, to a *point*. In other words, there wasn't necessarily a sense that the guys all got together and went drinking after the show. As a fan, you just watched what you watched - and you enjoyed it. You didn't sit there and analyze what the booking decisions were - you didn't even know what booking was.

Back then, there was no such thing as a six month build for a storyline. You had to draw houses in the same cities every week, and you couldn't do a three-month tease of a popular tag team turning on each other - not when you needed to make that next house. You had a show coming up Monday in West Palm, Tuesday in Tampa, Wednesday in Miami Beach, Thursday in Jacksonville, and then Sunday in Orlando. There was no time to map things out over a long period of time, and that's why one week, Ernie Ladd and Dusty Rhodes were the best of friends, and then the next week, Ernie turned on Dusty and nobody saw it coming.

That's a true angle from 1977, by the way - and it was incredible! Florida did *great* business with Ladd as a heel and Dusty as a babyface, and some of the interviews which came out of that *captivated* me as a young fan. Anyway, the point here is this: they were booking week-to-week, and the fans had very little information about how the magic happened.

In 1989, Vince McMahon famously admitted that wrestling was "sports entertainment," primarily as a way of avoiding the athletic commission taxes associated with 'real' sports. The *New York Times* treated his disclosure as a major revelation:

> The promoters of professional wrestling have disclosed that their terrifying towers in spandex tights, massive creatures like Bam Bam Bigelow, Hulk Hogan and Andre the Giant, are really no more dangerous to one another than Santa Claus, the Easter Bunny and the Tooth Fairy.

> But please don't repeat this. Millions of grown men and women just don't want to know.

> In an attempt to free their exhibitions from regulations that apply to boxing and other sports that cause serious injury, spokesmen for the World Wrestling Federation testified recently before the New Jersey Senate that professional wrestling is just "entertainment" and that participants are trained to avoid serious injuries.

Although less widely known, it wasn't the first time that McMahon had made such a statement. In 1985, for example, he answered this way to a question from the *Boston Globe* on wrestling's legitimacy:

> I really don't respond to that question. I think it was done to death in the '20s. But I hasten to say that we're in the sports entertainment field. It's not important to determine what wrestling is or not. It doesn't fall into one particular category. It's not in the category of sport, in the strictest sense of the word.

By the time of Vince's comments, the public-at-large were pretty smart - but again, to a point. There was still a lot of ambiguity around how certain aspects of the business took place, or how the illusion of certain moves was achieved in practice. Furthermore, much of the terminology used in the business - *face, heel, shoot, work, sell, get over, pop, gimmick, rib* - remained exclusive, for the most part, to those *in* the business.

Fast forward to the Monday Night Wars. Now, the guys are freely hanging out after episodes of *Nitro* or *Raw* - and often at the same hotel bar together. Fans would obviously see this and often join in on the festivities. At this point, the psychology of the business changed, in my opinion. It became less about generating *emotion*, and more about generating *intrigue* around storylines - and building towards pay-per-views on a monthly basis.

Funnily enough, a lot of people say it was easier to book in the territory days. To a certain extent, it definitely was, because you mostly had a captured audience. You didn't have the ability to switch channels - in real-time - and check out what the other wrestling show was doing (as was the case with *Nitro* and *Raw*). By the late '90s, you had to focus a lot more on portraying *realism* in order to capture people's emotions. They wouldn't be *as* emotionally invested in something like Ernie Ladd turning on Dusty, because they knew a lot more about the inner workings - plus, with so much wrestling on the airwaves, they were seeing angles play out all the time.

But even though so much was changing (and had changed) about the business, I *still* didn't want to be known as a dirtsheet subscriber. As I mentioned, nobody did - but when you're at the level that I was, you *especially* never wanted to 'show your hand'. You would never want to draw any kind of attention to yourself, because any attention, invariably, can quickly become *negative* attention. Part of that is the inherent paranoia of the wrestling business - you never know what someone could be thinking in the back of their head.

For me, I was all about just staying under the radar. I didn't have to be 'buddy-buddy' with the bosses, nor did I want to kiss anybody's ass (unless I had to). By staying under the radar, and more importantly, by focusing on doing my job, I managed to stay out of the way - and that's the formula for longevity in this business.

After so many years in WCW, I may have still been worried about my briefcase falling open, but I no longer worried about *everything*.

I had earned my stripes, and that meant this: I now took a picture with whoever I wanted.

In the early part of 1998, and with the Monday Night Wars at its highest point yet, more people than ever were familiar with David Penzer. Forget being a mark - *I* was now being asked for my picture. *I* was being asked to give an autograph. *I* was being recognized by wrestling fans all over the country.

All of that was a new and unexpected experience for me.

Funny story: I remember sitting in a Denny's with Jericho, Benoit and Malenko when one of the waitresses approached us. *My son is a really big fan*, she said. *If I bring over a napkin or something, will you guys all sign it?*

Sure, we said. *Of course!*

The waitress brought the napkin over and Jericho, Benoit and Malenko signed it, before I picked up a pen and signed it too.

179

Jericho gave me a funny look: *You signed it, Penzer?*

Yeah, I said, almost defensively. *I sign autographs sometimes - maybe he's that big of a fan, who knows?*

That's not the point, said Jericho. *He's not gonna know whose signature this is! You wrote David and a squiggly line, and then 'P' and a squiggly line! Put a microphone next to your name or something, Penzer!*

Alright, I said.

I grabbed the napkin and put a little microphone next to my name, with a little bass and a wire attached. It's how I've signed my name *every* time since!

Anyway, that kind of recognition followed us from town to town, and let me tell you something - it was intoxicating.

Not to mention: that roar of the crowd was something else, man. It almost became like a *drug*; in fact, some of the people I knew who were heavy drug users swore that those crowd reactions were up there, in terms of any possible 'high' you might live to experience. I got caught up in it too, as even though I wasn't a wrestler, my 'buzz' came from starting the show each night.

Getting that first 'pop' of the night became *my* adrenaline rush: *Good evening, Chicago - how you doin' tonight?*

Now let's be real - there's also a depression that comes with all that adrenaline. Obviously, a lot of wrestlers took pain pills in our era, and I dabbled in it too when I first got started. Very quickly, however, I realized that it was a really bad idea, and I went cold turkey - never to take a pain pill again.

Instead, I guess I was 'high' enough on what my life was turning into. The wrestling business had caught fire and at WCW's peak, we were traveling up to 25 days a month. We typically had a house show on Friday, another house show on Saturday, yet another on Sunday, then *Monday Nitro*, the tapings for *Thunder* on Tuesday (once it moved from being a live show on Thursdays), and then, every other Wednesday, we'd tape *two* episodes of *Saturday Night*.

If we had a week without those *Saturday Night* tapings, I'd get to be at home on Wednesday and Thursday (before leaving on Friday); alternatively, if those tapings were scheduled, I'd fly back Thursday, have less than 24 hours at home, and then start the cycle all over again on Friday morning. When you're running that hard, you don't even have time to think about what you're doing - you just do it.

Such an intense schedule provided little time for reflection, and consequently, we felt like the WCW run would last forever. In the process, all of us - present company *included* - became a little full of ourselves.

It probably speaks to the success of your company when the *ring announcer* develops an ego. I learned that fame and notoriety (even at my level) affects your personality in interesting ways; for example, let me remind you about Lenny Horowitz - the 'L' in *D and L Sound Productions*. As I alluded to earlier, Lenny was probably the best friend that I ever had - the best man at my wedding, as a matter of fact (I returned the favor at his wedding, incidentally). At one point, Lenny and I were as close as close could be, but once I was riding with Ric Flair and Arn Anderson - well, I don't know...

Maybe Lenny wasn't as cool anymore.

To his credit, Lenny would try and keep in touch regardless. *Dave*, he would say, *Why don't you call anymore, just to say 'hello' or something?*

In return, I basically blew him off: *Eh, I don't want to talk to Lenny Horowitz.* My son Dillon asked me once about my wedding day, and when Lenny's name came up, Dillon's response said it all: *Huh? Who the hell is that?*

At the time, I guess my mindset was something like, *Hey, I'm David Penzer. I'm the ring announcer for WCW, and Nitro is the highest rated show on cable television!*

People want my autograph, and I even have an 8x10 made. I have a trading card out on the market! I'm so important that Bobby Heenan makes jokes about me in WCW Magazine!

That leads me to that nerd David Penzer, that sad excuse of a ring announcer. Gee, I wonder who taught him how to speak...Rosanne Arnold or Pee Wee Herman? Come to think of it, Penzer kind of reminds me of both. Maybe I should become WCW's premiere ring announcer.

Here's one from the How Dumb Can He Really Be? file: David Penzer was staring at a can of frozen orange juice for two hours before Slamboree. When someone asked him why, he replied, "Because it says concentrate." I'm not going to pass judgment on Penzer, but let me tell you a

It's that time again, my monthly report on the ultimate moron in WCW, ring announcer David Penzer. I mean, when I say this kid is stupid, he's even surpassed Rey Mysterio, Jr., Kidman and Jim "The Anvil" Neidhart.

Dave Penzer popped along to see the Jerry Springer Show recently and asked Jerry if he could appear on the show. Springer naturally enquired about Penzer's "credentials" and on hearing them told him that he only has a one hour show and it would take at least a month to sort out Penzer's smallest problems. Negotiations are underway to produce a series of video tapes.

A certain ring announcer was a frequent target of gags in WCW Magazine (credit: Bryan Barrera)

(Those jokes, by the way, were actually written by the editor of the magazine - but I digress.)

But imagine what happened to my ego when I learned this: I had an action figure in the pipeline!

At the time, a line of WCW action figures was being sold, and they were typically marketed as including an 'extra' of some description. If you got Raven's action figure, for example, it came with a little trash can and chair, and for whatever reason, Konnan's action figure came with a little Rey Mysterio! As a way of playing off our interactions earlier in the year, Chris Jericho's action figure was going to come with - wait for it - David Penzer (*and* my removable tuxedo jacket)! The deal, as they say, was done - but for reasons that we'll get into later, it ultimately never occurred.

182

Speaking of my attire, it's one of the things that wrestling fans remember most about me. I was known for having these colorful bowtie and cummerbund sets, and in that sense, my appearance differed from how ring announcers traditionally dressed. The reason for it was simple: pretty early on, I realized that wrestlers could wear different outfits, but I had to wear the same thing every night: a white shirt, black jacket, black shoes and a black pair of pants. That was kind of tough for me, because I'm actually sort of a colorful guy - I mean, even back in high school, I was wearing pink shirts before they were cool! Therefore, mixing up the bow ties and cummerbunds was a way of making myself distinctive - *and* an effort to showcase my personality a little bit.

I bought them mostly from a tuxedo shop down in Fort Lauderdale, and at one time, I probably had about 60 or 70 different sets. Most of the time, there was no rhyme or reason to what I wore, other than the Disney tapings - where I sported something Mickey Mouse related - or a show around the holiday season. I would also give things a little more thought prior to a major event - like *Starrcade '97* - when Sting challenged Hogan for the title.

Many years later, I wore the *Starrcade* ensemble to ring announce a match between Kenny Omega and Rich Swann, and afterwards, Tony Khan happened to walk by me. Tony gave me a quick look and then shared an eerie observation: *Starrcade '97*, he said.

You wore that bowtie!

I mean…what do you even say to that? Tony is a savant when it comes to that stuff. We soon got to talking about an event from back in the day, and Tony went on to name - off the top of his head - the name of the pay-per-view, the date, and every single match on the show.

Talk about a head trip.

183

Hey, you ever hear this expression?

'If I knew then what I know now...'

For me, I often think the opposite - in some ways, I'm glad I *didn't* know then what I do know now. I'll give you an example. If I go to a wrestling convention today, someone will invariably say to me: *Hey, I used to pretend to be the WCW ring announcer. I used to do the 'David Penzer' voice!*

No, you didn't, I'll say in disbelief.

But it's true - and I've probably had 100 people say it to me over the years. Recently, Brett Lauderdale, the owner of Game Changer Wrestling, told me the exact same thing: *When I was a kid, I used to do you. I used to do impressions of David Penzer!*

If I had an awareness of *that* back then...well, let's put it this way: I *really* would have been full of myself.

Nonetheless, circa 1998, I thought I was *the shit* - to be honest with you.

Back then, I don't know...maybe I was?

Anyone who's been there will tell you this: there's a big difference between simply being in the business, and being there once it gets *hot*. After all, wrestling during a 'boom' period is a whole different animal - we're talking parties, celebrities, and mainstream recognition (true story: Wayne Gretzky once showed up at a *Nitro* and told me his son wanted to be a ring announcer. How cool is that?). Consequently, you start giving yourself permission to relax a little bit more, to enjoy your success, to celebrate whenever possible. It can be hard to maintain the same hunger when you're reveling in the moment: *Man, my life is so fucking cool...*

It's all kind of difficult for outsiders to understand, but around this time, I decided to give my dad a taste of the life we were living. WCW had a rare day off in the schedule, and we were all staying at the MGM Grand in Las Vegas. I brought Dad with me, and before I knew it, he was hanging out with a whole group of us - including Ric, Arn, Pee Wee, Bobby Heenan, Steven Regal and Bobby Eaton - down at the swimming pool bar. The hotel had one of those new flavored, frozen alcohol machines, and collectively, we went to fucking *town* that day. I think Bobby Eaton, from what I remember, drank 31 different flavors of frozen drinks - all by himself!

In no time, everybody was absolutely hammered - to the point where by four o'clock that afternoon, we all went back to our rooms and passed out. There was just one problem - the bar tab.

It was $3,000.

When we reconvened later, Flair was almost panicked about it: *Who paid the fucking bar tab?*

My dad did, I said.

Was he pissed about it?

No, I said, *not at all. I think he had one of the best times he ever had in his life!*

Whether in good times or bad - Dad was still there when I needed him.

While we were all busy glowing in our mainstream success, the WWF had gradually been closing the gap in the ratings war. In

January 1998, an unbelievable angle involving Mike Tyson and 'Stone Cold' Steve Austin gave them a huge wave of momentum - and by springtime, their 'Attitude Era' was firmly in effect.

Nonetheless, we still felt like WCW was on top of the world. We were selling out arenas left and right. Everyone was flying first class. Everything was spoken for. We stayed in four-star hotels. Celebrities attended our shows. Guys were getting paid more than ever before - and having a blast in the process. Even I was closing in on making six figures.

One day, I guess I felt compelled to place a phone call to an old friend: Gary Michael Cappetta.

Wow, said Gary, *You guys are really on fire, right?*

Yeah, I said, feeling pretty happy with myself. *We're just kicking ass right now.*

Gary had an interesting reply.

Enjoy it, he said.

I got nervous for a second: was Gary coming back to take my spot?

Why did you say that? I asked him.

Silence.

Why did you say, 'Enjoy it', Gary?

His response said everything.

Enjoy the ride, he told me.

...Because it's not gonna last.

186

SITTING RINGSIDE VOLUME 1

LIFE IN THE FAST LANE

Lynyrd Skynyrd

Gene Simmons

Chuck Norris

188

Shaquille O'Neal

Wade Boggs

Casey Kasem

James Brown

Jean-Claude Van Damme

Ed McMahon

Donnie & Marie

Cheap Trick

Billy Corgan

George Steinbrenner

193

13:
RATS ON A SINKING SHIP

"Personal issues draw money." - Jerry Jarrett

Historically, promoters in wrestling loved to exploit real-life conflicts between people. Some of the most memorable feuds ever, as a matter of fact, involved guys who *really* didn't like each other, but agreed, nonetheless, to work together for *business*. There were obviously exceptions to that rule, but generally speaking, the mindset was to capitalize on what fans knew (or thought they knew) about the backstage environment - and then make some money with it.

Hey, the thought process went, *if we can turn this into some business - and everyone agrees to it - let's do it.*

Throughout 1998, Ric Flair and Eric Bischoff found themselves entangled - as a shoot - in a well-publicized legal battle. It all stemmed from a disagreement regarding the nature of Ric's absence from an April 9 *Thunder* taping in Tallahassee, Florida. Ric claimed that due to his son's qualification in a national wrestling AAU tournament, he had asked the company, in advance, for permission to let him miss the show. On the other hand, WCW retorted by saying that Flair had breached his contract, as reflected in an April 17 legal complaint:

On or about November 11, 1997, Flair entered into a binding letter agreement with WCW. The Letter Agreement set forth the principal terms of a new Independent Contractor Agreement between WCW and Flair pursuant to which Flair would continue to provide wrestling services to WCW through February 15, 2001.

...Until April 9, 1998, both parties performed pursuant to the terms of the Letter Agreement.

Pursuant to [the agreement], Flair was scheduled to appear for WCW's nationally televised "Thunder" program in Tallahassee, Florida on April 9, 1998, which was telecast live. Flair informed WCW that for personal reasons he would not appear at this event. To accommodate Flair, WCW arranged at its expense for a private jet to transport Flair to Tallahassee and back after the show. Despite these arrangements, Flair, without notice or excuse, failed and refused to appear at and perform in this event. Flair's failure to appear caused WCW to have to re-work the content of this live program on extremely short notice.

After the April 9th incident, WCW ran Minneapolis for *Nitro* on April 13th, and according to the complaint, Flair "failed and refused to appear" on that show as well. Ric, of course, strongly disagreed with that version of events, but regardless, the dispute couldn't have come at a worse time. What made matters worse was something that happened before we went live. Eric called a talent meeting and went *off* on Flair, essentially saying that he was going to starve his family and prevent him from returning to TV.

At the time, it wasn't the best look for Eric. His comments came off as extremely vindictive, and his error was compounded by the fact that Flair was popular with most of the locker room. It was like a more extreme version of a previous meeting where Eric pointed out Hulk, Randy and Piper as "the only guys who had ever drawn money." Technically, you could probably make a case that Flair's drawing power was nowhere close to those three, but why say that out loud? In hindsight, I think Eric would admit that perhaps he should have avoided those meetings altogether.

Ultimately, that same April 13th show would become famous for another reason - a WWF ratings victory, and the first defeat suffered by *Nitro* in 83 straight weeks.

Beginning in May, the WWF began their own streak of consecutive ratings victories. With a massive *Nitro* episode coming up on July 6th, we suddenly had an opportunity to stop their momentum, as well as making a statement in front of 41,000 of our hometown fans. "*By last count*," announced J.J. Dillon, WCW's on-screen commissioner, "*there were some 35,000 tickets sold...but if*

195

you're not in the proximity of Atlanta, Georgia...I would suggest that you get on the phone, call your neighbors, call your friends and if there's ever a Nitro that you didn't miss...I would suggest that you don't miss this coming Monday night.

"It is now official: Hollywood Hulk Hogan - the WCW champion - is contractually obligated to be in the Georgia Dome, this coming Monday night for Nitro...to defend the WCW heavyweight title belt...against [who] I feel is the number one contender...Goldberg!"

Since his debut in September 1997, Bill Goldberg had become a certifiable phenomenon. He had come out of the NFL, and later, WCW's own Power Plant training facility, and got himself over to an unbelievable level. By April, he had captured the WCW United States title - and as of July, he remained unbeaten - helping to set the stage for a historic clash with Hogan. Goldberg had been on fire for at least six months, and the crowd reactions surrounding his appearances were simply mind-boggling. Even today, I think I can still hear the ringing in my ears: *Gold...berg...Gold...berg...*

After the *Starrcade* debacle with Sting, I'm sure a lot of people were skeptical that Hulk was going to do business with Goldberg. But while people can say whatever they want - including whether or not it was a good idea to 'give away' the match on *Nitro* - Hulk ultimately did the right thing that night. What happened afterwards is definitely suspect, in terms of how they treated Bill from a booking standpoint, but that specific night - with Goldberg pinning Hulk clean and winning the World Heavyweight title - it was the right finish for that crowd. Those 41,000 people went absolutely insane at the finish, and to this day - after nearly 50 years of watching professional wrestling - it's the most incredible crowd reaction that I personally ever witnessed.

Now, you could make an argument that *maybe* - if they had handled it correctly - Sting could have got a similar reaction in that spot. If *Starrcade* had taken place at the Georgia Dome, and there was none of the wacky booking that took place, you might have seen a similar scene unfold. Nonetheless, by the time we got to Goldberg vs.

Hogan, the crowd wanted Goldberg to go over *desperately*. They got what they wanted, went home happy, and at the end of the day - while not always the case - that's kind of the name of the game.

Simply put, it was a nice moment, and you need those kinds of moments to give back to your fan base. People had invested a lot of time into watching our shows, purchasing tickets to see us live, buying our merchandise, and even following the gossip on the 'WCW Hotline' (or the Internet, which was really in its infancy at that time). At some point, you need to pay off all of that support - and in that sense, Goldberg-Hogan was one *hell* of a payoff.

As it had been designed, the match also helped us break the WWF's winning streak, with over five million viewers watching *Nitro* live on TNT. What is often forgotten, however, is the fact that *Raw* won again (4.7-4.5) the very *next week*, followed by each company splitting three victories out of the next six (July 20-August 24). It was clear that to get back on track, we needed something more than just a 'hot shot' angle, and seemingly, there was only one man for the job.

It had long been observed that whenever WCW needed a boost - especially in the early years of the company - the booking team turned to Ric Flair. As per the ongoing lawsuit, WCW acknowledged that a "new storyline" for Ric had indeed been in the works:

> At the time of Flair's refusal to appear and perform in these events, WCW had been developing a new storyline involving several wrestlers. Flair was to be a key participant in this new storyline through the reinstatement of the highly successful "Four Horsemen" wrestling group, of which Flair was to be the leader.

As more and more time went on, the long-awaited Horsemen reunion seemed to be impossible. On July 10th, Flair filed a countersuit - the news of which made the *Atlanta Journal-Constitution* - alleging that he couldn't have breached his contract. He didn't have one!

197

[WCW] sent a "proposed agreement" letter to Plaintiff on November 11, 1997 outlining 'skeleton' terms of a future arrangement between the parties.

[Flair] was assured by [WCW] that [the agreement] was nothing more than an outline of basic economic terms of a future relationship between the parties...comprehensive documents were [needed] to describe the actual contractual relationship between the parties.

Ric's uncertain status led to speculation that he might make an appearance on WWF TV, and allegedly, it almost happened when they held a pay-per-view in Greensboro, NC. It remained to be seen how Ric could ever work with Eric again, particularly given the claims made in the courtroom:

The parties continued their negotiations after January. During these negotiations, the parties' relationship deteriorated drastically. [WCW] reduced the number of [Flair's] appearances at its promotions. [Flair's] appearances on [WCW's] weekly television programs, "Thunder", "Nitro" and Pay Per View were de-emphasized and for over a month, completely eliminated. Upon information and belief, [Flair's] role in such [events were] downplayed by [WCW]'s agents, in particular, Eric Bischoff, in order to satisfy demands made by, and commitments to, other wrestlers, including Terry 'Hollywood' Hogan.

Throughout the time period, Bischoff has been treating [Flair], off camera, in an increasingly hostile, rude, threatening and degrading manner. Bischoff asserts himself as a 'czar' and seems to believe he has dictatorial authority over [Flair]. His language is crude, rude and 'socially unacceptable' even in the world of professional wrestling. He has threatened to bankrupt [Flair], put [him] out of work, banish him to some foreign country and has referred to him as 'garbage'.

Fans were outraged that Flair was being kept off television, and the dispute dragged on for months. Journalist Mike Mooneyham summarized much of the feeling in an August 30 piece:

Pro wrestling is hotter than ever, ratings have never been higher, but something is wrong. Terribly wrong.

Pro wrestling's icon - a performer who has meant more to this generation than any other - has been removed from a landscape in which he has been 'the man' for the past three decades.

Ric Flair, through no fault of his own, has been on the shelf since April. That's when WCW boss Eric Bischoff banished him from WCW and threatened to sue him "into bankruptcy." Why? For missing a hastily scheduled appearance on a TBS

Thunder show that Flair found out about only three nights earlier while viewing Monday Nitro at his home, long after he had asked for that date off to watch his 10-year-old son compete in a national amateur wrestling tournament in Detroit.

…Ric Flair is loved, adored and admired by the wrestling public. To many of those fans, he's not bigger than pro wrestling, he is pro wrestling. Few wrestlers in the history of professional wrestling have meant more to the business than Ric Flair. No one has worked harder. Although he migrated to Charlotte from Minnesota nearly 25 years ago, Ric Flair is truly a Southern phenomenon, not unlike Elvis, and his character has become a part of the culture. The word 'icon' is loosely used in many circles, but it's no exaggeration in the case of the 'Nature Boy.'

…WCW most likely would be more than willing to take him back, but Flair is not comfortable with allowing his legend to be tarnished any more than it already has. If he returns, he wants to come back as 'champ,' not 'chump,' as WCW has less-than-subtlely portrayed him the past couple of years.

…. Meanwhile, the company wants to string out the litigation and financially bleed him. Flair, feeling the crunch of fighting a very expensive lawsuit, reportedly has already spent more than a hundred thousand dollars waging his legal battle against the seemingly unlimited financial resources of the Turner outfit.

Just two days later, on September 1st, 1998, a legal filing revealed that the litigation had been *stayed*, setting the table for a dramatic return like no other. Apparently, it appeared that Eric and Ric had finally agreed to work together, although officially, the lawsuit remained unresolved, and Ric, reportedly, was coming back only on a day-to-day contract.

Nonetheless, word began to spread that Ric would appear on the September 14th, 1998 edition of *Nitro* - set to emanate from the new BI-LO Center in Greenville, South Carolina - sparking anticipation of that long-awaited Horsemen reunion. It made for much conversation on the next house show loop, and fortuitously, I happened to be riding with Arn Anderson.

If the Horsemen were going to be put back together, Arn was the obvious choice to set it all up. He already had a lot of what he wanted to say, but he bounced his promo off me as we drove down the road. When it came to promos, and especially when it came to something this important, Arn was a perfectionist, and he probably practiced the speech over 100 times.

To be clear, I wouldn't say that I provided a lot of input - Arn was (and is) one of the best talkers in the business. I might have said, 'You might wanna pause here,' or something like that, but it wasn't anything Arn probably wouldn't have done anyway - purely by instinct - with or without me being there. He even had it down to where he knew, ahead of time, that he was going to 'forget' to bring Ric out to the live crowd (including the fact that he was going to knock on the side of his head and blame 'Alzheimers', just to give you an appreciation of prepared he was).

Arn was at a point where he was very frustrated - not with anybody in particular, but with what life had handed him. Due to injury, he had been forced to retire at a very young age, and that's hard to do at the top of your game - never mind with the business being as hot as it was. Arn had really struggled with all that, but reuniting the Horsemen gave him a chance to be more involved - to be a *player* again.

Arn took it very, very seriously. As has since become widely known, he was legitimately angry about an nWo segment which aired a year earlier, an in-ring skit where the group parodied his 'my spot' promo with Curt Hennig. The parody wasn't inaccurate, by the way, and I'll admit to laughing when Kevin Nash came out, dressed as Arn, holding that beer cooler under his arm. I don't know if I ever told Arn that though!

I knew from first-hand experience that on the road, assuming Arn was traveling with you, a certain order of operations would have to follow: *pick up the rental car, get a cooler and a bag of ice, put the beer in the bottom of the cooler, put the ice on top, and get that cooler in the back seat!*

Nonetheless, there were a couple of reasons why Arn was so affected by the parody. First, his family at home were watching, and his kids were young at the time. It's not a lot of fun to be portrayed as a drunk on national TV.

Secondly, there wasn't a way for Arn, in a wrestling context, to personally get *revenge*. Not real revenge - just so you understand me - but storyline revenge. That looked like it was never going to happen, and although he started working behind the scenes for WCW, Arn was left to deal with that frustration; to try and accept the hand he had been dealt.

Harnessing all of that, Arn stepped up to the plate, that night in Greenville, and delivered a promo for the ages:

Can you smell it, JJ [Dillon]? Take a breath - can you smell it? When fifteen thousand people blow the roof off a place, that's what a pop smells like. Take a bow. What you said to me is what all those people have been saying to me for a year and a half, and only a true friend would say that. They said, 'Arn Anderson, stand up and be a man - like you've always been!'

...I'm gonna start at the beginning, because you have to start at the beginning...tonight *is* a new beginning for the Four Horsemen.

Now when I was a kid, like all kids, people ask you, 'What do you wanna be when you grow up?' There was no gray area for me - I always knew I wanted to be a wrestler. And when that finally happened for me, it was the proudest day of my life, and in 1986 I started coming to these towns, just like Greenville, South Carolina, as a Horseman.

...About a year and a half ago, I laid down on an operating table and when I woke up, Arn Anderson the wrestler was dead, and I thought to myself, 'How could I be a horseman if I couldn't be a wrestler?' Well, the fact is I couldn't in my mind...

Arn paused briefly as the crowd began to chant: *We want Flair! We want Flair!*

Trust me, everybody's gonna get what they want tonight...[especially] Bischoff...Eric Bischoff.

So when I thought I could no longer be a Horsemen, Chris Benoit came to me first and said, 'This can all happen,' and with that prelude, I would like to bring the other three Horsemen out right now.

One by one, the other three Horsemen, each wearing tuxedos, received separate introductions: Chris Benoit, Mongo McMichael and Dean Malenko. Arn continued:

201

Ladies and gentlemen, through the year 2000, we're gonna do exactly what all of you across this nation have asked: 'Arn Anderson, bring back the Horsemen!' But I feel it fair to tell ya, I'm not gonna be responsible for what happens next. 'Cos we don't wear white hats - we're not nice guys - and I can tell you this: heads are gonna roll!

So, I've said it: Be careful what you wish for, because now you have it!

Just as he had prepared, Arn began to deliver the final line:

Ah, Whatagoof! Whatagoof! You know…I get accused of getting racked in the head a few times - and having a little touch of Alzheimer's...

…My God! I almost forgot the fourth Horseman!

Ric Flair, come on down here!

The roof nearly went off the place.

Dressed in the same attire as his fellow Horsemen, Flair enjoyed a thunderous ovation after walking through the curtain. *"One week ago, ladies and gentlemen,"* added Tony Schiavone on commentary, *"when Mark McGwire hit 62, you'd always know where you'd be on that day; well, at 10:38 pm Eastern time on Monday, September 14, you were a part of wrestling history. He is back!"*

Once Arn handed over the microphone, Ric was visibly moved to tears:

I'm almost embarrassed by the response, but when I see this…I know I spent 25 years trying to make you happy every night of your life, [and] it was worth every damn minute of it!

Now…someone told me…the Horsemen were having a party tonight in Greenville! Could that be true…that the most elite group - that Eric Bischoff said was dead - is alive and well?

Bischoff, this might be my only shot - but I gotta tell ya, I'm going to make it my best.

Is this what you call a great moment of TV? That's wrong - because this is real! This is not bought and paid for! It's a real…life…situation!

202

Referencing Arn's retirement in 1997, Flair continued:

Just like the night in Columbia, South Carolina, when you looked at me, tears in my eyes, and said, 'God, that's good TV.'

…That was real! Arn Anderson passed the torch! It was real, dammit! You think Sting would have been crying in the dressing room - like I was on TV - if it wasn't real?

This guy, Arn, my best friend, is one of the greatest performers to ever live. And you…you squashed him in one night.

Then you get on the phone and tell me, 'Disband the Horsemen - they're dead. Disband the Four Horsemen.'

You know what? I looked myself in the mirror the next day, and I saw a pathetic figure that gave up and quit. And for that, I owe you, the wrestling fans…I owe these guys…an apology. Because it won't happen again…

At this point, something happened that I didn't know about in advance - Eric came out. Presented as "the boss" (as opposed to his character), Eric played the role of trying to shut the segment down. In response, Flair absolutely unloaded in the ring, ad-libbing a string of insults in Bischoff's direction:

You're an overbearing asshole! You're an obnoxious, overbearing…

…Abuse of power! You! Abuse of power! Cut me off!

Abuse of power! You suck! I hate your guts!

You are a liar…you're a cheat…you're a scam. You…are a no good…son of a bitch!

The fans became unglued as Ric took it home:

Fire me! I'm already fired!

Fire me! I'm already fired!

In this business, you'll hear guys laying something out - and it'll sound great backstage - but for whatever reason, sometimes it just doesn't connect. That happens.

This was one of those times where everything was laid out perfectly, and it ended up *better* than you ever could have hoped for. Greenville was definitely considered 'Horsemen country', and the people were emotionally invested in the group coming back.

Hell, *I* was emotionally invested, both as a wrestling fan and a friend of those guys. Now sure, part of the exchange between Ric and Eric was a work, but part of it was a shoot, too - there was certainly no love lost between them.

It became one of my favorite angles of all-time.

"It was all out in the open," Ric later wrote of his promo, the unquestioned highlight of a night in which *Nitro* beat *Raw* (4.5 to 4.0) in the ratings.

"It was real.

"100 percent real."

Ultimately, the Horsemen reunion fizzled out, in my opinion, at a point way too far in advance. As a storyline, Ric's issue with Eric fell short, too - at least in terms of drawing TV ratings, over the long-term, and generating money on pay-per-view. If you look at a list of the highest drawing feuds in wrestling history, it's nowhere near the top - even though, based on their legitimate heat and the way that it all started, it arguably should have been.

It was just the latest in a series of missed opportunities for our company, and together with the WWF's resurgence in the ratings, morale was starting to take a hit. Guys were getting disgruntled with their lack of movement up the card. People like Ultimate Warrior were being brought in to 'pop' a number, only to disappear seemingly just a fast. Matches that WCW could have built towards, like Bret Hart vs.

204

Hogan, or Goldberg vs. Sting, were given away on *Nitro* without any buildup.

Hanging with Jay Leno at Road Wild '98

While mere months earlier, Goldberg had been a certifiable phenomenon, his streak was then broken, at the hands of Kevin Nash, in the main event of *Starrcade '98*. It followed a period where WCW had been losing the ratings war for two straight months.

On one hand, Goldberg was going to have to lose at *some* point. They couldn't keep him winning forever, because from a psychology standpoint, all the fun was in the *chase*. Then again: what do I know? At times in this business, you have to make difficult decisions - and I would hope that decision was made for the right reasons. I can't be in anyone else's head, and generally speaking, I try to think the best of people. That makes it difficult for me to speculate.

That said, I do know that suddenly, we were ending 1998 being *desperate* to draw, and wanting the ratings to turnaround *that week* if possible. When you're in that kind of mindset, you'll do anything to 'win' the night - you'll make a deal with the devil if necessary. Maybe they thought beating Goldberg was going to get the viewers back.

205

Ultimately, however, was it a mistake to end the streak? Probably. From where I was sitting, it only further turned off the audience.

It's kind of a crude observation, but once WCW got hot, you could tell the strength of our business by looking at the *ring rats*, or the groupies who hung around after shows. Going back to the territory days, it was a pretty simple dynamic: *The better the business, the better the broads.*

Oh, there's a correlation in there somewhere. You could have analyzed all the different metrics and statistics you wanted, but equally, you could have saved yourself some time and just stopped by the Marriott. That visual told you everything and then some.

Was it something that I involved myself in? No. With two little kids and a wife at home, I was deathly afraid of losing what I had. I didn't pay much attention to the 'rats', but it was fun to see different guys interacting with them - no names mentioned.

All of a sudden, though, the strangest thing happened one night. I was sitting at the bar with Arn when he paused to look around.

Penzer, he said, *Where did all the rats go?*

I looked around the bar myself, and sure enough - things had definitely changed. Other than maybe the bartender and our production people, there wasn't a single woman in sight.

There were still plenty of male fans around, but the rats, seemingly on a dime, had vanished - just like that.

In hindsight, maybe it was a sign of things to come.

14:
MOMENTUM LOST

Going into 1999, we found ourselves at a crossroads - either start to go in a different direction, or attempt, desperately, to recreate something that had already faded.

In theory, providing an end to the WCW vs. nWo storyline would have been a great launching-off point. We could have had one big 'World Series' - or one big 'Super Bowl' - the ultimate winner-take-all pay-per-view. It could have been a 'blow-off' event for the ages, with control of the company at stake - and WCW finally getting rid of the nWo.

It's easy to say that now, of course.

As they say, *hindsight is 20/20*. It's easy to sit back and say, 'We should have done this, or we should have done that,' but at the time, remember, we had *five hours* of prime-time television to fill - every single week. On top of that, we had two hours of *WCW Saturday Night* to worry about, all of the syndicated programming, house shows and, obviously, all of the egos, injuries and personal issues that came with it.

On that note, once the company started growing at an exponential rate, the egos spiraled out of control - as did the backstage politics. Even guys you wouldn't necessarily expect to be political got that way, because why wouldn't they? At first, you kind of had to be in the upper echelon to have an influence backstage - maybe if you were getting paid upwards of $250,000 per year - but once people saw you could plead your case and get things changed, *everyone* started bitching about *everything*.

The mentality of the entire company changed. When we first started *Nitro*, we almost saw ourselves as the small, little group that wanted to hang with the WWF - and everybody was 'all in' on the vision. That kind of 'little engine that could' mindset really spurred us on in the early days, but once we started selling out huge domes and arenas, that team atmosphere gave way to something else - a toxic mix of paranoia and skepticism.

People often talk about the level of disorganization in WCW, as if we could have generated hundreds of millions of dollars without having any kind of plan. That kind of talk is a little overblown, in my opinion, because at the height of our success, there was always a format for the entire three-hour show on Mondays. Unfortunately, a number of guys would come in with the, 'That doesn't work me, brother' routine, and if Eric is being totally honest, he probably should have been a little more like Vince McMahon in those situations: *The buck stops with me.*

At first, Eric *was* actually a bit more like that, but once he started socializing with the guys - and our company took off in the direction it did - he gave in on some things that he probably shouldn't have. Now, it *is* true that the show would sometimes get re-written while it was on the air, but I don't think that was down to disorganization. From my vantage point, I think there was a fear that certain guys might walk out on the company, or, at the very least, get disgruntled with what we were doing. We were in the middle of a ratings war, and therefore, you probably had to placate in certain situations when it wasn't always best to do so.

Furthermore, guys weren't always held accountable because of the competition we were in. A good example is some of the shenanigans that went on at house shows; specifically, the fact that a lot of guys who were advertised wouldn't actually perform. WCW killed a lot of towns because of that problem, and some of the most insane last-minute stuff went on due to those issues (for example, I have a vague recollection of Goldberg traveling via helicopter as a last-minute arrival one night). Of course, it often put pressure on me to make

208

'chicken salad out of chicken shit', as ultimately, *I* was the guy who had to tell the people that their favorite wrestlers weren't showing up.

Was it unprofessional? Absolutely. Everybody was making a ton of money, and sometimes, they kind of forgot about their obligations - especially when they were allowed to skip those shows. If I was in Eric's shoes, I probably would have been thinking: *Okay, I'm working 80 hours a week. I got the weight of the world on my shoulders - and now I have a guy who didn't show up for a weekend house show. I don't like what he did, but I don't want him to go to the competition either.*

What do you do?

I would never have wished to be in Eric's position. You had all these huge egos and established stars making millions of dollars, and at the time, I'm sure he was just trying to make everyone happy.

Ultimately, however, it just made everyone *nuts*.

Between the years of 1995 and 1999, WCW got too big, too fast. I know Eric has talked a lot about the lack of infrastructure that we suffered from - even basic things like our merchandising department (or lack thereof). In many ways, we were behind the WWF even as we were beating them in the ratings, and once the ratings flipped, that difference between us became clear for all to see.

The amount of first-run TV we produced was a lot for a company used to doing a *Saturday Night* taping every two weeks, or a syndicated taping once every three weeks. We didn't have enough people in production to fill all the spots that were needed, and a lot of people got burned out on the road.

Compared to years earlier, the announcers' trailer was no longer as fun as it used to be. I even saw Mike Tenay getting annoyed and pissed off about the product - which definitely hadn't been the case before - and ditto for Larry Zbyszko. Without question, however, I never saw *anyone* as miserable as Tony Schiavone. He wore that negativity on his sleeve - every freaking minute of every freaking day...of every freaking show. His entire body language, demeanor and mood screamed the exact same thing: *I hate this shit.*

Tony is a pretty laid-back guy in general, but by this point, he was anything but. I don't want to put words in his mouth, but as far as I could tell, he didn't like the direction of the company - nor did he like all the drama that came with it. He just got something in him - like a *demon* - almost like it entered his soul (hey, there's a wrestling storyline for you). He was cranky. He was irritable. He was forcing himself to do something that every ounce of his being - in my opinion - didn't want to do anymore. Basically, he wasn't Tony Schiavone anymore - or, at least, the guy we had previously all known.

But here's something that anyone who worked in WCW - particularly on the production side - will tell you if they're being honest. There was an ongoing situation involving a female producer which became a never-ending source of tension for everybody. Things got very weird, very uncomfortable, and very much out of control. This producer in particular got out of control. Eventually, her assistant got out of control, too - and you couldn't say a word to either one of them. It created a *horrible* work environment which made a bad situation ten times worse.

This producer had so much power over Tony's boss that she almost *became* Tony's boss, and I think Tony resented that. But nobody liked her having the power she had - not one person. It was a big bomb of negative energy every time she was around. The atmosphere was *poisonous,* and a lot of arguments happened as a result. I don't want to bury the poor girl, but it *is* an important part of the entire WCW story - and one of the reasons why Tony was so miserable.

If Tony could have won the lottery in 1999, he would have walked away from the business a happy man - and never, ever looked back.

210

One of the criticisms levied against WCW was our failure to turn over the top stars. While the usual big names dominated the main event scene, some of the most talented workers of all-time languished in the midcard - seemingly forever. There was very little mobility up the card, and I believe Eddie Guerrero said it best when he observed: *You couldn't tell what year it was on our show.*

We were kind of stuck in that same, post-nWo dynamic, and there's only so many times you can watch the same great matches - involving the same great wrestlers - before people want to check in on something new. A lot of the future stars that we should have been building went under the radar - including Chris Jericho, famously, who wrestled without a WCW contract for 17 months.

One night early in his run, Jericho and I showed up for a house show at the Target Center in Minneapolis, and somehow, we got around to talking about his contract situation: *By the way*, he said, *Eric never signed me to a deal.*

That was a shock to me: *You're not under contract?*

No, he said. *Isn't that crazy?*

Holy shit, I said. *You could show up on Raw if you wanted to.*

As Chris remembers it, he then said something to this effect: *Yeah, I could go to Raw tomorrow. Fuck Bischoff - it's his fault for not signing me.*

We finished talking momentarily, walked around the corner and saw someone standing next to a pay phone - right near the wrestler's entrance. Evidently, he had been listening to every word.

211

Yep, you guessed it - it was Eric. Like a bad movie scene, the person we had been talking about had been standing there the whole time! Eric never came to house shows, and I don't know if he ever went to one again. Even if you had told me he was going to show up at a house show, I wouldn't have expected him to arrive before five o'clock - which is when Jericho and I got there. The whole thing was preposterous, really.

But once I saw Eric, I basically just *froze*.

Chris and I looked at each other, and eventually, I turned to face the boss: *Hi…?*

Eric gave me the 'evil eyes', walked away and went upstairs to sit in an office.

Chris basically ignored it, but I decided it would be best to go see him: *Eric, I'm really sorry - we were just talking hypotheticals. Can I speak with you please?*

No, said Eric. *Don't talk to me right now.*

I did the show that night in the midst of a full-on panic and anxiety attack, spending most of my time trying to figure out how to tell Lisa that I screwed up so badly. At the end of the show, Eric finally called me into his office, and I trudged in expecting to be put out of my misery.

I want you to know, Eric said, *before…I was busting your chops a little bit.*

For a second, I exhaled a sigh of relief, but then…

I really was pissed off though, Eric continued. *Don't ever talk about stuff like that again - or you will be fired.*

This is your warning, he added.

212

Ironically, Jericho eventually did show up on *Raw* (signaling the end of that action figure idea I was telling you about!) in August 1999, debuting in a thrilling segment opposite Dwayne 'The Rock' Johnson. His departure seemed to underscore how far the tables had turned during the Monday Night Wars, as in a stunning reversal of fortunes, the WWF had now become the premier destination for wrestling's top talent.

As far as WCW was concerned, we had finally run out of surprise debuts of our own - and increasingly, it became difficult to mine for nostalgia. Pretty much all the big names of yesteryear had been brought in already, creating an imperative - you would think - to build up the younger guys. By the time we reached that realization, however, many of them had been worn down by all the politics, and those who could get out - like Jericho - did so with no regrets.

You know what? Gary Cappetta *had* predicted that our run wouldn't last.

With guys like Jericho leaving, it seemed like he may have just been on to something.

Jericho may have left on his own volition, but at one time, there had been a perception about WCW - under its Turner Broadcasting ownership - that no one ever really got *fired*. Although there were numerous counterexamples disproving that (including some high-profile names that went on to become big stars in the WWF, such as Steve Austin), it was kind of the widespread feeling amongst some of the boys. I never felt that way personally, but a lot of guys handled themselves like they were untouchable.

A lot of people felt like with Ted Turner's money, our resources were basically infinite, which probably explains much of the waste that happened on the financial side. I had heard that WCW spent

$50,000 on the outfit for 'Wildcat Willie', for example, and famously, you had guys like Lanny Poffo who got paid for *years* to sit at home.

Once our business started to slide, however, people did start getting let go with more regularity - including Pee Wee Anderson. While I don't quite remember the circumstances around his firing, I do remember this: the bitterness that Pee Wee had was unlike anything I had ever seen before. He felt like he was owed something, and consequently, he just couldn't accept losing his job. Unfortunately, it caused him to get even deeper into the drugs.

Like Joe Gomez was to Tampa - or Scott D'Amore was to Windsor, Ontario - Pee Wee had been *the man* in Rome, Georgia. That was his only saving grace after being terminated - but now, returning home, he had plenty of time to ruminate.

By mid-year, pretty much everyone acknowledged that our product had been overexposed. One of the casualties of that overexposure was *WCW Saturday Night*, which had once been the flagship show (or 'The Mothership' as Dusty would call it) in its historic 6:05pm EST time slot. With the addition of *Thunder* - and the subsequent expansion of *Nitro*, from January 1998 onwards, to a *three-hour* program - *Saturday Night* was ultimately relegated to 'C' show status.

In the July 10th, 1999 edition of the *Pro Wrestling Torch*, Wade Keller discussed that efforts were underway to revive the lame-duck program:

Jimmy Hart proposed to management that he be put in charge of booking *WCW Saturday Night*. There has been talk of overhauling the show. Hart wants to book it Memphis style by pushing some of the younger wrestlers with potential in weekly storylines. Supposedly, the idea is extremely popular in the locker room, but the feeling is those who are booking *Nitro* and *Thunder* (so poorly) will feel threatened by Hart producing a better show with a talent roster payroll less than one-tenth that of *Nitro*.

214

It was no secret that in WCW, the younger wrestlers were often given nothing to work with. I think about a guy like Jerry Lynn, a phenomenal worker who went on to star in ECW. I remember that the booking committee couldn't get a name cleared for him, so eventually, they settled on this little doozy: Mr. J.L.

I cringed at that, honestly. Mr. J.L.? Let me get this straight. The guy looks like Jerry Lynn - he wrestles like Jerry Lynn - but you want to call him Mr. J.L.? That meant he was dead in the water, as far as I was concerned, even before he started.

Jimmy had seen this pattern play out a number of times, and naturally, he wanted to change things. Therefore, a month later after the initial reports leaked, the *Torch* published a piece confirming the proposed changes:

Jimmy Hart will be taking over the booking duties for the *WCW Saturday Night* show. Hart asked for the job over a month ago but stressed he was only interested if he was allowed to do things his way. He will not be given any of the top names to work with but will instead try to get over the younger stars and mid-carders that are already appearing on the show. Most believe the show will have a 'classic Memphis feel' to it. Hart is telling some that he believes he can make the show good enough to draw better ratings than *Thunder*.

Around this time, Jimmy came up to me backstage and said: *Hey, baby - I'm gonna be booking Saturday Night.*

They're so busy, Jimmy said, speaking of the booking committee, *that Saturday Night is an afterthought, baby.*

So I asked Eric if I could take it over, *baby*, he continued, *to feature some of these guys who are hungry...the guys who aren't on Nitro every week.*

Jimmy mentioned that he would be working with Schiavone and Arn on the show, and then - to my surprise - he asked if I would be a part of it: *You think you can help us too, baby?*

What other answer could I give?

215

Sure, baby!

It ended up being the most fun I ever had in wrestling. Looking back, it's pretty funny to think about, but WCW gave us full autonomy over that show. We could do anything we wanted, essentially, as nobody bothered us or seemed to care about the people we were doing angles with. My sense was that Eric and the other decision-makers were just happy to have it off their plate. Basically, everybody was so busy that they didn't give a crap, meaning that *Saturday Night* - which was already scarcely referred to on television (and mostly operated as a standalone show) - became our own creative universe.

We never had official booking meetings, *per se*; instead, we worked on it at different times during the week. We would discuss things backstage before *Nitro* and *Thunder*, or on the weekend house show loops, or even via e-mail occasionally. We bounced ideas back-and-forth constantly - mostly on-the-fly - and then finalized everything in-person. That process made it fun to contribute, in a truly meaningful way, with people that I already liked and respected (in fact, Jimmy, Tony and Arn happened to be some of my closest friends in the business). I even hired another ring announcer (Keith Butler, for those of you who love obscure trivia) so that I could run 'Gorilla' (or the Jody position) backstage.

Personally, it was also pretty cool to have the responsibility of writing up the formats - especially after having years of making copies for everyone else (I guess my time riding with Kevin Sullivan had prepared me for the task). In truth, our shows followed a fairly simple structure, which after all the shenanigans elsewhere on WCW programming, is probably why it worked. There weren't a ton of huge angles on the show; rather, it was usually competitive matches between some undercard guys, a couple of squashes to get somebody over, and a main event that was built up over a couple of weeks.

We just had to keep track, on a week-to-week basis, of what we had done before and what we wanted to do moving forward. One thing that helped us is that the younger guys *loved* working on the show. On

Nitro (and to a lesser extent, *Thunder*), they had to deal with the presence of much bigger names on the card. On *Saturday Night*, conversely, the younger guys were the stars, and consequently, it gave them a platform to develop their talents. I think the record will show that many of the regulars on *Saturday Night* went on to become some of the biggest names in wrestling.

As the weeks went by, Jimmy started to warn us: *Be careful of success, boys. Once we start getting similar ratings to Thunder, they're gonna pull the plug. I'm telling you guys…*

Jimmy is so smart when it comes to the business. People have often suggested that he should have been given a larger role in creative, maybe even getting WCW's Head Booker job at some point. Here's the thing about Jimmy, though: he's not a confrontational person, and during this time, there was a *lot* of confrontation to deal with. There's a reason why, to this day, Jimmy doesn't give many interviews - it's because he doesn't like to give his opinion.

In Jimmy's mind - and he's told me this directly - if someone was to ask him about the favorite tag-team that he managed, for example, he would be worried about disappointing somebody: *If I say the Hart Foundation, now I'm pissing off the Nasty Boys*, he would say. *If I say the Nasty Boys, well, now I'm pissing off the Hart Foundation…*

Jimmy would rather not give an answer in that situation, because again, he doesn't like the prospect of confrontation or controversy. That doesn't take away from his amazing mind for the business, however. I learned so much from Jimmy and take all of that with me to this day.

Everything in wrestling now is so micromanaged, but our booking experience, led by Jimmy, could hardly have been more different. A multi-million-dollar company in WCW had basically handed over two hours of its programming to an announcer, a manager, an ex-wrestler and a ring announcer (a producer named Woody Kearce also helped us out) - and the funny thing is, the ratings went up!

217

Based on what Jimmy had been saying, we kind of got nervous about it. He believed that if we were *too* successful, people would start to take notice, look at what we were doing, and eventually tell us what we could and couldn't do.

Jimmy, I'd point out, *the ratings were good this week for Saturday Night.*

Yeah, baby, he'd say. *Too good.*

They're too good, baby...and now they're gonna start watching us.

Mere weeks into our tenure booking Saturday Night, word spread of a massive management shake-up. Apparently, after almost a year straight of losing in the Monday ratings - in addition to concerns over WCW's financial performance - Eric had been sent home by TBS. According to the *Atlanta Journal-Constitution*, the conglomerate had decided to "reassign" Eric out of its wrestling division altogether:

Eric Bischoff, who in five years helped transform World Championship Wrestling from a money-losing part of Ted Turner's empire to one that generated $200 million in 1998, was fired Friday as executive vice president, according to the WCW site on the World Wide Web.

In 1995, Bischoff was responsible for launching WCW Monday Nitro on TNT, which remains one of the most successful shows on cable television. He also generated mainstream publicity by using celebrities such as Jay Leno and Dennis Rodman in matches and helped steal Hulk Hogan from the rival World Wrestling Federation in 1994. But in the past year, the Atlanta-based WCW has fallen far behind the WWF in TV ratings and pay-per-view revenue.

Bischoff, who will be reassigned to another position within Time Warner, has been replaced by Bill Busch.

At the time, I thought that Eric had basically worn himself out - mentally and physically. He had been so *consumed* by the job that it

218

ate him up, I thought, and his burnout came at a detriment to the company. As the leader of WCW, he had been running at 100 miles per hour for so long, and in my opinion, he didn't delegate enough until it was too late. Even when he did delegate - like giving Kevin Nash 'the book' throughout 1999 - it wasn't like he stepped back entirely.

You often hear the phrase 'be careful what you wish for', and it was kind of like that for us in WCW. By virtue of our success, all kinds of opportunities opened up which had never been a possibility before: international deals, licensing agreements, celebrity tie-ins - and, of course, the increased television presence. Ultimately, all of that fell on Eric's shoulders, and he found himself doing a balancing act with a thousand different plates. Being in that position, you couldn't help but reach the point of exhaustion after a while, and in that sense, I'm surprised Eric lasted as long as he did.

An actual ad for Fall Brawl '99 – the first pay-per-view after Eric left.
"We're the advertising agency, and they won't even tell us who's going to be
there! For God's sake don't miss it!"

As the *Journal-Constitution* piece noted, Eric was replaced by Bill Busch - a long-time Turner accountant - whose primary purpose, as far as I could tell, was to come in and cut costs. It didn't take long for Busch to make a significant move, however, as on October 3rd, 1999, he announced the acquisition of the WWF's 'creative team': Vince Russo and his writing partner, Ed Ferrara.

At first, I didn't know much about Russo and Ed, at least other than what I had heard around the locker room. Some of our guys had worked with Russo before - when he was just the magazine guy at the WWF - and his reputation certainly preceded him. Furthermore, it was hard to argue with the WWF's ratings turnaround, and in the mainstream press, the defection of both was treated as a major coup for WCW.

For instance, *Variety* had this to say about the new creative direction:

Turner's World Championship Wrestling has decided that if you can't beat 'em, buy 'em.

WCW, which has been taking a beating in the ratings and losing consistently to rival World Wrestling Federation, has signed Vince Russo, head writer of such WWF shows as UPN's "WWF Smackdown" and USA Network's "Raw Is War" and "Sunday Night Heat," to a two-year deal valued in the high six-figure range.

The deal was inked Saturday, and co-writer Ed Ferrara joined the defection on Monday. The two are credited with helping to make the WWF an edgy, over-the-top show that has brought male teens flocking to UPN and USA. Russo's new title will be creative director for the WCW, and he'll supervise all television storylines.

Russo first came to the WWF in the early '90s to write for WWF magazine and was named editor four years ago. He eventually moved up to booking duties, creating controversial storylines involving strong sexual content as well as drugs and cults.

Everyone wanted to give the new regime a chance, but after only a few short weeks, I quickly came to a realization of my own - that shit didn't work for me, *brother*.

220

The whole 'Crash TV' thing - short matches, frequent backstage segments, and all-around controversial content - kind of flew in the face of the WCW audience. Previously, we had differentiated ourselves successfully from the WWF, but now, in my opinion, we were positioning WCW as *WWF-lite*. Much of the content tended to be silly and juvenile - and most of the big angles went nowhere.

Now, were the new guys being interfered with? Sure. There were always people pulling at their strings, and at the time, the Turner suits were really cracking down on the content of the show. I know that Russo and Ed wanted to be even *more* risqué - mostly because that had worked for them in the WWF - but in WCW, they had to deal with Turner's 'Standards and Practices' division. In any event, I didn't see how adding more shock value-type segments would move us in the right direction - and I think the WCW audience pretty much agreed with me.

Some of Russo's public comments probably didn't help matters either. Infamously, he professed to "not giving a shit" about the Mexican and Japanese talent, and in another interview, he promised that *Starrcade '99* would feature "something big…to lead WCW into the next year." Ultimately, however, Russo's *Starrcade* ended in a rehash of the Montreal Screwjob, and - after the following night's events on *Nitro* - another reformation of the nWo.

Because of these kinds of statements, Russo got most of the blame when the needle, so to speak, failed to move as expected. Fans started to see our product as a pale imitation of the 'Attitude Era', and the writing increasingly became more frantic. While Russo remained undeterred - continuing as the brash, confident and unapologetic spokesperson of the duo - I'm not *entirely* sure that Ed felt the same way.

For reasons that we'll get into later, I eventually got to know Ed pretty well on a personal basis. I've often wondered if he knew - to some extent, at least - that what they produced in WCW wasn't revolutionary, or groundbreaking.

221

It was garbage.

I don't know. Maybe I'm giving Ed the benefit of the doubt - because he's such a super guy - but I'm a pretty good judge of character. Something tells me that probably 85% of the stuff which made TV came from Russo, with maybe 15% of it coming from Ed. I could be totally wrong, by the way, but here's something interesting to think about: a lot of people don't even *remember* that Ed was Russo's writing partner at first. A lot of that had to do with their respective personalities - Ed was very laid-back, and he sort of carried himself like Russo's sidekick - with Russo, unquestionably, as the domineering presence.

After all, when Russo in particular came into WCW, the perception was that the young guys - after being 'held down' for so long - were finally going to get their shot. Russo was going to make them all *stars*, apparently - but there can only be so many stars on the show. Realistically, you can't make *everyone* a Hulk Hogan, or a Ric Flair, or a Randy Savage, but the younger talent saw him as their savior.

Ironically, however, those same younger guys were ultimately hamstrung - not by the more established talent - but by Russo's bad writing. Some of the gimmicks he gave to guys were just nonsensical; for example, although he was a veteran wrestler - and not in the group who had previously become disgruntled - 'Hacksaw' Jim Duggan became a *janitor*, for reasons that I don't really care to remember.

Over the last few months of Eric's run, there had been so much resentment in the locker room, mostly due to the feeling that Eric was *always* going to favor the same top guys. In turn, that allowed Russo to enjoy a 'honeymoon period' of sorts when he first arrived on the scene. While in my view, he went on to fail in his attempts to improve things, his support from the younger wrestlers - as of December 1999 - mostly remained intact.

At the same time, many of us who knew better were less optimistic - and we were *beyond* burned out. Compared to where WCW had been

222

at its peak, the houses were the absolute *shits*. The ratings had plateaued for the most part, and while not everyone saw it yet, the new direction wasn't *ever* going to pan out.

1999 had been an emotional roller coaster - but as we entered 2000, it was about to take *another* turn.

Less than two weeks into the new year, Russo was removed from his position as WCW's 'Creative Director', and after being given the option to work within a creative committee, he decided to go home instead.

"A decision was made by WCW management," summarized Bob Ryder of *1Wrestling.com*, "to bring more people into the creative process…and to reestablish a booking committee. Russo is said to have been unhappy with the prospect of booking by committee, and [he] expressed his feelings to WCW management."

That committee, I soon learned, was going to be led by a familiar face: Kevin Sullivan.

They're giving me the book, Kevin told me in confidence.

And here's the first thing I'm doing…

I'm putting the belt on Benoit.

15:
RADICAL CHANGES

Unlike most people in the industry, Kevin had the ability to separate his personal feelings from business. Nevertheless, he was fully aware of the dissension that was building in the locker room. *Some of these guys*, he predicted, *are not gonna like that I'm the booker. They're really into what Russo's doing - the way he's pushing the young guys - even though Russo doesn't have a fucking clue how to do it.*

On the one hand, I knew that Benoit being with Nancy was still a fresh wound - for everyone concerned. On the other hand, I truly believed that Kevin's intentions - relative to putting the belt on Chris - came from a good place.

I've heard of extending olive branches, I told Kevin when he told me of his plans, *but I never heard of giving up the whole tree!*

The guy deserves it, Kevin said, speaking of Benoit.

He's worked hard - and this is about business.

On Sunday, January 16th, 2000, the *Souled Out* pay-per-view ended as envisioned by Kevin, with Benoit, for the very first time, winning the WCW title after submitting Sid Vicious clean (crucially, Sid had been told to put his feet under the ropes, a prophetic decision given what was to come). To close the broadcast, Benoit exchanged words with Kevin Nash - WCW's newly crowned on-screen 'commissioner' - seemingly teasing a future program between them. "*Enjoy that belt for another hour and 40 minutes*," said Nash in a backstage segment, "*because at the stroke of midnight, your life becomes a living hell!*"

Fans never got to see that storyline develop, as amid a chaotic backstage scene, Benoit - along with the heart of the WCW midcard - left the company the very next night. It followed a series of backstage meetings - the first of which occurred on the actual day of the pay-per-view - where Benoit and a contingent of wrestlers voiced their anger at the booking change.

Everything *really* accelerated after Busch called an all-talent meeting before *Nitro* on Monday, January 17th. At the meeting, Busch explained that Russo wasn't coming back, and Kevin, for the foreseeable future, was going to be the booker. In response, as many as 20 guys - according to reports published at the time - expressed their desire for a contractual release, including Konnan (eventually convinced into staying by the luchadores), Rey Mysterio, Jr., Kidman and Juventud Guerrera. Five guys were especially unhappy: Benoit, Eddie Guerrero, Dean Malenko, Perry Saturn and Shane Douglas.

Penzer, Kevin said to me, knowing that I was friends with those five, *go talk to 'em.*

Now believe me, I tried my best to talk those guys out of leaving, and I pleaded with them *all fucking day*. Ultimately, it seemed not to matter what I had to say, because clearly, they had made up their minds already. As soon as they heard that Russo was gone, that was it - there was nothing really to talk about.

Like I said before, a lot of the younger guys thought Russo was the savior - and who's kidding who? Russo definitely took credit - and subsequently, *got* credit - for a lot of the stuff that turned the WWF around. Therefore, from the perspective of the wrestlers who wanted to leave, they pretty much thought, *Shit, this was the guy who got all those people in the WWF over. He promised us he'd do the same thing here - turning around the company in the process - but now they've sent him home and brought back Sullivan.*

To make matters worse, an incident allegedly occurred backstage involving Mike Graham - at this point, a WCW road agent - where he supposedly pulled a knife out on the group. For the record, I didn't personally witness that incident, but like I told you before - think back to Sid and the squeegee debacle - Mike didn't need much of an excuse to fucking *go*.

I'll just leave it at that.

When Chris and them started walking out of the building, I could hardly believe it - and thinking back on it now, the scene still replays in my mind. Up until the very last minute that they walked through those doors, I continued making my plea to no avail: *Guys, Kevin put the belt on Chris. Kevin's keeping the belt on Chris. Kevin's gonna use you guys - why can't you at least give him a chance?*

I understand why you're leery, I said, *but why do this tonight? What's the difference between walking out now - and walking out in two weeks?*

As a group, they presented themselves as being on the same page: *David, we appreciate it, and you might end up being right...but we just can't stay here.*

For the record, I thought it was the wrong move, but in a decision that had far-reaching consequences for our company, Busch agreed to give Benoit, Guerrero, Malenko and Saturn a slate of *unconditional* releases. Within weeks, they were appearing together on *Raw* as 'The Radicalz', and in their debut match (a multi-man tag involving The Rock, Triple H and Cactus Jack), the segment drew an insane 8.1 rating.

While the rest of the disgruntled wrestlers were convinced to stick around - for one reason or another - Shane Douglas was the one left hanging. He explained his perspective in an interview given shortly after the fact, shining further light on what happened that day:

When it started becoming clear to us that Kevin was going to take over, and when he finally did, we went to Bill Busch. We had all met earlier that day: me, Billy Kidman, Konnan, Juventud, Perry, Eddie, Chris and Dean. We sat up in the stands in the Cincinnati Gardens and we talked about what we were going to say in this meeting. My understanding before we went in there was we were going to tell

Bill Busch what was going on, [what] the heat with Kevin [was]…and just let him know that if we started getting misused, he understood why.

We had talked about that we had to be willing to walk away in order to back up [our position]. We went up into Bill's office…and everybody took their turn in talking and saying what their concern was. When it came time for me to talk, a couple of guys kept butting in and started talking. In the middle of this meeting, Perry Saturn said to Bill, 'You once told me Bill that you didn't want anybody unhappy in your dressing room - and you'd give anybody their release that wasn't happy here.'

Bill said, 'I don't remember exactly saying those words.'

Perry said, 'No, no - that's what you said. Don't go back on your word and not be a man, Bill.'

Bill said, 'I said something similar to that…so I'll agree with that.'

Perry said, 'Okay, fine - I want my release.'

Now that caught me completely off guard, because although we had covered our asses on the 'what if' situation, I didn't know we were going to go in there and tender any resignations. Chris Benoit then spoke up and said, 'That goes for me also.'

After that meeting let out…I went back in. I said, 'Bill, the first thing I want to tell you is that I definitely do not want to leave the company.' He thanked me for saying that. I apologized for the meeting and told him I didn't recognize that was where the meeting was going.

I didn't get a chance to talk in that first meeting. I told him, 'Here's my concern - you guys are paying me, over three years, well into seven figures to be here. I don't want to be a welfare case.

…He thanked me for being so candid with him, thanked me for clarifying my position from the other guys and he said [to] give him a week to come up with some sort of solution, and [that] he would meet with me in Atlanta.

According to Shane, Busch even offered to sequester Kevin into booking *Thunder* - thus limiting his interactions with the group, before later thinking better of it:

J.J. Dillon comes up and tells us, 'Bill would feel more comfortable if you guys weren't around. He'd like you all to go home and he will contact you later.

…We walked out of all those meetings and Mike Graham came up to us. Chris and I were talking in the hallway, and he pulled Chris across the hall and said, 'I heard you guys went in there and tried to get me, J.J. and Kevin fired.'

Chris said, 'First of all, what we talked about in that office is none of your business…but I will tell you this: your name and J.J.'s [name] never came up.'

[Mike] said, 'Well, that's not what I heard' - and he leaned up into Chris's face. He said, 'When I find out which of you [motherfuckers] said it, I'm going to slice your [fucking] throat and send you home in a body bag.'

Now we're in a whole different ball game. A Time Warner management-level person making threats against you is not going to fly very well in a court of law. That's the reason Bill Busch did not want us in the building [at *Nitro*]. He didn't know what was going to happen if we ran into Mike in the back.

We all went to the hotel, packed our bags, had dinner and swore we were going to stick together. My whole thing was I had worked with Vince [McMahon] on three different occasions. If there's any weakness at all, he'll find it and he'll capitalize on it. In other words, if we stick together, we stand to make a hell of a lot more money than if we stand apart. We all shook on it, we all hugged on it, we all drank a glass of wine on it and toasted to it.

Shane recalled returning home to Pittsburgh, only to receive a phone call from Russo:

[Russo] asked me where I was and I told him I was in Pittsburgh. He said, 'Are you sure about that?' I said, 'Well, why would I lie to you about that, Vince?'

He said a friend of his just called from New York, and told him [that] 'his boys' were in Stamford negotiating with Vince. He didn't know which guys…[but] he asked me if I knew where the other guys [were].

I said [that] I hadn't spoken with them for a couple of days.

[Russo] said, 'Well, you better call and find out.'

[So] I called Dean and asked him where he was. He said he was at his 'brother's beach house in Florida.' I said, 'Are you sure? Let me tell you what I've heard…'

[Dean] said, 'Shane, I would never fuck you over like that. If we did that, I'd be the first guy to have called and told you. You have my word - as a friend…I'm at my brother's beach house in Florida.'

I called Vince back and told him, 'Don't buy it. Dean is in Florida.'

228

[Russo] said, 'Shane, I don't want to call anybody a liar, but I know for a fact they're up there.'

On [Russo's] suggestion, I called the hotel and asked for those four guys. [Sure enough], the guy at the front desk told me all four had checked in.

In other words, the guys basically pulled a double-cross on Shane. That's a tough one to think about, because if Vince McMahon, especially at that time, said behind closed doors, *Here's the deal - I want you four guys but not Shane* - well, what do you do in that situation?

Now, if Vince had gone to Benoit and said, *Look - I only want you*, I guarantee that Benoit wouldn't have signed. He would have basically said, *Sorry, Vince - it's a package deal with me.*

The problem was that the four 'Radicalz' weren't really that tight with Shane - and unfortunately, he found that out the hard way.

Bill Busch was a real nice guy, but that kind of personality *cannot* lead a wrestling company. I think Bill thought he could do it his way - through leaning on a different style than Eric had deployed - but at the end of the day, he was just a total pushover. I mean, think about it: why would you ever release those guys?

Bill was way too nice for the job, and consequently, he got easily taken advantage of. That includes being swayed by those on the booking side of things - he was really getting it from all angles. It reminded me of when a hot girl arrives on a college campus, and all the fraternity guys are busy plotting, strategizing and diabolically planning about how they're going to get her into bed. In this case, everyone backstage was trying to figure out how to *play* Bill Busch - or trying to position themselves to be his *consigliere*.

Everybody was wining and dining him: *Hey Bill, why don't you come over here so I can talk to you?*

Hey Bill, let's go up in the stands and talk...

Hey Bill, could I get a meeting in your office?

When Bill replaced Eric, a lot of people perked up and said, '*A-ha - this is my opportunity - I'm gonna get in with the new boss.*'

That's just how the wrestling business is, and it almost makes me laugh because I've seen it so often. It's a great business in many ways - full of great people - but it's extremely *manipulative* as well.

Bill was probably too nice of a person to have ever been in that spot, and within two months, he gave *himself*, so to speak, an unconditional release.

Before Bill quit his position, the company went through a strange period where a lot of the top guys were out of action. In my opinion, some of them kind of gave up on WCW once our business went south.

Look, I'm not saying that I blame them. They had guaranteed contracts - and WCW was not a fun place to be anymore. That is my personal opinion of the situation, because listen - sometimes, lives (and careers) are too short. When you're making big money - and you know you have the ability to make big money other places - what do you need all the psychological, bullshit drama for? That can be something which affects your personal life, because you bring home all that work stress to a wife and kids at home. I don't want to accuse anyone of milking an injury or anything, and I respect anyone who has a different opinion. I'm just saying there was little incentive for guys to do what the company needed at that time.

In the early part of 2000, we were left with a rag-tag crew to run *Nitro* and *Thunder* with. Russo was gone, Sullivan (with the creative committee) was in, and we were doing it against a now-insurmountable enemy, with the WWF regularly *doubling* our viewership in the ratings.

Behind the curtain, things were unraveling, and increasingly, the disorganization came out on the screen. On the February 7th edition of *Nitro*, for example, Scott Steiner got on a live mic and tore into Ric Flair:

Now last week, I was watching TV, and I watched a 53-year-old man come out here - who has more loose skin than a Shar Pei puppy...and say he's still 'The Man.'

...When you walked down that aisle last week, I know I wasn't alone, 'cos the people at home, all they did, was grab the remote, and change the channel to the WWF, and watch Stone Cold - a person you and your old friends got fired from here, 'cos you're a jealous, old bastard!

So Ric Flair, remember this - in this wrestling business, there's never been a bigger ass-kissin', butt-suckin' bastard. In this business - but also in life - you're the biggest ass-kissin', back-stabbin', butt-suckin' bastard, and you belong where you're at, in WCW...because WCW sucks - and so do you.

Just eight days later, on February 15, a *Thunder* taping in Philadelphia went completely off the rails. *Alright, Philadelphia*, I said, having worked the crowd into a frenzy. *Here we go - it's time to start the show. You're on TV in five...four...three...two...one...*

The people went nuts, and the *Thunder* theme hit. The pyro went off, and then...*nothing*.

It was crickets - the show just didn't start.

I didn't know what the hell was going on until they got a message relayed to me: *Just kill time.*

Now, listen: a ring announcer can 'kill time' for five or ten minutes. Sometimes you have to stretch things out (such as during the show) and generally speaking, we're prepared for that kind of thing -

231

it happens. Personally, I could usually be good *enough* to make those situations appear seamless.

This time, however, I noticed that those five or ten minutes were turning into a much longer time period. Eventually, as the minutes ticked by - with no further communication in my earpiece - the crowd started to *turn*.

That would be bad news in Philadelphia. You just give them any excuse in that town, and they will happily go ahead and *torture* you. As the fans started to throw things towards the ring, I looked towards the hard camera for guidance: *Please, guys, you gotta help me out here…*

Left alone to think on my feet, I realized that I had two choices. It was either:

A) Let the fans turn on the promotion, including the event that we had yet to tape; or
B) Somehow get them to turn on *me*.

Looking over at the announcer's table, I noticed a copy of *Positively Page* - the autobiography written by Diamond Dallas Page. I guess I was inspired by that classic 'Great Gatsby' sketch by Andy Kaufman (look it up if you have a minute), because with little else to work with, I started reading out sections of Page's book!

Just to be clear, I wasn't trying to be Andy Kaufman in the sense of making our fans *leave* - as Andy would famously do to his audience from time to time - I was just trying to kill some time. I did it in kind of a funny way, and it gave the crowd an excuse to take out their frustration in my direction.

At the same time, once we hit the *half hour mark* (!), I kind of had to acknowledge being out of shit to say: *Sorry, Philadelphia…*

The *New York Daily News* picked up the story a few days later:

WCW hoped to work [Scott] Hall into the PPV main event at the taping of its TBS show 'Thunder' Tuesday night in Philadelphia, but that didn't happen…Hall was ready to go out to the ring when he got into a beef with WCW agent Terry Taylor.

WCW security broke it up and Hall went back to his hotel. This forced WCW to rewrite the show on the run and caused more than a 30-minute delay at the Spectrum.

In addition to our own, self-inflicted problems, there were still hangovers to deal with from the Russo era – such as the existence of the nWo, which Russo had reformed in late December. Russo had also got rid of the WCW Television Title - a belt traditionally used as a 'stepping stone' or midcard championship - following a segment where Scott Hall threw the belt in the trash. On February 19th, 2000, we decided to capitalize on that decision for an episode of *WCW Saturday Night*. *"When the Powers [that] Be came into WCW,"* explained 'Hacksaw' Jim Duggan. *"They made [me] the janitor…but that's ok with me…I've worked hard my whole life, and I'm not afraid of hard work. I know that every cloud has a silver lining, but in this case, it's gold!*

"When I was down in the basement of the WCW [building]," continued Duggan, *"cleaning up all that trash and all that garbage…I looked right over in the corner, and covered with goo was something real shiny.*

"It's the WCW Television Title!"

Okay - it didn't exactly make sense that Scott Hall dumped the belt on November 21st, 1999, and then 'Hacksaw' found it three months later, but nonetheless, that TV title became our *Saturday Night* championship!

We ended up doing a bunch of stuff with Duggan as the TV champion, but just like Jimmy said, our *Saturday Night* show ended up doing a little too good in the ratings. When it finally got close to eclipsing *Thunder* one week, it was swiftly turned into a 'package show' - and shortly thereafter, the show was canceled from TBS entirely.

I never really thought about it until now, but ultimately, I was on the last ever booking team for *Saturday Night*. That would have been a pretty wild thing to tell the 14-year-old me - the same kid who tuned in at 6:05pm religiously at his friend's house (before I convinced my parents we had to get cable ourselves!). For years, I sat there watching the Freebirds, Tommy Rich, Mr. Wrestling II and Ole Anderson, and seemingly in the blink of an eye, I was helping to format and book the show myself.

Who could have predicted *that?*

In light of all the chaos, and with ratings for *Nitro* and *Thunder* continuing to decline, it felt like another big change was imminent. There was speculation that Russo could be coming back, while in other circles, some predicted a dramatic return for Eric. In the end, however, WCW announced something that no one could have foreseen - *both* guys returning, this time in tandem, as part of a creative 'Dream Team'.

It's kind of funny how things work out. When Eric had been sent home originally, I think a lot of people in WCW breathed a sigh of relief. The atmosphere and morale had been steadily declining for a while, and it was nice to have some new blood coming in. I think that's part of the reason why a good amount of optimism came with Russo and Ed's arrival.

After just a few weeks of that first Russo regime, suddenly Eric didn't look so bad after all! In some ways, the best thing he ever did was go away, because at this point, WCW was practically begging him to come back. Comparatively speaking, Eric now looked like an Oscar-award winner - as opposed to the comic book writing that we had seen from Russo.

234

In any event, both of them were now going to be working together - almost out of necessity - as each of them were still on the WCW payroll. With that being said, I think the theory was solid on paper. Russo was going to be kept in check by Eric's oversight, and on the other hand, Eric would have a different voice to bounce some ideas off. Russo had been popular with the younger guys, while Eric had most of his support among the veterans. It seemed like a good way to spark the morale and get everyone hungry again. At first, I remember people kind of saying, *Okay - this is really it now. This is the fresh start we needed.*

That feeling didn't last very long. After two weeks of programming, the new partnership failed to deliver much in the ratings, leading to one of the most controversial creative decisions ever in wrestling.

First, some context. A WCW-themed movie called *Ready to Rumble* had just been released on April 7th, 2000, with David Arquette playing the lead role. It bombed at the box office, but because of that movie, I ended up experiencing (with the exception of my children being born), probably the greatest day (and night) of my life - the *Ready to Rumble* movie premiere at the famous Mann's Chinese Theater.

All kinds of celebrities were there, including Jon Voight, George S. Clinton and Paul Walker. I drove over there with Schiavone and Gene, and before long, I was strolling the red carpet in a pair of douchey sunglasses. I never wore sunglasses normally, but I figured that's what you do at a movie premiere. When in Rome - or in this case, Hollywood. Am I right?

I even did a live interview from the red carpet, courtesy of Chad Damiani from WCW.com:

Chad: I have a superstar guest who's just joined me - oh, I'm sorry. My peripheral vision is questionable - it's David Penzer. David, how you doin'?

Me: I'm ok. How you doin', Chad?

Chad: Welcome to Hollywood, California...

Me: This is amazing, isn't it?

Chad: You are a big star right now.

Me: No, I'm not.

Chad: Dave, question - was there a pre-cocktail party before this, because I wasn't invited, but certainly - it sounds like you were.

Me: No...I've been in my room all day.

Chad: Let's talk about this movie for a second - *Ready to Rumble*. You were an integral part of this movie.

Me: Not really...

Chad: Come on, help me out - we're waiting for Sting!

Later on in the broadcast, I decided to insert myself into Chad's interview with the Stinger himself:

Chad: Can you believe [this]? You are a huge star and David Penzer has squashed his ugly little face in between us for this interview.

Me: It's just 'WCW Live'. I can do this.

Chad [to Sting]: You are in the top 5 biggest stars in the company - maybe the top star - and this guy is taking your time!

But no question, the highlight of the broadcast came when Chad attempted an interview with our announce team:

Me: Ladies and gentlemen, Mike Tenay and Tony Schiavone from *WCW Monday Nitro*...

Chad: Get out of here!

Me: I'm their escort...

Chad: Tony, I apologize that this curtain-jerker is taking your time. Welcome to the broadcast.

236

At this point, Tony leaned over and whispered in my ear: *Tell him, 'Thanks a lot.'*

Me: He said, 'Thanks a lot.'

Mike: Wow! He's using Penzer as an interpreter?

Chad: You got the two veterans [here]. I'm on TV for the first time and they're workin' me over. What am I, 'pledging?'

Tony: Oh, that was too good! And Penzer went right with it...unbelievable!

Stylin' and Profilin' at the 'Ready to Rumble' Premiere!

We all went to watch the movie together, and that's where I learned that a lot of people come to these events for one reason - the free popcorn and hot dogs! Afterwards, we had an after-party with even more celebrities - musicians, entertainers, you name it - culminating in a private party back at the hotel bar. I might be a 'Z' list celebrity in real life, but for that one night, I got to live the life of an A-lister - with limousine rides, people yelling my name, autograph requests and, of course, the presence of the paparazzi.

All in all, it was a pretty damn cool experience.

One of my hazy memories from that night is somehow getting linked up with Chris Kanyon and David Arquette. We all ended up doing shots of vodka on the roof of the L.A. Hilton, and we parted ways hoping for a chance to do it again. None of us could have predicted what was just around the corner.

Ringside with Courtney Cox and David Arquette

Little did we know that David would soon become an integral part of WCW programming. On April 25th, 2000, he was booked to appear at a *Thunder* taping in Syracuse, NY, in order to take part in a tag-team match involving DDP, Jeff Jarrett and Eric. Originally, their match - the main event on the show that night - was laid out this way in the format:

Talent Note: Kimberly as Special Referee
Content Note: Jarrett Over Arquette (Arquette Not Legal Man)
Kimberly Fast Counts 1-2-3
Announcer Note: Ponder That If DDP Had Taken Out Kimberly Earlier, He Would Not Have Lost The Belt!!

You'll notice that plan is quite different from what ultimately made air, as in a last-minute call, a decision was made to put David over - making *him* the World Heavyweight champion. In an interview days later, Russo argued that it was all part of the plan:

If we put the title on a David Arquette, it's obviously going somewhere. It's obviously part of a story that's going to make sense in the big picture. Again, [there's] a lot of negativity, but that's okay – because they are talking about WCW…and they have no idea of where the story is going.

I know people will want me to bury the Arquette decision into the ground, but listen: by that point, it made about as much sense as anything else Russo was booking. It was a desperate publicity stunt, sure - but at least it got us a mention in *USA Today* and *Entertainment Tonight*. In a few months' time, Russo would be booking *himself* to be the World champion, and what did that get us? One 'champion' was a great guy who got us some publicity, and the other was a booker who doesn't know how to book. Which one was worse?

Like I said, David was a very nice guy, and that night, he covered the bar tab (plus pizza) for the entire talent and crew. It wasn't his decision to win the belt, but due to the backlash it received, he ultimately became convinced - *truly* convinced - that he had somehow killed the entire wrestling business.

Years later, we ended up connecting again and discussing the whole situation. It became a really significant conversation which I think affected David a lot, but I'll save that story for the next book - Volume 2 of *Sitting Ringside*.

By June, Russo was already having major issues working with Eric, and consequently, he went home on a two-week sabbatical. He returned just in time for *Bash at the Beach*, but by the end of that event, things had only gotten worse.

Originally, the pay-per-view had been advertised as featuring a Jeff Jarrett title defense against Hulk. On the day of the show, however, neither Eric, Russo nor Hulk could agree on the creative plans, leading to yet another clusterfuck in the ring. In the end, there was no real 'match' to speak of - Jeff simply laid down for Hulk, who then covered him, won the WCW World Heavyweight title, and swiftly left the arena.

Although Russo later admitted to not totally 'smartening up' Jeff (in order to provoke a so-called 'real' reaction out of him), everything until that point - relating to Russo, Eric and Hulk - had essentially been agreed upon. The disputed part came later, when Russo returned to the ring, delivered a scathing promo against Hogan, and then booked an impromptu title match between Jeff and Booker T.

Russo referred to Hulk's belt as a "memorial" championship and launched several personal insults in Hulk's direction. Those insults ultimately formed the basis of a legal complaint, relative to Hulk's contention that WCW had defamed his wrestling character. After leaving the building that night, Hulk never again appeared on WCW television.

The entire *Bash at the Beach* episode has been analyzed so many times - and in so many ways - but here's one thing that often goes unmentioned. Three days before the event, I received a phone call from Terry Taylor about the upcoming *Nitro* in Jacksonville, FL. Over the previous few months, I had started working as a talent relations assistant under Terry (in addition to everything else I was doing), so I was often relaying messages from the office to the boys. Over the phone, Terry advised that I should inform Booker to pack a *suit* with him for Monday. When I called Booker the next day with the news, I explained to him the reason - he was going to be made the champion. Between Booker and I, there was no doubt, ambiguity or confusion about that fact.

A long time after, I had the chance to tell Jeff that detail - and his reaction was *classic*.

That is unbelievable, Penzer, he said.

I was in the ring - and you knew more than I did!

240

At the time, some people speculated that Booker's title win had been motivated by something else - a series of racial discrimination lawsuits filed against the company.

I want to make a few points clear on this subject. First, let me address the situation from a general standpoint. Have I witnessed racial shit go on in the wrestling business? Yes.

Things have happened, back in the past, which are inexcusable and unforgivable - in many different aspects of society. Within wrestling specifically, people were definitely held down because of their race. As sad as it is to say, some of the African American workers sort of expected that kind of treatment - almost like it was just part of being in the wrestling business, especially in a Southern territory. They were treated as a 'less than' - and that is a horrible, horrible thing. That's why it was such a big deal, back in 1992, when Ron Simmons won the World Heavyweight title.

Now, have I known people in this business who are racist? Yes.

They aren't people who I ever surrounded myself with - just to be clear - and honestly, it was more the prior generation of guys, I thought, who carried some of those attitudes with them. There was a big difference between people who may have worked the territories in the '60s and '70s, as opposed to guys who were active in the '90s or early 2000s. The former group lived in places where words were thrown around that wouldn't be okay today. That's a good thing that we have evolved as a society.

The specific question here though is this: was there merit to a lot of the allegations in the racial discrimination lawsuits against WCW, circa 2000?

In my opinion - no.

Most of the talent viewed those lawsuits as nothing more than a corporate money grab. There was a perception that Turner would look to settle any legal issues in a heartbeat, and believe me - don't think that people didn't know that. Anyone who is being honest will say the same thing.

I remember Bobby Walker being one of the wrestlers involved in the whole deal. Jody Hamilton had taken that kid under his wing, mostly because he saw something in him - and therefore, Jody believed he could get over. It was like a project of Jody's to work with Bobby in the Power Plant, and he really tried hard to bring out his charisma. Jody was like the biggest Bobby Walker fan in the world, and he'd tell anyone who listened about Bobby's dropkick - he was really quite impressed by that.

The truth is that Bobby was a good wrestler, but ultimately, he never developed the charisma needed to connect with the fans. They tried different ways of trying to get him over, but it was just never going to happen for Bobby. He could work - and again, he threw one hell of a dropkick - but he simply had no charisma. Zero. In my view, his lack of advancement had nothing to do with the color of his skin.

As far as other people are concerned, were opportunities as equal then as they are now? That's definitely debatable. I'm not excusing anything, but I do know this: a lot of people were lied about in those lawsuits.

For example, I had never seen Arn Anderson doing anything *approaching* what was alleged in the courtroom, but they had one key witness willing to say otherwise.

Pee Wee.

Out of sheer spite, Pee Wee Anderson decided to go against Arn - his childhood friend.

In my opinion, Pee Wee also wanted to enact some revenge on the company that fired him: *I'll show these motherfuckers*, seemed to be his mindset.

There was no coming back from that, as far as we were concerned.

We never spoke to Pee Wee again.

After *Bash at the Beach*, Eric removed himself from the creative situation and went home, causing another shake-up in the booking department. For the next three months, Russo headed up a committee made up of different people - including Terry Taylor, Disco Inferno, Bill Banks and Jeremy Borash, and our shows became increasingly absurd. During commercial breaks of *Nitro*, Tony was at the point of taking off his headset, placing his head on the announcer's desk, and holding his head in his hands.

Even guys who had previously bitten their tongue - like Bobby and Gene, for instance - were starting to become a lot more vocal. For people who were the absolute best at what they did - like they were - I can't imagine how frustrated they must have been.

Wow, offered Gene sarcastically, looking over the format for one night's show. *Sounds like a million-dollar angle, boys!*

In case you missed it, Gene would then clarify his thoughts to you: *They don't know what the fuck they're doing, Penzer.*

While WCW remained as a distant number two to the WWF, Russo featured himself on television more than ever. He booked his character to get the upper hand on numerous top guys, and - as noted earlier - he even put the belt on himself come September.

The most absurd part is who Russo beat for the belt. You guessed it - Booker T.

Just two weeks later, Russo himself was gone - finally done with WCW, as WCW was with him.

Look - on a personal basis, I have nothing against Vince Russo. I hope he has a wonderful life. I hope he has tons of grandkids who go on to do wonderful things. I hope that all of his dreams come true - from now until the end of time.

Vince was a nice enough guy who treated me well, but on a professional level, I think he's the worst writer/booker in the history of the business - and it's not even close. I'm not afraid to say it, and, in fact, I've said it before on many occasions. It's not a personal thing with me - it's just honestly what I believe.

Now, Vince would give you a whole laundry list of reasons as to why that *isn't* the case. His story is that he was merely doing the things that he was hired to do - in other words, the things that had worked in the WWF. To that I say: okay, nice try - but in reality, you were just killing the fucking business.

To some extent, we all create stories in our mind as a way of dealing with different things, and maybe that's how Vince likes to remember it. But think about this: in 2024, there's *still* a ton of people - wrestlers and other figures within the industry - who remain convinced that Russo was a plant (i.e. that Vince McMahon purposefully sent him to destroy WCW).

For the record, I don't believe that myself, but I had that same discussion - on a phone call with a prominent person in the industry - as recently as two weeks ago. If you showed me proof that Russo was a 'spy', it wouldn't necessarily shock me (I've seen just about everything in this business), but realistically, I wouldn't bet the house on it.

His time in WCW *was* a disaster though.

Again, to reiterate, I'm not saying that Vince wasn't a good guy. I'm not saying I want him to burn in hell. I'm not saying I want to piss on his grave like Jim Cornette.

Speaking of which, that's a shoot, by the way - the Jim Cornette, pissing-on-the-grave thing. It's in Cornette's will. If Vince dies before he does, Cornette has it in writing that regardless of his condition - whether he's in a wheelchair or almost totally immobile - he wants to be transported to Russo's grave so he can piss on it. Could you imagine the lawyer writing that one up?

You might hear that and think, 'Oh, that's just Jim Cornette being Jim Cornette.' I thought the same too; that is, until Jim showed me the legal document confirming it.

No fucking way, I told him. *You got that on legal paper?*

Jim was deadly serious: *Fuck yeah, I did!*

But that's Jim. I don't hate Russo like that - I just hate what he did to the business.

He was just bad at what he did - and somehow, he stayed around much longer than he deserved.

By October 2000, an ominous feeling had enveloped the whole company. I still enjoyed coming to work, but it just wasn't the same for me. We had long ago lost our special spark, I thought, and a lot of the guys who had built WCW into what it was were no longer around. Things had changed in a major way, and now we had to worry about more than just a ratings war.

We had to worry about our jobs.

At this point, rumors were flying everywhere about WCW being sold. In a different era, that notion had been unthinkable, but after Turner merged with Time Warner - and then Time Warner merged with AOL - Ted Turner no longer had the same level of power he once had. That made us more vulnerable than ever before, especially if we were losing money - which WCW was at a record level.

After Bill Busch quit, Brad Siegel was supposedly the figurehead of WCW (as well as President of the Turner networks), but no one could ever get in touch with him. I got to see this first-hand when for several months (starting in October 2000), I actually became part of the WCW booking committee.

After Russo left, the decision had been made to re-create the committee, and since Terry Taylor was a big part of it already (and, as previously stated, I had been helping Terry in talent relations), I decided to throw my name in the hat too. Terry and I talked about the business often and therefore, I figured he might have seen I had a little bit of creative in me. *Hey, Terry*, I said, *is there any way I could sit in on these meetings?*

Terry agreed - and once I started showing up to the meetings, I noticed that questions would come up that only Siegel could answer. There was just one problem - the man wouldn't return anyone's phone calls. He was almost like this mythical figure that very few people could get to.

One day, I saw Craig Leathers walking around looking concerned: *I just came out of a meeting with Siegel*, he said, *and it's not looking good...*

That alone told me that our days were probably numbered. Nonetheless, we had no choice but to carry on, and every Wednesday, the booking committee met together in Atlanta. At this point, the ideas being thrown around the room were getting to be ridiculous at a different level entirely. At one meeting, Terry pitched a character named 'Bill Ding' - the evil architect. He was half-joking with that

246

one, but not to be outdone, Disco then pitched a wacky storyline of his own - *The Invisible Man*.

Disco explained his thought process in an interview with me years later:

> There would be times in these booking meetings where nobody would be saying anything and literally, it would be two minutes of silence because of writer's block. I just spoke up and said, 'What about this? Let's shoot 30 seconds of an empty locker room, and at the end: COMING SOON: The Invisible Man!'

> Everybody popped - but we never actually did it.

As Disco recalled, it wasn't the last of his ideas:

> We would meet at the Hilton in Atlanta in a meeting room every Wednesday after we got home from TV. One day, I got to the meeting about fifteen minutes early and I wrote out a six-month angle of a Martian invasion - on a flip chart pad - that would culminate at a PPV called *A Space Odyssey!*

Disco went on to tell us the big reveal: antennas were going to pop out of Mike Tenay's head, he said - revealing Tenay to be the Martian's leader!

He was kidding about that part...I think.

During my time on the booking committee, I managed to get through a couple of ideas. First, the ladder match at *Starrcade 2000* between 3 Count, the Jung Dragons and Evan Karagias and Jamie Knoble was all my idea. I was a big fan of those guys and if given the chance, I knew they would tear the house down together.

Secondly, I was one of the main people who *strongly* pushed for AJ Styles to appear on television. Obviously, AJ has gone on to have a legendary career - and that is 1000% him - but he was also one of the few highlights for WCW during this time. Other than that, I didn't have much of an influence, but I did learn to appreciate a lot about the booking process.

247

Looking back now, I think that throughout 1999 and 2000, there were various points where WCW got some positive attention for a storyline, only for things to all fall apart soon after. Often, angles that had some momentum behind them were abandoned due to political reasons, and other times, it was due to a lack of patience. The pressure of the ratings war had a lot to do with that.

I've never claimed to be any sort of great wrestling mind, but I can tell you about the challenges involved in booking - especially as it relates to WCW back then. I can't even begin to try and explain to you how hard it was. In our case, we had to put together an entertaining show for the fans, sure - but also a show that the guys would sign off on. Obviously, that was an issue because there were so many egos involved, frequent roster changes, and people with undue influence in the booking process.

There were also the *usual* considerations to worry about - guys getting hurt, or undergoing personal issues, or something happening with their contract. For every plan that we had, we basically had to have about 10 back-up plans - and those back-up plans sometimes made television. Sometimes, things went on the air that people knew weren't going to draw, simply because after dealing with all the egos and bullshit going on, there were no other options available.

Remember, WCW wasn't an environment like the WWF - where Vince McMahon was the boss and that was that. In our company, a significant number of people had a say - and seeing as they had guaranteed contracts, you kind of *had* to listen to them.

Our supposed leader - Brad Siegel - remained basically AWOL. Quite obviously, the boys were aware of that, and they took full advantage of it whenever they could. No one knew where the buck *really* stopped, because if one person said something to the talent, they could go around that person by talking to someone else. Therefore, anyone who joined the company around this time was left with an obvious question: *Who the hell is in charge here?*

248

Ed Ferrara was still with us - having rejoined the booking committee after Russo left - and in late 2000, he was the one literally putting pen to paper. In other words, Ed was the person actually writing up the formats, and it was in this capacity that I got to know him a lot better. In my opinion, once Ed had a chance to take the lead a little bit, some of his stuff was pretty damn good - especially compared to earlier in 2000. Yes, WCW was a shell of itself versus where it had been, but creatively, things *were* starting to stabilize a little.

Like everyone else though, I just hoped it wasn't too little, too late. We still didn't know what our future held, and at this point, we didn't even know if we would ever get an answer.

At the end of one booking meeting, a single comment kind of summed it all up.

Well, Ed said, shuffling his papers. *I'm the one writing the script...so hey, maybe I'm the one in charge!*

Around this time, I came to realize that all along, Eric really was the guy who had steered the ship. He might have steered it into rocky waters eventually, but he steered it for those 83 weeks of glory into the right direction. We were the little engine that could back then, and we deserved to become the winners that we were for all of those weeks.

In retrospect, it was simply never the same after Eric left in '99. It was never again the sense of, 'Okay - we're gonna win this war.' It was more like, 'Let's just hold on, and try to keep chugging along - if we can.'

By the end of 2000, it was hard not to go through the motions at times - almost as if we expected the inevitable.

Besides, Eric wasn't ever coming back.

After *Bash at the Beach*, we had all seen the last of him, unfortunately.

...Or had we?

16:
A FAIT ACCOMPLI

On January 11th, 2001, Eric dramatically burst back on to the scene, announcing that along with an investment group named Fusient Media Ventures, he had purchased WCW and was returning as President. "Wrestling fans can rest assured," he stated in a company press release, "that we will give WCW the adrenaline shot it needs to once again become the most exciting brand of wrestling in the world."

As part of the deal, Turner Broadcasting would be divesting itself *operationally* from WCW, but retaining a minority interest and long-term programming rights. It meant that even with its new ownership, WCW's home would remain on the Turner networks - putting an end, it appeared, to months of stress and speculation.

As part of the 'new' WCW, Eric's right-hand man figured to be John Laurinaitis (the former 'Johnny Ace'), who had initially been hired during the year 2000. In turn - and by virtue of my recent experience in talent relations - I started working as Johnny's assistant.

At first, my primary responsibility was to evaluate the Nielsen ratings; in other words, to keep track of the quarter-hour fluctuations in viewership, or even analyze some of the *minute-to-minute* changes in those numbers. For the time being, WCW wasn't really running any house shows, so in addition to still doing a little talent relations, I spent most of my time working on that with Johnny. Together, we developed a formula on how to plot out who was driving the ratings (and, conversely, who was causing people to change the channel), all based around data that Eric had provided to us.

I don't know this for sure, but I think that subsequently, Eric started to realize that I could be more of an asset for WCW - or at least something more than just the ring announcer. That's not to suggest

251

that Eric had some great epiphany about it - I'm sure he had a lot more on his mind, quite frankly - but regardless, I couldn't help but feel optimistic about my future. Suddenly, I was now 'in the mix', so to speak, more than ever before, and - after receiving a recent raise - I was finally making six figures.

Everything was going great - and part of me wondered if I could do even better.

Who knows, I thought.

Maybe one day, if things go my way...I could make a good 'VP' in this company.

As I approached the 10-year mark in my association with WCW, I was very proud of what I had accomplished. By 2001, I had spent eight years as a full-time ring announcer - and six years as the lead guy - without ever so much as missing a show. I guess it wasn't bad for someone who started just driving guys up from Florida.

After all those years, something occurred to me that deep down, I probably already recognized. Quite frankly, no matter how far up the ladder I went, I *still* suffered from anxiety and panic attacks. To different degrees of intensity, those negative feelings surfaced *every* time I faced a live audience - without any exception that I can think of.

Some shows were worse than others, and in the interest of transparency, it could also be affected by how much I may have drunk the night before. But all the way through WCW - whenever I had a microphone in front of people - there would come a time when the anxiety *tried* to kick my ass.

Thankfully, I managed to push through it - and if you're having similar issues, maybe that can be an example for you.

Look, if *I* can do it, believe me when I tell you - don't ever let your struggles keep you from a dream.

It was going to take some time for the Fusient deal to finalize, at which point WCW, according to Eric, would be going on *hiatus*. In the interim, Eric planned for all the major babyfaces to go away - and mainly at the hands of Scott Steiner, who we had established in recent months as our dominant heel champion. At one point, the plan was to come back with Goldberg and some of the other faces who had been off television, with Steiner and a group of younger heels to go up against them. It was kind of like a concept which Eric had tried already with Russo - *The Millionaires Club vs. The New Blood* - only *better*.

The Millionaires-New Blood storyline had been abandoned in mid-2000, and most fans agreed that it ended too quickly (case in point: we had a pay-per-view called *New Blood Rising*, and by the time it took place, the New Blood faction didn't even exist anymore!). This time around, I think Eric really wanted to take his time with everything, and he envisioned culminating his plans with a huge relaunch of the WCW brand. Following the planned hiatus, a pay-per-view called *The Big Bang* would air on May 6th, 2001, at which point all the big stars would return. At the event, some new faces would debut as well, and effectively, we would 'reboot' the entire company.

A magazine ad for the proposed 'Big Bang' pay-per-view

253

As per the plan, Steiner was positioned as an unstoppable monster on television. One by one, he destroyed all the top babyfaces in convincing fashion, restoring at least some credibility to a belt so devalued during 2000. In the process, I'm not afraid to say that Steiner *legitimately* scared me. I still don't know if he was truly losing his mind - due to all the politics and stress he had endured - or whether he was just playing his 'unhinged' character at a Hall of Fame level. If Scott *was* just playing a character, he never stopped playing it - as anyone who saw him backstage will tell you. Scott would punch the walls, yell, scream, push things over and freak out...and I wouldn't want anywhere near him.

My attitude towards Scott even extended beyond the arena. Shortly before the Fusient announcement, for example, there had been an incident on board a commercial airplane headed to Atlanta. All of WCW's Atlanta-based production crew and wrestlers were on the same 10 o'clock flight, and beforehand, everyone had been drinking at the bar. It quickly turned into a big party, but remember - it wasn't a chartered flight!

Once we got on board, it turned into *shenanigans central*, with Mickie Jay, one of our referees, even letting off a stink bomb in the aisle way. Complaints were subsequently filed by some of the other customers and flight attendants, and ultimately, Mickie ended up losing his job over it. The biggest rib of all was that I got blamed for it in the press! Just take this excerpt from Ohio's *Morning Journal:*

WCW suspended ring announcer David Penzer indefinitely for allegedly lighting a smoke bomb on a commercial airplane. He's lucky he didn't go to jail, since that is a federal offense.

What *actually* happened is that I got a one-week suspension - and it had nothing to do with the stink bomb. As we were a Turner company, numerous employees were subjected to post-mortem interviews - and at the time, I had no problem admitting to what I did. I had been sitting in the last row of first class, and Steiner happened to be seated in the bulkhead seat. *Hey, Penzer*, he said, *roll me down a couple bottles of vodka!*

254

Now listen, when Scott Steiner tells you to do something, you fucking *do it*. At the same time, our company had close to 90% occupancy of that flight. Why *couldn't* I roll down some vodka to our World champion? After all, the flight attendant in first class knew what I was doing. She kept the cap on both bottles, and we even had a conversation about it.

That's our World champion right there, I said. *I'm gonna roll these bottles down to him - is that a problem?*

I didn't see anything, she said.

That was kind of everyone's mentality in the moment. There were senior WCW employees like David Crockett and Craig Leathers on the plane, and I don't remember anyone stepping in, or even trying to shut anything down.

By the way, you might be wondering why I was in first class - and someone like 'Big Poppa Pump' wasn't. Well, because I had been so dedicated to WCW - including never missing a show - I had *Platinum Medallion* status with Delta. That meant that any Delta flight I was booked on got automatically upgraded - a nice little perk - but one which definitely caused some embarrassment at times. There were even occasions when *Eric* would walk past me, and I often heard grumblings coming from some of the bigger name talent.

But hey, what can I say? I had traveled to shows via Greyhound - I wasn't giving up *this* perk!

In any event, that airplane incident became a huge deal for Turner corporate. In the days of Jim Crockett Promotions - or in the 1980s, period - the whole thing would have been laughed off. Back then, they would have basically shrugged and said, *Eh - boys will be boys*, but that's not the mentality of corporate America.

We wouldn't have to worry about that much longer. Once the Fusient deal was finalized, the Turner suits - for the most part, anyway - would be mostly out of the picture.

It would be a new day in WCW - and it was just a matter of time.

On March 6th, 2001, everything suddenly changed. Jamie Kellner was appointed as the new CEO of Turner Broadcasting, and eleven days later, TBS announced (despite previous indications otherwise) that it was *canceling* WCW's programming. Apparently, there was simply no future for wrestling on the Turner networks, and - due to the time slots being removed - no sale to Fusient after all. "We've come to the decision," said TBS spokesperson Jim Weiss, "that professional wrestling, in its current style, is not consistent with the upscale brands we've created with TNT and the SuperStation TBS…therefore, we've made the decision that we're no longer going to carry professional wrestling in its current style."

I spent the next week trying to process everything - especially the news that the programming had been canceled. There was still vague talk of a 'hiatus' - but no one really knew what that meant. Rumors were rampant and everywhere, but we had very little in terms of concrete information. Evidently, it had all been done by the corporate people in secret.

Talk about a *fait accompli*.

On Friday, March 23rd, 2001, I was at home talking to Lisa about it all when the phone rang. It was one of the 'Peachtree City Gang' - our friend Jill, to the best of my recollection, whose husband worked backstage in production. I'll never forget what she had to say.

David, she said, *turn on your computer - and go to WCW.com.*

I walked across the kitchen, turned on the computer, and punched in the URL. The website loaded to the company 'splash page' which I had visited countless times before. This time, however, a large image took up the entire page. On the top left-hand side, the WWF logo was displayed, followed by the word 'purchases' - and then the WCW logo in the bottom-right side.

The WCW.com splash page, 3/23/01

Wait, they sold the company to Vince?

A wave of emotions passed through me: shock, sadness, confusion, fear. There might have even been a tear in my eye. I looked at Lisa, still stunned, and said aloud what probably both of us were thinking: *What are we gonna do now?*

My next thought was to try and get some answers.

I called Tony Schiavone: *no idea.*

I emailed Craig Leathers: *no idea.*

I contacted everyone else I could think of: *no idea.*

No one knew what the hell was going on.

As the day progressed, we were all left to grapple alone with the news. We understood there was a *Nitro* scheduled for Monday (the annual 'spring break' edition of the show, this time from *Club La Vela* in Panama City Beach), but other than that, there was zero

257

communication coming from the Turner suits. Zero details were given about our jobs. Personally, I was just as shocked by the speed at which everything had happened as I was with the fact that the WWF was the actual buyer. In time, I became even more shocked at learning what they paid for our company: a little over 4 million bucks.

I remember talking to Jeff Jarrett, whose prospects of a WWF return seemed outlandish at best. Jeff had left the WWF in controversial fashion in late 1999, and consequently, he knew that door was probably closed for him: *Well, I gotta figure something else out, Penzer...*

Among the production people, office staff and many other WCW employees whose names you've never heard of, there was obviously a tremendous amount of sadness. Everybody was tore up about it, with one notable exception: Tony Schiavone.

I don't care, Tony shrugged.

Good...it's gone.

Oh, it was gone alright - and this was *really* it this time.

WCW had finally been sold - and after years of going non-stop, we had but just one show remaining.

At the final *WCW Monday Nitro*, the backstage scene was very sad. The boys put on a brave face - for the most part - although certainly, some emotional moments went down in private. As the show progressed, there were a lot of messages flying back and forth, particularly about the skits in which Vince trashed Lex Luger and Jeff Jarrett (those skits were not included in WCW's version of the format, by the way). I still didn't dare talk to Luger about anything - even at the last show - but I did ask Jeff if he was surprised.

Hell no, Jeff said. *I held Vince up for money - what else is he gonna do?*

As I looked around, I noticed that the production people were especially upset, as in general, most of them believed their time in wrestling was over. In some cases, that sentiment actually proved to be accurate, and such an abrupt ending to things only compounded matters further. We were all like a family on the road, and if you were still traveling with WCW, circa 2001, you were basically one of the *true believers*.

To some extent, *I* was one of the truest believers of them all. Sure, I had become burned out and beaten down by the product, but in the back of my mind, I always had hope that we could turn things around. Therefore, I empathized with what the production crew were feeling, because for all I knew, this was it for *me* as well.

Despite all the uncertainty, I resolved that I was going to go out, do one hell of a job, and let the chips fall wherever they may. I gave that last show my absolute *best* - and at the end of the night, I came back through the curtain, removed my IFB, placed my microphone on the table, and took the first steps into my new life.

Before I could get too far, however, a familiar voice stopped me in my tracks: *Hey, you were pretty good out there.*

The voice belonged to someone that even a week earlier, you could never have convinced me that I'd see on our show - Shane McMahon.

Thank you, I said to Shane. *I really appreciate that.*

You got it, nodded Shane.

I'll keep that in mind.

At the time, it kind of made sense to me why Shane would have said that. As I mentioned earlier, there were a lot of differences between the WWF and WCW ring announcers, including the fact that in the WWF, the ring announcers didn't actually talk that much. During commercial breaks, most of what they conveyed to the audience came via the *Titantron* - or the giant video screen in each arena - and so what I did probably stood out in comparison.

After I had that exchange with Shane, I thought of my dad and an expression that he had. Dad would often talk about putting things in your 'pride bank', and after so many years without getting a lot of feedback, Shane's comments went *straight* in there. Under the circumstances, it was a nice way for things to wrap up, and with the show now over, I did the only thing left that was appropriate.

I got *hammered*.

As strange as it might sound, it ended up being a cathartic experience for all of us. We all sat upstairs drinking together at *Club La Vela* (well, other than Tony, of course, who immediately got in his car and drove back home), as by that point, the WWF officials, like Jerry Brisco, weren't anywhere in sight. It was obvious that Johnny Ace was going to be the liaison between the two companies, but once the show wrapped, he was off premises too. It was just us WCW people, and one by one, we each said our goodbyes for the very last time.

Everything after that is a little hazy, but in the wee hours of the morning, I found myself waking up Johnny Grunge - who had passed out in the dirt, or somewhere between the *Nitro* set and the club.

Grunge, I said, *what did you do?*

I took somas, he said.

How many?

About 25, he said.

Have you ever thought, I said, *about maybe taking one every half-hour? You know, maybe just enjoy the ride…instead of taking 25, passing out…getting up and taking 25 more?*

Nah, Grunge said.

Not really.

The advantage of being hungover on Tuesday was that I didn't have time to think about anything. When I arrived back in Atlanta, though, I soon found myself going down to the Power Plant (which in addition to being our training facility, also functioned as the company HQ) - mostly to find out something (anything!) about our collective futures.

If you've ever seen pictures of the Power Plant, you'll know there were multiple wrestling rings on the main floor - surrounded by a variety of pay-per-view and television banners on the walls: *Saturday Night, Monday Nitro, SuperBrawl, Starrcade…*

As I walked around the building, I took in all of that history before noticing Craig and some other staffers, who were busy packing things up nearby. *Here*, Craig said, tossing me in an nWo shirt. *This was one of the first ten ever printed - it's different than the other shirts.*

I hadn't really put 'two and two' together yet, in terms of the sheer finality of us vacating the offices. It only started to dawn on me once I held that shirt in my hands, but it *really* hit home after what Craig said next: *Hey, don't ask any questions - but if I were you, I'd ship two boxes of your WCW promo pics to your house.*

Get it done today, he emphasized.

Less than 24 hours later, we all gathered back at the Power Plant for a big HR meeting, and essentially, everyone was fired in unison.

There was a very short address by an HR representative, and then we were all taken back to our offices - where we found our computers disconnected. Our laptops were all taken, and they told us in no uncertain terms: *You can only walk out of this building once, and we're going to have you searched and escorted by security. If it isn't yours, don't even think about taking it!*

Like any wrestling company, there were two kinds of employees at WCW: those who spent most of their time on the road (and some time in the office), and those who spent most of their time in the office (and some time on the road). My main life was on the road, and whenever I had a day or two at home, I wanted to see my family in Peachtree City. For those who were in the latter category, they had more of a typical work experience - going to Happy Hours together, that sort of thing. Therefore, there were a lot of close relationships that more or less ended the day WCW closed.

Our only saving grace was learning about our severance agreements, and for me, it translated into eight months of severance pay. That ended up saving me as the year went on, but here's a detail that I wonder if Turner ever realized. In all my years working for WCW, I never actually had a contract! I certainly would have been a lot more comfortable if they ever got me to sign anything, but at the same time - and there's a theme here - I didn't want to tempt fate. Regardless of how much time went by, I was still worried that it might give someone the ammo to reevaluate my position.

None of the wrestlers were present at the final meeting, and as far as the big stars went, they could look forward to many months (and in some cases, years) of getting paid out from AOL-Time Warner. For example, Bill Goldberg ultimately got paid millions of dollars until the year *2003* - and I'm sure he wasn't broken up about it.

For a select few guys, the blow of WCW being sold was cushioned by the chance of getting a shot in the WWF. In that sense, there was probably some cautious optimism and excitement there - and why not? The morale in WCW had been so bad for so long, and for the guys

262

with talent - like Booker, for example - the WWF presented itself as a promising new frontier.

At the Power Plant, however, the only *visible* person who was happy about anything was Tony. Nobody else was celebrating the news, but Tony was - and he meant it.

At any rate, it was time for us all to go. I grabbed what I could, walked towards the exit, and stopped to look up at those banners - just one last time.

It had been the ride of a lifetime.

I was 11 years old when I first started dreaming: *could I somehow be a part of this?*

The path ahead offered no signposts or directions. The odds were unlikely at best. The chances to walk away were numerous.

But I didn't walk away; I didn't give up. I persevered through it all - professional disappointments, mental health struggles, time away from family - armed with nothing more than a dream and good luck.

And ultimately - against all possible odds - my dream came true.

Look, I'm not delusional. I always knew that my path to pro wrestling would never involve me being a *wrestler*. I didn't have the height or the athletic ability for it, but fortunately, an amazing alternative opened up for me. I got to be the ring announcer for World Championship Wrestling - at one time, the most successful wrestling company in the world - during the famous Monday Night Wars, no less!

In time, I ended up pairing my ring announcer role with working on the production end of WCW. I got to work in the talent relations department. I even got involved in the creative side of the business during the last year of our run. More importantly, I got to ride down the road with people like Arn Anderson, Ric Flair, Chris Jericho, Eddie Guerrero, Dean Malenko and many others – the list is endless, really. I became friends with so many people who are rightfully considered legends today.

Even now I can't believe it - *I did it.*

I'm one of the lucky few people who got to live their dream - but every dream, whether we like it or not, eventually comes to an end.

For me, it was finally time to wake up. The last show was over, the pink slips disbursed, the terminations now handled. Ten years of memories - over in an instant.

I took one last look around the building. Soon, I realized that everything would be gone - the banners, the rings, and - for all intents and purposes - something a little more personal to me.

A well-earned ringside seat.

SITTING RINGSIDE VOLUME 1

THE FINAL FORMAT

*6 Jott ⊘ Jhdrnde

8 Komm ⊘ Ditao
  Hughe Soeder

WCW MONDAY NITRO
CONFIDENTIAL SCRIPT **REVISED**

MARCH 26TH, 2001   PANAMA CITY, FL

1. WCW Logo Identification

2. Vince McMahon Vignette #1

3. WCW Nitro Open

4. Pyro/Ballyhoo

5. (GRAPHIC) "NIGHT OF CHAMPIONS" LOGO

6. BRIEF ON-CAMERA: TONY SCHIAVONE and SCOTT HUDSON
   - Talk about this historic night – scores will be settled
   - Night of Champions – every title on the line
   - Tonight Vince McMahon Will Address the troops live

7. RIC FLAIR Music & Entrance

1 int
6 min

8. RIC FLAIR PROMO (Agent: Terry Taylor)
   - This will not be CEO Ric Flair, it should be 14 time World champion and
     WCW Legend Ric Flair speaking
   - Classic Ric Flair promo- very emotional, tears
   - Ric Flair will announce that tonight he will wrestle Sting

   Ric music

9. (BUMPER) UP NEXT: Title v. Title- Booker T. v. Scott Steiner

---

SEGMENT #2:

10. (GRAPHIC) "Night of Champions" Logo

11. (GRAPHIC – FLY-IN) WCW UNITED STATES HEAVYWEIGHT
    CHAMPIONSHIP MATCH

12. (GRAPHIC – FLY-IN) WCW WORLD HEAVYWEIGHT CHAMPIONSHIP
    MATCH

13. BOOKER T. Music & Entrance

8 min

14. SCOTT STEINER Music & Entrance (w/Midajah)

266

15. TITLE-FOR-TITLE: WCW WORLD CHAMPIONSHIP vs. WCW UNITED
    STATES CHAMPIONSHIP
    SCOTT STEINER vs. BOOKER T. (Agent: Arn Anderson)
    - Booker T. Over
    - Booker T. Music On Out
    - Off hot

SEGMENT #3:

Charles 16. (GRAPHIC) "Night of Champions" Logo

17. Vince McMahon Vignette #2

18. 3 COUNT Music & Entrance

19. JUNG DRAGONS Music & Entrance

8 min 20. REY MYSTERIO JR. & KIDMAN Music & Entrance

21. CRUISERWEIGHT TAG-TEAM CHAMPIONSHIP QUALIFYING MATCH
    THREE-WAY DANCE
    REY MYSTERIO JR. & KIDMAN vs. JUNG DRAGONS vs. 3 COUNT (Agent:
    Fit Finlay)
    - Announcers: Tell how the winner of this match gets to face PrimeTime
      and Kid Romeo later this evening for the Championship – this qualifying
      match was specifically requested by the Champions (so that they'll be
      going into their match fresh against opponents who have already been
      through a war tonight)
    - Rey Mysterio Jr. scores pinfall 1-2-3 *over Shannon Moore*
    - Rey/Kidman over
    - Rey/Kidman music on out

22. (BUMPER) TONIGHT: RIC FLAIR vs. STING

SEGMENT #4:

23. Vince McMahon Vignette #3

24. (GRAPHIC) "Night of Champions" Logo

7 min 25. (B-ROLL) Chavo defeating Shane Helms at WCW Sin PPV; Helms winning 6-
    Man at SuperBrawl; Chavo getting heat on Helms over weeks leading up to
    Greed; Helm defeats Chavo at Greed

267

26. (GRAPHIC – FLY-IN) WCW CRUISERWEIGHT CHAMPIONSHIP MATCH

27. CHAVO GUERRERO JR. Music & Entrance

28. "SUGAR" SHANE HELMS Music & Entrance (w/SugarBabies)

29. WCW CRUISERWEIGHT CHAMPIONSHIP MATCH
"SUGAR" SHANE HELMS vs. CHAVO GUERRERO JR. (Agent: Ricky Santana)
- Helms over 1-2-3
- Helms Music on out

30. (BUMPER) UP NEXT: WCW WORLD TAG TEAM TITLE MATCH- TEAM CANADA V. SEAN O'HAIRE & CHUCK PALUMBO... PLUS LATER TONIGHT- RIC FLAIR V. STING

SEGMENT #5:

31. (PRETAPE) Booker T. With Both Belts (:30)

32. (GRAPHIC) "Night of Champions" Logo

33. (GRAPHIC) WCW WORLD TAG-TEAM CHAMPIONSHIP MATCH

34. LANCE STORM & MIKE AWESOME Music & Entrance

35. (B-ROLL) Storm/Awesome over O'Haire and Palumbo last week on Nitro (non-title)

36. SHORT LANCE STORM PROMO
- "If I can be serious for a moment..."
- Calls for playing of Anthem
- **Anthem Starts to play**
- **Off Hot To Commercial Break While Anthem Is Playing**

SEGMENT #6:

37. Vince McMahon Vignette #4

38. (GRAPHIC) "Night of Champions" Logo

39. SEAN O'HAIRE & CHUCK PALUMBO Music & Entrance

40. WCW WORLD TAG-TEAM CHAMPIONSHIP MATCH
SEAN O'HAIRE & CHUCK PALUMBO vs. LANCE STORM & MIKE
AWESOME (Agent: Ricky Santana)
- O'Haire & Palumbo over clean
- O'Haire/Palumbo Music On Out

41. (BUMPER) TONIGHT: RIC FLAIR vs. Sting

SEGMENT #7:

42. (B-ROLL) Footage from Spring Break-Out Bikini Contest (shot earlier this afternoon)

43. (B-ROLL) Bam Bam Bigelow's challenge to Stasiak for Tattoo Match tonight –
Stasiak accepts – Bam Bam reveals he was talking about Stasiak, not Stacy –
Stasiak freaks

44. STACY Music & Entrance

45. Stacy Promo
- Will Introduce Shawn "The Star" Stasiak

46. SHAWN "THE STAR" STASIAK Music & Entrance
- Stasiak doesn't want any part of this match – Stacy is encouraging him – he can do it!

47. BAM BAM BIGELOW Music & Entrance
- Bringing tattoo machine with him – sets it up on announce table

48. TATTOO MATCH
BAM BAM BIGELOW vs. SHAWN "THE STAR" STASIAK (Agents: Terry
Taylor & Johnny Ace)
- Shawn Stasiak Over 1,2,3
- Shawn Stasiak music on out

49. Vince McMahon Vignette #5 #4

SEGMENT #8:

50. (PRETAPE) Diamond Dallas Page Interview (:30)

51. (PACKAGE) WCW Champions Montage

52. (BUMPER) UP NEXT: WCW CRUISERWEIGHT TAG TEAM MATCH...
"PRIMETIME" & KID ROMEO V. REY MYSTERIO, JR. & KIDMAN...
PLUS STILL TO COME: RIC FLAIR V. STING

SEGMENT #9:

53. Vince McMahon Vignette #6 *t/ 5*

7 mn
Pak
Spott

54. (GRAPHIC) "Night of Champions" Logo

55. (GRAPHIC – FLY-IN) WCW CRUISERWEIGHT TAG-TEAM
CHAMPIONSHIP MATCH

56. (B-ROLL) Rey/Kidman over 3 Count and Dragons earlier this evening

57. PRIMETIME Music & Entrance

58. KID ROMEO Music & Entrance

59. REY MYSTERIO JR. & KIDMAN Music & Entrance

60. WCW CRUISERWEIGHT TAG-TEAM CHAMPIONSHIP MATCH
PRIMETIME & KID ROMEO vs. REY MYSTERIO JR. & KIDMAN (Agent:
Ricky Santana)
   - Billy Kidman catches the fall 1-2-3
   - Rey/Kidman over – New Champs!
   - Rey/Kidman music on out

61. (PRETAPE) Sting Interview (:30)

SEGMENT #10:

62. Vince McMahon Vignette #7 *t/ 6*

1 min

63. RIC FLAIR Music & Entrance
- Announcer Throw To "Coming Up Next, The Return of Sting!"

270

SEGMENT #11:   8:33

THIS NEEDS TO START AT 9:33 EASTERN TIME (8:33 PM Local)

Dut

charles   64. STING Music & Entrance

10 min   RIC FLAIR V. STING (Agent: Johnny Ace)
                    • Finish TBA

            65. Copyright

17 min End

271

EPILOGUE

There's that famous phrase about things happening gradually - and then *suddenly*. For me, the end of WCW kind of unfolded in similar fashion, but given the alternative, the speed at which everything occurred may have actually been a good thing.

Obviously, WCW being sold was a devastating event in my life, but in hindsight, the circumstances could have been worse. If I had six months to think about the WWF purchasing our company, I would have driven myself *crazy*. For a guy like me, it was probably best *not* to have the time to process anything.

For a long while, I used to think that 'WCW killed WCW', but let's just be honest here - the suits were *looking* for a reason to bury us. Once our business started to go south, we were on life support, essentially - and in that sense, we never really had a chance. Again, it was probably better that I didn't know that, but I think there were a subset of people who did recognize what we were up against. To continue doing one's job under those type of conditions is no easy thing, and now that I think about it, maybe that's *another* reason why Tony was so miserable.

When I told my dad the news of the WCW sale, he was supportive as always, but after such a prolonged period of speculation, he wasn't exactly shocked. At the same time, we both realized that I needed to figure something out - and relatively quickly. I wanted my dream to continue, but effectively, the wrestling business was now down to one company - and I had a wife and two kids to think about.

Nonetheless, it initially appeared that the WWF was going to run WCW as a separate entity, anchored around the launch of a new show on the TNN network. "It looks like the new WCW," reported the *Trentonian* on April 1, "has chosen to begin right here in Trenton, [New Jersey]. WCW, which previously was not allowed to perform at

Sovereign Bank Arena (SBA) out of respect to WWF, will be taping a TV show on May 9 at the SBA. The show is tentatively set to air on TNN on Saturday May 12 from 11 p.m. to 1 a.m. Not exactly prime time, but still, it will be good to get WCW back on TV."

Almost as soon as it was announced, the Trenton show was canceled - or "postponed" according to the WWF - with a tentative date of June 9 provided as an alternative. Ironically, it seemed like the more things had changed, the more they were staying the same. "I haven't heard anything from anybody," revealed Ernest 'The Cat' Miller to a reporter. "It's about the same as it was before the sale. Nobody is saying anything."

The *Richmond Times-Dispatch* summarized the situation on April 12:

Jim Ross, who is in charge of talent for the WWF, said last week that so far, the WWF has picked up the contracts of 24 WCW wrestlers. While Ross did not list any names, it has been reported that they included members of the Natural Born Thrillers and Team Canada.

Ross said he expects that employment of WCW support staff, including agents, referees, ring crew, writers and announcers, will be decided on in the next several weeks.

He also confirmed that a tentative date of June 9 has been set as the first night of production for WCW. The show would be broadcast at 11 p.m. June 9 on TNN. Ross said it is likely that WCW house shows will resume by early fall and that the company's first pay-per-view could come as early as September.

Shortly thereafter, Jim flew to Atlanta, flanked by Johnny Ace, for the purpose of conducting meetings with various WCW employees. I met them myself at a ritzy hotel in Marietta, and what they said seemed to confirm what we had all been hearing. *Well, David*, Jim said, *I understand you have severance pay right now, but the plan is for WCW to be a separate brand. If and when that happens - because we have to work out a lot of logistics - the plan is for you to be the ring announcer. Is that something you want to do?*

Is that something I wanted to do?

Abso-fucking-lutely, it was!

Jim and Johnny told me they would be in touch, but for the next few months, it was basically radio silence from the WWF. The next thing I knew, the company was booking Booker T and Buff Bagwell to do a match in Washington State - hardly a WCW stronghold - with the final 20 minutes of *Raw* given over to a WCW 'takeover'.

Unsurprisingly, the match absolutely bombed in front of the live audience, and seemingly across the board, critics eviscerated the entire 'takeover' concept. Some found it particularly bizarre that the following *Raw* episode was scheduled in our former backyard - Atlanta, GA. If the WWF was serious about WCW being a separate brand, why not just wait a week?

I suspect you might know the answer to that one.

Anyway, a few days after the Booker-Buff match, Johnny Ace called me on the phone: *Hey, why don't you come by Raw on Monday?*

Why would I do that?

At the production meeting, Johnny said, *someone asked Vince who was gonna ring announce the WCW match.*

Vince said, 'Well, who's the WCW ring announcer?'

The reply came back: 'That would be David Penzer.'

'Well,' Vince said, 'Is David Penzer here?'

Obviously, I wasn't there - and they ended up using Stacy Keibler as the ring announcer instead. It's a close call, but I don't know - maybe she happened to be a *little* easier on the eyes or something.

I guess.

In any event, Johnny seemed to indicate that all was not lost. *For Monday*, he continued, *I can tell them you're here. Come by the building - and bring your tux with you.*

That Monday, July 9th, 2001, I arrived at the Philips Arena before *Monday Night Raw*. I started looking for some familiar faces backstage, but almost instantly, I met Howard Finkel for the very first time. Howard and I traded notes for about forty minutes or so, and I remember he was so kind in putting me over. To get that kind of praise from the greatest in my profession made showing up worthwhile - in and of itself!

While Howard and I got to know each other, the WWF brass had been holding a production meeting that went *way* over time. I was anxiously hoping for an update, and finally - at about three o'clock - Johnny emerged from a room backstage with some news.

We're killing the whole angle, he said.

So there's no WCW tour? I asked. *No separate brand?*

Not right now, Johnny said, *and I don't see how that could happen.*

I can't say I was surprised, but Johnny offered me a concession: *do you wanna stay and watch the show?*

I wasn't going to stay and watch the show. You don't do that in this business - not if you're not booked to be there - and ultimately, I guess I missed what became a historical episode of *Raw*. At the end of the night, it was revealed that in storyline, WCW had 'merged' with the former *ECW*, and thus 'The Alliance' - led by Shane and Stephanie McMahon - was born.

The reason for the pivot was simple, I thought - WCW wasn't getting over in the WWF. They didn't have the talent to make it work, quite frankly, and Vince wasn't going to pay our guys what they had been making in Atlanta. Then again, you didn't need *everybody*, and in my opinion, they could have pulled it off with just a few big names: Booker T (the final WCW champion), Sting and Ric Flair.

Nonetheless, the WWF was clearly not in my future, and therefore, I went to Memphis to do some stuff for Jimmy Hart. Jimmy and Jerry Lawler were restarting the territory up there, and halfway through one live, 90-minute show, I got the chance to step up for them in a major way.

Up until that point, they had some news guy working as their producer, but evidently, he didn't really know what the hell he was doing. The whole live show was falling apart, and Lawler got so desperate that he eventually turned to me: *Penzer, go in there and replace him!*

Jerry is famous for never putting anyone over - other than maybe Jimmy or Lance Russell - but the rest of that show ran pretty smoothly with me in the producer's chair. Therefore, I guess Jerry made an exception in my case: *Penzer, you know I don't usually dole out compliments...but you saved our ass today!*

After all the shit I had been through in 2001, getting that compliment really meant a lot to me. Jimmy was just as encouraging, and if not for him, I might have walked away from the business entirely - especially after my WWF misadventure.

Come September - and with only two months left of my severance pay - I got to achieve another ambition of mine in wrestling.

I got to be a heel!

It happened when I showed up for the second anniversary show of Bill Behrens' *NWA Wildside* promotion. After launching a comment in the direction of Jeremy Borash on commentary (Jeremy and I had a friendly rivalry in WCW - almost like Seinfeld and Newman - and whatever we said was a 90% shoot), I turned to address my attention on the local ring announcer:

Kid: Let me give you some advice - from 15 years all over the world. A real ring announcer wears a tuxedo - not a shirt with stars on it. A real ring announcer doesn't screech like Joey Styles. A real ring announcer talks from here...you'll grow into that as you get older.

But let me ask you a couple questions, 'cos I hear them chanting your name - and they seem to like you.

...Have you ever been on network television...live every week?

I know you haven't.

Have you ever introduced legends like Ric Flair, Hulk Hogan, Bill Goldberg, Sting...have you done that?

I know you haven't.

...Have you ever been on a world tour, played Sydney, Australia...London, England...Germany...Canada...and every major arena in the United States, in front of a sold-out crowd?

I know you haven't.

As much fun as that was, I still didn't have a regular gig, and time was starting to run out. I decided that maybe I should take a turn at promoting, and on October 4th, 2001, I put together a card featuring several of the old WCW talent, with the *Atlanta-Journal Constitution* picking up the story:

Southside wrestling fans can enjoy a night of eyeball-gougin', airplane-spinnin', pile-drivin' fun Saturday at the Kiwanis Fayette County Fairgrounds.

The South Atlanta Showdown will feature pro wrestlers such as Disco Inferno and Buff Bagwell slugging it out for a good cause. Some of the money raised will go to the New York Fire 911 Disaster Relief Fund and the Fayette County High wrestling team.

...The [event] is organized by Fayette resident David Penzer, who's worked 15 years in the wrestling world. He says parents should not hesitate to bring their children.

277

"This will be family-friendly," Penzer said. "What I'm going to promote is old-style wrestling, good guys vs. bad guys and theatrics without the vulgarity and obscenity."

Among the scheduled wrestlers are Flyboy Rocco Rock, Johnny Grunge, Sgt. Buddy Lee Parker, David Young, Adam Jacobs and the Iceman.

Matches start at 8 p.m., but fans will get a chance to meet and get autographs from the wrestlers starting at 6:45 p.m. Fayette residents Chris 'The Crippler' Benoit, who is recovering from an injury, and Paul "Mr. Wonderful" Orndorff, a retired star, will meet the fans but won't wrestle.

I more or less broke even on the event - mostly as a result of Benoit showing up to sign autographs - and overall, it did okay as a first effort. A familiar old face even showed up to do a promo - albeit with a radically new look, and newly installed braids in his hair.

And his name, you ask?

Only the hottest manager on the local independent scene: Ed 'Hip Hop' Ferrara!

But by the time Ed introduced one of our main eventers that night, the big star he had hyped up was in no condition to perform.

In that moment, I learned something about myself - promoting shows just wasn't for me.

By late October, I was down to only a few weeks left of my severance pay. Through hanging out with Jimmy, I had been hearing about a new promotion *potentially* starting up, but nothing ever seemed to materialize. *Don't get excited, baby,* said Jimmy whenever we talked about it. *I don't know if it's really gonna happen, but here's where things are at...*

Finally, Jimmy came to me with something more definitive.

Okay, he said, *there's a real chance we're gonna be starting something, baby!*

I smiled at the thought.

Somewhere, there was a briefcase - probably covered in padlocks - in need of dusting off.

Maybe it was time to pack up my bags, pick up that microphone, and embrace the next chapter - wherever that led me.

After all, it appeared that my dream had been extended - and the best part?

It wasn't quite time - not near time, *baby* - for me to wake up just yet.

ACKNOWLEDGMENTS

This book is dedicated to my mom (Ronnie) and late father (Bill). They were 1000% supportive of my crazy journey filled with obstacles, severe anxiety, panic attacks and some success. My heartfelt love and gratitude for their never wavering love and support.

To my amazing wife Lisa. Not sure how I got so lucky, but you are an incredible woman, an amazing mom, and a wonderful partner. I will always be grateful that I shared this crazy ride with you and can't wait to continue our journey.

Thank you to Bob Roop, who took this total mark under his learning tree - and for being a man of his word.

To Jody Hamilton, my favorite wrestler growing up. As I've said many times, in 1991, in a vastly different business, you saw something in me that wasn't there. You were the key that opened the door to living my dream and my utmost appreciation of your guidance, mentorship, and friendship will always be cherished.

To Tony Schiavone, Craig Leathers, Kevin Sullivan and Eric Bischoff, once Jody opened the door you all played significant roles in my WCW journey. My forever appreciation for the doors that you opened, the opportunities you provided, and for our friendships.

Mental health issues affect millions of people around the world. My battle is ongoing and well documented in this book. Never give up the fight, reach out to someone, even if it's a mental health hotline, and know that you are NOT alone!

Guy Evans would like to thank:

My wife, Aysha, for your amazing love, inspiration and support.

Nicky and Matthew for being everything to us.

David Penzer for believing in the concept - and for being so great to work with.

Craig Lynas, Bryan Barrera and Mark Curi – very much appreciated.

Every single person who checked out this book!

Thank you for reading *Volume 1* of *Sitting Ringside!*

SITTING RINGSIDE: VOLUME 2

Release Date: October 2024

ORDER NOW AT DAVIDPENZERBOOK.COM/RINGSIDE2

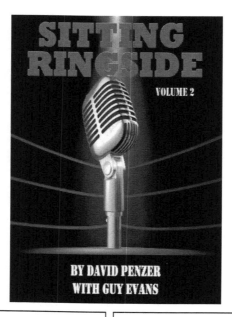

TNA BOOKING INFORMATION SHEET

Wrestling Name _C M PUNK_

Real Name _PHIL BROOKS_

TNA IMPACT
SHOW 133
AIRDATE: 05/11/06

HIGHLY CONFIDENTIAL—ROUGH DRAFT
X WRESTLING FEDERATION.

SCAN ME

ALSO BY GUY EVANS

NITRO: The Incredible Rise and Inevitable Collapse of Ted Turner's WCW

Publisher: WCWNitroBook.com (ISBN-13: 978-0692139172)

Print Length: 590 pages

Format: Paperback, Hardcover, E-book, Audiobook (Audible and Apple Books)

For more: WCWNitroBook.com / guyevanswcwbook@gmail.com

283

ALSO BY GUY EVANS

Grateful (with Eric Bischoff)

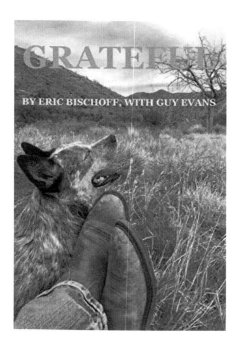

Publisher: WCWNitroBook.com (ISBN-13: 979-8218091781)

Print Length: 270 pages

Format: Paperback, Hardcover, E-book

For more: WCWNitroBook.com / guyevanswcwbook@gmail.com

BONUS MATERIALS

PERRY, GA   TV TAPING
1 7/91
                              INTERVIEWS TO PRE-TAPE

1.	:30	SOLIE W/DOOM	RE:		WWW 1/26
2.	:20	SOLIE	RE:		WWW 2/2
3.	:30	TONY/SOLIE	RE: DOOM INT		WWW 2/9
4.	:30	TONY/BARRY	RE: SHOW OPEN		WWW 1/26
5.	:30	TONY/SULLIVAN	RE: SHOW OPEN		WWW 2/2
6.	:30		RE: RECAP STING/FLAIR MEADOWLANDS		WWW 2/2
7.	1:00	~~TONY~~ W/DOOM	RE:		WWW 2/9
8.	1:00	~~RICH~~	RE:		WWW 1/26
9.	1:00	~~Z-MAN~~	RE:		WWW 1/26
10.	:15	WALLSTREET/ALEX	RE:		WWW 1/26
11.	1:00		RE:		WWW 2/2
12.	:15		RE:		WWW 2/9
13.	:15	RICK STEINER	RE:		WWW 1/26
14.	1:00	~~STEINERS~~	RE:		WWW 2/9
15.	1:00	~~MANFIELD~~	RE:		WWW 1/26
16.	1:00	~~JUICEMEN DOG~~	RE:		WWW 2/2
17.	:15	VICIOUS	RE:		WWW 2/2
18.	:15		RE:		WWW 2/9
19.	1:00	~~SOUTHERN BOYS~~	RE:		WWW 2/2
20.	:15	TEDDY LONG	RE:		WWW 2/2
21.	1:00	~~FLYIN BRIAN~~	RE:		WWW 2/9

Freebirds✓   Paul El Flair
Doom/Long   Sullivan
Vicious✓   Windham
R. Steiner   Solie
Wallstreet✓   Sting/Pittman/JStein.
                  HorseMen

285

PERRY, GA   TV TAPING
1/7/91   7:00PM
                                    ORDER OF EVENTS

---

1.   VS.   DOOM   WWW 1/26

2. EATON   VS.   ARN

    LIVE - TONY & WINDHAM

3.   VS.   WALLSTREET

4. SCOTT STEINER   VS.

5. LUGER   VS.

6.   VS.   VICIOUS

    LIVE CLOSE - ANNOUNCERS

---

7. PILLMAN/   VS.   FREEBIRDS   WWW 2/2
    B ARMSTRONG

8.   VS.   VICIOUS

9.   VS.   DOOM

10. Z-MAN   VS.   ARN

11. RICH   VS.

12. STEINERS   VS.   MASTER BLASTERS

---

13. FLAIR/ARN/WINDHAM/SID   VS.   LUGER/STING/STEINERS   DARK MATCH

---

14.   VS.   WALLSTREET   WWW 2/9

15. SOUTHERN BOYS   VS.

16.   VS.   VICIOUS

17. WINDHAM   VS.   SIMMONS

18. RICH/MORTON/JYD   VS.   MASTER BLASTERS/HOROWITZ

19.   VS.   FLAIR

20. LUGER/STING   VS.   LANDELL/MANTELL

---

21.   VS.   DARK MATCH

286

PERRY, GA

SYNDICATED SHOW

SHOW: World Wide Wrestling
REC: 1/7/91
DATE OF AIR: 1/26/91

HOT OPEN - :30 DRESSING ROOM INT SOLIE & DOOM - TO SET

SEGMENT #1 | ANNOUNCER OPEN :30/SHOW BILLBOARD :30

VS.   DOOM
W/TEDDY LONG

SLO-MO TO BREAK

1:00 WCW THIS WEEK OR INT W/TOMMY RICH

POSITION #1 (2:02)

SEGMENT #2
ONE FALL X 15 MINUTES - #1 CONTENDER FOR TV TITLE

BOBBY EATON   VS.   ARN ANDERSON

POSITION #2 (2:32)

SEGMENT #3

MATCH CONTINUES

TO SET - LIVE TONY & WINDHAM TO SLO-MO RECAP - TO BREAK

1:00 WCW THIS WEEK OR INT W/Z-MAN

POSITION #3 (2:32)

SEGMENT #4   [:15 WALLSTREET & ALEXANDRIA]

VS.   MICHAEL WALLSTREET

POSITION #4 (2:32)

SEGMENT #5
[:15 RICK STEINER]
SCOTT STEINER   VS.

POSITION #5 (2:02)

SEGMENT #6

LEX LUGER   VS.

1:00 WCW THIS WEEK OR INT W/DUTCH MANTELL

POSITION #6 (3:15)

SEGMENT #7 | NEXT WEEK BILLBOARD :15

VS.   SID VICIOUS

LIVE CLOSE - ANNOUNCERS (SHOT IN RING, GOING CRAZY, TO SET)

TOTAL RUNNING TIME & LENGTH 58:57

287

PERRY, GA

SYNDICATED SHOW   SHOW: *World Wide Wrestling*
REC: 1/7/91
DATE OF AIR: 2/2/91

HOT OPEN - FLAIR/STING FROM MEADOWLANDS - TO SET

SEGMENT #1 | ANNOUNCER OPEN :30/SHOW BILLBOARD :30

FLYIN' BRIAN   VS.   FABULOUS
BRAD ARMSTRONG   FREEBIRDS

1:00 WCW THIS WEEK OR INT W/JUNKYARD DOG
POSITION #1   (2:02)

SEGMENT #2
[:15 VICIOUS]
VS.   SID VICIOUS

SLO-MO TO BREAK

POSITION #2   (2:32)

SEGMENT #3   SET - TONY/SULLIVAN :30 TO VTR W.T. STING/FLAIR
@ MEADOWLANDS 5:00 - TO

SET - TONY/SULLIVAN RECAP

1:00 WCW THIS WEEK OR INT W/SOUTHERN BOYS
POSITION #3   (2:32)

SEGMENT #4
[:15 TEDDY LONG]
VS.   DOOM
W/TEDDY LONG

POSITION #4   (2:32)

SEGMENT #5
WORLD TV TITLE
Z-MAN   VS.   ARN ANDERSON

SLO-MO TO BREAK

POSITION #5   (2:02)

SEGMENT #6   [:20 GORDON SOLIE]

TOMMY RICH   VS.

1:00 WCW THIS WEEK OR INT W/WALLSTREET
POSITION #6   (3:15)

SEGMENT #7 | NEXT WEEK BILLBOARD :15

RICK STEINER   VS.   MASTER
SCOTT STEINER   BLASTERS
LIVE CLOSE - ANNOUNCERS RECAP

TOTAL RUNNING TIME & LENGTH   58:57

PERRY, GA

SYNDICATED SHOW

SHOW: World Wide Wrestling
REC: 1/7/91
DATE OF AIR: 2/9/91

HOT OPEN - HORSEMEN/DOOM ACTION FROM STARRCADE - TO SET

SEGMENT #1	ANNOUNCER OPEN :30/SHOW BILLBOARD :30

                            [:15 WALLSTREET & ALEXANDRIA]
                    VS.   MICHAEL WALLSTREET
                          W/ALEXANDRIA YORK

1:00 WCW THIS WEEK OR INT W/STEINERS
POSITION #1   (2:02)

SEGMENT #2

    SOUTHERN BOYS   VS.

SLO-MO TO BREAK

POSITION #2   (2:32)

SEGMENT #3

                            [:15 VICIOUS]
                    VS.   SID VICIOUS

1:00 WCW THIS WEEK OR INT W/FREEBIRDS
POSITION #3   (2:32)

SEGMENT #4   SET - TONY/GORDON SOLIE :30 TO 1:00 VTR INT TONY W/DOOM

    BARRY WINDHAM   VS.   RON SIMMONS
                                 W/TEDDY LONG & BUTCH REED

POSITION #4   (2:32)

SEGMENT #5
                    SIX MAN TAG TEAM
        TOMMY RICH   MASTER
        RICKY MORTON   VS.   BLASTERS
        JUNKYARD DOG   BARRY HOROWITZ

POSITION #5   (2:02)

SEGMENT #6

                    VS.   RIC FLAIR
TO - FLAIR ON P.A. (TONY IN) - TO BREAK

1:00 WCW THIS WEEK OR INT W/FLYIN' BRIAN
POSITION #6   (3:15)

SEGMENT #7	NEXT WEEK BILLBOARD :15

    LEX LUGER   VS.   BUDDY LANDELL
    STING   DUTCH MANTELL

LIVE CLOSE - ANNOUNCERS

            TOTAL RUNNING TIME & LENGTH   58:57

ORDER OF EVENTS
TUESDAY Jan. 8

NCW 1/20   6 1. ZMAN vs. BLADE   (Eaton)
5 2. MIKE HART vs. WALLSTREET w/ York
5 3. TAYLOR vs. DALE JOHNSON
      LIVE INT (1:00) PauL E w/ TAYLOR (morton)
5 4. BRIAN WORLEY & RAY DIAMOND vs. Doom w/ Long
      Live INT (1:00) Paul E w/ Birds
8 5. Renegade Warriors vs. MAGNUM FORCE

Main Event 1/20 6 +4. Horner & Armstrong vs. Freebirds   6:00

VCW 1/26   8 7 Morton vs. RIP ROGERS
      Live INT Paul E w/ Morton (Taylor)
3 8. GREG SAWYER vs. Sid Vicious   (stretcher)
6 9. Horner vs. SHEIK ALI SHIKAR
5 10. SCOTT ALLEN vs. Wallstreet w/ York
5 11. MIKE SAMPLES & MIKE HART vs Doom w/ Long
      Live INT (1:00) Paul E w/ Doom
4 12. Pillman vs. CAJUN PREDATOR
6 13. DAVID ISLEY & JOHN FAULKNER V Freebirds
4 14. S Steiner vs JOHN PETERSON
7 15. LARRY SANTO & KEITH HART vs Royal Family
      Live INT (1:30) Paul E w/ Sting & Luger
5 16. RICK FORD & CARL ROBERTS vs. AA & Windham
7 17. BRETT SAWYER vs. EATON
9-2 18. Renegade Warriors vs. STATE & PATROL (AA & Windham)

290

Pre-tapes
Tues. JAN 8

WCW 1/20	Ross-Caudle	:30	open
	Ross-Caudle	:30	(seq. 2) to Paul E/Missy
	Ross-Caudle	:15	(seq 2) recap Paul E/Missy
	Doom	:15	(seq.) Clash Jan 30
	Rom-Caudle	:30	(seqs) to Renegade-Horsemen

WCW 1/26	Ross-Caudle	:30	seq 1	open
	Vicious	:15	seq. 2	'Stretcher'
	S Steiner	:30	seq 3	Clash vs Flair
	Hyatt-Wallstreet-York	:60	seq. 4	Clash- computers
	Ross-Caudle	:30	seq 9	to Paul E Missy PKG
	Ross-Caudle	:15	seq. 9	recap Armwrestling
	Rom-Caudle	:30	seq. 10	to last wk Z-Eaton
	ZMAN	:30	seq 10	re: last wk's incident
	Eaton	:15	seq. 10	Clash vs Z
	AA-BWindham	:15	seq.	

| Power Hour | Eaton | 1:15 seq3 | Clash vs ZMAN |
| 1/26 | ZMAN | :15 seq3 | " " " |

WCW WORLDWIDE

PROGRAM NUMBER:	B-4896
AIR DATE:	January 6-7, 1995
DATE RECORDED:	Saturday, November 4, 1995

(:10) OPEN / (:20) HOT OPEN

SEGMENT #1

1-M		In Ring *Ring Announce On Line*
Scott Norton	VS	_____
Set: Tony and Bobby (:45)		

(:10) BUMP

CM POSITION #1 (2:32)

SEGMENT #2

1-M		In Ring
American Males	VS	_____

(2:00) WCW MAGAZINE INTERVIEW: GENE OKERLUND W/

(:10) BUMP

CM POSITION #2 (3:02)

SEGMENT #3

Clash of the Champions Update #1 (2:00)

1-M		In Ring
Bunkhouse Buck	VS	Men
Dirty Dick Slate		At Work
W/Col. Parker		(NOTE: Sherri)

(:10) BUMP

CM POSITION #3 (3:02)

SEGMENT #4

(:33) PROMOTIONAL CONSIDERATIONS

1-M		2-M
Taskmaster	VS	Dave Sullivan

(:10) BUMP

CM POSITION #4 (2:32)

SEGMENT #5

Set: Tony and Bobby (:45) to		
1-M		2-M *Ring Announce On Line*
Sgt. Craig Pittman	VS	Sting
NOTE: Match Needs to be Shot on 11/5/95		

(2:00) WCW MAGAZINE INTERVIEW: Gene Okerlund w/

(:10) BUMP

CM POSITION #5 (3:02)

SEGMENT #6

PROMO: (:30) NEXT WEEK

Close: Randy Savage (To Be Done Later) (2:00)

(:43) PROMOTIONAL CONSIDERATIONS

(:07) SHOW CLOSE TO (:03) DISNEY END PAGE TO (:05) BOLT

RT 58:57 CM 14:10

292

WCW WORLDWIDE

PROGRAM NUMBER:	B-4897
AIR DATE:	January 13-14 1995
DATE RECORDED:	Saturday , November 4, 1995

(:10) OPEN/(:20) HOT OPEN

SEGMENT #1

1-M		In Ring *Ring Announce On Line*
Hacksaw Jim Duggan	VS	_____
Set: Tony and Bobby (:45)		

(:10) BUMP

CM POSITION #1 (2:32)

SEGMENT #2

1-M		In Ring
Big Bubba	VS	

(2:00) WCW MAGAZINE INTERVIEW: GENE OKERLUND W/

(:10) BUMP

CM POSITION #2 (3:02)

SEGMENT #3   Clash of the Champions Update #2(2:00)

1-M		2-M
V.K. Wallstreet	VS	Frankie Lancaster
		(WITH D.D.P.ROBE)

(:10) BUMP

CM POSITION #3 (3:02)

SEGMENT #4

(:33) PROMOTIONAL CONSIDERATIONS

1-M		In Ring
Diamond Dallas	VS	

(:10) BUMP

CM POSITION #4 (2:32)

SEGMENT #5

Set: Tony and Bobby (:45) to		
2M		1-M *Ring Announce On Line*
Eddie Guerrero	VS	Chris Benoit

(2:00) WCW MAGAZINE INTERVIEW: Gene Okerlund w/

(:10) BUMP

CM POSITION #5 (3:02)

SEGMENT #6

PROMO: (:30) NEXT WEEK

Close:	Sting (To Be Done Later) (2:00)	

(:43) PROMOTIONAL CONSIDERATIONS

(:07) SHOW CLOSE TO (:03) DISNEY END PAGE TO (:05) BOLT

TRT 58:57   CM 14:10

293

WCW WORLDWIDE

PROGRAM NUMBER:	B-4898	
AIR DATE:	January 20-21 1995	
DATE RECORDED:	Saturday , November 4, 1995	

(:10) OPEN /(:20) HOT OPEN

SEGMENT #1

1-M		In Ring *Ring Announce On Line*
Hugh Morrus	VS	_____
Set: Tony and Bobby (:45)		

(:10) BUMP

CM POSITION #1 (2:32)

SEGMENT #2

1-M		In Ring
Arn Anderson	VS	Bart Sawyer
NOTE: Four Horsemen		

(2:00) WCW MAGAZINE INTERVIEW: GENE OKERLUND W/

(:10) BUMP

CM POSITION #2 (3:02)

SEGMENT #3

Clash of the Champions Update #3 (2:00)

1-M		In Ring
Shark	VS	_____ .
w/Jimmy Hart		

(:10) BUMP

CM POSITION #3 (3:02)

SEGMENT #4

(:33) PROMOTIONAL CONSIDERATIONS

1-M		In Ring
Flyin' Brian	VS	_____
Chris Benoit		

(:10) BUMP

CM POSITION #4 (2:32)

SEGMENT #5

Set: Tony and Bobby (:45) to		
1-M		2-M *Ring Announce On Line*
Super Assassins	VS	American Males
W/Col. Parker		
NOTE: THIS MATCH MUCH BE SHOT ON 11/2/95		

(2:00) WCW MAGAZINE INTERVIEW: Gene Okerlund w/

(:10) BUMP

CM POSITION #5 (3:02)

SEGMENT #6

PROMO: (:30) NEXT WEEK

Close: Giant (To Be Done Later) (2:00)

(:43) PROMOTIONAL CONSIDERATIONS

(:07) SHOW CLOSE TO (:03) DISNEY END PAGE TO (:05) BOLT

TRT 58:57 CM 14:10

294

1996 Strategic Plan

(Re-printed from the book, 'NITRO: The Incredible Rise and Inevitable Collapse of Ted Turner's WCW')

World Championship Wrestling/ Mission Statement...

WCW VISION-- TO DOMINATE SHARE IN OUR TRADITIONAL BUSINESS, WRESTLING, WHILE EXPLOITING THE ASSETS AND CHARACTERS IN OUR CORE BUSINESS TO EXPAND INTO OTHER FORMS OF FAMILY ENTERTAINMENT.

Mission Statement

World Championship Wrestling is an action-based entertainment company. Its PRIMARY PURPOSE is to provide television programming to be distributed through WTBS, TNT, domestic and international syndication, home video, and domestic and international Pay Per View.

To every extent, WCW should also endeavor to develop revenue streams from secondary sources such as:

1. Sponsorships

2. Merchandising and licensing

3. 900 Numbers

The key driving forces are the popularity of talent, production quality, interesting stories, and the emotional involvement of a large and loyal audience.

WCW should be positioned as an "Athletic Soap Opera" targeted toward a core audience between the ages of 12 and 49, skewed heavily toward children.

WCW's PRIMARY PURPOSE is programming, although ancillary sources can contribute significantly to earnings enhancement.

295

World Championship Wrestling/ Marketing...

IN THE PAST, BRANDING AND MARKETING HAVE NOT BEEN EFFECTIVELY USED TO MANAGE THE BUSINESS.

RECENT ANALYSIS BY ROSS ROY COMMUNICATIONS HAS PROVIDED IMPORTANT DIRECTIONAL INDICATORS.

1. Wrestling, in general, has lost some of its audience to other forms of entertainment. The major challenge is to re-seed the audience by re-inventing the business-- making it "cool" again.

2. WCW must re-seed a younger audience for "life cycle" marketing. The only other significant competitor, The WWF, has a stronger appeal to younger viewers.

3. Market research indicates a strong perception that The WWF has a better show in many respects--venues, signage, product branding, production values, event staging, action, excitement. WCW must upgrade the product in order to dominate core business.

4. Significant investment may be required to provide a competitive production capacity.

CONCLUSION: Core business domination will require fundamental strategic change and repositioning, not just against The WWF, but against other forms of entertainment which are appealing to a younger audience.

World Championship Wrestling/ Historical Trends...

INCONSISTENT LEADERSHIP AND MULTIPLE DIRECTION CHANGES HAVE CHARACTERIZED WCW OVER THE LAST FIVE YEARS.

Where we were:

1. Six executive management changes in four years resulting in lack of direction and lost opportunity

2. Inappropriate "Arena-driven" strategy

3. Lack of Television experience and vision resulting in inability to produce compelling programming

4. Syndication markets falling from 170 to less than 120

5. Unrealistic budgeting, crippling underdelivery

Where we are:

1. Acquisition of talent pool consisting of the biggest names in the history of professional wrestling

2. Elimination of significant underdelivery

3. Pay per View revenues up 70%

4. Closing gap with WWF

5. First sponsorship program an unqualified success

6. Station list up-- overdelivery against ad sales budget

7. Core product repositioned for a younger audience

8. Improved focus on expense control

9. "Farm system" for developing new talent

10. Branding/ marketing effort with Ross Roy

CONCLUSION: WCW has emerged from a troubled and unstable past with strategic clarity of purpose and strong indicators of potential success.

World Championship Wrestling/ Strategic Directions...

1994 AND 1995 WERE YEARS IN WHICH THE FUNDAMENTALS OF THE COMPANY WERE REINVENTED.

1996 AND BEYOND ARE PERIODS OF POTENTIAL PROSPERITY AS PAST EFFORTS ARE LEVERAGED.

Where we need to be:

1. Continue and expand the marketing/ branding effort
2. Expand programming into other genres-- Kid's Team Challenge, NASCAR, Animation, Monster Trucks
3. Greatly strengthened production capacity-- increased ability
4. Deeper strategic alliance with Disney Organization
5. Capitalize on international opportunity
6. Expand Sponsorship development efforts

CONCLUSION: The future for WCW is based on broader programming options aimed at a younger audience.

World Championship Wrestling/ Strategic Directions...

1. CONTINUE AND EXPAND THE MARKETING/ BRANDING EFFORT

A. Continue the 18 month re-branding campaign

B. Re-position WCW as the place "Where the Big Boys Play"

C. Add bundled Pay-Per View Value Added Packages capitalizing on retail merchandising efforts

D. Develop Frequent Buyer Pay-Per-View packages that offer volume-based price breaks

E. Identify retail-oriented potential partnerships for sponsorships, joint promotions

F. Generate in-store retail activities consistent with younger audience

G. Sports promotion budget for re-branding activities should approach $500,000 for 1996

SUMMARY: The most cost effective gateway for branding efforts and re-energized marketing appears to be sponsorship arrangements and partnerships with nationally based retail establishments.

World Championship Wrestling/ Strategic Directions...

2. EXPAND PROGRAMMING INTO OTHER GENRES

A. Kids' Team Challenge

-- Opens politically correct avenue to European market

-- Logical extension of action based character oriented entertainment to a younger market

B. NASCAR Sponsorship

-- An attempt to broaden appeal within traditional demographic group

-- 1995 sponsorship results are encouraging

C. Animation/ Monster Trucks

-- Uniquely effective way to leverage characters for the critical 5-11 children's market

SUMMARY: For longer term success, it is essential to transition our audience from one form of action based entertainment to another, capitalizing on our assets, our images, and our characters.

World Championship Wrestling/ Strategic Directions...

3. GREATLY STRENGTHEN PRODUCTION AND POST-PRODUCTION CAPABILITIES

Market research indicates a strong perceived gap in production quality when WCW is compared to WWF. Closing the gap requires a combination of three tactics:

-- Take the show on the road so that we will always have a "fresh" audience

-- Incorporate more special effects, i.e. audio and video enhancement packages, pyro, etc.

-- Use advanced technical equipment-- digital audio, digital video, "chip" cameras, etc.

Actions necessary by 1996 to close the gap:

-- Install digital audio and video equipment currently held in storage because of executive mandate

-- Develop capital plan for high tech production truck

-- Expand current production facilities to meet existing requirements, enhance production values, and   minimize outside production expense

CONCLUSION: The perceived production quality gap is material when comparing WCW and WWF programming.

Some combination of the three quality improvement tactics should be employed immediately.

4. EXPLORE DEEPER STRATEGIC ALLIANCE WITH THE DISNEY ORGANIZATION

During the last two years, WCW has established a mutually beneficial arrangement with Disney World in Orlando.

WCW Worldwide and portions of WCW Pro are produced at the Disney/ MGM Studios. A more permanent arrangement offers the following advantages:

A. Post Production strength and availability will be limited in Atlanta during 1996 because of the Olympics. Resources are readily available at Disney.

B. An action based daily attraction at a major entertainment park complements our programming. 80% of people who view production in progress at a studio become viewers.

C. Disney legitimizes our product.

D. Database development and research opportunities become more significant.

E. Potential savings from Disney production, post production, and theme park participation can yield net savings up to $500,000 per year.

SUMMARY: A move to the Disney/ MGM Studios for post production strength offers major strategic advantage as WCW moves to close the perceived gap in production quality.

World Championship Wrestling/ Strategic Directions...

5. CAPITALIZE ON INTERNATIONAL OPPORTUNITY

In order to leverage existing assets and images WCW must develop the infrastructure to capitalize on TV, PPV, licensing and arena revenue streams in Europe and Japan. Activities over the last two years, for a variety of reasons, have been disappointing.

Changes in programming content and access to alternative distribution systems offer compelling advantages:

A. The Kids' Team Challenge is essential to reach children in Europe because of a culturally different view of the acceptability of television violence.

B. TNT International offers an opportunity to reach 25 million homes that were previously unreachable.

C. Distribution of product on a non-exclusive basis through other non-Turner channels should be explored.

D. Potential annual net revenue that can be harvested internationally is material:

-- Kid's Team Challenge	$ 500,000
-- International Licensing and merchandising	$ 500,000-
1,000,00	
-- Tour revenue	$ 1,000,000

> **CONCLUSION: The development of an infrastructure to leverage our assets and images in television, arenas, and merchandising offers $2- 2.5 million in potential net revenue over the next 5 years.**

World Championship Wrestling/ Strategic Directions...

6. EXPAND SPONSORSHIP DEVELOPMENT EFFORTS

During 1995 WCW successfully engaged Slim Jim in our first sponsorship event. The arrangement has been an unqualified success bringing a net contribution of $250,000 to the bottom line. At a minimum, this cost abatement strategy offers earnings improvement of over $1,000,000 exclusive of ad buys in 1996.

The Sponsorship Package:

-- Structured like entertainment road show tour promotion

-- Includes participation in all WCW venues: Arena, telecast, PPV

-- Strategy involves primary sponsor and secondary complementary sponsorships

1996 Tactical Plan:

-- 9 Pay-Per-Views, all merchandizable

-- Slim Jim already committed for one event

-- Other high potential prospects include:

Snack Foods	Toys
Juices	Trucks
Soft Drinks	Auto Parts
Fast Food	Personal Care Products
Retailers	Cereals
Cameras	Beer

CONCLUSION: Early successes indicate that we have just scratched the surface on this previously unharvested opportunity. The potential is extraordinary for reducing the net cost of producing an event.

WCW MAIN EVENT

:55 Format with Terminal Break

SHOW#: T-796		EDIT DATE: 1/2/96		AIRDATE: 1/7/96	

SOURCE: Various

		Elem Time	Seg Time	Run Time	Back Time
SEGMENT 1	Hot Open (Giant/Hogan/Savage from Nitro 096)	0:00:41			
	Gene Okerlund and Bobby Heenan on Set	0:00:58			
	Hugh Morris VS Dino Cassanova	0:05:07			
	Voices of Tony Schiavone and Dusty Rhodes				
	Eric Bischoff interviews Mike Ditka	0:02:00			
	Opening Billboard	0:00:07	0:08:53	0:08:53	
COMMERCIAL BREAK 1			0:02:15	0:11:08	
SEGMENT 2	Clash of the Champions Update #1 (TBS VERSION)	0:02:00			
	Promotional Considerations	0:00:33			
	Gene Okerlund and Bobby Heenan on Set	0:00:49			
	Sting VS Sgt. Craig Pittman	0:06:21			
	Voices of Tony Schiavone and Bobby Heenan				
	Bumper #2	0:00:05	0:09:48	0:20:56	
COMMERCIAL BREAK 2			0:02:30	0:23:26	
SEGMENT 3	Gene Okerlund and Bobby Heenan on Set	0:01:34			
	World TV Title				
	Johnny B. Badd VS Dave Taylor	0:04:14			
	Voices of Tony Schiavone & Dusty Rhodes				
	Bumper #3	0:00:05	0:05:53	0:29:19	
COMMERCIAL BREAK 3			0:02:30	0:31:49	
SEGMENT 4	Gene Okerlund and Bobby Heenan on Set	0:00:53			
	Four VS Men at Work	0:03:23			
	Horsemen Joey Maggs, Frankie Lancaster				
	Voices of Chris Cruise; Larry Zbyszko & Dusty Rhodes				
	Bumper #4	0:00:06	0:04:22	0:36:11	
COMMERCIAL BREAK 4			0:03:00	0:39:11	
SEGMENT 5	Gene Okerlund and Bobby Heenan on Set	0:01:13			
	Disco Inferno VS Alex Wright	0:07:05			
	Voices of Tony Schiavone & Dusty Rhodes				
	Closing Billboard	0:00:08			
	Bumper #5	0:00:10	0:08:36	0:47:47	
COMMERCIAL BREAK 5			0:02:45	0:50:32	
SEGMENT 6	Promotional Considerations	0:00:43			
	Gene Okerlund and Bobby Heenan on Set	0:01:22			
	Music Close	0:00:08	0:02:13	0:52:45	
TERMINAL BREAK			0:02:15	0:55:00	
				UNDER	########
	TOTAL RUN TIME	0:55:00		OVER	0:00:00

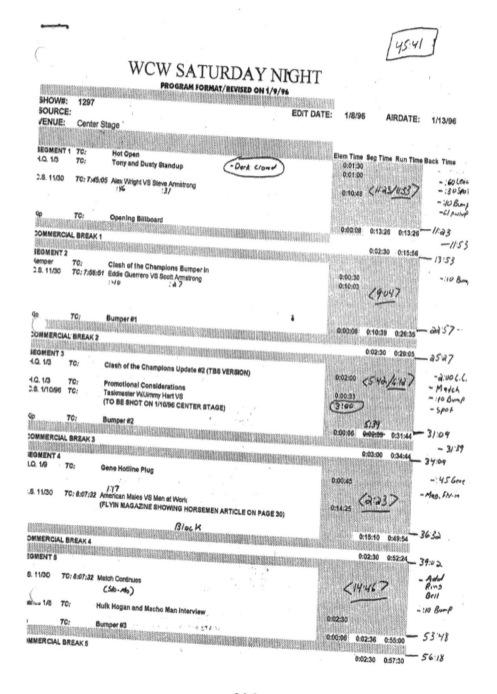

45:41

WCW SATURDAY NIGHT
PROGRAM FORMAT/REVISED ON 1/9/96

SHOW#: 1297
SOURCE:
VENUE: Center Stage

EDIT DATE: 1/8/96   AIRDATE: 1/13/96

SEGMENT 1	TC;	Hot Open		Elem Time	Seg Time	Run Time	Back Time
A.Q. 1/3	TC;	Tony and Dusty Standup	-Dark crowd	0:01:30			
				0:01:00			-:60 Lesee
C.S. 11/30	TC: 7:43:05	Alex Wright VS Steve Armstrong					-:30 Spot
		:16 :31		0:10:48	11:23/11:53		-:10 Bump
							-:61 pullup
Op	TC;	Opening Billboard					
				0:00:08	0:13:26	0:13:26	11:23
COMMERCIAL BREAK 1							
							-11:53
SEGMENT 2					0:02:30	0:15:56	13:53
Kemper	TC;	Clash of the Champions Bumper in					
C.S. 11/30	TC: 7:56:51	Eddie Guerrero VS Scott Armstrong		0:00:30			-:10 Bum
		:41 :27		0:10:03	9:47		
Op	TC;	Bumper #1					
				0:00:06	0:10:39	0:26:35	22:57
COMMERCIAL BREAK 2							
					0:02:30	0:29:05	25:27
SEGMENT 3							
A.Q. 1/3	TC;	Clash of the Champions Update #2 (TBS VERSION)		0:02:00	5:40/6:12		-2:00 C.C.
A.Q. 1/3	TC;	Promotional Considerations					- Match
C.S. 1/10/96	TC;	Tasiemaster W/Jimmy Hart VS		0:00:33			-:10 Bump
		(TO BE SHOT ON 1/10/96 CENTER STAGE)		3:00			- Spot
Op	TC;	Bumper #2			5:39		
				0:00:06	0:02:39	0:31:44	31:09
COMMERCIAL BREAK 3							
							- 31:39
SEGMENT 4					0:03:00	0:34:44	34:09
I.Q. 1/8	TC;	Gene Hotline Plug					
				0:00:45			-:45 Gene
C.S. 11/30	TC: 8:07:32	American Males VS Men at Work					- Mag. Fly-in
		:17			2:23		
		(FLYIN MAGAZINE SHOWING HORSEMEN ARTICLE ON PAGE 30)		0:14:25			
		Black					
COMMERCIAL BREAK 4				0:15:10	0:49:54		36:32
SEGMENT 5					0:02:30	0:52:24	39:02
C.S. 11/30	TC: 8:07:32	Match Continues					- Add
		(Slo-Mo)			14:46		Ring
							Bell
Gene 1/8	TC;	Hulk Hogan and Macho Man Interview					-:10 Bump
	TC;	Bumper #3		0:02:30			
				0:00:06	0:02:36	0:55:00	53:48
COMMERCIAL BREAK 5							
					0:02:30	0:57:30	56:18

	TC:	Tony Cover Pitch	0:00:15		— 56:18
2/26	TC:	Kensuke Sasaki VS One Man Gang	0:02:00	~ :10 B~
		(Match was shot in Nashville AFTER Starrcade and must be voiced by		⟨2:03/2:53⟩	~ Spot
		Tony and Dusty)		~vo Repay

| p | TC: | Bumper #4 | 0:00:06 0:02:21 0:59:51 — 58:41 |

COMMERCIAL BREAK 6 — 59:1
0:03:00 1:02:51 — 0:00:0

SEGMENT 7

Q. 1/10/96	TC:	Tony and Dusty On Camera	0:01:00	— :60 Leo
ro 097	TC:	Nitro Footage (Hulk/Savage VS Flair/Arn) – Giant after* / 2ed/ac – hold,	0:01:30	⟨12:31⟩	— :10 Bump
S. 11/30	TC: 8:22:50	V.K. Wallstreet VS J.L. (Slo-Mo) '87	0:09:05	— Spot+
	:37	(CHRYON PHONE NUMBERS FOR SUPERBRAWL TIXS DURING MATCH)		— 2:30 Fl
er 1/6	TC:	Ric Flair and Giant interview	0:02:30	— h31
	TC:	Bumper #5 O+H~	0:00:06 0:14:11 1:17:02

COMMERCIAL BREAK 7
0:02:30 1:19:32 — 15:01

SEGMENT 8

2. 1/10/96	TC:	Tony and Dusty On Camera	0:01:00	⟨6:24/7:59⟩	— :60 Lead
#1	TC:	Mike Ditka interview Part #2 (5:18)	0:00:00	— :10 Bum/
				— Spot
	TC:	Bumper #6 :10	6:28 0:00:06 0:00:06 1:20:38	— 21:30
				— 22

COMMERCIAL BREAK 8
0:03:00 1:31:38 — 24:30

SEGMENT 9

	TC:	Gene Hotline Plug and Main Event Promo	0:01:00	— :60 Gene
L	TC:	Promotional Considerations	0:00:43	⟨6:07⟩
. 1/6/96	TC: 8:35:30	Meng W/Hugh Morris VS Dusty Wolfe	0:03:10	— 1:30
	:50			M+o
	TC:	Nitro Package – Luger/Sting / Finish / Benoit / Sting DDT/ Hogan	0:01:00	
		Friction / ROH / Finish		
	TC:	Nitro Promo Lehsh	0:00:30	
			0:06:23 1:38:01 — 30:37

COMMERCIAL BREAK 9
0:03:15 1:41:16 — 33:52

SEGMENT 10

1/10	TC:	Gene W/Col. Parker and Sherri	0:02:30
1/6/96	TC:	Ric Flair VS Macho Man Randy Savage
		(TO BE SHOT ON 1/10/96 CENTER STAGE)
		0:02:30 1:43:46

COMMERCIAL BREAK 10
0:03:15 1:47:01

SEGMENT 11   :11 B.B.

1	TC:	Match Begins and Ends
1/3	TC:	(Slo-Mo)	⟨2:51⟩
1/10	TC:	Tony Close with Hogan and Savage (2:30)
		(TO BE SHOT ON 1/10/96 CENTER STAGE)
	TC:	Music Close
		0:00:10 0:00:10 1:47:11

FINAL BREAK

307

PROGRAM NUMBER: 1298 Page #1
PROGRAM AIR DATE: Saturday, January 20, 1996
PROGRAM RECORDED: Wednesday, January 10, 1996 Center Stage
Note: This Program Airs Two Days Before The Clash Of The Champions
Crowd Warm Up
TC: 6:24:04 Cheers
TC: 6:25:22 Boos
Reel Name: 1297-1298-1299 Center Stage 1/10/96

SEGMENT #1

PRE-BUILT:	(1:31) OPEN		
H.Q. TBA:	(1:00) TONY-DUSTY OPEN & Pitch To Ring		
RING:	1-M		2-M *Ring Announce On Line*
	CHRIS BENOIT	VS	EDDIE GUERRERO
	w/Flyin Brian		
Match Note:	Match Begins...		

TC: 6:52:42
RT: 7:35 w/o Slo Mo
Notes: 6:53:48 Crane Cam In Shot   6:53:45 Crane
        Need To Break Match In Post   6:54:25 Cam 1-Lose Crane
        6:56:47 Weak Boot   6:55:28 VT Z-Lose Crane Shot Of Eddie w/Two Horsemen
        6:58:19 Pilman Chokes Eddie On The Floor   6:56:47 Boot
        6:59:03 Talk   6:57:13 Cam 1
        6:59:31 Pilman Pushes Benoit Accidentally On Ring Apron   6:57:54 Cam 1
                                          6:59:00 Talk-Cam 1
                                          6:59:47
                                          7:00:00

BILLBOARDS: (12) OPENING   Twix
BUMPER: (:06)

CM POSITION #1   (2:30)/Spot A (:30) Calling Card Spot

SEGMENT #2

RING: MATCH CONTINUES & ENDS...
PRETAPE: (1:30) GENE OKERLUND W/EDDIE GUERRERO re: Flyin' Brian & Clash Of The Champions
        Pitch To Break
TC: 4:16:14
RT: 1:28
BUMPER: (:06)

CM POSITION #2   (2:30)

SEGMENT #3

TAPE: (33) PROMOTIONAL CONSIDERATIONS
CONTROL CENTER: (2:00) CLASH OF THE CHAMPIONS UPDATE #3

RING:	1-M	In Ring
	SCOTT NORTON VS	Bill Payne
Match Note:	Match Begins & Ends In This Segment	

TC: 7:03:16
RT: 2:23 w/o Slo Mo
Notes: 7:04:40 Talk   7:03:54 Good Boos VT Z
PRETAPE: (1:30) GENE OKERLUND W/SCOTT NORTON re: I'm Here In WCW!
TC: 4:06:06
RT: 1:17
BUMPER: (:06)

CM POSITION #3   (3:00)/Spot A (:30) 1-900 Spot

PROGRAM NUMBER: 1298   Page #2
PROGRAM AIR DATE: Saturday, January 20, 1996
PROGRAM RECORDED: Wednesday, January 10, 1996   Center Stage
Note: This Program Airs Two Days Before The Clash Of The Champions
Crowd Warm Up
TC: 6:24:04 Cheers
TC: 6:25:22 Boos
Reel Name: 1297-1298-1299 Center Stage 1/10/96

SEGMENT #4

HOTLINE: (:45) GENE OKERLUND W/HOTLINE PLUG Pitch To Ring
RING: 1-M   In Ring
    BUNKHOUSE BUCK   VS   MEN AT WORK
    DIRTY DICK SLATER
    W/COL. ROBERT PARKER
Match Note: Sister Sherri Out During This Match
    Match Begins & Ends During This Segment
TC: 7:08:00
RT: 5:25 w/Slo Mo
Notes: Sister Sherri Didn't Come Out   Sherri At Entrance (To Be Added) TC: 8:54:44
BUMPER: (:05)

CM POSITION #4   (2:30)

SEGMENT #5

BUMP IN: (:30) CLASH OF THE CHAMPIONS
RING: 1-M   2-M   Ring Announce On Line
    BIG BUBBA   VS   ARN ANDERSON
Match Note: Hacksaw Jim Duggan Out & V.K. Wallstreet Out During This Match
    Match Begins & Ends In This Segment
TC: 7:14:23
RT: 7:10 w/o Slo Mo
Notes: 7:20:00 Wallstreet Out
    7:20:16 Hacksaw Jim Duggan Out- VT Z
    7:20:29 Hacksaw Taped Arn's Fist
    7:21:00 Arn Hits Bubba w/Punch By Taped Fist
NITRO 1/15:   (3:00) GENE OKERLUND W/HULK HOGAN & MACHO MAN RANDY SAVAGE
    re: WCW Monday Nitro 1/22/96 & Clash Of The Champions
    Pitch To Break
    (To Be Done On Monday 1/15/96 Miami, Florida)-Neal's Project
BUMPER: (:05)

CM POSITION #6   (2:30)

SEGMENT #6

PRETAPE: (1:00) GENE OKERLUND W/DIAMOND DALLAS PAGE
TC: 4:52:54   RT: 1:15
RING: 1-M   In Ring
    TASKMASTER W/HART   VS   Chris Nelson
Match Note: Match Begins & Ends In This Segment
TC: 7:22:41
RT: 2:46 w/o Slo Mo
Notes: 7:23:44ish Taskmaster Uses Chair
    7:24:22ish Taskmaster Uses Hulk's Ear Sign
PRETAPE: (2:30) GENE OKERLUND W/TASKMASTER & JIMMY HART re: Disco Inferno
    Gene Pitch To Break
TC: 4:09:00
RT: 2:09
CM POSITION #8   (3:00) (Spot A (:30) Calling Card Spot

PROGRAM NUMBER:	1298 Page #3
PROGRAM AIR DATE:	Saturday, January 20, 1996
PROGRAM RECORDED:	Wednesday, January 10, 1996 Center Stage

SEGMENT #7

TBA:	(:30) TONY-DUSTY Pitch To Nitro Footage	
PACKAGE:	(1:00) WCW MONDAY NITRO FOOTAGE	
PROMO:	(:30) WCW MONDAY NITRO	
RING:	1-M U.S. Champion	In Ring
(1:30)	ONE MAN GANG VS	GIANT NINJA WARRIOR
Match Note:	Match Begins & Ends In This Segment	
TC:	7:27:22	
RT:	2:56 w/o Slo Mo	
Notes:	Gang w/ U.S. Title Belt	
PRETAPE:	(1:30) GENE OKERLUND W/ONE MAN GANG re: WCW Monday Nitro vs. Hulk Hogan	
	& U.S. Title	
	Gene Pitch To Ring	
TC:	4:02:01	
RT:	1:17	
RING:	1-M	In Ring
	FLYIN' BRIAN VS	Todd Morton
Match Note:	Match Begins & Ends In This Segment	
TC:	7:32:55	
RT:	6:25 w/o Slo Mo	
Notes:	7:35:20 Good Pillman Four Horsemen Sign Shot On Line	
	Pillman Flips Off Crowd At The End Of Match	
	Finish Screwed Up	
PRETAPE:	(1:30) GENE OKERLUND W/FLYIN' BRIAN re: Paul Orndorff & Eddie Guerrero	
	Gene Pitch To Break	
TC:	4:25:00	
RT:	1:54	
BUMPER:	(:08)	

CM POSITION #7   (2:30)

SEGMENT #8

BUMP IN:	(:30) CLASH OF THE CHAMPIONS		
RING:	1-M	2-M	Ring Announce On Line
	DEAN MALENKO VS	ALEX WRIGHT	
Match Note:	Match Begins & Ends In This Segment		
TC:	7:41:04		
RT:	7:45 w/o Slo Mo		
Notes:	7:42:08ish Good Alex Chant On Line	7:57:13 Fuck	8:06:38 Cam 1
	Malenko Trying To Break Alex's Leg-Alex Submits	7:57:46 Back	8:07:50 Cam 1
		8:04:40 VT Z Sooner	
		8:05:37 Spit	
		8:05:55 Cam 1	
PRETAPE:	(1:00) GENE OKERLUND W/JOHNNY B. BADD & DIAMOND DOLL		
TC:	4:55:20		
RT:	1:18		
BUMPER:	(:08)		

CM POSITION #8   (3:00)

PROGRAM NUMBER: 1298   Page #4
PROGRAM AIR DATE: Saturday, January 20, 1996
PROGRAM RECORDED: Wednesday, January 10, 1996   Center Stage
Note: This Program Airs Two Days Before The Clash Of The Champions
Crowd Warm Up
TC: 6:24:04 Cheers
TC: 6:25:22 Boos
Reel Name: 1297-1298-1299 Center Stage 1/10/96

SEGMENT #9

SET: (1:00) HOTLINE PLUG & MAIN EVENT PROMO Pitch To Jim Belushi Feature
FEATURE: (6:00) JIM BELUSHI INTERVIEW W/ERIC BISCHOFF-Neal's Project
COVER PITCH: (:15) TONY
PRETAPE: (1:30) TONY SCHIAVONE W/LEX LUGER & STING re: WCW Monday Nitro 1/22 & Clash
                Tony Pitch To Break

TC: 4:58:50
RT: 1:28
RING: WCW World Tag Team Title Match
                1-M World Tag Champions   2-M   Ring Announce On Line
                HARLEM HEAT   VS   LEX LUGER
                W/SISTER SHERRI   STING-Use Sting's Music
Match Note: Match Begins...
TC: 7:56:43
RT: 11:57 w/o Slo Mo
Notes: 7:57:07ish Harlem Heat Says FUCK
        Harlem Heat Tells Sherri That She Isn't With Them Anymore...Go Get Married
        7:57:33 Sherri Leaves Arena
        There Will Be A Return Match At The Clash Of The Champions 1/23/96 In Las Vegas, NV
        8:07:40 Lex Dumps Heat Over Top Rope..D.Q. (Sting Thinks They Have Won)
BUMPER: (:08)

CM POSITION #9   (3:15)/Spot A (:30)1-900 Spot

SEGMENT #10
RING: MATCH CONTINUES & ENDS...
BUMPER: (:08)

CM POSITION #10 (3:15)

SEGMENT #11
BILLBOARDS: (:12) CLOSING Slim Jim
TAPE: (:33) PROMOTIONAL CONSIDERATIONS
PROMO: (:30) NEXT WEEK PROMO
CLOSE: (2:00) SPLIT SCREEN INTERVIEW W/RANDY SAVAGE & RIC FLAIR
                re: WCW Monday Nitro 1/22 & Clash
                (This Interview To Be Done In The Studio On 1/17/95) -Neal's Project
MUSIC CLOSE   (:10)

TERMINAL BREAK   (2:15)

PROGRAM NUMBER: 1299   Page #1-Revised 1/13/96
PROGRAM AIR DATE: Saturday, January 27, 1996
PROGRAM RECORDED: Wednesday, January 10, 1996   Center Stage
Notes: WCW main Event Is Pre-Empted Tomorrow Night Due To An Andy Griffith Marathon
         Directly Following WCW Saturday Night...Jaws On TBS Award Saturday
         This Program Airs One Week After The Clash Of The Champions!!!
         SuperBrawl 2 Weeks Away...St. Petersburg, FL-Bayfront Center-Sunday, Feb. 11th

SEGMENT #1

PRE-BUILT:	(1:31) OPEN From WCW Monday Nitro 1/22/96 TNT099
H.Q. TBA:	(1:00) TONY-DUSTY OPEN & Pitch To Ring
RING:	1-M In Ring
	DIAMOND DALLAS PAGE VS Steve Armstrong
Match Note:	Match Begins & Ends In This Segment
TC: 8:09:37	
RT: 4:39 w/o Slo Mo	
Notes: 8:11:03 Page Falls Down & Weak Punches 8:12:23 Cam 1 To VT Z 8:13:28 Talk	
PRETAPE 1/17/96:	(1:30) GENE OKERLUND W/DIAMOND DALLAS PAGE re: SuperBrawl -Challenge To Badd
Interview Note:	Needs To Be Spritz Down, They Just Wrestled
	Gene Pitch To Break
BILLBOARD	(:12) OPENING
BUMPER:	(:06)

CM POSITION #1   (2:30)/Spot A (:30) Calling Card Spot

SEGMENT #2

CLASH UPDATE:	(2:00) FOOTAGE FROM THE CLASH OF THE CHAMPIONS
RING:	1-M In Ring
	LORD STEVEN REGAL VS Dusty Wolff
	w/Jeeves
Match Note:	Belfast Bruiser Out During This Match
TC: 8:15:38	
RT: 4:55 w/o Slo Mo	
Notes: 8:19:05 Belfast Bruiser Out Pull Up Entrance	
	8:19:40 Clothesline On Floor
	Decks Pee Wee 8:20:10 Drops Elbow On Regal 8:20:26 Great Kick...Out On Kick
	Mentions His Name Is Dave Findley...
BUMPER:	(:06)

CM POSITION #2   (2:30)

SEGMENT #3

TAPE:	(:33) PROMOTIONAL CONSIDERATIONS
CONTROL CENTER:	(1:30) SUPERBRAWL #1-PART #1 Pitch To Ring
RING:	WCW World Television Title Match
	1-M 2-M Ring Announce On Line
	JOHNNY B. BADD VS MENG
	W/DIAMOND DOLL
Match Note:	Match Begins & Ends During This Segment...
TC: 8:24:03	
RT: 10:55 w/o Slo Mo	
Notes: 8:29:09 Badd Over The Top Rope On Meng	
	8:32:35 Meng Tags DDP In & Badd Pins DDP ??? Weird
	8:27:06 VT Z 8:27:40 Back 8:31:50 Cam 1
PRETAPE 1/18/96:	(1:30) GENE OKERLUND W/JOHNNY B. BADD & DIAMOND DOLL re: SuperBrawl
Interview Note:	Needs To Be Spritz Down, They Just Wrestled...Gene Pitch To Break Badd Turns Down
BUMPER:	(:06) Challenge From Page

CM POSITION #3   (3:00)/Spot A (:30) 1-900 Spot

PROGRAM NUMBER: 1299   Page #2-Revised 1/13/96
PROGRAM AIR DATE: Saturday, January 27, 1996
PROGRAM RECORDED: Wednesday, January 10, 1996   Center Stage
Notes: WCW Main Event Is Pre-Empted Tomorrow Night Due To An Andy Griffith Marathon
Directly Following WCW Saturday Night...Jaws On TBS Award Saturday
This Program Airs One Week After The Clash Of The Champions!!!
SuperBrawl 2 Weeks Away...St. Petersburg, FL-Bayfront Center-Sunday, Feb. 11th

SEGMENT #4

COVER PITCH:	(:15) TONY
PRETAPE 1/18/96:	(2:00) GENE OKERLUND W/LEX LUGER & STING re: SuperBrawl vs. Harlem Heat In Return
Interview Note:	Sting Needs To Wear Same Face Paint To The Ring Tonight In World Tag Team Title
	Gene Pitch To Ring
FOOTAGE:	(1:00) HARLEM HEAT VS. STING & LUGER FINISH FROM 1298 SEGMENT #10
RING:	1-M 2-M Ring Announce On Line
	BARRIO BROTHERS VS **LEX LUGER**
	STING (Use Sting's Music)

Match Note:	Match Begins & Ends During This Segment
TC:	8:33:54
RT:	4:50 w/o Slo Mo
Notes:	8:38:00ish Great Stinger Splash & Goes Into Lex Torture & Scorpion Death Lock... Finish COOL
	8:36:50 Cam 1
	8:37:18 VT Z
	8:38:10 Cam 1
	8:38:33 Cam 1
BUMPER:	(:06)

CM POSITION #4   (2:30)

SEGMENT #5

HOTLINE:	(:45) GENE OKERLUND W/HOTLINE PLUG Pitch To Ring
RING:	1-M 2-M Ring Announce On Line
	JOEY MAGGS VS V.K. WALLSTREET
	W/TEDDY LONG
Match Note:	Disco Out Dancing First
	Sgt. Craig Pittman Out During This Match...Follow Pittman Backstage To Talk With Teddy Long
	Match Begins & Ends In This Segment

TC:	8:40:24		
RT:	9:58 w/o Slo Mo		
Notes:	8:41:27 Disco Inferno Out??? Screwd Up	8:42:46 Cam 1	8:42:55 VT X
	8:42:07 Wallstreet's Music	8:47:05 Jump Iso	
	8:42:30 Wallstreet Tells Disco To Get Outta Here...	8:47:53 Cam 1	
	8:46:36 Bell Rings For DQ		
	8:26:57 Pittman Out		
	8:47:30 Stockmarket Crash On Pittman		
	8:48:01 Teddy On Wallstreet's Back		
	8:49:05 Pittman Asks Pittman "Will You Manage Me"?		
	Teddy Long "I Trust You"!		

TAKE #2 Pittman	
TC:	8:52:16
RT:	1:00-Use This One!
Notes:	Will You Manage Me? By Pittman
	Teddy Can I Trust Ya?
	Handshake...
BUMPER:	(:06)

CM POSITION #5   (2:30)

PROGRAM NUMBER:	1299 Page #3
PROGRAM AIR DATE:	Saturday, January 27, 1996
PROGRAM RECORDED:	Wednesday, January 17, 1996 Center Stage

SEGMENT #6

BUMP IN:	(:30) SUPERBRAWL
RING 1/17/96:	Handicap Match

1-M			In Ring
GIANT		VS	_____
W/TASKMASTER & JIMMY HART			

Match Note:	Three Additional Men Out During This Match-They Will Come Out Of Shoot Not Entrance
	Match Begins & Ends In This Segment
PRETAPE 1/17/96:	(2:30) GENE OKERLUND W/TASKMASTER - GIANT & JIMMY HART re: SuperBrawl
	Gene Pitch To Break

CM POSITION #6   (3:00) /Spot A (:30)

SEGMENT #7

TBA:	(:30) TONY-DUSTY Pitch To Nitro Footage
PACKAGE:	(1:00) WCW MONDAY NITRO FOOTAGE
PROMO:	(:30) WCW MONDAY NITRO

RING 1/17/96:	1-M		2-M	Ring Announce
	ALEX WRIGHT	VS	RIC FLAIR	On Line

Match Note:	Match Begins...

CM POSITION #8   (3:00)

SEGMENT #9

RING:	MATCH CONTINUES & ENDS...
LIVE INTERVIEW:	(2:30) TONY SCHIAVONE W/RIC FLAIR re: SuperBrawl
	Tony Pitch To Steve Michael Interview
FEATURE:	(5:00) STEVE MCMICHAEL INTERVIEW W/ERIC BISCHOFF-To Be Taped On 1/15/96 In Miami
BUMPER:	(:06)

CM POSITION #9   (3:15)/Spot A (:30)

SEGMENT #10

COVER PITCH:	(:15) TONY
CONTROL CENTER:	(1:30) SUPERBRAWL #1-PART #2 Pitch To Ring

RING 1/17/96:				Ring Announce On Line
	1-M		2-M	
	AMERICAN MALES	VS	HARLEM HEAT	

Match Note:	Match Begins & Ends In This Segment
PRETAPE:	(1:30) GENE OKERLUND W/HARLEM HEAT re: SuperBrawl
	Gene Pitch To Break
BUMPER:	(:06)

CM POSITION #10 (3:15)

SEGMENT #11

BILLBORDS:	(:12) CLOSING
TAPE:	(:33) PROMOTIONAL CONSIDERATIONS
COVER PITCH:	(:15) TONY
FEATURE:	(2:00) HULK HOGAN FROM WCW MONDAY NITRO
TBA:	(2:30) HULK HOGAN INTERVIEW
LIVE INTERVIEW:	(2:00) TONY SCHIAVONE W/MACHO MAN RANDY SAVAGE re: SuperBrawl
Interview Note:	Ric Flair Out During Interview
	Tony Closes Program
PROMO:	(:30) NEXT WEEK PROMO
MUSIC CLOSE:	(:10)

PROGRAM NUMBER: 1299   Page #3-Revised 1/13/96
PROGRAM AIR DATE: Saturday, January 27, 1996
PROGRAM RECORDED: Wednesday, January 17, 1996   Center Stage
Notes: WCW main Event Is Pre-Empted Tomorrow Night Due To An Andy Griffith Marathon
         Directly Following WCW Saturday Night...Jaws On TBS Award Saturday
         This Program Airs One Week After The Clash Of The Champions!!!
         SuperBrawl 2 Weeks Away...St. Petersburg, FL-Bayfront Center-Sunday, Feb. 11th

SEGMENT #10

TAPE:	(:33) PROMOTIONAL CONSIDERATIONS
COVER PITCH	(:15) TONY
FEATURE:	(2:00) HULK HOGAN FROM WCW MONDAY NITRO
TBA 1/22/96:	(2:30) HULK HOGAN INTERVIEW-This Interview Needs To Be Done On Monday 22, 1996 In Las Vegas, Nevada re: SuperBrawl vs. Giant
BILLBORDS:	(:12) CLOSING

CM POSITION #10   (3:15)

SEGMENT #11

LIVE INTERVIEW 1/17/96:	(2:00) TONY SCHIAVONE W/MACHO MAN RANDY SAVAGE re: SuperBrawl vs. Ric Flair
Interview Note:	Ric Flair Out During Interview World Title-Cage, Return
	Tony Closes Program
PROMO:	(:30) NEXT WEEK PROMO
MUSIC CLOSE:	(:10)

TERMINAL BREAK   (2:15)

PROGRAM NUMBER: 1300   Page #1

PROGRAM AIR DATE: Saturday, February 3, 1996

PROGRAM RECORDED: Wednesday, January 17, 1996   Center Stage

Notes: SuperBrawl One Week Away...St. Petersburg, FL Bayfront Arena...Sunday, Feb. 11th
Coming Up Next On TBS...TBS Award Saturday...True Grit

[handwritten top right: 51:00]

SEGMENT #1
[handwritten: 65714-BACK]

PRE-BUILT:	(1:31) OPEN
H.Q. TBA:	(1:00) TONY-DUSTY OPEN & Pitch To Footage
FOOTAGE:	(2:00) PUBLIC ENEMY VIDEO-This Video Will Be Completed By Neal Pruitt
RING: *65245 (5:40)*	1-M In Ring Ring Announce On Line
	PUBLIC ENEMY VS _____
	&
Match Note:	Match Begins & Ends In This Segment
PRETAPE 1/17/96:	(1:30) GENE OKERLUND W/PUBLIC ENEMY re: SuperBrawl - vs. Nasty Boys (Street Fight)
Interview Note:	Needs To Be Spritz Down, They Just Wrestled
	Gene Pitch To Break
BILLBOARD	(:12) OPENING
BUMPER:	(:05)

CM POSITION #1   (2:30) Spot A (:30) Calling Card Spot

SEGMENT #2
[handwritten: 70133-Back 76215-Butt 70303-Missed, 70353-Tail19 70346-70519 70413-61]

COVER PITCH:	(:15) TONY
FEATURE:	(3:00) DIAMOND DALLAS PAGE VIDEO...Neal Pruitt Project Needs To Be Complete On 1/29/96
RING: *70055 3:37*	1-M In Ring
	STING VS _____
Match Note:	Match Begins & Ends In This Segment
PRETAPE 1/17/96:	(2:00) GENE OKERLUND W/MACHO MAN RANDY SAVAGE re: SuperBrawl vs. Ric Flair
Interview Note:	Gene Pitch To Break WCW World Title-Cage
BUMPER:	(:05) This Is A Return Match

CM POSITION #2   (2:30)

SEGMENT #3
[handwritten: 70321-Backcrowd Fix start of smark'n Lose shot of Barriel in bulk 70322-Quit 71110-Back]

TAPE:	(:33) PROMOTIONAL CONSIDERATIONS
CONTROL CENTER:	(1:30) SUPERBRAWL #2-PART #1 Pitch To Ring
RING: *705400 5:48*	-WCW World Television Title Match
	1-M 2-M Ring Announce On Line
	BARRIO BROTHERS VS NASTY BOYS
Match Note:	Match Begins & Ends During This Segment
PRETAPE 1/17/96:	(1:30) GENE OKERLUND W/NASTY BOYS re: SuperBrawl vs. Public Enemy (Street Fight)
Interview Note:	Needs To Be Spritz Down, They Just Wrestled
	Gene Pitch To Break
BUMPER:	(:05)

CM POSITION #3   (3:00) Spot A (:30) 1-900 Spot

SEGMENT #4
[handwritten: 71314-12 seconds 71583-1:00]

PREATPE 1/18/96:	(1:30) GENE OKERLUND W/JOHNNY B. BADD re: SuperBrawl vs. DDP World TV Title
Interview Note:	Pitch To Footage Maggs vs. DDP From WCW Main Event Accepts Challenge
FOOTAGE:	(1:00) MATCH FROM WCW Main Event T-791 Segment #5 DDP vs. Maggs (Maggs 1st Win)
RING: *71236 4:36*	Raw Footage Info. Center Stage 11/18 (9:17)=RT TC In = 6:43:50 TC Out = 6:53:07
	1-M 2-M Ring Announce On Line
	JOEY MAGGS VS DIAMOND DALLAS PAGE
	W/TEDDY LONG
Match Note:	Match Begins & Ends During This Segment
PRETAPE 1/17/96:	(1:30) GENE OKERLUND W/DIAMOND DALLAS PAGE re: SuperBrawl Challenge To Badd
Interview Note:	Needs To Be Spritz Down, They Just Wrestled re: WCW World TV Title
	Gene Pitch To Break
BUMPER:	(:05)

CM POSITION #4

PROGRAM NUMBER: 1300   Page #2
PROGRAM AIR DATE: Saturday, February 3, 1996
PROGRAM RECORDED: Wednesday, January 17, 1996   Center Stage
Notes: SuperBrawl One Week Away...St. Petersburg, FL Bayfront Arena...Sunday, Feb. 11th
        Coming Up Next On TBS...TBS Award Saturday...True Grit   -31:19

SEGMENT #5
                                                                    71922-C1
HOTLINE:	(45) GENE OKERLUND W/HOTLINE PLUG Pitch To Ring
RING:	WCW United States Title Match
	1-M In Ring
	ONE MAN GANG VS
Match Note:	Match Begins & Ends In This Segment
PRETAPE 1/17/96:	(2:00) GENE OKERLUND W/ONE MAN GANG re: SuperBrawl vs. Konan U.S. Title
Interview Note:	Needs To Be Spritz Down, They Just Wrestled
	Gene Pitch To Break
BUMPER:	(05)

CM POSITION #5   (2:30)

SEGMENT #6
                                            72942-C1
                                            72455-Giant Slipped
BUMP IN:	(30) SUPERBRAWL
RING:	Handicap Match
	1-M In Ring
	GIANT VS
	W/TASKMASTER & JIMMY HART
Match Note:	Match Begins & Ends In This Segment
BUMPER:	(05)

CM POSITION #6   (3:00) /Spot A (:30) WCW Magazine

SEGMENT #7
COVER PITCH:	(15) TONY
FOOTAGE:	(2:30) SPECIAL VIDEO ON HULK HOGAN & THE GIANT
PRETAPE: 1/17	(2:00) GENE OKERLUND W/TASKMASTER, THE GIANT, & JIMMY HART re: SuperBrawl
Interview Note:	Needs To Be Spritz Down, They Just Wrestled vs. Hulk Hogan
	Gene Pitch To Break
BUMPER:	(05)

CM POSITION #7   (2:30)

                                                                          -25:46

SEGMENT #8
                        72924-Shot   72937B+C/M
RING:	1-M 73122-C/+2	2-M	Ring Announce On Line
	MEN AT WORK VS	HARLEM HEAT	
PRETAPE 1/17/96:	(2:00) GENE OKERLUND W/HARLEM HEAT re: SuperBrawl vs. Sting & Lex Luger		
Interview Note:	Needs To Be Spritz Down, They Just Wrestled WCW World Tag Team Title-Return Match		
	Gene Pitch To Break		
BUMPER:	(05)		

CM POSITION #8   (3:00) /Spot A (:30) SuperBrawl

PROGRAM NUMBER: 1300   Page #3
PROGRAM AIR DATE: Saturday, February 3, 1996
PROGRAM RECORDED: Wednesday, January 17, 1996   Center Stage
Notes: SuperBrawl One Week Away...St. Petersburg, FL Bayfront Arena...Sunday, Feb. 11th
         Coming Up Next On TBS...TBS Award Saturday...True Grit

SEGMENT #9

TBA: (30) TONY-DUSTY Pitch To Nitro Footage
PACKAGE: (1:00) WCW MONDAY NITRO FOOTAGE
PROMO: (30) WCW MONDAY NITRO
RING: 1/18/95   (9:52)

                1-M   Ring Announce On Line
EDDIE GUERRERO *   VS.   ALEX LUGER
                                           W/JIMMY HART

Match Note: Match Begins & Ends In This Segment
BUMPER: (:05)

CM POSITION #9   (3:15)

SEGMENT #10

COVER PITCH: (:15) TONY
CONTROL CENTER: (1:30) SUPERBRAWL #2-PART #2 (Please Note We Will Release The Badd vs. Rage World TV Title Match Here...Badd Accepts In Segment #9) Pitch To Ring
RING: (10:58)
                1-M   2-M   Ring Announce On Line
DEAN MALENKO   VS   RIC FLAIR
Match Note: Match Begins & Ends In This Segment
BUMPER: (:05)

CM POSITION #10 (3:15)

SEGMENT #11

BILLBOARDS: (:12) CLOSING
TAPE: (:33) PROMOTIONAL CONSIDERATIONS
PRETAPE 1/17/96: (2:30) GENE OKERLUND W/RIC FLAIR re: SuperBrawl vs. Randy Savage For World Title-Cage
Interview Note: Needs To Be Spritz Down, They Just Wrestled   This Is A Return Match
               Gene Close Out The Program
PROMO: (30) NEXT WEEK PROMO
MUSIC CLOSE: (:10)

TERMINAL BREAK   (2:15)

318

TO-KIP BISSELL
Peachtree Post

WCW SATURDAY NIGHT

PROGRAM FORMAT/REVISED ON 2/4/96

SHOW:	1301		EDIT DATE:	2/5/96	Airdate: 2/10/96
SRCE:	1/18/96				
VENUE:	Center Stage				

			Elem Time	Seg Time	Run Time	Back Time
SEGMENT 1						
Kip	TC:	Hot Open	0:01:31			
H.Q. 1/30	TC:	Tony and Dusty Standup	0:01:00			
Nitro 101	TC:	Footage from Road Warriors VS Lex and Sting	0:01:00			
C.S. 1/18	TC: 7:04:48	Barrio Brothers VS Lex Luger and Sting	0:06:38			
		DO NOT PUT RING ANNOUNCE ON LINE				
Lakeland	TC:	Gene W/Lex and Sting	0:02:00			
H.Q.	TC:	Opening Billboard	0:00:12	0:12:21	0:12:21	
COMMERCIAL BREAK 1				0:02:30	0:14:51	
SEGMENT 2						
C.S. 1/18	TC: 4:48:25	Gene W/Belfast Bruiser	0:01:37			
		B-ROLL BELFAST BRUISER ATTACKING REGAL FROM 1299				
C.S. 1/18	TC: 7:12:53	Belfast Bruiser VS Mike Marcello	0:05:03			
Kip	TC:	Konan Music Feature	0:01:30			
Kip	TC:	BUMPER	0:00:06	0:08:16	0:23:07	
COMMERCIAL BREAK 2				0:02:30	0:25:37	
SEGMENT 3						
H.Q. 2/6	TC:	Superbrawl Control Center #3 Part A	0:01:30			
H.Q.	TC:	Promotional Considerations	0:00:33			
C.S. 1/18	TC: 7:40:55	Giant W/Jimmy Hart VS Pepe Prado and Larry Santo	0:02:47			
Lakeland	TC:	Gene W/Giant and Hart	0:02:00	① ITAKE		
Kip	TC:	BIG BOYS PLAY BUMPER	0:00:10	0:07:00	0:32:37	
COMMERCIAL BREAK 3				0:03:00	0:35:37	
SEGMENT 4						
Kip	TC:	Superbrawl VI Bumper In	0:00:15			
C.S. 1/18	TC: 24:38	Johnny B. Badd W/Diamond Doll VS Bill Payne	0:05:04			
C.S. 1/18	TC: 4:51:26	Gene W/Johnny B. Badd and Diamond Doll	0:01:46			
Kip	TC:	BUMPER	0:00:06	0:07:11	0:42:48	
COMMERCIAL BREAK 4				0:02:30	0:45:18	
SEGMENT 5						
H.Q.	TC:	Gene Hotline Plug	0:00:45			
C.S. 1/18	TC: 7:31:00	V.K. Wallstreet VS Sgt. Craig Pittman	0:07:55			
Lakeland	TC:	Gene W/Road Warriors	0:02:00	② ITAKE		
Kip	TC:	BUMPER	0:00:06	0:10:46	0:56:04	
COMMERCIAL BREAK 5				0:02:30	0:58:34	

SEGMENT 6

Kip	TC:	Superbrawl VI Bumper In	0:00:15		
H.Q. 1/29	TC:	Tony Cover Pitch	0:00:15		
Nitro	TC:	Hulk Hogan gets attacked during interview	0:01:13		
Lakeland	TC:	Gene W/Hulk Hogan	0:03:00		
Kip	TC:	BUMPER	0:00:06	0:04:49	1:03:23

COMMERCIAL BREAK 6 | | | | 0:03:00 | 1:06:23 |

SEGMENT 7

H.Q. 2/6	TC:	Tony and Dusty Standup	0:00:45		
Pruitt	TC:	Public Enemy Video	0:01:30		
C.S. 1/18	TC: 7:18:07	Nasty Boys VS Red Tyler and Manny Fernandez	0:03:21		
Lakeland	TC:	Gene W/Ric Flair	0:02:00		
Kip	TC:	Nitro Package	0:01:00		
Kip	TC:	Nitro Promo	0:00:30		
Kip	TC:	Bumper	0:00:06	0:09:12	1:15:35

COMMERCIAL BREAK 7 | | | | 0:02:30 | 1:18:05 |

SEGMENT 8

H.Q. 2/6	TC:	Superbrawl VI Control Center #3-Part B	0:01:30		
H.Q.	TC:	Promotional Considerations	0:00:33		
H.Q. 2/6	TC:	Cover Pitch	0:00:15		
Nitro 101	TC:	Horsemen VS Dungeon of Doom	0:01:00		
C.S. 1/18	TC: 6:37:14	Joey Maggs & Cobra W/Teddy Long VS Arn Anderson & Flyin' Brian	0:06:44		
Lakeland	TC:	Gene W/Arn Anderson and Flyin' Brian	0:02:30		
Kip	TC:	BUMPER	0:00:06	0:12:38	1:30:43

COMMERCIAL BREAK 8 | | | | 0:03:00 | 1:33:43 |

SEGMENT 9

H.Q. 2/5	TC:	Tony and Dusty Standup	0:01:00		
Pruitt	TC	Diamond Dallas Package from 1300	0:03:30		
Kip	TC:	BIG BOYS PLAY BUMPER	0:00:10	0:04:40	1:38:23

COMMERCIAL BREAK 9 | | | | 0:03:15 | 1:41:38 |

SEGMENT 10

H.Q. 2/6	TC:	Superbrawl VI Bumper In	0:00:15		
H.Q. 2/6	TC:	Tony Cover Pitch	0:00:15		
H.Q. 2/6	TC:	Gene Hotline Plug	0:01:00		
Nitro 101	TC:	Benoit VS Savage from Nitro 101	0:01:00		
C.S. 1/17	TC: 7:56:53	Chris Benoit VS Macho Man Randy Savage			
Kip	TC:	Closing Billboard	0:00:12	0:02:42	1:44:20

COMMERCIAL BREAK 10 | | | | 0:03:15 | 1:47:35 |

SEGMENT 11

Kip	TC:	Next Week Promo	0:00:30		
C.S. 1/17	TC: 7:56:53	Chris Benoit VS Macho Man Randy Savage	0:09:30		
Kip	TC:	Music Close	0:00:10	0:10:10	1:57:45

TERMINAL BREAK | | | | 0:02:15 | 2:00:00 |

				UNDER	########
				OVER	0:00:00
		TOTAL RUN TIME		2:00:00	

320

PROGRAM NUMBER: 1302   Page #1
PROGRAM AIR DATE: Saturday, February 17, 1996
PROGRAM RECORDED: Thursday, January 18, 1996   Center Stage

SEGMENT #1

PRE-BUILT:	(1:31) OPEN *Stills From SuperBrawl-Cage Match*	
H.Q. TBA:	(1:00) TONY-DUSTY OPEN & Pitch To Ring	
RING:	1-M	2-M *Ring Announce On Line*
	STATE PATROL VS	AMERICAN MALES
Match Note:	Match Begins & Ends In This Segment	
BILLBOARD	(12) OPENING	
BUMPER:	(06)	

CM POSITION #1   (2:30)/Spot A (:30) Calling Card Spot

SEGMENT #2

UPDATE:	(2:00) STILLS FROM SUPERBRAWL	
RING:	1-M	In Ring
	TASKMASTER VS	
	w/Jimmy Hart	
Match Note:	Match Begins & Ends In This Segment	
BUMPER:	(06)	

CM POSITION #2   (2:30)

SEGMENT #3

TAPE:	(33) PROMOTIONAL CONSIDERATIONS	
RING:	1-M	2-M *Ring Announce On Line*
	MEN AT WORK VS	SCOTT & STEVE ARMSTRONG
Match Note:	Match Begins & Ends During This Segment...	
BUMPER:	(06)	

CM POSITION #3   (3:00)/Spot A (:30) 1-900 Spot

SEGMENT #4

RING:	1-M	In Ring
	ALEX WRIGHT VS	
Match Note:	Match Begins & Ends During This Segment	
BUMPER:	(06)	

CM POSITION #4   (2:30)

SEGMENT #5

HOTLINE:	(45) GENE OKERLUND W/HOTLINE PLUG Pitch To Ring	
RING:	1-M	In Ring
	SHARK VS	
Match Note:	Match Begins & Ends In This Segment	
BUMPER:	(06)	

CM POSITION #5   (2:30)

321

PROGRAM NUMBER: 1302   Page #2
PROGRAM AIR DATE: Saturday, February 17, 1996
PROGRAM RECORDED: Wednesday, February 14, 1996   Center Stage

SEGMENT #6

BUMP IN:	(:30) UNCENSORED		
RING:	1-M		In Ring
	ARN ANDERSON		
	FLYIN' BRIAN	VS	
	CHRIS BENOIT		
Match Note:	Match Begins & Ends In This Segment		
BUMPER:	(:08)		

CM POSITION #6   (3:00) /Spot A (:30)

SEGMENT #7

TBA:	(:30) TONY-DUSTY Pitch To Nitro Footage		
PACKAGE:	(1:00) WCW MONDAY NITRO FOOTAGE		
PROMO:	(:30) WCW MONDAY NITRO		
RING:	1-M		In Ring
	PUBLIC ENEMY	VS	
Match Note:	Match Begins & Ends In This Segment		
BUMPER:	(:08)		

CM POSITION #7   (2:30)

SEGMENT #8

RING:	1-M		In Ring
	EDDIE GUERRERO	VS	
Match Note:	Match Begins & Ends In This Segment		
BUMPER:	(:08)		

CM POSITION #8   (3:00)/Spot A (:30)

SEGMENT #9

RING:	1-M		2-M Ring Announce On Line
	BLUE BLOODS	VS	STING (Sting's Music)
			LEX LUGER
Match Note:	Match Begins & Ends In This Segment		
BUMPER:	(:08)		

CM POSITION #9   (3:15)

SEGMENT #10

RING:	1-M		2-M Ring Announce On Line
	RIC FLAIR	VS	MACHO MAN RANDY SAVAGE
Match Note:	Match Begins & Ends In This Segment		
BUMPER:	(:08)		

CM POSITION #10 (3:15)

SEGMENT #11

BILLBOARDS:	(:12) CLOSING
TAPE:	(:33) PROMOTIONAL CONSIDERATIONS
TBA:	(2:00) GENE OKERLUND W/MACHO MAN RANDY SAVAGE
Interview Note:	Closes Program
PROMO:	(:30) NEXT WEEK PROMO
MUSIC CLOSE:	(:10)

TERMINAL BREAK   (2:15)

PROGRAM NUMBER:	1303 Page #1
PROGRAM AIR DATE:	Saturday, February 24, 1996
PROGRAM RECORDED:	Wednesday, February 14, 1996 Center Stage

SEGMENT #1

PRE-BUILT:	(1:31) OPEN		
H.Q. TBA:	(1:00) TONY-DUSTY OPEN & Pitch To Ring		
	WCW World Television Title		
RING:	1-M		2-M *Ring Announce On Line*
	JOHNNY B. BADD	VS	CHRIS BENOIT
	W/DIAMOND DOLL		
Match Note:	Match Begins In This Segment		
BILLBOARD	(:12) OPENING		
BUMPER:	(:06)		

CM POSITION #1   (2:30)/Spot A (:30)

SEGMENT #2

RING:	Match Continues & Ends From Segment #1
BUMPER:	(:06)

CM POSITION #2   (2:30)

SEGMENT #3

TAPE:	(:33) PROMOTIONAL CONSIDERATIONS	
CONTOL CENTER:	(1:30) UNCENSORED #1-Part #1 Pitch To Ring	
RING:	1-M	In Ring
	ONE MAN GANG	VS Pistol Pez Whatley
Match Note:	Match Begins & Ends During This Segment...	
BUMPER:	(:06)	

CM POSITION #3   (3:00) Spot A (:30)

SEGMENT #4

	WCW United States Heavyweight Title		
RING:	1-M		2-M *RAOL*
	SCOTT ARMSTRONG	VS	KONAN
Match Note:	Match Begins & Ends During This Segment		
BUMPER:	(:06)		

CM POSITION #4   (2:30)

SEGMENT #5

HOTLINE:	(:45) GENE OKERLUND W/HOTLINE PLUG Pitch To Diamond Dallas Page		
RING:	1-M		2-M *Ring Announce On Line*
	DIAMOND DALLAS PAGE	VS	SGT. CRAIG PITTMAN
			W/TEDDY LONG
Match Note:	Match Begins & Ends In This Segment...		
BUMPER:	(:05)		

CM POSITION #5   (2:30)

SEGMENT #6

BUMP IN:	(:30) UNCENSORED		
	WCW World Tag Team Title		
RING:	1-M		2-M *RAOL*
	PUBLIC ENEMY	VS	STING-Use Sting's Music
			LEX LUGER
BUMPER:	(:06)		

CM POSITION #6   (3:00) /Spot A (:30)

PROGRAM NUMBER: 1303 Page #2
PROGRAM AIR DATE: Saturday, February 24, 1996
PROGRAM RECORDED: Wednesday, February 14, 1996 Center Stage

SEGMENT #7

RING: Match Continues & Ends From Segment # 6
TBA: (:30) TONY-DUSTY Pitch To Nitro Footage
PACKAGE: (1:00) WCW MONDAY NITRO FOOTAGE
PROMO: (:30) WCW MONDAY NITRO
BUMPER: (:06)

CM POSITION #7 (2:30)

SEGMENT #8

CONTOL CENTER: (1:30) UNCENSORED #1-Part #2 Pitch To Ring
FEATURE: Footage From Universal Studios Florida ICE TRAIN VS. SCOTT NORTON
Announcer Note: Recently In Orlando, Florida This Match Took Place...
RING: 1-M 2-M
SCOTT NORTON VS ICE TRAIN **RAOL**
PRETAPE: (2:00) GENE OKERLUND W/SCOTT NORTON re: Partners...
Interview Note: Pitch To Break
BUMPER: (:06)

CM POSITION #8 (3:00)/Spot A (:30)

SEGMENT #9

RING: 1-M
ROADWARRIORS VS In Ring ~~Ring Announce On Line~~
_____

Match Note: Match Begins & Ends In This Segment
BUMPER: (:06)

CM POSITION #9 (3:15)

SEGMENT #10

RING: 1-M 2-M Ring Announce On Line
MARCUS BAGWELL VS LOCHNESS
W/JIMMY HART

Match Note: Match Begins & Ends In This Segment
BUMPER: (:06)

CM POSITION #10 (3:15)

SEGMENT #11

BILLBORDS: (:12) CLOSING
TAPE: (:33) PROMOTIONAL CONSIDERATIONS
TBA: (1:30) GENE OKERLUND W/LOCHNESS & JIMMY HART re: 3rd Person Destroyed
Interview Note: Closes Program
PROMO: (:30) NEXT WEEK PROMO
MUSIC CLOSE: (:10)

TERMINAL BREAK (2:15)

WCW [PRO] WRESTLING

Show:	TA-1202		EDIT:	2/14/96		
Venue:	Universal Studios 2-6A		AIRS:	2/17/96		

			Element	Segment	Run Time	Backtime
Segment #1		UNIVERSAL STUDIOS				
Kip	TC:	Hot Open-Stills -Superbrawl W/Commentary	0:00:41			
HQ 2/13	TC:	Cruise, Legend and Dusty Standup	0:01:00			
2-7D	TC:16:44:53	V.K. Wallstreet VS Cobra	0:05:42			
Kip	TC:	Opening Billboard	0:00:12	0:07:35	0:07:35	
CM BREAK #1		Spot A (:30)		0:02:15	0:09:50	
Segment #2						
Kip	TC:	Superbrawl Encore Bump In	0:00:15			
		WCW World TV Title				
2-6A	TC:11:57:15	Johnny B. Badd VS Squire David Taylor	0:08:41			
HQ 2/14	TC:	Nasty Boys Bumper-TONIGHT ON SAT.NIGHT	0:00:10	0:09:06	0:18:56	
CM BREAK #2				0:02:30	0:21:26	
Segment #3						
HQ 2/13	TC:	Cruise Cover Pitch	0:00:10			
Nitro102	TC:	Arn VS Hulk Hogan from Nitro	0:01:30			
HQ 2/16	TC:	Hulk Hogan Interview	0:02:00			
HQ	TC:	Promotional Considerations	0:00:33			
2-6A	TC:	Taskmaster W/Jimmy Hart VS Scott Armstrong	0:02:50			
HQ 2/14	TC:	UNIVERSAL STUDIOS BUMPER	0:00:10	0:07:13	0:28:39	
CM BREAK #3		Spot A (:30)		0:02:30	0:31:09	
Segment #4						
2-6A	TC:11:27:20	Men At Work VS Public Enemy	0:06:44			
HQ 2/14	TC:	Okerlund Hotline Plug and Pitch to Break	0:00:45			
HQ 2/14	TC:	Flair/Arn Bumper-TONIGHT ON SAT.NIGHT	0:00:10	0:07:39	0:38:48	
CM BREAK #4				0:03:00	0:41:48	
Segment #5		Cruise, Legend and Dusty Standup	0:01:00			
Kip	TC:	Superbrawl VI Stills	0:01:52			
HQ	TC:	Cruise React/Cover Pitch	0:00:15			
HQ 2/16	TC:	Macho Man Interview	0:01:30			
HQ	TC:	Promotional Considerations	0:00:33			
2-6A	TC:11:35:25	Earl Robert Eaton VS Konan	0:01:48			
HQ	TC:	Closing Billboard	0:00:12	0:07:10	0:48:58	
CM BREAK #5				0:02:45	0:51:43	
Segment #6						
2-6A	TC:11:37:26	Match Begins and Ends	0:06:25			
	TC:	Universal Studio Close	0:00:10	0:06:35	0:58:18	
TERMINAL BREAK				0:02:15	1:00:33	
					Over:	0:00:33
			1:00:00		Under:	#####

WCW [PRO] WRESTLING

| Show: | A-1203 | | EDIT: | 2/14/96 |
| Venue: | Universal Studios 2-6A | | AIRS: | 2/24-25/96 |

			Element	Segment	Run Time	Backtime
Segment #1		UNIVERSAL STUDIOS				
Kip	TC:	Hot Open-Stills -Superbrawl W/Commentary	0:00:41			
HQ 2/13	TC:	Cruise, Legend and Dusty Standup	0:01:00			
2-7D	TC:16:44:53	V. K. Wallstreet VS Cobra	0:05:42			
HQ	TC:	WCW MAGAZINE POSITION #1	0:02:00			
Kip	TC:	Opening Billboard	0:00:12	0:09:35	0:09:35	
CM BREAK #1				0:02:32	0:12:07	
Segment #2						
Kip	TC:	Superbrawl Encore Bump In	0:00:15			
		WCW World TV Title				
2-6A	TC:11:57:15	Johnny B. Badd VS Squire David Taylor	0:08:41			
wOODY	TC:	BUMPER	0:00:10	0:09:06	0:21:13	
CM BREAK #2				0:03:02	0:24:15	
Segment #3						
HQ	TC:	Promotional Considerations	0:00:33			
2-6A	TC:	Taskmaster W/Jimmy Hart VS Scott Armstrong	0:02:50			
HQ 2/14	TC:	UNIVERSAL STUDIOS BUMPER	0:00:10	0:03:33	0:27:48	
CM BREAK #3		Spot A (:30)		0:03:02	0:30:50	
Segment #4						
2-6A	TC:11:27:20	Men At Work VS Public Enemy	0:06:44			
HQ 2/14	TC:	WCW MAGAZINE POSITION #2	0:02:00			
HQ 2/14	TC:	BUMPER	0:00:10	0:08:54	0:39:44	
CM BREAK #4				0:02:32	0:42:16	
Segment #5		Cruise, Legend and Dusty Standup	0:01:00			
Kip	TC:	Superbrawl VI Stills	0:01:52			
HQ 2/14	TC:	Ric Flair W/Woman and Liz	0:01:30			
HQ	TC:	Promotional Considerations	0:00:33			
2-6A	TC:11:35:25	Earl Robert Eaton VS Konan	0:01:48			
HQ	TC:	Closing Billboard	0:00:12	0:06:55	0:49:11	
CM BREAK #5				0:03:02	0:52:13	
Segment #6						
2-6A	TC:11:37:26	Match Begins and Ends	0:06:25			
	TC:	Universal Studio Close	0:00:10	0:06:35	0:58:48	
TOTAL TIME					0:58:48	
					Over:	#####
		PROGRAM RUN TIME:	0:58:57		Under:	0:00:09

Program #: B-4902
Air Date: 2/17-18/96

SEGMENT #1

HOT OPEN/OPEN:	(:30)	
RING:	1-M	In Ring Ring Announce On Line
	Roadwarriors vs.	
		_____
Match Note:	This Match Will Be Recorded On Sunday, February 4th	
TAPE:	(:12) Opening Billboards	
BUMP:	(:10)	

CM POSITION #1   (2:32)

SEGMENT #2

RING:	1-M	In Ring
	Faces Of Fear vs.	
		_____
Match Note:	Meng & Barbarian Are The Faces Of Fear	
BUMP:	(:10)	

CM POSITION #2   (3:02)

SEGMENT #3

TAPE:	(:33) Promotional Considerations	
RING:	1-M	In Ring
	Ice Train vs.	
		_____
Match Note:	First Appearance Since Return On WCW Worldwide	
BUMP:	(:10)	

CM POSITION #3   (3:02)

SEGMENT #4

RING:	1-M	In Ring
	Renegade vs.	The Gambler
BUMP:	(:10)	

CM POSITION #4   (2:32)

SEGMENT #5

TAPE:	(:33) Promotional Considerations	
TAPE:	(:12) Closing Billboards	
RING:	1-M	2-M Ring Announce On Line
	Hugh Morrus vs.	The Giant
FLY-IN:	(:20) Hugh Morrus	
Fly-in Note:	To Be Done On Sunday, February 4th	
Match Note:	Spin The Ring...	
	Intros Only In This Segment	

CM POSITION #5   (3:02)

SEGMENT #6

RING:	MATCH BEGINS & ENDS
CLOSE(TBA):	(2:00) Gene Okerlund w/The Giant
TAPE:	(1:05) Next Week Promo & Program Close

TRT: 58:57   CM: 14:12

327

WCW MAIN EVENT

SHOW:	T-803	**EDIT:**	2/22/96
SOURCE:	Various	**AIRS:**	2/25/96

			Element	Segment	Run Time	Backtime
Segment #1						
		Hot Open	0:00:41			
		Gene and Bobby On Set	0:01:03			
		Blue Bloods VS Brad and Steve Armstrong	0:06:27			
		Voices of Tony Schiavone and Dusty Rhodes				
		WCW MOTORSPORTS	0:01:30			
		Opening Billboard	0:00:12	0:09:53	0:09:53	
CM BREAK #1		Spot A (:30)		0:02:15	0:12:08	
Segment #2						
		Uncensored Control Center-Part A	0:01:30			
		Promotional Considerations	0:00:33			
		Bobby on Set	0:00:38			
		Johnny B. Badd VS Disco Inferno	0:03:08			
		Voices of Tony Schiavone and Bobby Heenan				
		BUMPER	0:00:06	0:05:55	0:18:03	
CM BREAK #2				0:02:30	0:20:33	
Segment #3		Gene and Bobby On Set	0:00:50			
		Gene Wild Line				
		Ric Flair W/Woman VS Scotty Riggs	0:04:42			
		Voices of Chris Cruise, Dusty Rhodes & Larry Zbyszko				
		BUMPER	0:00:06	0:05:38	0:26:11	
CM BREAK #3		Spot A (:30)		0:02:30	0:28:41	
Segment #4						
		Gene and Bobby On Set	0:01:10			
		Marcus Bagwell VS Lochness	0:02:21			
		Voices of Tony Schiavone and Dusty Rhodes				
		BUMPER	0:00:06	0:03:37	0:32:18	
CM BREAK #4				0:03:00	0:35:18	
Segment #5		Gene and Bobby On Set	0:01:08			
		Promotional Considerations	0:00:33			
		Nasty Boys VS Public Enemy	0:07:33			
		Voices of Tony Schiavone and Dusty Rhodes				
		Closing Billboard	0:00:12			
		Uncensored Control Center-Part B	0:01:30			
		BUMPER	0:00:11	0:11:07	0:46:25	
CM BREAK #5				0:02:45	0:49:10	
Segment #6						
		Gene and Bobby On Set	0:00:29			
		Hulk, Macho and Buti Man Interview	0:02:00			
		Gene and Bobby On Set	0:00:55			
		Music Close	0:00:11	0:03:35	0:52:45	
TERMINAL BREAK				0:02:15	0:55:00	
					Over:	0:00:00
			0:55:00		Under:	#####

328

Program #: B-4903
Air Date: 2/24-25/96

SEGMENT #1
HOT OPEN/OPEN:	(:30)	
RING:	1-M	2-M Ring Announce On Line
	Public Enemy vs.	American Males
TAPE:	(:12) Opening Billboards	
BUMP:	(:10)	
CM POSITION #1	(2:32)	

SEGMENT #2
CONTROL CNTR:	(1:30) Uncensored #1-Part #1	
RING:	WCW United States Heavyweight Title-Return Match	
	1-M	2-M Ring Announce On Line
	One Man Gang vs.	Konan
Match Note:	*This Match Will Be Taped On Sunday, February 4th...*	
	Konan Became Champion On The Main Event Program On 2/14/96	
	They Will Wrestle At SuperBrawl On 2/11/96 For The Title Again!	
BUMP:	(:10)	
CM POSITION #2	(3:02)	

SEGMENT #3
TAPE:	(:33) Promotional Considerations	
RING:	WCW World Television Title Match	
	1-M	2-M Ring Announce On Line
	Johnny B. Badd vs.	Disco Inferno
	w/Diamond Doll	
BUMP:	(:10)	
CM POSITION #3	(3:02)	

SEGMENT #4
RING:	1-M	2-M
	Shark vs.	Dave Sullivan
BUMP:	(:10)	
CM POSITION #4	(2:32)	

SEGMENT #5
TAPE:	(:33) Promotional Considerations	
TAPE:	(:12) Closing Billboards	
CONTROL CNTR:	(1:30) Uncensored #1-Part #2	
RING:	WCW World Tag Team Title Match	
	1-M	2-M Ring Announce On Line
	Nasty Boys vs.	Lex Luger
		Sting-*Use Sting's Music*
Match Note:	*Intros Only In This Segment*	
	Jimmy Hart Out During This Match	
CM POSITION #5	(3:02)	

SEGMENT #6
RING:	MATCH BEGINS & ENDS
CLOSE(TBA):	(2:00) Gene Okerlund w/Lex Luger & Sting
TAPE:	(1:05) Next Week Promo & Program Close
TRT: 58:57	CM 14:12

329

Program #: B-4904
Air Date: 3/2-3/96

SEGMENT #1

HOT OPEN/OPEN:	(:30)		
RING:	1-M		2-M Ring Announce On Line
	Pat Tanaka	vs.	Flyin' Brian
	Lifeguard		Chris Benoit
TAPE:	(:12) Opening Billboards		
BUMP:	(:10)		
CM POSITION #1	(2:32)		

SEGMENT #2

CONTROL CNTR:	(1:30) Uncensored #2-Part #1		
RING:	1-M		In Ring
	Bobby Walker	vs.	_____
Match Note:	*Use Generic Music*		
BUMP:	(:10)		
CM POSITION #2	(3:02)		

SEGMENT #3

TAPE:	(:33) Promotional Considerations		
RING:	1-M		In Ring
	Diamond Dallas Page	vs.	_____
BUMP:	(:10)		
CM POSITION #3	(3:02)		

SEGMENT #4

RING:	1-M		In Ring
	Hacksaw Jim Duggan	vs.	Chris Kanyon
BUMP:	(:10)		
CM POSITION #4	(2:32)		

SEGMENT #5

TAPE:	(:33) Promotional Considerations		
TAPE:	(:12) Closing Billboards		
CONTROL CNTR:	(1:30) Uncensored #2-Part #2		
RING:	1-M		2-M Ring Announce On Line
	Alex Wright	vs.	Rich Flair
Match Note:	*Spin The Ring...*		
	Intros Only In This Segment		
CM POSITION #5	(3:02)		

SEGMENT #6

RING:	MATCH BEGINS & ENDS
CLOSE(TBA):	(2:30) Gene Okerlund w/Four Horsemen
TAPE:	(1:05) Next Week Promo & Program Close
TRT: 58:57	CM: 14:12

Program #: B-4905
Air Date: 3/9-10/96

SEGMENT #1

HOT OPEN/OPEN:	(:30)		
RING:	1-M		2-M Ring Announce On Line
	Barrio Brothers	vs.	American Males
TAPE:	(:12) Opening Billboards		
BUMP:	(:10)		
CM POSITION #1	**(2:32)**		

SEGMENT #2

CONTROL CNTR:	(1:30) Uncensored #3-Part #1		
RING:	1-M		2-M
	Pat Tanaka	vs.	Brad Armstrong
BUMP:	(:10)		
CM POSITION #2	**(3:02)**		

SEGMENT #3

TAPE:	(:33) Promotional Considerations		
RING:	1-M		In Ring
	V.K. Wallstreet	vs.	_____
BUMP:	(:10)		
CM POSITION #3	**(3:02)**		

SEGMENT #4

RING:	1-M		In Ring
	Roadwarriors	vs.	_____
Match Note:	To Be Recorded On Sunday, February 4th		
BUMP:	(:10)		
CM POSITION #4	**(2:32)**		

SEGMENT #5

TAPE:	(:33) Promotional Considerations		
TAPE:	(:12) Closing Billboards		
CONTROL CNTR:	(1:30) Uncensored #3-Part #2		
RING:	1-M		2-M
	Taskmaster		Arn Anderson
	Hugh Morrus	vs.	Chris Beniot
	Meng		Flyin' Brian
Match Note:	Spin The Ring...		
	Intros Only In This Segment		
CM POSITION #5	**(3:02)**		

SEGMENT #6

RING:	MATCH BEGINS & ENDS
Match Note:	Wrestling Action Continues Off The Air...
TAPE:	(1:05) Next Week Promo & Program Close
TRT: 58:57	**CM: 14:10**

Program #: B-4906
Air Date: 3/16-17/96

SEGMENT #1

HOT OPEN/OPEN:	(:30)	
RING:	WCW World Television Title	
	1-M	2-M Ring Announce On Line
	Johnny B. Badd vs.	Brad Armstrong
	w/Diamond Doll	
TAPE:	(:12) Opening Billboards	
BUMP:	(:10)	
CM POSITION #1	(2:32)	

SEGMENT #2

CONTROL CNTR:	(1:30) Uncensored #4-Part #1	
RING:	1-M	In Ring
	Kurasawa vs.	_____
	w/Col. Parker	
BUMP:	(:10)	
CM POSITION #2	(3:02)	

SEGMENT #3

TAPE:	(:33) Promotional Considerations	
Match Note:	*From Segment #2 Kurasawa Still In The Ring (Trance)*	
RING:	1-M	2-M
	Mark Starr vs.	Sgt. Craig Pittman
		w/Teddy Long
BUMP:	(:10)	
CM POSITION #3	(3:02)	

SEGMENT #4

RING:	1-M	2-M
	One Man Gang vs.	Cobra
BUMP:	(:10)	
CM POSITION #4	(2:32)	

SEGMENT #5

TAPE:	(:33) Promotional Considerations	
TAPE:	(:12) Closing Billboards	
CONTROL CNTR:	(1:30) Uncensored #4-Part #2	
RING:	1-M	2-M
	Public Enemy vs.	Nasty Boys
Match Note:	*Spin The Ring...*	
	Intros Only In This Segment	
CM POSITION #5	(3:02)	

SEGMENT #6

RING:	MATCH BEGINS & ENDS
CLOSE (TBA):	(2:00) Gene Okerlund w/Public Enemy
TAPE:	(1:05) Next Week Promo & Program Close
TRT: 58:57	CM: 14:10

Program #: B-4907
Air Date: 3/23-24/96

SEGMENT #1

HOT OPEN/OPEN:	(:30)	
RING:	1-M	2-M Ring Announce On Line
	Shark vs.	Hulk Hogan
Match Note:	*Match To Be Recorded on Sunday, February 4th*	
TAPE:	(:12) Opening Billboards	
BUMP:	(:10)	

CM POSITION #1 — (2:32)

SEGMENT #2

CONTROL CNTR:	(1:30) Uncensored #5-Part #1	
RING:	1-M	In Ring
	Big Bubba vs.	_____
BUMP:	(:10)	

CM POSITION #2 — (3:02)

SEGMENT #3

TAPE:	(:33) Promotional Considerations	
RING:	1-M	2-M
	Men At Work vs.	Harlem Heat
BUMP:	(:10)	

CM POSITION #3 — (3:02)

SEGMENT #4

RING:	1-M	2-M
	Marcus Bagwell vs.	Ric Flair
Match Note:	*Match To Be Recorded On Sunday, February 4th*	
BUMP:	(:10)	

CM POSITION #4 — (2:32)

SEGMENT #5

TAPE:	(:33) Promotional Considerations	
TAPE:	(:12) Closing Billboards	
CONTROL CNTR:	(1:30) Uncensored #5-Part #2	
RING:	1-M	2-M
	Hugh Morrus vs.	Sting
Match Note:	*Spin The Ring...*	
	Intros Only In This Segment	

CM POSITION #5 — (3:02)

SEGMENT #6

RING:	MATCH BEGINS & ENDS
Match Note:	*Dungeon Of Doom Out During This Match...*
CLOSE (TBA):	(2:00) Gene Okerlund w/Sting
TAPE:	(1:05) Next Week Promo & Program Close

TRT: 58:57   **CM: 14:10**

333

Program #: B-4908
Air Date: 3/30-31/96

SEGMENT #1		
HOT OPEN/OPEN:	(:30)	
RING:	1-M	2-M Ring Announce On Line
	Disco Infemo vs.	Brad Armstrong
TAPE:	(:12) Opening Billboards	
BUMP:	(:10)	
CM POSITION #1	(2:32)	
SEGMENT #2		
RING:	1-M	In Ring
	Ice Train vs.	_____
BUMP:	(:10)	
CM POSITION #2	(3:02)	
SEGMENT #3		
TAPE:	(:33) Promotional Considerations	
RING:	1-M	In Ring
	Scott Norton vs.	_____
BUMP:	(:10)	
CM POSITION #3	(3:02)	
SEGMENT #4		
RING:	1-M	2-M
	Barrio Brothers vs.	Sting-Use Sting's Music
		Lex Luger
BUMP:	(:10)	
CM POSITION #4	(2:32)	
SEGMENT #5		
TAPE:	(:33) Promotional Considerations	
TAPE:	(:12) Closing Billboards	
RING:	WCW United Stated Heavyweight Title	
	1-M	2-M
	Flyin' Brian vs.	Konan
Match Note:	Match To Be Recorded On Sunday, February 4th	
	Spin The Ring...	
	Intros Only In This Segment	
CM POSITION #5	(3:02)	
SEGMENT #6		
RING:	MATCH BEGINS & ENDS	
Match Note:	Wrestling Action Off The Air...	
CLOSE (TBA):	(2:00) Gene Okerlund w/Konan	
TAPE:	(1:05) Next Week Promo & Program Close	
TRT: 58:57	CM: 14:10	

Program #: T-1208
Air Date: 3/30/96

SEGMENT #1		
HOT OPEN/OPEN:	(:30)	
TBA:	(1:00) Announcers Open	
PACKAGE:	(2:00) WCW Monday Nitro Highlights	
RING:	1-M	2-M Ring Announce On Line
	State Patrol vs.	Harlem Heat
TAPE:	(:12) Opening Billboards	
BUMP:	(:10)	
CM POSITION #1	(2:15)/Spot A (:30)	
SEGMENT #2		
COVER PITCH:	(:15)	
PACKAGE:	(1:00) Still From Uncensored	
RING:	1-M	2-M
	Mark Starr vs.	Chris Benoit w/Flyin' Brian
BUMP:	(:10)	
CM POSITION #2	(2:30)	
SEGMENT #3		
TAPE:	(:33) Promotional Considerations	
RING:	1-M	2-M
	Lifeguard Steve Collins vs.	Dirty Dick Slater w/Col. Parker
BUMP:	(:10)	
CM POSITION #3	(2:30)/Spot A (:30)	
SEGMENT #4		
HOTLINE:	(:45)	
RING:	1-M	In Ring
	Hugh Morrus vs.	_____
BUMP:	(:10)	
CM POSITION #4	(3:00)	
SEGMENT #5		
TAPE:	(:33) Promotional Considerations	
TAPE:	(:12) Closing Billboards	
RING:	1-M	2-M
	Ric Flair vs.	Sting-Use Sting's Music
	Arn Anderson	Lex Luger
Match Note:	Spin The Ring...	
	Intros Only In This Segment	
CM POSITION #5	(2:45)	
SEGMENT #6		
RING:	MATCH BEGINS & ENDS	
CLOSE (TBA):	(2:00) Lex Luger & Jimmy Hart Interview	
TAPE:	(1:05) Next Week Promo & Program Close	
TERMINAL BREAK	(2:15)	

335

WORLD CHAMPIONSHIP WRESTLING
MONTHLY Line-Up REPORT
March 1996

Rank	Market	DMA %	Station	Chan	Affil	Show	Day	Time
1	New York	6.987	WCBS	2	CBS	WWW	Sat	12:30 am
2	Los Angeles	5.132	KNBC	4	NBC	WWW	Sun	1:15 am
3	Chicago	3.216	WCIU	26	Ind	WCWP	Sat	10:30 pm
	Chicago			26	Ind	WWW	Sun	6:00 pm
4	Philadelphia	2.761	WPSG	57	UPN	WWW	Sat	9:00 am
5	San Francisco	2.355						
6	Boston	2.214	WSBK	38	UPN	WWW	Fri	2:30 am
7	Washington DC	1.966	WDCA	20	Ind	WWW	Sat	10:00 am
8	Dallas/Ft. Worth	1.901	KDFI	27	IND	WWW	Sat	12:00 n
	Dallas/Ft. Worth			27	Ind	WCWP	Sun	1:30 pm
9	Detroit	1.813	WDIV	4	NBC	WWW	Sat	3:00 am
10	Atlanta	1.652	WTBS	17	CBL	WCWSN	Sat	6:05 pm
	Atlanta			17	CBL	WCWP	SAT	9:05 am
	Atlanta			17	CBL	WCWME	Sun	6:05 pm
	Atlanta/LaGrange	1.644	WGBN	33	Ind	WCWP	Sat	10:00 pm
11	Houston	1.643	KRIV	26	FOX	WWW	Sat	11:00 am
	Houston		SprtSth		Cbl	WCWP	Wed	12:30 am
12	Seattle/Tacoma	1.528	KTZZ	22	IND	WCWP	Fri	1:30 am
	Seattle/Tacoma			22	Ind	WCWSN	Sat	3a-5a
13	Cleveland/Akron	1.515	WAKC	23	ABC	WCWP	Sat	2:05 am
	Cleveland/Canton		WOAC	67	Ind	WWW	Sat	9:00 pm
14	Minneapolis	1.473	KLGT	23	Ind	WCWP	Sat	2:00 pm
	Minneapolis		KMSP	9	UPN	WWW	Sat	11:00 am
15	Tampa-St.Pete-Sar	1.456	WBSV	62	IND	WCWP	Sat	11:00 pm
	Tampa/St. Pete		WTTA	38	IND	WCWP	Sun	2:00 am
	Tampa		WTVT	13	FOX	WWW	Sat	12:00 n
16	Miami/Ft. Lauderdale	1.399	WBFS	33	UPN	WWW	Sat	4:00 am
	Miami/Ft. Lauderdale		WSVN	7	FOX	WCWP	Sun	6:00 am
17	California	1.220	KNBC	27	IND	WCWP	Sat	10:00 am
	Phoenix		KSAZ	10	FOX	WCWP	Sat	12:30 am
	Phoenix		KTVK	3	ABC	WWW	Fri	3:00 am

336

Rank	Market	DMA %	Station	Chan	Affil	Show	Day	Time
17	Phoenix		KSAZ	10	FOX	WCWP	Sat	12:30 m
	Phoenix		KUSK		Ind	WCWP	Sat	10:00 am
18	Denver	1.210						
19	Pittsburgh	1.201	WPTT	22	UPN	WWW	Sat	11:00 am
20	St. Louis	1.157						
21	Sacramento/Stockton	1.149						
22	Orlando	1.041	WRBW	65	UPN	WCWP	Sun	12:00 n
	Orlando			65	UPN	WWW	Sat	4:00 pm
	Orlando			65	UPN	WCWME	Sun	1:00 pm
23	Baltimore	1.023	WBFF	45	FOX	WWW	Sat	1:00 pm
24	Portland, OR	0.974	KWBP	32	WB	WWW	Sat	2:00 pm
25	Indianapolis	0.966	WAV	53	Ind	WCWP	Fri	8:00 pm
	Indianapolis		WTTV	4	UPN	WWW	Sun	9:00 am
26	Hartford/New Haven	0.951						
27	San Diego	0.949						
28	Charlotte	0.837	WFVT	55	WB	WCWP	Sat	11:00 am
	Charlotte			55	WB	WWW	Sat	12:30 am
	Charlotte/Hickory		WHKY	14	IND	WCWP	Fri	7:00 pm
	Charlotte/Hickory			14	IND	WWW	Thu	6:00 pm
29	Cincinnati	0.827	WBQC	25	Ind	WCWP	Sun	8:00 pm
	Cincinnati		WSTR	64	UPN	WWW	Sat	11:00 am
30	Raleigh/Durham	0.826	WKFT	40	IND	WWW	Sat	1:00 pm
	Raleigh/Durham		WRDC	28	NBC	WCWP	Sat	11:00 pm
	Raleigh/Durham		WLFL	22	FOX	WWW	Sat	12:00 n
31	Milwaukee	0.817	WDJT	58	CBS	WWW	Sat	1:00 am
	Milwaukee		WVTV	18	Ind	WCWP	Sat	12:00 n
32	Kansas City	0.814	KSMO	62	UPN	WWW	Sat	12:30 am
33	Nashville	0.799	WKZX	28	WB	WCWP	Fri	5:00 pm
	Nashville		WNAB	58	Ind	WCWP	Sat	11:00 am
	Nashville		WXMT	30	UPN	WWW	SAT	11:30 am

337

Rank	Market	DMA %	Station	Chan	Affil	Show	Day	Time
33	Nashville/Hopkinsville	0.785	WKAG	43	IND	WWW	Sun	11:00 am
	Nashville/Hopkinsville			43	IND	WCWP	Mon	5:00 pm
34	Columbus, OH	0.757	WCLS	62	LPTV	WCWP	Sat	10:00 am
	Columbus, OH		WWHO	53	WB	WWW	Sun	1:00 pm
35	Greenville/Spar/Ash	0.721	WFBC	40	Ind	WCWP	Sat	10:00 pm
	Greenville/Spar/Ash		WSPA	7	CBS	WWW	Sat	12:00 m
36	Salt Lake City	0.685						
37	San Antonio	0.666	KABB	29	UPN	WWW	Sun	11:00 am
38	Grand Rapids	0.665						
39	Buffalo, NY	0.663	W58AV	58	LPTV	WCWP	SAT	11:00 am
40	Norfolk/Portsmouth	0.646	WPEN	68	Ind	WCWP	Sun	5:00 pm
	Norfolk/Portsmouth		WTVZ	33	FOX	WWW	Sat	12:00 n
41	New Orleans	0.640	WUPL	54	UPN	WWW	Sun	1:00 pm
42	Memphis	0.632	WHBQ	13	FOX	WWW	Sat	12:00 n
43	Oklahoma City	0.611	KOKH	25	FOX	WWW	Sun	11:00 am
44	Harrisburg/Lancaster	0.604	WLYH	15	CBS	WWW	Sat	12:00 n
45	West Palm Beach	0.602	WAQ	19	Ind	WCWP	Sat	11:00 pm
	West Palm Beach		WTVX	34	UPN	WWW	Sat	10:00 am
46	Providence, RI	0.581	WPRI	12	ABC	WWW	Sun	12:30 pm
47	Greensboro/W.S.	0.577						
48	Albuquerque	0.577	KASA	2	FOX	WWW	Sun	3:30 am
49	Wilkes-Barre/Scranton	0.577	PCTN	11	LPTV	WWW	SAT	12:00 n
50	Louisville	0.567	WBNA	21	Ind	WCWP	Fri	8:00 pm
	Louisville		WFTE	58	FOX	WWW	Sat	11:30 pm
51	Birmingham	0.548	WTTO	21	FOX	WWW	Sat	12:00 n
52	Albany/Schenectady	0.529						
53	Dayton	0.523	WRGT	45	FOX/UPN	WWW	Sat	1:00 pm
54	Richmond/Petersburg	0.523						
55	Jacksonville-Brnswick	0.507	WNFT	47	UPN	WWW	Sun	11:00 pm

Rank	Market	DMA %	Station	Chan	Affil	Show	Day	Time
55	Jacksonville-Brnswick	0.507	WNFT	47	UPN	WCWP	Sat	11:00 pm
56	Fresno/Visalia	0.503	KAIL	53	UPN	WWW	Sat	9:00 am
57	Charleston/Huntington	0.500	WVAH	11	FOX/UPN	WWW	Sat	5:00 pm
58	Little Rock	0.493	KASN	38	UPN	WWW	Sat	11:00 am
59	Tulsa	0.479						
60	Flint-Saginaw-Bay Cty	0.470						
61	Pensacola/Mobile	0.455	WEAR	3	ABC	WWW	Sat	3:35 am
62	Knoxville	0.448	WKXT	8	CBS	WWW	Sat	12:00 n
63	Wichita/Hutchinson	0.443	KWCH	12	CBS	WWW	Sat	12:35 am
64	Austin	0.435						
65	Toledo	0.423						
66	Las Vegas	0.417	KUPN	21	UPN	WWW	Sun	12:00 n
67	Roanoke/Lynchburg	0.414	WSLS	10	NBC	WWW	Sat	12:00 n
68	Lexington	0.404						
69	Syracuse	0.401	WSYT	68	FOX	WWW	Sat	1:00 am
70	Honolulu	0.398						
71	Green Bay/Appleton	0.388						
72	Des Moines-Ames	0.385						
73	Rochester	0.383						
74	Spokane	0.382	KDQ	58	Ind	WCWP	Sun	1:00 pm
75	Omaha, NE	0.376						
76	Shreveport	0.374	KTBS	3	ABC	WWW	Sat	1:07 am
77	Springfield, MO	0.369	KTV	56	WB	WWW	Sun	10:30 pm
	Springfield, Mo		KTV	56	WB	WCWP	Sun	12:00 n
78	Paducah-CP Girardeau	0.366						
79	Portland/Auburn, ME	0.359						
80	Tucson	0.359						
81	Champaign/Springfield	0.349						
82	Chattanooga	0.334	WDSI	61	FOX	WWW	Sat	12:00 n

339

Rank	Market	DMA %	Station	Chan	Affil	Show	Day	Time
83	Madison, WI	0.322						
84	Ft. Myers	0.319	WSWF	10	WB	WCWP	Sat	1:00 pm
85	South Bend-Elkhart	0.318						
86	Huntsville/Dec/Flo	0.319	WYLE	26	WB	WCWP	Sat	1:00 pm
	Huntsville/Dec/Flo	0.318	WYLE	26	WB	WWW	Sat	2:00 pm
87	Cedar Rapids/Waterloo	0.317						
88	Davenport/Rock Is.	0.312						
89	Columbia	0.312	WOLO	25	ABC	WWW	Sat	11:00 am
90	Johnstown/Altoona	0.300	WWCP	8	FOX	WWW	Sun	11:00 am
91	Jackson, MS	0.299	WJTV	12	CBS	WWW	Sat	11:35 pm
92	Burlington/Plattsburg	0.299	WWIN		WB	WWW	Sun	11:00 am
	Burlington/Plattsburg	0.298	WWIN		WB	WCWP	Sat	11:00 am
93	Tri Cities	0.296	WKPT	19	ABC	WWW	Sat	11:00 am
94	Evansville	0.288						
95	Youngstown, OH	0.287						
96	Waco/Temple	0.285	KCEN	6	NBC	WWW	Sat	1:00 am
97	Colorado Springs	0.280	KOAA	5	NBC	WWW	Sat	12:05 am
98	Baton Rouge	0.274						
99	El Paso	0.268	KJLF	65	WB	WWW	Sat	5:00 pm
	El Paso	0.261	KJLF	65	WB	WCWP	Sun	11:00 pm
100	Savannah	0.265	WJCL	22	ABC	WWW	Sat	12:00 n
	Savannah		WTOC	11	CBS	WCWP	Sat	2:00 am
101	Lincoln/Hastings, NE	0.260						
102	Springfield/Holyoke	0.253						
103	Ft. Wayne	0.249	WFFT	55	FOX	WCWP	Sat	2:00 am
	Ft. Wayne			55	FOX	WWW	Sat	1:00 am
104	Greenville/N.Brn/Wash	0.247						
105	Sioux Falls, SD	0.239						
106	Lansing, MI	0.238						
107	Harlingen, TX	0.237	KGBT	4	CBS	WWW	Sat	10:30 pm

340

Rank	Market	DMA %	Station	Chan	Affil	Show	Day	Time
108	Charleston	0.245	WCIV	4	NBC	WCWP	Sat	1:30 am
	Charleston	0.235	WTAT	24	FOX/UPN	WWW	Sat	12:00 n
109	Peoria/Bloomington,IL	0.234						
110	Tyler, TX	0.233						
111	Augusta	0.231	WFXG	54	FOX	WWW	Sun	11:00 am
112	Fargo/Valley City, ND	0.227						
113	Montgomery	0.226	WCOV	20	FOX	WWW	Sat	11:00 am
114	Florence, SC	0.220	WBTW	13	CBS	WWW	Sat	12:30 pm
	Florence/Myrtle B		WGSE	43	IND	WCWP	Sat	4:00 pm
115	Santa Barbara	0.220	KSTB	57		WCWP	Sat	11:00 pm
	Santa Barbara			57	Ind	WWW	Sun	11:00 pm
116	Tallahassee	0.219	WCTV	6	CBS	WWW	Sat	6:00 am
117	Traverse City, MI	0.215						
118	Ft. Smith, AR	0.214						
119	Eugene/Roseburg	0.213	KROZ	36	IND	WCWP	Sun	8:00 pm
120	Reno	0.210						
121	Lafayette, LA	0.210						
122	Monterey/Salinas, CA	0.209						
123	Macon	0.202	WMGT	41	NBC	WWW	Sat	12:00 n
124	Yakima, WA	0.202						
125	Columbus	0.194	WRBL	3	CBS	WWW	SUN	12:00 n
	Columbus		WSWS	66	WB	WCWP	Sat	4:00 pm
126	Amarillo	0.193	KFDA	10	CBS	WWW	Sat	1:05 am
127	Boise	0.193						
128	Corpus Christi	0.186						
129	Columbus/Tupelo	0.184	WTVA	9	NBC	WWW	Sat	12:00 m
	Columbus/Tupelo	0.176	WCBI	4	CBS	WCWP	Sat	3:30 am
130	Chico/Redding, CA	0.181						
131	Wausau/Rhinelander	0.180						

	Market	DMA %	Station	Chan	Affil	Show	Day	Time
132	Bakersfield, CA	0.179						
133	Monroe/El Dorado	0.177	KNOE	8	CBS	WWW	Sun	11:00 pm
134	Duluth/Superior	0.176						
135	LaCrosse/Eau Claire	0.172						
136	Rockford, IL	0.171						
137	Beaumont/Pt Arthur	0.168						
138	Wheeling/Steubenville	0.164						
139	Wichita Flls/Lawton	0.161						
140	Topeka	0.160						
141	Sioux City	0.160						
142	Terre Haute	0.160						
143	Erie	0.160	WJET	24	ABC	WWW	Sun	1:00 am
144	Medford/Klamath Falls	0.154						
145	Joplin/Pittsburg	0.150						
146	Columbia/Jeff City,MO	0.146						
147	Mason City	0.144	KIMT	3	CBS	WWW	SAT	12:00 n
148	Bluefield	0.143	WVVA	6	NBC	WWW	Sat	2:00 pm
149	Odessa-Midland	0.143	KMID	2	ABC	WWW	Sat	11:30 pm
150	Lubbock	0.142	KJTV	34	FOX	WWW	SAT	11:00 am
151	Binghampton, NY	0.139						
152	Albany	0.138	WSST	55	IND	WCWP	Sat	3:00 pm
	Albany		WGVP	44	WB	WWW	SAT	12:30 pm
153	Minot/Bismarck, ND	0.137						
154	Bangor, ME	0.132						
155	Wilmington	0.129						
156	Anchorage	0.129	KYES	5	IND	WWW	Sun	12:00 n
157	Biloxi/Gulfport	0.126	WLOX	13	ABC	WWW	Sat	10:30 pm
158	Quincy/Hannibal	0.122						

	Market	DMA %	Station	Chan	Affil	Show	Day	Time
	Panama City	0.115						
	Ada-Ardmore, OK	0.114						
	Abilene/Sweetwater	0.113						
	Clarksburg/Weston	0.108						
163	Salisbury	0.107	WBOC	16	CBS	WWW	Sat	2:00 pm
164	Palm Springs	0.105						
165	Hattiesburg/Laurel	0.102	WHLT	22	CBS	WCWP	Sat	11:00 pm
166	Utica	0.102	WUPN	33	FOX	WWW	Fri	9:00 pm
167	Gainesville, FL	0.099						
168	Idaho Falls/Pocatello	0.098						
169	Elmira, NY	0.097						
170	Billings, MT	0.097						
171	Watertown	0.091						
172	Dothan	0.089	WTVY	4	CBS	WWW	Sat	6:00 am
173	Rapid City, SD	0.089						
174	Missoula, MT	0.087						
175	Marquette, MI	0.086						
176	Yuma/El Centro	0.086						
177	Alexandria	0.083						
178	Greenwood/Greenvile	0.081	WXVT	15	CBS	WWW	Sat	12:35 am
179	Lake Charles	0.079	KVHP	29	Fox	WWW	Sat	1:00 am
180	Jonesboro, AR	0.077						
181	Bowling Green	0.071	WGRB	34	FOX	WWW	Thu	10:00 pm
182	Meridian, MS	0.069						
183	Great Falls	0.066						
184	Parkersburg	0.064						
185	Jackson, TN	0.063						
186	Mankato, MN	0.061						

343

Rank	Market	DMA %	Station	Chan	Affil	Show	Day	Time
187	Tuscaloosa	0.060						
188	Eureka, CA	0.057						
189	Gd Junction/Montros	0.056						
190	St. Joseph	0.056						
191	Butte, MT	0.056						
192	Casper-Riverton	0.052						
193	Cheyenne(WY)/Sterling	0.052						
194	San Angelo	0.052						
195	Twin Falls, ID	0.050						
196	Lafayette, IN	0.049						
197	Laredo, TX	0.048						
198	Charlottesville	0.045						
199	Anniston, AL	0.045						
200	Ottumwa/Kirksville	0.045						
201	Harrisonburg	0.042						
202	Lima, OH	0.040						
203	Bend, OR	0.038						
204	Zanesville, OH	0.033						
205	Fairbanks	0.032						
206	Victoria, TX	0.029						
207	Presque Isle, ME	0.029						
208	Helena, MT	0.021						
209	Alpena	0.017						
210	North Platte, NE	0.015						
211	Glendive, MT	0.005						
999	Kingman	0.000	KMOH	6	IND	WCWP	Sat	2:00 pm
	Branson		KO5JQ		IND	WWW	Sat	9:00 am
	Branson				IND	WCWP	Sat	8:00 am
	St. George, UT		KSGI	4	Ind	WCWP	Sat	12:00 n

Rank	Market	DMA %	Station	Chan	Affil	Show	Day	Time
999	Ashland/Mansfield	0.000	WBP	59	Ind	WWW	Sun	12:00 n
	Fayetteville, NC		WFAY	62	FOX	WCWP	Sat	2:00 pm

WCW AT A GLANCE

World Championship Wrestling (WCW), operated by Turner Sports, has been a division of Turner Broadcasting System, Inc. since 1988. WCW built on the tradition of the National Wrestling Alliance, which began in 1906. Wrestling first started on TBS Superstation (then WTCG) in 1971 with *Georgia Championship Wrestling*.

WCW **"Where The Big Boys Play,"** features the biggest names in professional wrestling, such as Hulk Hogan, Sting, Lex Luger and Ric Flair, along with the best new talent in the world.

Each week over **20 million people** watch the heroes of WCW through one hour live on TNT prime time, four hours on TBS Superstation and three hours in syndication reaching 94 percent of U. S. television households in over 190 markets. WCW programming is also available on Prime Regional Sports Network.

WCW Monday Nitro Live On TNT is the leading prime time wrestling show in the country and the fourth highest franchise on TNT behind NFL Football, TNT Original Movies and NBA Playoffs. *WCW Saturday Night,* seen on TBS Superstation, attracts the most viewers of any weekend wrestling show.

The most watched wrestling event in history was *Clash Of The Champions* (Jan. '95) live on TBS Superstation with a 4.5 rating/6.0 share. The *Clash* special, seen twice a year, typically ranks among the top programs on basic cable.

Attracting a wide range of **demographics,** WCW programming ranks among the top five in reaching males (18-49). WCW also draws attractive audiences for kids, teens and families.

As a leader in the **pay-per-view** industry, WCW produces 10 live pay-per-view specials annually, such as *Bash At The Beach, Halloween Havoc, WCW Uncensored* and *Superbrawl.*

Fans stay aware of the latest breaking WCW news through an **interactive phone line.** The 900 number is available seven days a week, 24 hours a day.

Internationally, WCW programming reaches 85 countries in 10 languages on TNT and in syndication.

WCW sponsors the #29 Chevrolet Monte Carlo for the Diamond Ridge Motorsports team in the **NASCAR Busch Series.** WCW won the Goody's 300 in Daytona and the Hummingbird 500 in Talladega.

Licencees of **WCW products** include trading cards, posters, action figures, calling cards, apparrel and video games. **WCW Magazine** is distributed in the U.S., Canada and the UK.

Across the country each year, WCW superstars appear in over 150 live **arena shows.**

WCW releases 12 **home videos** annually through Turner Home Entertainment.

Wild Cat Willy (WCW) is the **official mascot.**

TBS WRESTLING

Date	Day	Program	Time	Notes
03/02	Sat	WCW Pro Wrestling	9:05 am - 10:05 am	
		WCW Saturday Night	6:05 pm - 8:05 pm	
03/03	Sun	WCW Main Event	Pre-Empted	
03/09	Sat	WCW Pro Wrestling	9:05 am - 10:05 am	
		WCW Saturday Night	6:05 pm - 8:05 pm	
03/10	Sun	WCW Main Event	Pre-Empted	
03/16	Sat	WCW Pro Wrestling	9:05 am - 10:05 am	
		WCW Saturday Night	6:05 pm - 8:05 pm	
03/17	Sun	WCW Main Event	6:05 pm - 7:00 pm	
03/23	Sat	WCW Pro Wrestling	9:05 am - 10:05 am	
		WCW Saturday Night	6:05 pm - 8:05 pm	
03/24	Sun	WCW Main Event	6:05 pm - 7:00 pm	Live
03/30	Sat	WCW Pro Wrestling	9:05 am - 10:05 am	
		WCW Saturday Night	6:05 pm - 8:05 pm	
03/31	Sun	WCW Main Event	6:05 pm - 7:00 pm	
04/06	Sat	WCW Pro Wrestling	9:05 am - 10:05 am	
		WCW Saturday Night	6:05 pm - 7:05 pm	- 1 Hour
04/07	Sun	WCW Main Event	6:05 pm - 7:00 pm	
04/13	Sat	WCW Pro Wrestling	9:05 am - 10:05 am	
		WCW Saturday Night	6:05 pm - 8:05 pm	
04/14	Sun	WCW Main Event	pre-empted	
04/20	Sat	WCW Pro Wrestling	9:05 am - 10:05 am	
		WCW Saturday Night	6:05 pm - 7:05 pm	- 1 Hour
04/21	Sun	WCW Main Event	6:05 pm - 7:00 pm	
04/27	Sat	WCW Pro Wrestling	9:05 am - 10:05 am	
		WCW Saturday Night	6:05 pm - 8:05 pm	
04/28	Sun	WCW Main Event	6:05 pm - 7:00 pm	
05/04	Sat	WCW Pro Wrestling	9:05 am - 10:05 am	
		WCW Saturday Night	6:05 pm - 7:05 pm	- 1 Hour
05/05	Sun	WCW Main Event	6:05 pm - 7:00 pm	
05/11	Sat	WCW Pro Wrestling	9:05 am - 10:05 am	
		WCW Saturday Night	6:05 pm - 7:00 pm	- 55 MINUTES
05/12	Sun	WCW Main Event	6:05 pm - 7:00 pm	
05/18	Sat	WCW Pro Wrestling	9:05 am - 10:05 am	
		WCW Saturday Night	6:05 pm - 7:05 pm	1 Hour
05/19	Sun	WCW Main Event	6:05 pm - 7:00 pm	
05/25	Sat	WCW Pro Wrestling	9:05 am - 10:05 am	
		WCW Saturday Night	6:05 pm - 7:00 pm	- 55 MINUTES
05/26	Sun	WCW Main Event	pre-empted	
06/01	Sat	WCW Pro Wrestling	9:05 am - 10:05 am	
		WCW Saturday Night	6:05 pm - 8:05 pm	2
06/02	Sun	WCW Main Event	6:05 pm - 7:00 pm	
06/08	Sat	WCW Pro Wrestling	9:05 am - 10:05 am	
		WCW Saturday Night	6:05 pm - 8:05 pm	2
06/09	Sun	WCW Main Event	6:05 pm - 7:00 pm	
06/15	Sat	WCW Pro Wrestling	9:05 am - 10:05 am	
		WCW Saturday Night	6:05 pm - 8:05 pm	2
06/16	Sun	WCW Main Event	6:05 pm - 7:00 pm	
06/22	Sat	WCW Pro Wrestling	9:05 am - 10:05 am	
		WCW Saturday Night	6:05 pm - 7:05 pm	- 1 Hour
06/23	Sun	WCW Main Event	6:05 pm - 7:00 pm	
06/29	Sat	WCW Pro Wrestling	9:05 am - 10:05 am	
		WCW Saturday Night	6:05 pm - 7:00 pm	55 MINUTES
06/30	Sun	WCW Special	8:00 pm - 9:00 pm	

346

Program #: T-1209
Air Date: 4/6/96

SEGMENT #1

HOT OPEN/OPEN:	(:30)
TBA:	(1:00) Announcers Open
PACKAGE:	(2:00) WCW Monday Nitro Highlights
RING:	1-M 2-M Ring Announce On Line
	Barrio Brothers vs. Hacksaw Jim Duggan
	Sgt. Craig Pittman
	w/Teddy Long
TAPE:	(:12) Opening Billboards
BUMP:	(:10)
CM POSITION #1	(2:15)/Spot A (:30)

SEGMENT #2

RING:	1-M 2-M
	Scott Norton vs. One Man Gang
BUMP:	(:10)
CM POSITION #2	(2:30)

SEGMENT #3

TAPE:	(:33) Promotional Considerations
RING:	1-M 2-M
	Men At Work vs. Public Enemy
BUMP:	(:10)
CM POSITION #3	(2:30)/Spot A (:30)

SEGMENT #4

HOTLINE:	(:45)
RING:	1-M In Ring
	Shark vs. _____
BUMP:	(:10)
CM POSITION #4	(3:00)

SEGMENT #5

TAPE:	(:33) Promotional Considerations
TAPE:	(:12) Closing Billboards
RING:	1-M 2-M
	Ice Train vs. Lex Luger w/Jimmy Hart
Match Note:	Spin The Ring...
	Intros Only In This Segment
CM POSITION #5	(2:45)

SEGMENT #6

RING:	MATCH BEGINS & ENDS
CLOSE (TBA):	(2:00) Lex Luger & Jimmy Hart Interview
Interview Note:	Sting Out During This Interview
TAPE:	(1:05) Next Week Promo & Program Close
TERMINAL BREAK	(2:15)

PROGRAM NUMBER:	1310 Page #1 (Rvd. 4/10/96)
PROGRAM AIR DATE:	Saturday, April 13, 1996
PROGRAM RECORDED:	Birmingham, AL 4/10/96

SEGMENT #1

PRE-BUILT:	(1:31)	OPEN Tease Ric Flair, Liz, Woman One On One Int. From 1309
STANDUP:	(1:00)	TONY-DUSTY OPEN/Welcome Pitch To Ring
MATCH:	(6:00)	1-M 2-M Ring Announce On Line
		AMERICAN MALES VS RIC FLAIR & GIANT Use Flair's Music
B-roll:		During Males Entrance Use (:15) Of Males Video Built By Kemper
Match Note:		Match Begins & Ends In This Segment
INTERVIEW:	(2:30)	GENE OKERLUND W/GIANT & RIC FLAIR, WOMAN, JIMMY HART,
		MISS ELIZABETH re: Nitro (TNT111) In Charleston vs. Sting & Luger
		Gene Pitch To Break
BILLBOARD:	(:12)	OPENING
BUMPER:	(:30)	Where The Big Boys Play
CM POSITION #1	(2:30)	Includes Spot A (:30) WCW May Magazine

SEGMENT #2

COVER PITCH:	(:15)	TONY Pitch To WCW Cruiserweight Package
PACKAGE:	(1:30)	WCW CRUISERWEIGHT TOURNAMENT
MATCH:	(8:00)	WCW CRUISERWEIGHT TITLE MATCH
		1-M 2-M Ring Announce On Line
		J.L. VS EDDIE GUERRERO
Match Note:		Match Begins & Ends In This Segment
BUMPER:	(:10)	Sting & Lex Luger Promoting vs. Flair & Giant This Monday On Nitro
CM POSITION #2	(2:30)	

SEGMENT #3

COVER PITCH:	(:15)	TONY Pitch To Macho Man Randy Savage One On One
FEATURE:	(3:00)	MACHO MAN RANDY SAVAGE ONE ON ONE Built By Neal Pruitt
MATCH:	(4:00)	1-M 2-M Ring Announce On Line
		DAVE SULLIVAN VS CHRIS BENOIT
Match Note:		Match Begins & Ends In This Segment
		Arn Anderson Out During This Match
INTERVIEW:	(2:00)	GENE OKERLUND W/CHRIS BENOIT & ARN ANDERSON
		re: Taskmaster
		Taskmaster/Jimmy Hart Out During Interview
		Gene Pitch To Break
BUMPER:	(:10)	Nasty Boys Promoting vs. Public Enemy This Monday On Nitro
CM POSITION #3	(3:00)	Includes Spot A (:30) N'tional Arena Combo/Local Rollover

PROGRAM NUMBER:	1310 Page #2 (Rvd. 4/10/96)
PROGRAM AIR DATE:	Saturday, April 13, 1996
PROGRAM RECORDED:	Birmingham 4/10/96

SEGMENT #4

PROMO CONSIDERATIONS:	(:33)	
HOTLINE: (4/10 HQ)	(:30)	GENE W/PLUG Pitch To Ring
MATCH:	(8:00)	1-M 2-M Ring Announce On Line
		BELFAST BRUISER VS LORD STEVEN REGAL W/JEEVES
B-roll:		During Head Of This Match (:20) Footage From 1308 Ent...1309 Int.
Match Note:		Match Begins & Ends In This Segment
		Eaton & Taylor Out During This Match
BUMPER:	(:10)	Giant/Flair/Liz/Woman Promoting vs. Sting/Luger On Nitro

CM POSITION #4   (2:30)

SEGMENT #5

BUMP IN:	(:15)	Graphics Announcing New Matchup For Slamboree...
		Tony v/o...Taskmaster & Chris Benoit vs. Public Enemy
MATCH:	(4:00)	1-M 2-M Ring Announce On Line
		COL. PARKER VS MADUSA
		W/DIRTY DICK SLATER
Match Note:		Match Begins & Ends In This Segment
BUMPER:	(:30)	Where The Big Boys Play

CM POSITION #5   (2:30)

SEGMENT #6

COVER PITCH:	(:15)	TONY Pitch To Hulk Hogan Package
FEATURE:	~~(1:00)~~	~~HULK HOGAN...Footage Showing Hogan Over Taskmaster/Arn~~
INTERVIEW: (4/10 HQ)	~~(2:00)~~	HULK HOGAN (4:15)
MATCH:	(8:00)	WCW CRUISERWEIGHT TITLE MATCH
		1-M 2-M Ring Announce On Line
		DEAN MALENKO VS BRAD ARMSTRONG
Match Note:		Match Begins & Ends In This Segment
		Need Slo Mo For 1-800 Collect...Announcers Pitch To Mo
BUMPER:	(:10)	Public Enemy Promoting vs. Nasty Boys This Monday On Nitro

CM POSITION #6   (3:00) Includes Spot A (:30) BBJ 900# Spot

349

PROGRAM NUMBER:		1310 Page #3 (Rvd. 4/10/96)
PROGRAM AIR DATE:		Saturday, April 13, 1996
PROGRAM RECORDED:		Anderson, SC 4/10/96

SEGMENT #7

COVER PITCH:	(:15)	TONY Pitch To Taskmaster/Arn Anderson Package
PACKAGE:	(1:00)	Footage From 1308 & 1309 Trouble Between Taskmaster & Arn
		Interviews Then Match Following...Start w/Huntsville Nitro Footage
		TNT108...
MATCH:	(4:00)	1-M In Ring
		TASKMASTER VS _____
		ARN ANDERSON _____
B-roll:	(:30)	Footage Showing Spine Busters, Double Stomps During Their Ent.
Match Note:		Match Begins & Ends In This Segment
INTERVIEW:	(2:30)	GENE OKERLUND W/TASKMASTER & ARN ANDERSON w/HART
		re: Nitro...Last Week On Sat. Night (Booty)
B-roll:	(:15)	B-roll From Last Week 1309 Booty/Flair Match
		Gene Pitch To Break
BUMPER:	(:10)	Hulk Hogan Promoting vs. Arn/Taskmaster This Monday On Nitro
CM POSITION #7	(2:30)	

SEGMENT #8

STANDUP:	(:30)	TONY-DUSTY Pitch To WCW Monday Nitro Footage
PACKAGE:	(1:00)	WCW MONDAY NITRO FOOTAGE Last Nitro TNT109 Booty/Hulk vs.
		Arn/Taskmaster
PROMO:	(:30)	WCW MONDAY NITRO Pitch To Gene
HOTLINE: (4/10 HQ)	(:45)	GENE OKERLUND Pitch To Ring...No Main Event Tomorrow
MATCH:	(4:00)	1-M In Ring
		STING VS Chris Kanyon
Match Note:		Mike Winner Out During This Match
		Match Begins & Ends During This Segment
INTERVIEW:	(2:00)	GENE OKERLUND W/STING & LEX LUGER re: Nitro...vs. Giant/Flair
BUMPER:	(:10)	Arn/Taskmaster Promoting vs. Hulk Hogan This Monday On Nitro
CM POSITION #8	(3:00)	Includes Spot A (:30) N'tional Arena Combo/Local Rollover

350

PROGRAM NUMBER:	1310 Page #4 (Rvd. 4/10/96)
PROGRAM AIR DATE:	Saturday, April 13, 1996
PROGRAM RECORDED:	Anderson, SC 4/10/96

SEGMENT #9

COVER PITCH:	(:15)	TONY Pitch To Ric, Liz, Woman Feature
FEATURE:	(1:30)	RIC FLAIR, MISS ELIZABETH & WOMAN Showing Woman & Liz
		Helping Ric Flair
MATCH:	(12:00)	EIGHT MAN TAG TEAM MATCH

		1-M	2-M	Ring Announce On Line
		STEINER BROTHERS	VS	ROADWARRIORS
		NASTY BOYS		PUBLIC ENEMY

Match Note:		Match Begins In This Segment....
BUMPER:	(:10)	Hulk Hogan Promoting vs. Arn/Taskmaster This Monday On Nitro
CM POSITION #9	(3:15)	

SEGMENT #10

Match Note:		Match Continues From Segment #9 & Ends In This Segment...
BUMPER:	(:30)	Where The Big Boys Play
CM POSITION #10	(3:15)	

SEGMENT #11

BILLBOARDS:	(:12)	CLOSING
NEXT WEEK PROMO	(:30)	
INTERVIEW:	(2:00)	GENE OKERLUND W/MACHO MAN RANDY SAVAGE re: Ric Flair
		Gene This Is The Closing Interview Of The Program!
MUSIC CLOSE:	(:10)	
TERMINAL BREAK	(2:15)	

Big Boys Play

Vader
Cactus Jack

Program #: B-4910
Air Date: 4/13-14/96

SEGMENT #1			
HOT OPEN/OPEN:	(:30)		
RING:	1-M		In Ring Ring Announce On Line
	Roadwarriors	vs.	
			_____
Match Note:	*Match To Be Recorded On Sunday, February 4th*		
TAPE:	(:12) Opening Billboards		
BUMP:	(:10)		
CM POSITION #1	(2:32)		
SEGMENT #2			
RING:	1-M		2-M
	Blue Bloods	vs.	Brad & Steve Armstrong
BUMP:	(:10)		
CM POSITION #2	(3:02)		
SEGMENT #3			
TAPE:	(:33) Promotional Considerations		
RING:	1-M		2-M
	Shark	vs.	Sting
BUMP:	(:10)		
CM POSITION #3	(3:02)		
SEGMENT #4			
RING:	1-M		In Ring
	Cobra	vs.	
BUMP:	(:10)		_____
CM POSITION #4	(2:32)		
SEGMENT #5			
TAPE:	(:33) Promotional Considerations		
TAPE:	(:12) Closing Billboards		
RING:	1-M		2-M
	Taskmaster		Ric Flair
	Meng	vs.	Arn Anderson
	Barbarian		Chris Benoit
	Hugh Morrus		Flyin' Brian
Match Note:	*Match To Be Recorded On Sunday, February 4th*		
	Spin The Ring...		
	Intros Only In This Segment		
CM POSITION #5	(3:02)		
SEGMENT #6			
RING:	MATCH BEGINS & ENDS		
Match Note:	*Wrestling Action Off The Air...*		
TAPE:	(1:05) Next Week Promo & Program Close		
TRT: 58:57		CM: 14:10	

352

Program #: B-4911
Air Date: 4/20-21/96

SEGMENT #1

HOT OPEN/OPEN:	(:30)		
RING:	1-M		2-M Ring Announce On Line
	Disco Inferno	vs.	Alex Wright
TAPE:	(:12) Opening Billboards		
BUMP:	(:10)		
CM POSITION #1	(2:32)		

SEGMENT #2

RING:	1-M		2-M
	Ice Train	vs.	Bunkhouse Buck w/Col. Parker
BUMP:	(:10)		
CM POSITION #2	(3:02)		

SEGMENT #3

TAPE:	(:33) Promotional Considerations		
RING:	1-M		2-M
	Lifeguard Steve Collins vs.		Lex Luger w/Jimmy Hart
BUMP:	(:10)		
CM POSITION #3	(3:02)		

SEGMENT #4

RING:	WCW United States Heavyweight Title		
	1-M		2-M
	Dick Slater	vs.	Konan
	w/Col. Parker		
Match Note:	*Bunkhouse Buck Out During This Match*		
BUMP:	(:10)		
CM POSITION #4	(2:32)		

SEGMENT #5

TAPE:	(:33) Promotional Considerations		
TAPE:	(:12) Closing Billboards		
RING:	WCW United Stated Heavyweight Title		
	1-M		2-M
	V.K. Wallstreet	vs.	Sgt. Craig Pittman
	Big Bubba		Hacksaw Jim Duggan
			w/Teddy Long
Match Note:	*Spin The Ring...*		
	Intros Only In This Segment		
CM POSITION #5	(3:02)		

SEGMENT #6

RING:	MATCH BEGINS & ENDS
Match Note:	*Nasty Boys Out During This Match..*
CLOSE (TBA):	(2:00) Gene Okerlund w/V.K. Wallstreet & Big Bubba
TAPE:	(1:05) Next Week Promo & Program Close
TRT: 58:57	CM: 14:10

PROGRAM NUMBER:	1311 Page #1
PROGRAM AIR DATE:	Saturday, April 20, 1996
PROGRAM RECORDED:	Gainesville, GA 4/3/96

SEGMENT #1

PRE-BUILT:	(1:31)	OPEN
STANDUP:	(1:00)	TONY-DUSTY OPEN/Welcome Pitch To Ring
MATCH:		1-M 2-M Ring Announce On Line
		MEN AT WORK VS AMERICAN MALES
Match Note:		Match Begins & Ends In This Segment
INTERVIEW:	(2:00)	GENE OKERLUND W/MACHO MAN RANDY SAVAGE re: Ric Flair
		Gene Pitch To Break
BILLBOARD:	(:12)	OPENING
BUMPER:	(:10)	Promoting Next Week On WCW Monday Nitro

CM POSITION #1   (2:15)/Spot A (:30) WCW May Magazine

SEGMENT #2

MATCH:		1-M In Ring
		BOOTY MAN VS _____
		W/BOOTY BABE
Match Note:		Match Begins & Ends In This Segment
INTERVIEW:	(1:30)	GENE OKERLUND W/BOOTY MAN & BOOTY BABE re:
		Gene Pitch To Break
BUMPER:	(:15)	Promoting Next Week On WCW Monday Nitro

CM POSITION #2   (2:30)

SEGMENT #3

HOTLINE:	(1:00)	GENE OKERLUND W/HOTLINE PLUG & MAIN EVENT PROMO Pitch To Ring
MATCH:		NO DISQUALIFICATION MATCH
		1-M 2-M Ring Announce On Line
		COL. PARKER VS MADUSA
Match Note:		Match Begins & Ends In This Segment
PROMO CONSIDERATIONS:	(:33)	
BUMPER:	(:10)	Promoting Next Week On WCW Monday Nitro

CM POSITION #3   (2:30)/Spot A (:30) N'tnl Arena Combo

SEGMENT #4

PROMO CONSIDERATIONS:	(:33)	
COVER PITCH:	(:15)	TONY Pitch To Short Nitro Package
PACKAGE:	(:30)	WCW MONDAY NITRO FOOTAGE TNT 110 Charleston, WV
PROMO:	(:30)	WCW MONDAY NITRO Pitch To Ring
MATCH:		1-M In Ring
		FIRE & ICE VS _____ & _____
		(Scott Norton & Ice Train)
BUMPER:	(:30)	Where The Big Boys Play

CM POSITION #4   (3:00)

PROGRAM NUMBER: 1311 Page #2
PROGRAM AIR DATE: Saturday, April 20, 1996
PROGRAM RECORDED: Gainesville, GA 4/3/96

SEGMENT #5

COVER PITCH:	(:15)	TONY Pitch To One On On w/ Macho Man Randy Savage
FEATURE:	(3:00)	ONE ON ONE W/MACHO MAN RANDY SAVAGE
MATCH:		1-M 2-M Ring Announce On Line
		PUBLIC ENEMY VS THE STEINER BROTHERS
Match Note:		Match Begins & Ends In This Segment
		Knobs Out During This Match
		Need Slo Mo For This Match...TWIX (Announcers Pitch During Mo)
BUMPER:	(:10)	Promoting Next Week On WCW Monday Nitro
CM POSITION #5	(2:45)	

SEGMENT #6

BILLBOARDS:	(:15)	CLOSING
MATCH:		WCW WORLD HEAVYWEIGHT TITLE MATCH
		1-M 2-M Ring Announce On Line
		HACKSAW JIM DUGGAN VS RIC FLAIR
		W/WOMAN & MISS ELIZABETH
Match Note:		Match Begins & Action Off The Air...
		Macho Man Randy Savage Out During This Match
COPYRIGHT/MUSIC:	(:10)	
CM POSITION #6	(2:15)	

355

PROGRAM NUMBER:	1312
PROGRAM AIR DATE:	Saturday, April 27, 1996
PROGRAM RECORDED:	Anderson, SC 4/17/96

SEGMENT #1

PRE-BUILT:	(1:31)	OPEN Tease One On One w/ Randy Savage
STANDUP:	(1:00)	TONY-DUSTY OPEN/Welcome
RING:	( )	1-M	2-M	Ring Announce On Line
		SHARK	VS	RANDY SAVAGE
INTERVIEW:	(1:30)	GENE OKERLUND W/MACHO MAN RANDY SAVAGE
Interview Note:		re: Lord Of The Ring
		Pitch To Break
BILLBOARD:	(:12)	OPENING
BUMPER:	(:10)	LORD STEVEN REGAL Promoting Nitro vs. Belfast Bruiser
CM POSITION # 1	(2:30)/Spot A (:30)	

SEGMENT #2

COVER PITCH:	(:15)	TONY Pitch To Highlight Package Nastys vs. Public Enemy
PACKAGE: (Kip)	(1:00)	Footage Of Nastys vs. Public Enemy From Gainesville,
		Birmingham, Charleston
RING:	( )	1-M	2-M	Ring Announce On Line
		PUBLIC ENEMY	VS	NASTY BOYS
FLY-IN:	(:20)	Public Enemy re: Nasty Boys
INTERVIEW:	(1:30)	GENE OKERLUND W/NASTY BOYS
		re: Lord Of The Ring
		Pitch To Break
BUMPER:	(:10)	BELFAST BRUISER Promoting Nitro vs. Lord Steven Regal
CM POSITION # 2	(2:30)	

SEGMENT #3

COVER PITCH:	(:15)	TONY
FEATURE: (Neal)	(1:00)	CRUISERWEIGHT TOURNAMENT
RING:	( )	1-M	In Ring Ring Announce On Line
		EARL ROBERT EATON VS	STEVE DOLL
BUMPER:	(:10)	Promoting WCW Monday Nitro
CM POSITION #3	(3:00)/Spot A (:30) N'tional Arena Combo/Local Rollover	

SEGMENT #4

PROMO CONSIDERATIONS:	(:33)	
COVER PITCH:	(:15)	TONY
PACKAGE:	(1:00)	BELFAST BRUISER/ LORD STEVEN REGAL
RING:	( )	1-M	2-M	Ring Announce On Line
		BELFAST BRUISER	VS	LORD STEVEN REGAL
BUMPER:	(:10)	Promoting WCW Monday Nitro
CM POSITION # 4	(2:30)	

356

PROGRAM NUMBER:	1312
PROGRAM AIR DATE:	Saturday, April 27, 1996
PROGRAM RECORDED:	Anderson, SC 4/17/96

SEGMENT #5

COVER PITCH:		(:15)	TONY
FEATURE:	(Neal)	(1:30)	GIANT CHOKESLAMS
RING:		( )	1-M 2-M Ring Announce On Line
			DIRTY DICK SLATER VS GIANT W/JIMMY HART
INTERVIEW:		(1:30)	GENE OKERLUND W/GIANT re: Sting
			Pitch To Break
BUMPER:		(:30)	WCW...Where The Big Boys Play
CM POSITION #5		(2:30)	

SEGMENT #6

BUMP IN:		(:15)	SLAMBOREE
FEATURE:	(Neal)	(2:00)	RIC FLAIR, WOMAN, & MISS ELIZABETH
RING:		( )	1-M *C/W Tourny* 2-M Ring Announce On Line
			CHRIS BENOIT VS ALEX WRIGHT
INTERVIEW:		(1:30)	GENE OKERLUND W/CHRIS BENOIT
Interview Note:			Arn Anderson & Taskmaster Out
BUMPER:		(:10)	Promoting WCW Monday Nitro
CM POSITION #6		(3:00) /Spot A (:30)	

SEGMENT #7:

COVER PITCH:		(:15)	TONY
PACKAGE:	(Kip)	(1:00)	Footage From Gainesville Ric Flair & Jimmy Hart
			Hurts Booty Man 1309
RING:		( )	1-M 2-M Ring Announce On Line
			BOOTY MAN VS BIG BUBBA
			W/BOOTY BABE
INTERVIEW:		(1:30)	GENE OKERLUND W/BOOTY MAN re: Taskmaster & Arn
			Pitch To Break
BUMPER:		(:10)	Promoting WCW Monday Nitro
CM POSITION #7		(2:30)	

SEGMENT #8

STANDUP:	(:30)	TONY-DUSTY Pitch To WCW Monday Nitro Footage
PACKAGE:	(1:00)	WCW MONDAY NITRO FOOTAGE
PROMO:	(:30)	WCW MONDAY NITRO
RING:	( )	1-M 2-M Ring Announce On Line
		SCOTT & STEVE VS FACES OF FEAR
		ARMSTRONG
BUMPER:	(:10)	Promoting WCW Monday Nitro
CM POSITION #8	(3:00)/Spot A (:30)	

PROGRAM NUMBER:	1312
PROGRAM AIR DATE:	Saturday, April 27, 1996
PROGRAM RECORDED:	Anderson, SC 4/17/96

SEGMENT #9   *WTCh*

RING: ( )1-M   2-M   Ring Announce On Line
                                     HARLEM HEAT   VS   STING & LEX LUGER

Match Note: Jimmy Hart Out & Throws In The Towel
                                     Match Begins In This Segment...

BUMPER: (:10)   Promoting WCW Monday Nitro

CM POSITION #9   (3:15)

SEGMENT #10

RING: ( )   MATCH CONTINUES & ENDS IN THIS SEGMENT

BUMPER: (:30)   WCW...Where The Big Boys Play

CM POSITION #10   (3:15)

SEGMENT #11

BILLBOARDS: (:12)   CLOSING

 NEXT WEEK PROMO   (:30)

INTERVIEW: (2:00)   GENE OKERLUND W/STING & LEX LUGER
                                     re: Harlem Heat
                                     Pitch To Break

Interview Note: Harlem Heat Out

MUSIC CLOSE: (:10)

TERMINAL BREAK   (2:15)

PROGRAM NUMBER:	1313 Page #1
PROGRAM AIR DATE:	Saturday, May 4, 1996
PROGRAM RECORDED:	Rome, GA 4/24/96

SEGMENT #1

PRE-BUILT:	(1:31)	OPEN		
STANDUP:	(1:30)	TONY-DUSTY OPEN/Welcome Pitch To Ring		
Standup Note:		Marcus Bagwell To Set w/Tony & Dusty!		
MATCH:		1-M	2-M	Ring Announce On Line
		BARBARIAN VS	CHRIS BENOIT	
		w/Taskmaster & Jimmy Hart	w/Arn Anderson	
Match Note:		Match Begins & Ends In This Segment		
INTERVIEW:	(2:00)	GENE W/CHRIS BENOIT, ARN ANDERSON, TASKMASTER, & JIMMY HART re:		
BILLBOARD:	(:12)	OPENING		
BUMPER:	(:10)	Sting Promoting Next Week On WCW Monday Nitro		

CM POSITION #1 (2:15)/Spot A (:30) WCW Power Plant

SEGMENT #2

COVER PITCH:		(:15)	TONY Pitch To Konan Feature		
FEATURE:	(Neal)	(1:30)	KONAN		
MATCH:			1-M	In Ring	
			THE STEINER BROTHERS VS	_____ & _____	
Match Note:			Match Begins & Ends In This Segment		
			Marcus Bagwell To Annouce Position During This Match...		
			Need Slo Mo Replay On This Match For Pep Boys!!!		
			(Announcers Need To Pitch)		
INTERVIEW:		(1:00)	GENE OKERLUND W/THE STEINER BROTHERS re:		
			Gene Pitch To Break		
BUMPER:		(:30)	Where The Big Boys Play		

CM POSITION #2 (2:30)

SEGMENT #3

HOTLINE:	(HQ)	(1:00)	GENE OKERLUND W/HOTLINE PLUG & MAIN EVENT PROMO Pitch To Ring		
MATCH:			1-M	2-M	Ring Announce On Line
			BILLY KIDMAN VS	ALEX WRIGHT	
Match Note:			Match Begins & Ends In This Segment		
			Show Great White Hype Signage At Head Of This Match		
			For Announcer Mention		
			Marcus Bagwell To Announce Position During This Match...		
PROMO CONSIDERATIONS:		(:33)			
BUMPER:		(:10)	Ric Flair & Ladies Promoting Next Week On WCW Monday Nitro		

CM POSITION #3 (2:30)/Spot A (:30) N'tnl Arena Combo

SEGMENT #4

PROMO CONSIDERATIONS:		(:33)		
COVER PITCH:		(:15)	TONY Pitch To Short Nitro Package	
PACKAGE:	(Kip)	(:30)	WCW MONDAY NITRO FOOTAGE TNT 113 Recorded In Albany, GA	
PROMO:		(:30)	WCW MONDAY NITRO Pitch To Break	

CM POSITION #4 (3:00)

PROGRAM NUMBER: 1313 Page #2
PROGRAM AIR DATE: Saturday, May 4, 1996
PROGRAM RECORDED: Rome, GA 4/24/96

SEGMENT #5

CONTROL CENTER: (HQ)	(1:30)	GENE Pitch To Ring
MATCH:		1-M 2-M Ring Announce On Line
		LEX LUGER VS GIANT w/Jimmy Hart
Match Note:		Intros Only...In This Segment
BUMPER:	(:10)	Giant & Jimmy Hart Promoting Next Week On WCW Monday Nitro

CM POSITION #5   (2:45)

SEGMENT #6

BILLBOARDS:	(:15)	CLOSING
MATCH:		Match Begins & Action Off The Air...
Match Note:		This Match Will Conclude On WCW Main Event!!!
		Sting Out During This Match
COPYRIGHT/MUSIC:	(:10)	

CM POSITION #6   (2:15)

Jan 2, 1997

RING NAME	LAST NAME	FIRST NAME
	DELLINGER	DOUG
	ENGLE	JANIE
	PENZER	DAVID
	TACHE	CHUCK
AMERICAN MALE - MARCUS BAGWELL	BAGWELL	MARCUS
AMERICAN MALE - SCOTTY RIGGS	ANTOL	SCOTT
ARMSTRONG, BRAD	JAMES	BRAD
ARMSTRONG, SCOTT	JAMES	SCOTT
ARMSTRONG, STEVE	JAMES	STEVE
AWESOME PROMOTIONS	BRESLOFF	ZANE
BENOIT, CHRIS	BENOIT	CHRIS
BIG BUBBA	TRAYLOR	RAY
BOOKING DEPT - ARN ANDERSON	LUNDE	MARTY
BOOKING DEPT - J.J. DILLON	MORRISON	JAMES
BOOKING DEPT - JIMMY HART	HART	JIMMY
BOOKING DEPT - KEVIN SULLIVAN	SULLIVAN	KEVIN
BOOKING DEPT - PAUL ORNDORFF	ORNDORFF	PAUL
BOOKING DEPT - TERRY TAYLOR	TAYLOR	TERRY
BOOTY GIRL	FALKINBURG	KIMBERLY
BOOTY MAN	LESLIE	EDDIE
BROCK, CHAD	BROCK	CHAD
CANADIANS	OUELLET	CARL
CANADIANS	ROUGEAU	JACQUES
CANYON, CHRIS MoRtis/Wrath	KLUCSARITS	CHRISTOPHER
DISCO INFERNO	GILBERTI	GLENN
DUGGAN, HACKSAW JIM	DUGGAN	JIM
EATON, BOBBY	EATON	BOBBY
ELIZABETH	HULETTE	ELIZABETH
FACES OF FEAR - BARBARIAN	VAILAHI	SIONE

361

WCW Great American Bash {Show Confidential Format}

Moline, IL The Mark of the Quads (Sunday, June 15, 1997)
Page 1 of 3
As Of: 6/14/97

STILLSTORE:	(:15)	FBI Warning
Tape:	(1:00)	Pre-built WCW Great American Bash Open
Audio Note:		Track Op Reel
Live:	(:20)	Arena Wide Shot w/Pyrotechnics
Pyro Note:		Go Pyro w/PPV Open Look
Audio Note:		Track Announcers Headsets @ Set
Infiniti Note:		Needs Live Chyron Moline, IL ID
Live:	(1:00)	~~Dusty Rhodes-Tony Schiavone-Bobby Heenan~~ @ Set
Audio Note:		Track Announcers Headsets @ Set
Infiniti Note:		Needs Live Chyron w/Announcers Name Bar
Announcer Note:		Tony Pitch To David Penzer w/Ring Announce

6-16.28 PM

~~Respect Match~~

Match:	(16:00)	1-M 6:03.18 2-M 6:04:01
6:12:00 X 6:13.48		Psychosis v. Ultimate Dragon
		w/ Sonny Onoo

Z
Y 6:17:38

Referee:	Scott Dickinson
Infiniti Note:	Voice Of Mike Tenay
Audio Note:	Track Announcers Headsets @ Set & Share Mic For Mike Tenay
Announcer Note:	Mike Tenay Joins Announcers

Tape: (Op Reel)	(:15)	Website Pretape w/Chris Benoit
Audio Note:		Track Op Reel 1:14:00
Tape Note:		Show Full screen
Infiniti Note:		Needs Lower 3rd WCW Website Address Chyron
Match:	(17:00)	#1 Contenders for the WCW World Tag Team Title Match
		1-M 6:21' 2-M Ring Announce On Line
		Harlem Heat v. The Steiner Brothers
1:03:40		w/ Sister Sherri
		6:22:25 1'05

Referee:	Randy Anderson
Audio Note:	Track Announcers Headsets @ Set
	Track Penzer's wireless mic

WCW Great American Bash {Show Confidential Format}
Moline, IL The Mark of the Quads (Sunday, June 15, 1997)
Page 2 of 3
As Of: 6/14/97   *1:24:00*

Match:	(14:00)	1-M *6:39:05*		2-M *6:39:48*
		Konan *1:20* v.		Hugh Morrus
				1:22:

Referee: Mickie Hensen
Audio Note: Track Announcers Headsets @ Set
Announcers Note: Tony Pitch To Gene Okerlund

Interview:	(2:00)	Gene Okerlund w/ Public Enemy @ the Videowall

Audio Note: Track Gene's wireless mic

Includes (:30) WCW Hotline Promo @ Beginning Of Interview

Audio Note: Track Gene Okerlund's Mic at Videowall
Infinit! Note: Needs Live Chyron Hotline Information Lower 3rd
Announcer Note: Gene Pitch To Ring

Match:	(16:00)	1-M		2-M *6:58:20*
		Wrath *1:25* v.		Glacier *1:27*
7:05 X *2:04*		w/ James Vandenberg		

Referee: *7:05* Z *7:04*   Nick Patrick
Audio Note: Track Announcers Headsets @ Set & Share Mic For Mike Tenay
Announcers Note: *Y*   Mike Tenay Joins Announcers
Infinit! Note: Needs Voice Of Mike Tenay

Match:	(18:00)	Title v. Career Match		*7:17:06*
		1-M		2-M Ring Announce On Line
		Akira Hokuto	v.	Madusa
		7:18:52 w/ Sonny Onoo *1:32*		*1:34*

Referee: Mickie Hensen
Audio Note: Track Announcers Headsets @ Set/ Track Penzer's Wireless Mic
                               Track Spare Mic For Lee Marshall
Announcer Note: Lee Marshall Joins Announcers
Infinit! Note: Needs Voice Of Lee Marshall

Match:	(20:00)	Return Death Match		2-M *1:39:0*
		1-M		
		Meng *1:36:#* v.		Chris Benoit

Referee: Nick Patrick
Audio Note: Track Announcers Headsets @ Set
Announcers Note: Tony Pitch To Gene Okerlund

Live:	(:30)	Gene Hotline Promo at the Videowall

Announcers Note: Tony Pitch To David Penzer w/Ring Announce
Audio Note: Track Announcers Headsets @ Set
Infinit! Note: Needs Live Chyron *Hotline Information * Lower 3rd

WCW Great American Bash {Show Confidential Format}

Moline, IL The Mark of the Quads (Sunday, June 15, 1997)
Page 3 of 3
As Of: 6/14/97

Tape:	(:30)	WCW Bash at the Beach Spot	
Audio Note:		Track Op Reel	
Match:	(12:00)	1-M	2-M
		Steve McMichael	v.	Kevin Greene
		w/ Debra McMichael	
Referee:		Randy Anderson	
Audio Note:		Track Announcers Headsets @ Set	
MATCH:	(18:00)	WCW World Tag Team Title Match	
		1-M	2-M
		Scott Hall	v.	Ric Flair
		Kevin Nash	Rowdy Roddy Piper
Referee:		Mark Curtis	
Audio Note:		Track Announcers Headsets @ Set	
Announcer Note:		Pitch to Michael Buffer w/ Ring announce for tonight's Main Event	
MATCH:	(23:00)	Lights Out- No Disqualification - Falls Count	
		Anywhere- Non-Sanctioned- Must Be a Winner Match	
		1-M	2-M Ring Announce on Line
		Macho Man Randy Savage	v.	Diamond Dallas Page
		w/ Miss Elizabeth	w/ Kimberly
Referee:		Mickie Hensen	
Audio Note:		Track Announcers Headsets @ Set / Track Buffer's Wireless Mic	
Live:	(1:00)	Dusty Rhodes-Tony Schiavone-Bobby Heenan @ Set	
Audio Note:		Track Announcers Headsets @ Set	
Tape:	(1:30)	WCW Great American Bash Credit Roll	
Audio Note:		Track Op Reel	

CONFIDENTIAL FORMAT

WCW MONDAY NITRO (TNT 240) Columbia, SC

ORDER OF EVENTS

Monday, October 5, 1998

7:40pm Eastern Time   (2:00)   Wild Cat Willie Crowd Warm Up

7:45pm Eastern Time   (3:00)   Nitro Girls Pre-Show Introductions
"Intros" DC #5000 Universal Love Full Cut

7:59:50pm Eastern Time   **Monday Nitro begins!**

10:59:50pm Eastern Time   **Monday Nitro off air!**

Document Created 10/05/98 @ 7:31 PM

365

TAPE: (Op Reel) (1:26) Hot Open- Bret Hart/Sting/Hogan Package From TNT 239 (Last Week)
Audio Note: Track Op Reel
Tape Note: Fades Up From Black & Show Full Screen & Fades To Black

RING: (:36) Nitro Girls Performance #1 Floor Show
Audio Note: Track Nitro Girls Cut DC #8048 (:36 Version) Seven Daze / Track Announcer's Mic's @ Set

TAPE: (Op Reel) (:30) WCW/NWO Halloween Havoc Image Spot- TBS
Audio Note: Track Op Reel
Tape Note: Fades Up From Black & Show Full Screen & Fades To Black
Audio Note: Needs Chuckie Laugh Track In The Middle Of This Spot

LIVE: (:20) Pyro Arena Wide Shot
Audio Note: Track Announcer's Mic's @ Set & Pyro Audio & Needs Live Nitro Music
Infinit! Note: Needs Live Chyron w/ WCW Monday Nitro ID w/Columbia, SC
Pyro Note: Go Pyro Program Open

ANNOUNCE POSITION: (1:00) Mike Tenay, Tony Schiavone, & Larry Zbyszko
Audio Note: Track Announcer's Mic's @ Set
Announcer Note: Announcer's Should Talk About Chuckie Laugh track...Bret Hart/Sting/Hogan Situation

TAPE: (Op Reel) (1:30) Fgt. From TNT 235 & 237- Piper Speaking To Bret Hart(As A Good Guy)
Audio Note: Track Op Reel
Tape Note: Show Full Screen

ANNOUNCE POSITION: (:45) Mike Tenay, Tony Schiavone, & Larry Zbyszko
Audio Note: Track Announcer's Mic's @ Set

TAPE: (Op Reel) (1:30) Bumper From TNT 235 (TC 11:03:52) Hart Takes Belt Away From Hogan...
Audio Note: Hogan Is Beating Sting With The Belt
Tape Note: Track Op Reel
Show Full Screen & Fades To Black

366

| TNT 240 | Page #2 | Columbia, SC | Monday, October 5, 1998 | Air Time & Program Length: | 7:59:50-10:59:50pm Eastern Time |

TAPE: (Op Reel) (:09) Open Sponsor Billboards- Twix
Audio Note: *Needs Live WCW Monday Nitro Music & Track Op Reel*
Tape Note: *Fades Up From Black & Show Full Screen & Tied To WCW Credit Card Spot*

08:09:57

TAPE: (Op Reel) (:30) WCW Credit Card Spot
Audio Note: *Track Op Reel*
Tape Note: *Show Full Screen & Fades To Black*

TAPE: (Op Reel) (:28) WCW Monday Nitro Open W/O Closed Captioning
Audio Note: *Track Op Reel*
Tape Note: *Fades Up From Black & Show Full Screen & Fades To Black*

RING: (7:00) 1-M Lizmark, Jr. Lizmark, Jr. Music   v.   2-M Saturn Saturn Music
Match Note: *Match Begins And Ends In This Segment...*
Announcer Note: *Announcer's Should Tell The Recent History of Saturn & Focus On His Wrestling Skills... Explain The Man That We Have Come To Find Out Saturn Is. Announcers Should Anticipate Where Saturn Will Go From Here.*

TAPE: (Op Reel) (:30) Castrol Slo-Mo Replay Vignette
Audio Note: *Track Announcer's Mic's @ Set*
Tape Note: *Show Full Screen*

TAPE: (Op Reel) (1:00) Halloween Havoc Controls Center From 1439
Audio Note: *Track Op Reel*
Tape Note: *Fades Up From Black & Show Full Screen & Fades To Black*

LIVE: (:08) Locator (Needs Announcer's V/O) Pitch To Starburst Road Report
Audio Note: *Needs WCW Monday Nitro Music & Track Announcer's Mic*
Infinit! Note: *Needs WCW Monday Nitro ID*

TAPE: (Op Reel) (:30) Snickers Road Report (Chicago, IL)
Audio Note: *Track Op Reel*
Tape Note: *Fades Up From Black & Show Full Screen & Fades To Black*

08:19:42

367

page #3 — Columbia, SC — Monday, October 5, 1998 — Air Time & Program Length: 7:59:50-10:59:50pm Eastern Time

TAPE: (Op Reel) (:52)
Promotional Considerations #1
Audio Note: Needs Live WCW Monday Nitro Music & Track Op Reel
Tape Note: Fades Up From Black & Show Full Screen & Tied To Power Plant Spot

08:21:57

TAPE: (Op Reel) (:30)
WCW/NWO Halloween Havoc Image Spot- TBS
Audio Note: Track Op Reel
Tape Note: Fades Up From Black & Show Full Screen & Fades To Black

ENTRANCE: (:40)
Nitro Girls Performance #2
Audio Note: Track Nitro Girls Cut DC #5003 (:40 Version) Universal Love / Track Announcer's Mic's @ Set

TAPE: (Op Reel) (:15)
Nitro Party Pack Graphics Revised
Audio Note: Track Announcer's Mic's @ Set & Transition To Nitro Music
Tape Note: Show Full Screen

RING: (7:00)
1-M Kaz Hayashi Music   2-M The Cat Music
Kaz Hayashi   v.   The Cat
w/ Sonny Onoo
Match Note: Match Begins And Ends In This Segment...

LIVE: (:08)
Locator (Needs Announcer's V/O) Pitch To Break
Audio Note: Needs WCW Monday Nitro Music & Track Announcer's Mic
Infinit) Note: Needs WCW Monday Nitro ID

TAPE: (Op Reel) (:30)
Nitro Party Pack Winner # 37 (Jake Lovingood)
Audio Note: Track Announcer's Mic's @ Set & Transition To Nitro Music
Tape Note: Fades Up From Black & Show Full Screen & Tied To Closed Captioning

TAPE: (Op Reel) (:15)
Closed Caption Promotional Considerations- Jollytime Popcorn
Audio Note: Track Op Reel
Tape Note: Show Full Screen & Fades To Black

08:32:07

368

line 2nd   Page #4   (Formate) St.   Monday, October 5, 1998   Air Time & Program Length: 7:59:50-10:59:50pm Eastern Time

TAPE: (Op Reel)   (:30)   WCW Merchandise Spot- Goldberg Heavyweight Champion T-shirt
Audio Note:
Tape Note: Track Op Reel / Fades Up From Black & Show Full Screen & Tied To DDP/Goldberg Package

TAPE: (Op Reel)   (:58)   DDP v. Goldberg Pkg. For Halloween Havoc (Moves)
Audio Note:
Tape Note: Track Op Reel / Show Full Screen & Fades To Black

RING: (6:00)   1-M Jerry Flynn Music   Jerry Flynn   v.   Juventud Guerrera   2-M Juventud Guerrera Music
Match Note:
Announcer Note: Match Begins And Ends In This Segment... / Good Sell Job For Jury Here...Also Recap All The Match-Ups For Halloween Havoc!

TAPE: (Op Reel)   (:30)   Diamond Dallas Page v. Goldberg Pkg. For Halloween Havoc
Audio Note:
Tape Note: Track Op Reel / Fades Up from Black & Show Full Screen & Tied To Mike Tenay Bumper

TAPE: (Op Reel)   (:20)   Bumper- Mike Tenay w/ Fans Earlier Outside The Building #1
Audio Note:
Tape Note: Show Full Screen & Fades To Black

EXPOSITION #4   (2:30)   Nitro Girls Leonard's New dance DC #8019 Yati cut Off

08:42:10

TNT 240   Page #5   Columbia, SC   Monday, October 5, 1998   Air Time & Program Length: 7:59:50-10:59:50pm Eastern Time

POSITION #5

ANNOUNCE POSITION:	(:30)	Bobby Heenan, Tony Schiavone, & Larry Zbyszko
Audio Note:		Track Announcer's Mic's @ Set
		08:45:10

TAPE: (Op Reel)	(1:09)	Warrior v. "Hollywood" Hogan Package #2
Audio Note:		Track Op Reel
Tape Note:		Show Full Screen

RING:	(6:00)	In-Ring v. 1-M Wrath Music
		Villano IV Wrath
Match Note:		Match Begins And Ends In This Segment...

TAPE: (Op Reel)	(1:04)	Warrior v. "Hollywood" Hogan @ Halloween Havoc
Audio Note:		Track Op Reel
Tape Note:		Show Full Screen

TAPE: (Op Reel)	(:20)	Bumper- Mike Tenay w/ Fans Earlier Outside The Building #2
Audio Note:		Track Op Reel
Tape Note:		Fades Up From Black & Show Full Screen & Tied To Arena Combo

TAPE: (Op Reel)	(:30)	WCW National Arena Combo Spot
Audio Note:		Track Op Reel
Tape Note:		Show Full Screen & Fades To Black
		08:54:13

POSITION #5 (2:15)

page #6   Columbia, SC   Monday, October 5, 1998   Air Time & Program. Length: 7:59:50-10:59:50pm Eastern Time

LIVE:
Producer/Director Notes:

(5-6:00) NWO Wolfpac Outside

08:56:58

Outside The Building, We See The NWO Wolfpac Lead By Sting Pulling Up In Wolfpac Hummer Limo. As Wolfpac Exits Limo, They Charge The NWO Building Looking For NWO Hollywood Group. The Wolfpac Bust Into The First NWO Hollywood Locker Room To Find Scott Norton, Vincent, Brian Adams, Giant, Stevie Ray, Scott Steiner, Buff Bagwell. Fight Ensues With Everyone Except Sting...Who Continues Looking For Bret Hart...Sting Opens The Door To The Second NWO Locker Room To Find Bret Hart Lacing His Boots. Sting Attacks. Fight Ensues. Mass Chaos In & Out Of The Locker Rooms And In The Hallways.

LIVE:
Producer/Director Notes:

(4-5:00) Security Backstage

Backstage Security On The' Way To Help Contain The Situation. Security Separates Both Factions, But Both Get Free & Start Brawling Again....Security In Again....This Time Successful In Getting The Two Factions Separated.

LIVE:
Audio Note:
Infinit Note:

(:03) Locator *(Needs Announcer's V/O) Pitch To Break*

09:08:01

Needs WCW Monday Nitro Music & Track Announcer's Mic
Needs WCW Monday Nitro ID

Document Created 10/05/98 @ 7:11 PM

TUESDAY, OCTOBER 3, 1998   Air Time & Program Length: 7:59:50-10:59:50pm Eastern Time

LIVE:
Producer/Director Note:

(5:00) NWO Wolfpac Outside
Outside The Building Again, We See The NWO Wolfpac & Security Trying To Calm Them. NWO Wolfpac Goes After NWO Hollywood Limo...Beat It Up. Camera Follows Sting From The Group To A Forklift. Sting Gets On The Forklift, Starts It Up & Rams It Into The Side Of The NWO Hollywood Limo...Then Proceeds To Pick The Limo Up.

09:10:31

LIVE:
Audio Note:
Infiniti Note:

(:03) Locator *(Needs Announcer's V/O) Pitch To Break*
Needs WCW Monday Nitro Music & Track Announcer's Mic
Needs WCW Monday Nitro ID

09:15:34

Document Created 10/05/98 @ 7:31 PM

09:17:49

LIVE: (:30) Arena Wide Shot-Big 2nd hour Pyro/Ring Post Pyro
Audio Note: *Track Announcer's Mic's @ Set & Pyro Audio & Needs Live Nitro Music*
Pyro Note: *Go Pyro For 2nd Hour Look*
Director's Note: *This Shot Should Happen @ 9:00:00 PM*

RING: (8:00) 1-M Damian Music   2-M Hector Garza Music
                    Damian   v.   Hector Garza
Match Note: *Match Begins And Ends In This Segment...*
Announcer: Note: *Tony Schiavone Announces At The Beginning Of This Match That He Is Trying To Get An Interview With The NWO Wolfpac*

RING: Eddie Guerrero Interview
Audio Note: *Track David Penzer's Wireless Mic*

LIVE: (:03) Locator *(Needs Announcer's V/O) Pitch To Break (This Locator Will Be Interrupted)*
Audio Note: *Needs WCW Monday Nitro Music & Track Announcer's Mic*
Infinit Note: *Needs WCW Monday Nitro ID*

LIVE: (5:00) Mike Tenay Backstage
Audio Note: *Track Mike Tenay Wireless Mic*
Producer/Director Note: *Backstage Mike Tenay Will Be With A Camera Crew Trying To Get A Statement From Kevin Nash. Kevin Nash Then tells Mike Tenay He Is Looking For Scott Hall...Nash And Konnan Walk Outside The Building To Get To The Hummer Limo...Mike Tenay Goes With Them.*

LIVE: (:03) Locator *(Needs Announcer's V/O) Pitch To Break*
Audio Note: *Needs WCW Monday Nitro Music & Track Announcer's Mic*
Infinit Note: *Needs WCW Monday Nitro ID*

09:31:25

Monday, October 5, 1998   Air Time & Program Length: 7:59:50-10:59:50pm Eastern Time

[Position #8]   (2:30)   Nitro Girls / WcWRaddica / 500/Hedmo First

TAPE: (Op Reel)   (:20)   Bump-In- Bret Hart/Sting
Audio Note: Track Op Reel
Tape Note: Fades Up From Black & Show Full Screen & Fades To Black
                                                                          09:31:55

RING: (:43)   Nitro Girls Performance #3 Strobelight
Audio Note: Track Nitro Girls Cut DC #8007 (:43 Version) Talking Bout You / Track Announcer's Mic's @ Set

RING: (9:00)   WCW Cruiserweight Title Match
                                1-M Psychosis Music
                                Psychosis   v.   Kidman
                                                      2-M Kidman Music
Match Note: Match Begins And Ends In This Segment...

LIVE: (:03)   Locator (Needs Announcer's V/O), Pitch To Break
Audio Note: Needs WCW Monday Nitro Music & Track Announcer's Mic
Initial Note: Needs WCW Monday Nitro ID

TAPE: (Op Reel)   (3:00)   Warrior One-On-One
Audio Note: Track Op Reel
Tape Note: Fades from Black & Show Full Screen & Fades To Black
                                                                          09:47:01

HH ZH   Page #10   Columbia, SC   Monday, October 5, 1998   Air Time & Program Length: 7:59:50-10:59:50pm Eastern Time

TAPE: (Op Reel)   (2:02)   The Better Brother - Scott Steiner Package
Audio Note: *Track Op Reel*
Tape Note: *Fades Up From Black & Show Full Screen & Fades To Black*
09:49:31

TAPE: (:30)   Nash And Konnan On Way To Bar #1
Audio Note: *Track Op Reel*
Producer/Director Note: *Tape Will Be Brought Back To Site From Runner*

RING: (6:00)   Scott Steiner & Buff Bagwell Interview
Audio Note: *Track Wireless Mic. & Needs NWO Wolfie & Black Music*

RING: Brian Adams   v.   Rick Steiner
w/ Vincent
Match Note: *Intros And Match Begins In This Segment...*

TAPE: (Op Reel)   (:52)   Promotional Considerations #2
Audio Note: *Needs Live WCW Monday Nitro Music & Track Op Reel*
Tape Note: *Fades Up From Black & Show Full Screen & Fades To Black*
09:58:55

IN POSITION #10 (2:15)

Document Created 10/05/98 @ 7:31 PM

375

TNT 240	Page #11	Columbia, SC	Monday, October 5, 1998	Air Time & Program Length: 7:59:50-10:59:50pm Eastern Time

RING: (7:00) Brian Adams v. Rick Steiner
w/ Vincent

Match Note: *Match Continues And Ends In This Segment....*

10:01:10

LIVE: (:15) Arena Wide Shot-3rd hour Pyro open

Audio Note: *Track Announcer's Mic's @ Set & Pyro Audio & Needs Live Nitro Music*
Pyro Note: *Go Pyro For 3rd Hour Look*
Director's Note: *This Shot Should Happen @ 10:00 After This Match*

TAPE: (:30) Nash And Konnan Arrive At Bar #1

Audio Note: *Track Op Reel*
Producer/Director Note: *Tape Will Be Brought Back To Site From Runner*

POSITION #1 (4:30)

10:08:55

Document Created 10/05/98 @ 2:31 PM

Program Length: 7:59:50-10:59:50pm Eastern Time

TAPE: (Op Reel)	(:08)	Closing Sponsor Billboards- Wendy's Spicy Chicken
Audio Note:		*Needs Live WCW Monday Nitro Music & Track Op Reel*
Tape Note:		*Fades Up From Black & Show Full Screen & Tied To NWO Merchandise*

10:11:25

RING:	(6:00)	Eric Bischoff w/ "Hollywood" Hogan Interview
Audio Note:		*Track Wireless Mic & Needs I AM NWO VOODOO Chile Music For Intro & NWO For Exit*

TAPE:	(:49)	4 Horsemen Package
Audio Note:		*Track Op Reel*
Tape Note:		*Fades Up From Black & Show Full Screen & Fades To Black*

10:18:22

POSITION #13

Air Time & Program Length: 7:59:50-10:59:50pm Eastern Time

ENTRANCE: (:40) Nitro Girls Performance #4 Rerun

Audio Note: *Track Nitro Girls Cut DC #0038 (:40 Version) Fat Beat / Track Announcer's Mics @ Set*

10:20:52

RING: (9:00) 1-M Kanyon Music   2-M Diamond Dallas Page Music

Kanyon   v.   Diamond Dallas Page

Match Note: *Match Begins And Ends In This Segment...*

10:30:32

TNT 240	Page #14	Columbia, SC	Monday, October 5, 1998	Air Time & Program Length: 7:59:50-10:59:50pm Eastern Time

TAPE: (:30) Nash And Konnan Arrive At Bar #2   10:32:47
Audio Note:
Producer/Director Note: *Track Op Reel*
Tape Will Be Brought Back To Site From Runner

RING: (6:00) In-Ring
Lenny Lane   v.   1-M *Generic Disciple Music (NO NWO HOLLYWOOD MUSIC)*
     Disciple
Match Note: *Match Begins And Ends In This Segment...*
Producer/Director Note: *Disciple Will Speak To Hogan In The Camera Going Down The Aisleway "You Don't Own Me!" Following Match, Hogan Comes Out To Aisleway And Meets Disciple And Then camera Will Follow Disciple & Hogan Backstage*

ENTRANCE: (6:00) Gene Okerlund w/ Arn Anderson & Reid Flair (Eric Bischoff)   10:45:17
Audio Note: *Track Gene's Wireless Mic & Needs NEW Horsemen Music*

DIGITAL MIX (2:30) Nitro Girls "Studio /5089 out there..."

379

All Time & Program Length: 7:59:50-10:59:50pm Eastern Time

ENTRANCE: (6:00) Eric Bischoff w/ Miss Elizabeth (Arn, Ric & Reid, & JJ) 10:47:47
Audio Note: Track Wireless Mic

TAPE: (3:00) Nash And Konnan Arrive At Bar #3
Audio Note: Track Op Reel
Producer/Director Note: Tape Will Be Brought Back To Site From Runner

TAPE: (Op Reel) (:30) NWO Merchandise Spot- Big, Sexy Kevin Nash T-shirt 10:57:17
Audio Note: Track Op Reel
Tape Note: Fades Up From Black & Show Full Screen & Fades To Black

...Eastern Time

TAPE: (Op Reel) (:20) Bump-In- Bret Hart/Sting 10:59:32
Audio Note: Track Op Reel
Tape Note: Fades Up From Black & Show Full Screen & Fades To Black

RING: (12:00) WCW United States Heavyweight Title Match
Match Note: 1-M NWO Wolfpac Music 2-M Bret Hart Music
Sting v. Bret Hart
Match Begins And Ends In This Segment...

LIVE: (:05) Copyright 11:09:52
Audio Note: Need WCW Monday Nitro Music
Infinit Note: Need Copyright Chyron

Initial Break (:10)

Document Created 10/05/98 @ 7:31 PM
This Information Is Subject To Change

CONFIDENTIAL Format

Thunder TBS 121
Syracuse, NY
Tuesday, April 25, 2000- (To Air On Wednesday, April 26, 2000)

7:30 Eastern Time	(3:00)	David Penzer With Announcements & Music
7:33 Eastern Time		:30- Mike Tenay & Bobby Heenan On Camera
		:30 Mike Tenay & Bobby Heenan On Camera

(6:00)

1-M		2-M
Cory Williams	v.	Van Hammer
Cassidy Riley		Hugh Morrus
Rick Michaels		Chavo Guerrero, Jr.
James Storm		Lash LeRoux

<u>Handicap Match</u>

(6:00)

1-M		2-M
Shane Eden	v.	Mike Awesome
PW Douglas		

7:45 Eastern Time   David Penzer With Nitro Girl Introduction & Dance
8:00 Eastern Time   "Kid Rock"
                    Thunder Begins!!
10:00 Eastern Time Thunder Ends!!!

TBS 121   Page #1   Syracuse, NY   Tuesday, April 24, 2000   Air Time & Program Length: 9:05:00-11:04:45 Eastern Time   09:05:00

SEGMENT #1

1. TAPE: (Op Reel)   (:10)   **WCW Logo Identification**
Audio Note: *Track Op Reel...Self Contained*
Tape Note: *Fades Up From Black & Show Full Screen & Fades To Black /Tied To Package*

2. TAPE: (Op Reel)   (1:00)   **(Package) WCW Monday Nitro Recap - TNT 321 Rochester**
Audio Note: *Track Op Reel.....Self Contained*
Tape Note: *Fades Up From Black & Show Full Screen & Fades To Black/Tied To Open*
Production Note: **SHOW THIS TO THE HOUSE AS WELL.**

3. TAPE: (Op Reel)   (:54)   **(Package) WCW Thunder Open**
Audio Note: *Track Op Reel......Self Contained*
Tape Note: *Fades Up From Black & Show Full Screen & Fades To Black*

3a. BACKSTAGE: (Live)   **Pyro Arena Wide Shot**
Audio Note: *Track Announcer's Mic's @ Set & Track Pyro Audio & Needs Live Thunder Music*
Infinit Note: *Needs Live Chyron W/ Thunder Id W/ Syracuse, NY*
Pyro Note: *Go Pyro Program Open*

3aa. LIVE: (:30)   **(Outside) Eric Bischoff, Jeff Jarrett, & Kimberly Drag David Arquette Out Of The Car**
Audio Note: *Track Camera Mic & Track Announcer's Mic's & MUST HAVE CROWD CHEERING UNDER SHOT*
Production Note: **Camera Follows Them All The Way To The Entrance & Then To Ring**
Content Note: **David Is Badly Beaten**

6. ENTRANCE: **Jeff Jarrett w/ Eric Bischoff & Kimberly Music & Entrance**
Audio Note: *Track Announcer's Mic's @ Announce Position & Track Jeff Jarrett Music For Intro*

Segment #1 Continued On Next Page...

| TBS 121 | Page #2 | Syracuse, NY | Tuesday, April 24, 2000 | Air Time & Program Length: 9:05:00-11:04:45 Eastern Time |

SEGMENT #1 Continued

6a. RING: (8:00) **Jeff Jarrett Monologue**
Audio Note: *Track Wireless Mic*

6b. ENTRANCE: Diamond Dallas Page Music & Entrance
Audio Note: *Track Announcer's Mic's @ Announce Position & Track DDP Music For Intro*

6c. RING: Diamond Dallas Page Monologue
Audio Note: *Track Wireless Mic*
Content Note: Buff Bagwell & The Franchise Out to Stage
Jarrett: "You Aren't Leaving Till I Get An Answer"
Bagwell & Franchise After Page
The Total Package & Ric Flair Out
Package & Flair Take Out Buff & Franchise
Jarrett, Bischoff & Arquette Take Off Through Crowd
As Kim Starts to Leave The Ring, DDP Sets Her Up For The Diamond Cutter
DDP Can't Do It
She Nails DDP With A Low Blow
Kimberly Stands Over Page As WE Go To Announcer's

7. Announce Position: (1:00) **Tony Schiavone, Mike Tenay & Bobby Heenan**
Audio Note: *Track Announcer's Mic's @ Set*
Infiniti! Note: *Needs Announcer's Name Bar When Director/Producer Calls For It*
Announcer Note: Also – An Exclusive Interview With Bret "The Hitman" Hart Conducted From His Home In Calgary Earlier This Week!
Plus – For The First Time Ever On Thunder – The Wall V. Sting – In A Tables Match!

8. TAPE: (Pretape) (1:00) **(Backstage Interview Pos.) Gene Okerlund w/ The Cat**
Audio Note: *Track Pretape Audio & MUST HAVE CROWD CHEERING UNDER SHOT*
Tape Note: *Show Full Screen & Fades To Black*
Content Note: Cat Talks About Upcoming Match Against Bam Bam Bigelow.
Also Talk About Possible Heat With Bischoff & Russo

8aa. Infiniti!: (:03) **Thunder ID Logo ID Shot Over Pretape**
Audio Note: *Track Announcer's Mic & Needs Live Thunder Music*
Infiniti! Note: *Needs Thunder ID*

CM Position #1 (3:00) 09:18:34

TBS 121   Page #3   Syracuse, NY   Tuesday, April 24, 2000   Air Time & Program Length: 9:05:00-11:04:45 Eastern Time

SEGMENT #2

8a. TAPE: (Pretape)   (:30)   (Bowels Of The Building) Jeff Jarrett And Eric Bischoff 09:21:34
Torturing Arquette

Audio Note: Track Pretape Audio & Track Announcer's Mic's & MUST HAVE CROWD CHEERING UNDER SHOT

Tape Note: Fades Up From Black & Show Full Screen & Fades To Black/Tied To B-Roll

Content Note: Jarrett Tells Page That This Will Go On All Night Till Page Accepts The Challenge!

9. TAPE: (Op Reel)   (:15)   (B-Roll) The Cat/Bam Bam Bigelow Story From Spring
Stampede & Nitro TNT 321

Audio Note: Track Op Reel & Track Announcer's Mic's @ Announce Position

Tape Note: Fades Up From Black & Need Transition Thunder Animation On In & Out & Show Full Screen

10. ENTRANCE: 1-M The Cat Music
The Cat

Audio Note: Track Announcer's Mic's @ Announce Position

11a. RING: The Cat Monologue

Audio Note: Track Wireless Mic

Content Note: Short Cat Promo & Cat Dance

11. ENTRANCE: 2-M Bam Bam Bigelow Music
Bam Bam Bigelow

Audio Note: Track Announcer's Mic's @ Announce Position

12. RING: (5:00)   The Cat   v.   Bam Bam Bigelow

Match Note: Match Begins And Ends In This Segment!...

Content Note: Cat Over 1-2-3

Bam Bam Bigelow Gets Some Heat After The Bell

Segment #2 Continued On Next Page....

TBS 121   Page #4   Syracuse, NY   Tuesday, April 24, 2000   Air Time & Program Length: 9:05:00-11:04:45 Eastern Time

SEGMENT #2 Continued

13. TAPE: (Pretape)   (:15)   (Outside) Billy Kidman & Torrie Wilson Arrive @ The Building
Audio Note: *Track Pretape Audio & Track Announcer's Mic's & MUST HAVE CROWD CHEERING UNDER SHOT*
Tape Note: *Show Full Screen & Tied To Pretape*
Production Note: *Drive Up In A Porsche*

13a. TAPE: (Pretape)   (:10)   (Backstage) Diamond Dallas Page Searching For Arquette
Audio Note: *Track Pretape Audio & Track Announcer's Mic's & MUST HAVE CROWD CHEERING UNDER SHOT*
Tape Note: *Show Full Screen & Fades To Black*

13aa. Infiniti: (:03)Thunder ID Over Pretape
Audio Note: *Track Announcer's Mic & Needs Live Thunder Music*
Infiniti Note: *Needs Thunder ID*

CM Position #2   (3:01)   Nitro Girls- Cage- "Thong" Music From DJ Ran   09:27:59

TBS 121   Page #5   Syracuse, NY   Tuesday, April 24, 2000   Air Time & Program Length: 9:05:00-11:04:45 Eastern Time

SEGMENT #3

14. TAPE: (Pretape)   (:20)   **(Bowels Of The Building) Jarrett, Bischoff & Kimberly** 09:31:00

Audio Note: **STILL Torturing Arquette**

Tape Note: *Track Pretape Audio & Track Announcer's Mic's & MUST HAVE CROWD CHEERING UNDER SHOT*

Fades Up From Black & Show Full Screen

15. ENTRANCE: **1-M** Shawn Stasiak Music

Shawn "The Perfect One" Stasiak

Audio Note: *Track Announcer's Mic's @ Announce Position*

15a. TAPE: (Op Reel)   **(:15) (B-Roll) Clips Of Shawn "The Perfect One" Stasiak Win**

Over Curt Hennig TNT 320

Audio Note: *Track Op Reel & Track Announcer's Mic's @ Announce Position*

Tape Note: *Need Transition Thunder Animation On In & Out & Show Full Screen As Soon As Shawn Reach The Bottom*

Of The Ramp & After Chyron

16. ENTRANCE: **2-M** CCK Music

Chris "Champagne" Kanyon

Audio Note: *Track Announcer's Mic's @ Announce Position*

17. ENTRANCE: **3-M** Curt Hennig Music

Curt Hennig

Audio Note: *Track Announcer's Mic's @ Announce Position*

Content Note: Curt Hennig To Announce Position To Do Color

17a. GRAPHICS: **WCW Magazine Cover & Story Of Curt Hennig**

Audio Note: *Track Announcer's Mic's @ Announce Position*

Tape Note: *Show Full Screen During Curt Hennig Intro*

Infinit! Note: *Needs Live Chyron With "Now Available" & Phone #*

Segment #3 Continued On Next Page....

TBS 121	Page #6	Syracuse, NY	Tuesday, April 24, 2000	Air Time & Program Length: 9:05:00-11:04:45 Eastern Time

SEGMENT #3 Continued

18. RING: (7:00) **Shawn Stasiak** v. **Chris Kanyon**

Production Note:

Match Begins And Ends In This Segment!!

Audio Note:

Need A Shot Of Marc Mero During This Match!!

Content Note:

Match Gets Completely Out Of Control – Referee Throws It Out

Hennig Comes Over Announce Table After Bell

Hennig & Kanyon Double Team Stasiak

Mike Awesome To The Ring

Awesome Takes Out Hennig – Then Puts Kanyon Through Announce Table

18aa. Announce Position:

Audio Note:

Track Announcer's Mic's @ Set

Shot Of Curt Hennig With The Announcer's

Audio Note:

Track Announcer's Mic's @ Set

18a. ENTRANCE:

Audio Note:

Track Announcer's Mic's @ Announce Position & Track DDP Music For Intro

Diamond Dallas Page Music & Entrance

Diamond Dallas Page Monologue

Content Note:(

Audio Note:

Track Wireless Mic

Page Hits The Ring

Page & Awesome Go

Page Hits Stasiak With A Diamond Cutter

Page Cuts A Quick Promo And Accepts The Match For Tonight!

Off Hot

Production Note:

Diamond Dallas Page Music On Out

19. TAPE: (Pretape) (:07) **(Hallway) Billy Kidman w/ Torrie Wilson On Their Way To The Arena**

Audio Note:

Track Pretape Audio & Track Announcer's Mic's & Track Thunder Music Under & MUST HAVE CROWD CHEERING UNDER

Tape Note:

SHOT

Show Full Screen & Fades To Black

19a. Infiniti!: (:03)Thunder ID Over Pretape

Audio Note:

Track Announcer's Mic & Needs Live Thunder Music

Infiniti! Note:

Needs Thunder ID

CM Position #3 (2:30)

09:38:27

388

| TBS 121 | Page #7 | Syracuse, NY | Tuesday, April 24, 2000 | Air Time & Program Length: 9:05:00-11:04:45 Eastern Time |

SEGMENT #4

19b. TAPE: (:30) — Slo-Mo Replay Vignette Of Highlights From Seg. #3 That Took Place During The Match

09 40 57

Content Note: Show Awesome Putting Kanyon Through The Table
Infiniti Note: Needs Live Chyron With "Moments Ago" In Lower 3rd
Tape Note: Fades Up From Black & Show Full Screen
Audio Note: Track Announcer's Mic's & MUST HAVE CROWD CHEERING UNDER SHOT

20. ENTRANCE: — Billy Kidman w/ Torrie Wilson Music & Entrance

Pyro Note: Needs Billy Kidman Pyro Here
Audio Note: Track Announcer's Mic's @ Announce Position & Track Billy Kidman Music For Intro

21a. TAPE: (Op Reel) — (:24) (B-Roll) Clips Billy Kidman Putting Hogan Through A Table On TNT 321

Tape Note: Need Transition Thunder Animation On In & Out & Show Full Screen As Soon As Billy Reach The Bottom Of The Ramp & After Chyron
Audio Note: Track Op Reel & Track Announcer's Mic's @ Announce Position

21. RING: (7:00) — Billy Kidman Monologue

Audio Note: Track Wireless Mic

Billy Kidman: "It's Real Simple – The Legend Is Dead. Nobody Could Put Hulk Hogan Out Of The Business Until Billy Kidman Came Along. Interview After Interview Hogan Ran Me Down, Saying That I Couldn't Draw At A Flea Market. Well Hogan, Who's Drawing Now? These People Love Me – They Adore Me – Embrace Me. I Am The Guy That Their Kids Want To Be. They Idolize Me Hogan – While Your Red And Yellow Ass Finds Itself Once Again In A Hospital Bed Somewhere Down In Tampa. But Public – Don't Despair – Even Though My Victim Tonight Won't Be Hulk Hogan – I'm Throwing Out A Challenge To Anybody Back In That Locker Room Who Thinks They Can Swat This Flea. Let's Go Boys Put Your Potatoes In And Send Somebody Out Here – Torrie Can't Wait To See Me Sweat."

Production Note: After About A 10 Second Wait

21aa. ENTRANCE: — 1-M Hulk Hogan Music / Horace Boulder

Content Note: Horace In Street Clothes
Audio Note: Track Announcer's Mic's @ Announce Position

Segment #4 Continued On Next Page…

TBS 121   Page #8   Syracuse, NY   Tuesday, April 24, 2000   Air Time & Program Length: 9:05:00-11:04:45 Eastern Time

SEGMENT #4   Continued

22. RING:

Match Note: **Billy Kidman**   v.   **Horace Boulder**

Content Note: *Match Begins And Ends In This Segment...*

Kidman Dominates Match – Very Impressively – Until Horace Turns The Tide

Horace Goes For A Hulk-Like Finish On Kidman

Eric Hits The Ring – Nails Horace With Bat

Referee Calls For Bell – Eric Nails Referee With Bat

Kidman Then Annihilates Horace – High Spot After High Spot

Kidman Covers Horace

Eric Counts 1-2-3

Kidman Grabs A Table And Puts It In The Ring

Kidman Puts Horace On The Table

Kidman Dives Off The Turnbuckle Onto Horace On The Table

Torrie Then Kisses Horace

Kidman Music On Out

Production Note:

23. TAPE: (Pretape)   (:07)

(Hallway) Tank Abbott On His Way To The Arena

Audio Note: *Track Pretape Audio & Track Announcer's Mic's & Track Thunder Music Under & MUST HAVE CROWD CHEERING UNDER*

Tape Note: SHOT

Show Full Screen & Fades To Black

23a. Infinit!:

(:03)Thunder ID Over Pretape

Audio Note: *Track Announcer's Mic & Needs Live Thunder Music*

Infinit! Note: *Needs Thunder ID*

CM Position #4   (2:30)   09:48:34

TBS 121   Page #9   Syracuse, NY   Tuesday, April 24, 2000   Air Time & Program Length: 9:05:00-11:04:45 Eastern Time

SEGMENT #5

24. TAPE: (:30) Castrol GTX Slo-Mo Replay Vignette Of Highlights From Seg. #4 That Took Place During The Match   09:51:04

Audio Note: Track Announcer's Mic's & MUST HAVE CROWD CHEERING UNDER SHOT
Tape Note: Fades Up From Black & Show Full Screen
Infiniti! Note: Needs Live Clayton With "Moments Ago " In Lower 3rd
Announcer Copy: "Brought To You By The Motor Oil That Provides Maximum Protection, Castrol GTX, Drive Hard."
Content Note: See Eric Nailing Horace. Eric Nails Referee 1-2-3. And Kidman Dive On Horace.

25. ENTRANCE: Tank Abbott Music & Entrance

Audio Note: Track Announcer's Mic's @ Announcer Position & Track Tank Abbott Music For Intro

25a. RING: (5:00) Tank Abbott Monologue

Audio Note: Track Wireless Mic
Content Note: Short Tank Promo
Tank Gets Out Of Ring & Goes Over To Railing
Tank Pie Faces Marc Mero And Pulls His Friend And Trainer Ray Renaldo Over Barricade.
Marc & Ray Should Have Been Established Earlier
Announcer Note: Tank Mauls 70 Year Old Ray Renaldo
Marc Mero (Formerly Johnny B. Badd) Hits The Ring
Mero/Tank Exchange Punches
Security Hits The Ring
Off Hot
Production Note: Johnny B. Badd Music On Out

26. TAPE: (Pretape) (:20) (Backstage) A Red Liquid Covered Sting Walks Into The Building

Audio Note: Track Pretape Audio & MUST HAVE CROWD CHEERING UNDER SHOT
Tape Note: Show Full Screen & Fades To Black

26a. Infiniti! (:03)Thunder ID Over Pretape

Audio Note: Track Announcer's Mic & Needs Live Thunder Music
Infiniti! Note: Needs Thunder ID

CM Position #5 (3:00)   09:55:54

SEGMENT #6

27. TAPE: (Pretape) (:20) **(Bowels Of The Building) DDP Finds A Beaten Arquette** 09:58:54

Audio Note:
Tape Note: Track Pretape Audio & Track Announcer's Mic's & MUST HAVE CROWD CHEERING UNDER SHOT
Fades Up From Black & Show Full Screen

28. ENTRANCE: **1-M** The Wall Music
The Wall
Audio Note: Track Announcer's Mic's @ Announce Position

29. ENTRANCE: **2-M** Sting Music
Sting
Audio Note: Track Announcer's Mic's @ Announce Position

29a. TAPE: (Op Reel) (:24) (B-Roll) Clips From TNT 321- End Of Nitro- Sting v.
Vampiro First Blood Match
Audio Note: Track Op Reel & Track Announcer's Mic's @ Announce Position
Tape Note: Need Transition Thunder Animation On In & Out & Show Full Screen As Soon As Sting Reach The Bottom
Of The Ramp & After Chyron

30. RING: (7:00) **Tables Match**
The Wall   v.   Sting
Match Note: Match Begins And Ends In This Segment...
Content Note: Sting Dominates – Sting Puts Wall Through Table
Wall No Sells
Wall Gets On Sting
Vampiro Hits The Ring
Wall & Vampiro Double Team Sting
Wall & Vampiro Get Out Of Dodge
Off Hot
Sting Music On Out

Production Note:

Segment #6 Continued On Next Page...

TBS 121 Page #11 Syracuse, NY Tuesday, April 24, 2000 Air Time & Program Length: 9:05:00-11:04:45 Eastern Time

SEGMENT #6 Continued

31. TAPE: (Pretape) (:07) **(Hallway) Vince Russo, Buff Bagwell & "The Franchise" Shane Douglas On Their Way To The Arena**

Audio Note: Track Pretape Audio & Track Announcer's Mic's & Track Thunder Music Under & MUST HAVE CROWD CHEERING UNDER

Tape Note: SHOT

Show Full Screen & Fades To Black

31aa. Infiniti: **(:03)Thunder ID Over Pretape**

Audio Note: Track Announcer's Mic & Needs Live Thunder Music

Infiniti Note: Needs Thunder ID

31ab. TAPE: (Op Reel) (1:06) Promotional Considerations #1

Audio Note: Needs Live Thunder Music & Track Op Reel

Tape Note: Fades Up From Black & Show Full Screen & Fades To Black

CM Position #6 (2:30) **Nitro Girls- Ring- "Girls, Girls, Girls" Music From DJ Ran**

10 07 27

04/25/00 5:08 PM
This Information Is Subject To Change!!

TBS 121 | Page #12 | Syracuse, NY | Tuesday, April 24, 2000 | Air Time & Program Length: 9:05:00-11:04:45 Eastern Time

SEGMENT #7

31ac. TAPE: (Op Reel) (:18)
Closed Caption PC- Meineke

Audio Note:
Profile Note: *Needs Live Thunder Music & Track Announcer's Mic's @ Set*
Tape Note: *Needs Closed Captioning Graphics Over Arena Wide Shot*
Announcer Note: *"Closed Captioning Where Available Sponsored By Meineke Discount Muffler Shops."*

10 09 57

31ad. TAPE: (Op Reel) (:30)
WCW Merchandise Spot- Vampiro T-shirt VAMP-0400

Audio Note: *Track Op Reel...Self Contained*
Tape Note: *Fades Up From Black & Show Full Screen & Fades To Black*

31a. BACKSTAGE: (Live)(:15)
(Hallway) Sting Leaves The Building Into The Darkness

Audio Note: *Track Camera Mic & Track Announcer's Mic's & MUST HAVE CROWD CHEERING UNDER SHOT*

32. ENTRANCE:
Vince Russo w/ Buff Bagwell & "The Franchise" Shane Douglas Music & Entrance

Audio Note: *Track Announcer's Mic' s @ Announce Position & Track Vince Russo- Jimmy Hart Cut Music For Intro*

Content Note: *Before Russo Can Get A Word Out Edgewise...*

32a. ENTRANCE:
Ric Flair w/ The Total Package & Liz Music & Entrance

Audio Note: *Track Announcer's Mic' s @ Announce Position & Track Ric Flair Music For Intro*
Pyro Note: *Needs Ric Flair Pyro Here*

Segment #7 Continued On Next Page...

TBS 121 | Page #13 | Syracuse, NY | Tuesday, April 24, 2000 | Air Time & Program Length: 9:05:00-11:04:45 Eastern Time

SEGMENT #7 Continued

33. RING: (8:00)
Audio Note:

Ric: ## Ric Flair Monologue
Track Wireless Mic

"Russo, For The Past Three Weeks I've Had To Listen To You Come Out Here And Spew Your New York Venom – Well Tonight, Boy, You're Gonna Shut Your Mouth And Listen. You See Punk, I Was Headlining This Business While Your Momma Was Still Breast Feeding You. For The Past 20 Years I've Run Guys Like You Out Of This Business Before They Even Knew What Hit Them. You're Nothing More Than A Flash In The Pan – Here Today – Gone Tomorrow. The Nature Boy Is A Legend – And That's What's Eating You Up Inside. I'll Be Standing Tall In The Middle Of This Ring – When You're Long Gone. But Russo – My Patience Is Running Real Thin – Real Fast – So I Tell You What I'm Going To Do, Being That It's Obvious That The Franchise Can't Beat Me On His Own – At Slamboree – If You In Any Way Stick Your New York Attitude In My Business – Then After The Match - Win, Lose Or Draw – I Get Five Minutes With You. What Do You Say Hot-Shot?"

Russo: "I Say – I Look Forward To It. Do You Really Think I Sweat You Flair? Is This Where I'm Supposed To Be Afraid? Scared? I'd Love To Get You In The Ring For 5 Minutes. You See – I'm Not Wahoo Or Dusty, I'm A New Yorker. Not Only Am I Better Than You - But I Can Take You. One Way Or Another – Whether It's The Franchise – Or Me – Slamboree Will Be The Beginning Of Your End."

Package: You Know, Russo – You Were Nothing In New York – And You're Nothing Now. I Don't Know What You're On – But You Need A Reality Check Real Fast. I Advise You To Start Showing A Little Respect Around Here – Before Your Mouth Writes A Check That Your Ass Can't Cash."

Russo: "Lex Speaks! You Know, Package – It's Nice To See You Survived The Car Wreck Known As The Lex Express. But You're Right – Maybe I Was Nothing In New York - But I'm Everything Now. The Fact Is – That Just Looking At You Kinda Pisses Me Off. So Let Me Hit You With A Dose Of Reality Here – Liz Story."

Russo Takes Liz

Liz, Russo, Buff & Franchise Leave

¼ Way Up The Ramp – Lex/Flair Attack Buff Bagwell & The Franchise

Russo Spoots With Liz

Off Hot

33a. Infiniti: (:03)Thunder ID Over Hot Action
Audio Note:
Infiniti Note: Needs Thunder ID
Track Announcer's Mic & Needs Live Thunder Music

33b. TAPE: (Op Reel) (:30) **WCW National Arena Combo**
Audio Note:
Tape Note: Track Op Reel - Self Contained
Fades Up From Black & Show Full Screen & Fades To Black

CM Position #7 (2:31)

10:19:30

SEGMENT #8

33c. TAPE: (Op Reel) (1:30) WCW Motorsports Package   10:22:01
Audio Note:
Tape Note: Track Op Reel...Self Contained
Fades Up From Black & Show Full Screen & Fades To Black

34. TAPE: (Shot During Break) (:15) (Outside) Russo Hops Into The Getaway Car With Liz & Powders
Audio Note:
Tape Note: Track Pretape Audio & Track Announcer's Mic's & MUST HAVE CROWD CHEERING UNDER SHOT
Infiniti Note: Fades Up From Black & Show Full Screen
Needs Lower 3" Chyron With "During The Break"

34a. TAPE: (Pretape) (:20) (Backstage) DDP Takes David Arquette To The Trainer
Audio Note:
Tape Note: Track Pretape Audio & Track Announcer's Mic's & MUST HAVE CROWD CHEERING UNDER SHOT
Tape Note: Show Full Screen

35. ENTRANCE: Short Tammy Monologue
Audio Note: Track Wireless Mic

35a. RING: W/ "Hard Knox" Chris Candido
Audio Note: Track Announcer's Mic's @ Announce Position

36. ENTRANCE: 1-M "Strip Tease" Music
Tammy
Audio Note:

37. RING: (5:00) 2-M The Artist Music
Paisley
W/ The Artist
Audio Note: Track Announcer's Mic's @ Announce Position
Needs The Artist Pyro Here
Pyro Note:

Content Note: **Tammy   v.   Paisley**
Match Begins And Ends In This Segment....
Paisley Over
Tammy/Chris Get Heat Back After Match
Off Hot
Production Note: "Strip Tease" Music On Out

Segment #8 Continued On Next Page...

TBS 121   Page #15   Syracuse, NY   Tuesday, April 24, 2000   Air Time & Program Length: 9:05:00-11:04:45 Eastern Time

SEGMENT #8 Continued

38. TAPE: (Pretape)   (1:00)   **(Backstage Interview Pos.) Gene Okerlund w/ Booker**

Audio Note: *Track Pretape Audio & Track Announcer's Mic's & MUST HAVE CROWD CHEERING UNDER SHOT*
Tape Note: *Show Full Screen & Tied To Pretape*
Content Note: **Tylene Walks Into The Interview &. Tells Gene That She Is There To Help Interview- Then Starts to Interview Booker**

Regarding Upcoming Match With Mike Awesome

Scott Steiner Match At Slamboree

39. TAPE: (Pretape)   (:07)   **(Hallway) Scott Steiner w/ Midajah & Kim On Their Way To The Arena**

Audio Note: *Track Pretape Audio & Track Announcer's Mic's & Track Thunder Music Under & MUST HAVE CROWD CHEERING UNDER*
Tape Note: *Show Full Screen & Fades To Black*

39aa. Infinit!:   **(:03)Thunder ID Logo ID Shot Over Pretape**

Audio Note: *Track Pretape Audio & Track Announcer's Mic's & Track Thunder Music Under & MUST HAVE CROWD CHEERING UNDER SHOT*
Infinit! Note: *Track Announcer's Mic & Needs Live Thunder Music Needs Thunder ID*

39ab. TAPE: (Op Reel)   (:37)   **1-800-Call ATT Road Report**

Audio Note: *Track Op Reel... Self Contained*
Tape Note: *Fades Up From Black & Show Full Screen & Fades To Black*

CM Position #8   (2:45)   10:30:50

TBS 121 Page #16 Syracuse, NY Tuesday, April 24, 2000 Air Time & Program Length: 9:05:00-11:04:45 Eastern Time

SEGMENT #9

39a. TAPE: (Pretape) (:20) (Arquette Locker Room) DDP Talking With Arquette 10:33:35

Audio Note: *Track Pretape Audio & Track Announcer's Mic's If Necessary & MUST HAVE CROWD CHEERING UNDER SHOT*
Tape Note: *Fades Up From Black & Show Full Screen*
Content Note: DDP Is Telling David That There Is No Way David Can Go Out There
David Is Pissed- Says That There Is No Way He is NOT Going Out There

40. ENTRANCE:

1-M Booker Music
Booker
Audio Note: *Track Announcer's Mic's @ Announce Position*
Pyro Note: Needs Booker Pyro Here

40a. TAPE: (Op Reel) (:15) (B-Roll) Clips Of Booker/Scott Steiner Action From TNT
319 & TNT 321
Audio Note: *Track Op Reel & Track Announcer's Mic's @ Announce Position*
Tape Note: *Need Transition Thunder Animation On In & Out & Show Full Screen As Soon As Booker Reach The Bottom*
Of The Ramp & After Clayton
Announcer Note: Tell Booker Story – Caught Between Rock And Hard Place With Eric Bischoff

41. ENTRANCE:

2-M Mike Awesome Music
Mike Awesome
Audio Note: *Track Announcer's Mic's @ Announce Position*
Pyro Note: Needs Mike Awesome Pyro Here

42. ENTRANCE:

3-M Scott Steiner Music
Scott Steiner
Audio Note: *Track Announcer's Mic's @ Announce Position*
Content Note: Scott To Announce Position To Do Color

Segment #9 Continued On Next Page...

TBS 121   Page #17   Syracuse, NY   Tuesday, April 24, 2000   Air Time & Program Length: 9:05:00-11:04:45 Eastern Time

SEGMENT #9 Continued

43. RING: (8:00)   Booker   v.   Mike Awesome

Match Note: *Match Begins And Ends In This Segment....*

Content Note:
With Help From Scott – Awesome Over 1-2-3
Awesome/Scott Get Heat On Booker After The Bell
Hugh Morrus/Lash LeRoux/Hammer/Chavo Guerrero Hit The Ring
Booker Looks Surprised!
Schmazz
Morrus/LeRoux/Hammer/Guerrero/Booker Run Off Awesome & Steiner
Off Hot!

43a. Announce Position:
Audio Note: *Track Announcer's Mic's @ Set*

Shot Scott Steiner With The Announcer's

44. TAPE: (Op Reel)   (:15)   Bumper- "Up Next" Short Tease Of Bret Hart Interview w/
Audio Note: Scott Hudson
Tape Note: *Track Op Reel - Self Contained*
Fades Up From Black & Show Full Screen & Fades To Black

44a. Infiniti!   (:03)Thunder ID Logo ID Shot Over Bumper
Audio Note: *Track Announcer's Mic & Needs Live Thunder Music*
Infiniti! Note: *Needs Thunder ID*

44b. TAPE: (Op Reel)   (1:06)   Promotional Considerations #2
Audio Note: *Needs Live Thunder Music & Track Op Reel*
Tape Note: *Fades Up From Black & Show Full Screen & Fades To Black*

CM Position #9   (2:15)   Nitro Girls- Ring- "I Feel Like A Woman" Music From DJ Ran

10:43:16

TBS 121   Page #18   Syracuse, NY   Tuesday, April 24, 2000   Air Time & Program Length: 9:05:00-11:04:45 Eastern Time

SEGMENT #10

45. TAPE: (Op Reel)   (6:00)   (4/21/00) Scott Hudson w/ Bret "The Hitman" Hart   10:45:31

Audio Note:
Tape Note: *Track Op Reel...Self Contained*
Fades Up From Black & Show Full Screen & Fades To Black

**46. BACKSTAGE: (Live)(:07)   (Hallway) Eric Bischoff & Jeff Jarrett On Their Way To The
Arena**

Audio Note: *Track Camera Mic & Track Announcer's Mic's & Track Thunder Music Under & MUST HAVE CROWD CHEERING UNDER
SHOT*

**47. BACKSTAGE: (Live)(:07)   (Hallway) Diamond Dallas Page & David Arquette On Their
Way To The Arena**

Audio Note: *Track Camera Mic & Track Announcer's Mic's & Track Thunder Music Under & MUST HAVE CROWD CHEERING UNDER
SHOT*

47a. Infiniti!:   (:03)Thunder ID Over Live Shot

Audio Note: *Track Announcer's Mic & Needs Live Thunder Music*
Infiniti! Note: *Needs Thunder ID*

CM Position #10   (3:16)   Nitro Girls- Stage- "Thong" Music From DJ Ran   10:51:45

400

TBS 121   Page #19   Syracuse, NY   Tuesday, April 24, 2000   Air Time & Program Length: 9:05:00-11:04:45 Eastern Time

SEGMENT #11

48. ENTRANCE:

1-M Diamond Dallas Page Music

Diamond Dallas Page

Audio Note: *Track Announcer's Mic's @ Announce Position*
Pyro Note: *Needs DDP Pyro Here*

48a. TAPE: (Op Reel)

(:25) (B-Roll) Clips From TNT 321- DDP Winning World Title

Audio Note: *Track Op Reel & Track Announcer's Mic's @ Announce Position*
Tape Note: *Need Transition Thunder Animation On In & Out & Show Full Screen As Soon As DDP Reach The Bottom*
               Of The Ramp & After Chyron

49. ENTRANCE:

2-M Jeff Jarrett Music

Jeff Jarrett
Eric Bischoff

Audio N/nte: *Track Announcer's Mic's @ Announce Position*
Pyro Note: *Needs Jeff Jarrett Pyro Here*
Content Note/: *DDP Goes To The Announce Position Or To Penzer*
               DDP Won't Start The Match Because There Is No Referee
               Hit Eric Bischoff Music Here

49a. GRAPHICS:

WCW Magazine Cover & Story Of Jeff Jarrett

Audio Note: *Track Announcer's Mic's @ Announce Position*
Tape Note: *Show Full Screen During Jeff Jarrett Intro*
Info\it/ Note: *Needs Live Chyron With "Now Available" & Phone #*

50. ENTRANCE:

3-M Eric Bischoff "White Train" Music

Kimberly

Audio Note: *Track Announcer's Mic's @ Announce Position*
Content Note: *Kimberly In Referee Outfit*

Segment #11 Continued On Next Page...

10:55:01

TBS 121   Page #20   Syracuse, NY   Tuesday, April 24, 2000   Air Time & Program Length: 9:05:00-11:04:45 Eastern Time

SEGMENT #11   Continued

51. RING: (10:00)   WCW World Heavyweight Title Match

Diamond Dallas Page   v.   **Jeff Jarrett**
David Arquette   **Eric Bischoff**

Match Note:	Match Begins In This Segment...
Talent Note:	Kimberly As Special Guest Referee
Content Note:	Jarrett Over Arquette (Arquette Not Legal Man)
	Kimberly Fast Counts 1—2-3
	Ponder That! If DDP Had Taken Out Kimberly Earlier, He Would Not Have Lost The Belt!
Announcer Note:	Jarrett Music On Out
Production Note:	DDP Backs Kimberly Into Corner
	Cut Jarrett's Music
Production Note:	DDP Gets Kimberly By Throat
	Bischoff Nails DDP With Guitar
	Bischoff/Jarrett

52. Infiniti!:   (:05)Copyright- Shown Over Last Action Shot

Audio Note:	Needs Thunder Music
Infiniti Note:	Needs Copyright Chyron

Terminal Break: Hard Out @ 11:04:45   11:05:01

CONFIDENTIAL Format

WCW Monday Nitro (TNT 343) Uniondale, NY

Order Of Events

Monday, September 25, 2000

7:40:00 PM Eastern Time (3:00) David Penzer Welcome

7:43:00 PM Eastern Time (:30) WCW Master Card Credit Card

7:43:30 PM Eastern Time (3:00) wcw.com "Nitro Preview" Promo

7:46:30 PM Eastern Time (2:30) David Penzer With Announcements & DJ Ran Intro

7:49:00 PM Eastern Time (2:00) Nitro Girls Performance "Get Naked"

7:51:00 PM Eastern Time (9:00) DJ Ran Plays

8:00:00 PM Eastern Time Monday Nitro Begins!

10:00:00 PM Eastern Time Monday Nitro Off Air!

403

TNT 343 Page #1 Unionsdale, NY Monday, September 25, 2000 Air Time & Program Length: 8:00:00-10:00:00 PM Eastern Time

Segment #1 08:00:00 Eastern

1. TAPE: (Op Reel) *Audio Note:* *Tape Note:*	**(:10)**	**WCW Logo Identification** *Track Op Reel...Self Contained* *Fades Up From Black & Show Full Screen & Fades To Black/Tied To Package*
2. TAPE: (Op Reel) *Audio Note:* *Tape Note:*	**(:45)**	**(Package) Vince Russo "The Man, The Myth, The Legend"** *Track Op Reel...Self Contained* *Fades Up From Black & Show Full Screen & Fades To Black/Tied To Pretape*
Content Note:		**Package—Vince Russo—"The Man, The Myth, The Legend"** **(VO By Jeremy Borash—Way, Way, Over The Top)**
3. TAPE: (Pretape) *Audio Note:* *Tape Note:* *Infinit! Note:*	**(:30)**	**(Backstage)Vince Russo w/ Jeremy Borash Arriving At Nassau Coliseum** *Track Pretape Audio & Track Announcer's Mic's & NEEDS LOW CROWD CHEERING UNDER* *Fades Up From Black & Show Full Screen & Fades To Black/Tied To Open* *Needs Live Chyron With "Earlier Today"*
Content Note: ***Producer: Woody Kearce***		**Russo Arriving At Nassau Coliseum Via Limo With Security Entourage (A "Mike Tyson" Shot)**
4. TAPE: (Op Reel) *Audio Note:* *Tape Note:*	**(:43)**	**NEWLY REVISED- WCW Monday Nitro Open** *Track Op Reel ...Self Contained* *Fades Up From Black & Show Full Screen & Fades To Black*
5. LIVE: (Stage/Ring) *Audio Note:* *Infinit! Note:* *Pyro Note:*	**(:30)**	**Pyro Open Arena Wide Shot** *Track Announcer's Mic's @ Set & Pyro Audio & Needs Live Nitro Music & MUST HAVE CROWD CHEERING UNDER SHOT* *Needs Live Chyron W/ WCW Monday Nitro ID W/Uniondale, NY* *Go Pyro Open When Director Calls For It*
6. ENTRANCE: *Audio Note:*		**1-M** **Big Vito Music** **Big Vito** *Track Announcer's Mic's @ Announce Position*
7. ENTRANCE: *Audio Note:*		**2-M** **Johnny "The Bull" Music** **Johnny "The Bull"** *Track Announcer's Mic's @ Announce Position*

Reno

Document Created 09/25/00 @ 5:01 PM
This Information Is Subject To Change!

TNT 343   Page #2   Uniondale, NY   Monday, September 25, 2000   Air Time & Program Length: 8:00:00-10:00:00 PM Eastern Time

Segment #1   **(5:00)**   **Continued**

8. RING: **"I Quit" Stickball Bat v. Kendo Stick Match**

Big Vito   **v.**   **Johnny "The Bull"**

Match Note: *Match Begins And Ends In This Segment. . .*

Content Note: On Way To Ring Vito Needs To Hug And Kiss Girl In Front Row—Announcers Need To Sell That

Girl Is His Younger Sister

Brutal Match

Vito Begins To Brutally Beat Johnny With Stickball Bat

Vito Is Screaming At Johnny To Quit

Reno To Ring With Kendo Stick

Reno Viciously Attacks Vito

Reno Screams For Vito To Quit

Vito Won't Quit

Vito's Sister Gets In The Ring And Covers Vito

Ring Bell

Reno Goes To Swing At Vito And Stops

Vito's Sister Tearfully Pleads With Reno—"Rick—Why Are You Doing This. . .Why Do You

Always Have To Be This Way With Him?."

9. BACKSTAGE: (Live)   **(:10)**   **(Hallway) Vince Russo w/ Jeremy & Security On His**

Way To The Arena

Audio Note: *Track Camera Mic & Track Announcer's Mic's & Needs Nitro Music Under & NEEDS LOW CROWD CHEERING*

UNDER

Producer: Woody Kearce

9a. TAPE: (Op Reel)   **(:30)**   **WCW Magazine Spot**

Audio Note: *Track Op Reel...Self Contained*

Tape Note: *Fades Up From Black & Show Full Screen & Fades To Black*

9b. INFINITI: **(:03)WCW Nitro Logo I.D. Over Tape**

Audio Note: *Needs WCW Monday Nitro Music*

Infiniti Note: *Needs WCW Monday Nitro I.D.*

CM Position #1   **(2:33)**   **DJ Ran Performs- House Only**

08:08:18

Document Created 09/25/00 @ 5:01 PM
This Information Is Subject To Change!

405

| TNT 343 | Page #3 | Uniondale, NY | Monday, September 25, 2000 | Air Time & Program Length: | 8:00:00-10:00:00 PM Eastern Time |

08:10:51

Segment #2

10. ANNOUNCE POS.: (1:00) **Scott Hudson, Tony Schiavone, & Mark Madden**
Audio Note: Track Announcer's Mic's @ Announce Position
Infiniti Note: Needs Announcer Name Bar When Director Calls For It
Tape Note:
Content Note: Sell Tonight's Main Event—Russo/Booker T.
Update & Tell David Flair Story

11. TAPE: (Pretape) (:41) **(Shot 9/24/00) Vignette #1- David Flair At A Pay Phone**
Audio Note: Track Pretape Audio & Track Announcer's Mic's @
Tape Note: Show Full Screen

12. ENTRANCE: **Vince Russo w/ Security & Jeremy Borash Music & Entrance**
Audio Note: Track Vince Russo Music For Intro & Track Announcer's Mic's @ Announce Position

13. RING: (12:00) **Vince Russo Monologue**
Audio Note: Track Wireless Mic
Content Note: "New York—If You Can Make It Hear—You'll Make It Anywhere"

14. ENTRANCE: **Scott Steiner w/ Jeff Jarrett & Midajah Music & Entrance**
Audio Note: Track Scott Steiner Music For Intro & Track Wireless Mic(s) & Track Announcer's Mic's
Content Note: Steiner & Jarrett Tell Russo That They Got His Back— As Long As They Are Both Promised A Title
Shot After He Becomes The WCW Champion—Russo Agrees
Group Hug

15. TAPE: (Pretape) **(On NITROVISION) Sting & Booker T. Come Up On Screen**
Audio Note: TRACK STING MUSIC WHEN THIS COMES UP & Track Pretape Audio & Track Wireless
Mic(s) & Track Announcer's Mic's & NEEDS LOW CROWD CHEERING UNDER
Tape Note: Show Full Screen
Content Note: Sting Music & Entrance (With Booker) On NitroVision
Sting Tells Russo/Steiner/Jarrett That He's Got Booker's Back— And By The Way Russo—You'd
Better Have Eyes In The Back Of Your Head—Turn Around Jackass—

Document Created 09/25/00 @ 5:01 PM
This Information Is Subject To Change!

406

TNT 343   Page #4   Uniondale, NY   Monday, September 25, 2000   Air Time & Program Length::   8:00:00-10:00::00 PM Eastern Time

Segment #2   Continued

16. ARENA: (Live)   (Arena) Spotlight Of Goldberg In The Crowd

Audio Note: *Track Wireless Mic(s) & Track Announcer's Mic's & NEEDS LOW CROWD CHEERING UNDER*

Content Note: **Way Up In The People—**

Production Note: *HIT GOLDBERG MUSIC HERE*

A Spotlight Revels Goldberg—Go Off Hot With Shot Of Russo's Face.

16a. TAPE: (Op Reel)   (:30)   WCW Halloween Havoc

Audio Note: *Track Op Reel...Self Contained*
Tape Note: *Fades Up From Black & Show Full Screen & Fades To Black*

16b. INFINITI!:   (:03)WCW Nitro Logo I.D. Over Tape

Audio Note: *Needs WCW Monday Nitro Music*
Infinit' Note: *Needs WCW Monday Nitro I.D.*

CM Position #2   (2:30)   B-Truck- Play Credit Card Spot To House   08:25:02
Send Battle Royal Guys To Ring

Document Created 09/25/00 @ 5:01 PM
This Information Is Subject To Change!

407

| TNT 343 | Page #5 | Uniondale, NY | Monday, September 25, 2000 | Air Time & Program Length: | 8:00:00–10:00:00 PM Eastern Time |

Segment #3

17. TAPE: (Pretape)   (:30)   (Locker Room) "Above Average" Mike Sanders 08:27:32
Talks w/ Kronik

Audio Note: *Track Pretape Audio & NEEDS LOW CROWD CHEERING UNDER*
Tape Note: *Fades Up From Black & Show Full Screen & Fades To Black*
Content Note: *"Above Average" Mike Sanders Informs Kronik (Who's Warming Up) That He Hates To Be The Bearer Of Bad News—But Due To Their Screw Up On Thunder This Past Wednesday—Mr. Russo Has Removed Them From The Tag Team Battle Royal. Kronik Is Hot—Sanders Answers—"Hey, I'm Only The Messenger" And Walks Off.*

Producer: Woody Kearce

17a. GRAPHICS:
Audio Note:
Graphics Note: *Show Full Screen Before Entrances*
WCW World Tag Team Title (Title Page)

18. RING:
Audio Note: *Track Announcer's Mic's*
Content Note: **Shot Of The Following Already In Ring:**
Jung Dragons (Kaz & Yang) w/ Leia Meow, Jaime-San
3 Count w/ Evan
Corp. Cajun/Lt. Loco w/ Sarg A-WALL
Harris Brothers
Mark Jindrak/Sean O'Haire
Referee Sends The Seconds To The Back— Leia Whips Jaime-San All The Way To The Back

19. ENTRANCE:
Audio Note:
1–M Filthy Animals Music
Filthy Animals
Track Announcer's Mic's @ Announce Position

Segment #3 Continued On Next Page…

Document Created 09/25/00 @ 5:01 PM
This Information Is Subject To Change!

408

Segment #3   Continued

20. RING: (6:00)   **WCW Tag Team Battle Royal**
Jung Dragons   **3 Count**
Corp. Cajun/Lt. Loco   **Harris Brothers**
Mark Jindrak/Sean O'Haire

Match Note:	*Match Begins And Ends In This Segment...*
Announcer Note:	*Both Men Of Each Team Have TO Be Eliminated For The TEAM To Be Eliminated- Eliminated By*
Content Note:	*Going Our Of The Ring And Must Hit The Floor*
	Konnan & Tygress To Color
	At App. Time Kronik To Ring Cleans House—Leaving Animals/Jindrak & O'Haire
	Security To Ring—Mace And Arrest Kronik
	Disqo To Ring—Though People—Screws Rey & Juvy With Duck
	Jindrak & O'Haire Last 2 Survivors– WCW World Tag Team Champs
Production Note:	*Jindrak/O'Haire Music On Out*
	Off Hot

20a. GRAPHICS:
Audio Note:
Graphics Note: **"Bull Contest" Promo (Graphic)**
Track Announcer's Mic's
Show Full Screen When Producer Calls For It During Match

21. TAPE: (Pretape)   (:10)   **(Ladies Locker Room) Torrie Wilson Oiling Her Legs**
For The Miss WCW Contest
Audio Note: *Track Pretape Audio & Track Announcer's Mic's & Needs Nitro Music Under & MUST HAVE CROWD*
CHEERING UNDER SHOT
Tape Note: *Show Full Screen & Fades To Black*
Producer: Chris Larson

21a. INFINIT!:   (:03) **WCW Nitro Logo I.D. Over Pretape**
Audio Note: *Needs WCW Monday Nitro Music*
Infinit! Note: *Needs WCW Monday Nitro I.D.*

CM Position #3   (2:33)   **Nitro Girls-STAGE-"Hey Mr. DJ" Music From DJ**
08:34:12

TNT 343   Page #7   Uniondale, NY   Monday, September 25, 2000   Air Time & Program Length: 8:00:00-10:00:00 PM Eastern Time

Segment #4

21b. TAPE: (Op Reel)   (:55)   **Promotional Considerations #1**   08:36:45
Audio Note: *Needs Live WCW Monday Nitro Music & Track Op Reel...Self Contained*
Tape Note: *Fades Up From Black & Show Full Screen & Fades To Black*

22. BACKSTAGE: (Live)   (1:00)   **(Backstage Interview Pos.) Pamela & Gene Okerlund w/ Howard Stern's Whack Pack Interview**
Audio Note: *Track Stick Mic & Track Announcer's Mic's When Needed & MUST HAVE CROWD CHEERING UNDER SHOT*
Content Note: Pamela (In Full Length Fur Coat) & Mean Gene Interview Howard Stern's Whack Pack--The
    Judges For Tonight's Contest.
    Kevin Nash & The NBT's Walk Through This Shot- Jindrak & O'Haire Are The New Tag Team
    Champs

Producer: Darryl Marshall

23. ENTRANCE: 1-M ICP Music
Audio Note: Insane Clown Posse
    Track Announcer's Mic's @ Announce Position

24. TAPE: (:14) (B-Roll) Clips From Vampiro & Awesome Last
Audio Note: Week On Nitro TNT 342
    Track Tape... Nat's Only & Track Announcer's Mic's
    Needs Nitro Transition For In & Out & Show Full Screen During Entrance

25. RING: ICP Short Promo
Audio Note: Track Wireless Mic

26. ENTRANCE: 2-M Mike Awesome Music
Audio Note: That 70's Guy Mike Awesome
    Track Announcer's Mic's @ Announce Position
Content Note: That 70's Guy Mike Awesome Drives Bus Into Arena

Segment #4 Continued On Next Page...

Document Created 09/25/00 @ 5:01 PM
This Information Is Subject To Change!

BONUS MATERIALS

TNT 343   Page #8   Uniondale, NY   Monday, September 25, 2000   Air Time & Program Length: 8:00:00-10:00:00 PM Eastern Time

Segment #4   Continued

27. RING: (5:00) **Hardcore Match**

ICP   v.   That 70's Guy Mike Awesome

Match Note: Match Begins And Ends In This Segment....

Content Note: (If Possible) Awesome Powerbombs Shaggy D On Top Of Bus
Awesome Over 1-2-3

Production Note: Awesome Music On Out

Off Hot

28. TAPE: (Pretape) (:10) **(Locker Room) Major Gunns Oiling Up For The Miss WCW Contest**

Audio Note: Track Pretape Audio & Track Announcer's Mic's & Needs Nitro Music Under & MUST HAVE CROWD CHEERING UNDER SHOT

Tape Note: Show Full Screen

29. BACKSTAGE: (Live) (:10) **(Hallway) The Cat & Ms. Jones On Their Way TO The Arena**

Audio Note: Track Camera Mic & Track Announcer's Mic's & Needs Nitro Music Under & NEEDS LOW CROWD CHEERING UNDER

Producer: Chris Larson

29a. TAPE: (Op Reel) (:30) **WCW MasterCard Spot**

Audio Note: Track Op Reel...Self Contained

Tape Note: Fades Up From Black & Show Full Screen & Fades To Black

29b. INFINITI: (:03) **WCW Nitro Logo I.D. Over Tape**

Audio Note: Needs WCW Monday Nitro Music

Infiniti Note: Needs WCW Monday Nitro I.D.

CM Position #4 (3:03) **Nitro Girls- Stage- "Hey Mr. DJ" Music From DJ**

08:44:30

Document Created 09/25/00 @ 5:01 PM
This Information Is Subject To Change!

411

TNT 343   Page #9   Uniondale, NY   Monday, September 25, 2000   Air Time & Program Length: 8:00:00-10:00:00 PM Eastern Time

Segment #5

30. TAPE: (Pretape)   (1:27)   (Shot 9/24/00) Vignette #2– David Flair At Chuckie Cheese   08:47:33

Audio Note: Track Pretape Audio & NEEDS LOW CROWD CHEERING UNDER

Tape Note: Fades Up From Black & Show Full Screen

31. ENTRANCE: The Cat w/ Ms. Jones Music & Entrance

Audio Note: Track The Cat Music For Intro & Track Wireless Mic(s) & Track Announcer's Mic's @ Announce Position

32. RING: (5:00)   The Cat Short Promo

Audio Note: Track Wireless Mic

Content Note:

- Russo–This Is Not A Warning–But A Promise, If Your Three Stooges, Nash, Jarrett And Steiner Along With Gang Green–The Natural Born Thrillers Set One Foot In That Cage In Your Match With Booker T–They Will All Be Fired On The Spot.

33. ENTRANCE: "Above Average" Mike Sanders Music & Entrance

Audio Note: "Above Average" Mike Sanders With Russo's Bat

Content Note:

- Sanders Has A Problem With The Cat's Decision
- The Cat Tells Sanders To Screw Off
- The Cat Turns His Back On Sanders–Sanders Goes To Nail Cat With Bat–The Cat Catches It
- The Cat Get Heat On Sanders

34. ENTRANCE: "Coach" Kevin Nash Music & Entrance

Audio Note: Track Kevin Nash Music For Intro & Track Wireless Mic(s) & Track Announcer's Mic's @ Announce Position

Content Note:

- Kevin Powerbombs The Cat Twice
- Kevin Carries Off Mike Sanders

Production Note: Kevin Music On Out

Off Hot

35. BACKSTAGE: (Live)   (:10)   (Backstage) Paisley & Tygress Wearing Provocative Robes

Audio Note: Track Camera Mic & Track Announcer's Mic's & Needs Nitro Music Under, & NEEDS LOW CROWD CHEERING UNDER

Producer: Chris Larson

Document Created 09/25/00 @ 5:01 PM
This Information Is Subject To Change!

412

TNT 343   Page #10   Uniondale, NY   Monday, September 25, 2000   Air Time & Program Length: 8:00:00-10:00:00 PM Eastern Time

Segment #5   Continued

35a. INFINITI!:   **(:03)WCW Nitro Logo I.D. Over Live Shot**

Audio Note: *Needs WCW Monday Nitro Music*

Infiniti Note: *Needs WCW Monday Nitro I.D.*   08:54:10

CM Position #5   (2:30)   Send Miss WCW Contestants To The Ringside W/

Robes On

413

TNT 343   Page #11   Uniondale, NY   Monday, September 25, 2000   Air Time & Program Length: 8:00:00-10:00:00 PM Eastern Time

Segment #6

35b. TAPE: (Op Reel)   (:55)   Promotional Considerations #2   08:56:40

Audio Note:
Tape Note: *Needs Live WCW Monday Nitro Music & Track Op Reel... Self Contained*
Fades Up From Black & Show Full Screen & Fades To Black

36. RING: (8:00)   Pamela & Mean Gene Okerlund MC The Miss WCW Contest

Audio Note: *Track Wireless Mic's*
Content Note: **Pamela (Still In Fur Coat) & Mean Gene MC Miss WCW Contest**
Introduce Judges (Whack Pack—Who Should Be Sitting At Table Inside The Ring)
Production Note: *Chyron Their Names On Screen*

AUDIO NOTE: *Play Dancing Music Under The Entire Break So Girls Can Dance*

Gene Calls Each Girl Into The Ring & To The Mic-
One By One, The Girls Take Off Their Robe & Do A Little Dance - Major Gunns Is last

37. ENTRANCE: "Oh Canada" Music & Entrance

Audio Note: *Track Canadian National Anthem Music For Intro & Track Wireless Mic & Track*
Announcer's Mic's @ Announce Position

Content Note: "Oh Canada" Music & Entrance—Lance Storm Brings An Overcoat To Ring And Takes Major
Gunns Out Of Contest
Right Before Voting Pamela Takes Off Fur Coat Claiming To Be "Hot"
Pamela Revels The Skimpiest Bikini Of All
Whack Pack Votes For Pamela
Leia Attacks Pamela
Midajah To Ring Makes Save For Pamela
Midajah/Leia Go
Referees Break It Up
Off Hot

37a. GRAPHICS: "Bull Contest" Promo (Graphic)

Audio Note:
Graphics Note: *Track Announcer's Mic's*
Show Full Screen When Producer Calls For It During Contest

Segment #6 Continued On Next Page...

Document Created 09/25/00 @ 5:01 PM
This Information Is Subject To Change!

414

TNT 343　Page #12　Uniondale, NY　Monday, September 25, 2000　Air Time & Program Length:　8:00:00-10:00:00 PM Eastern Time

Segment #6　Continued

38. TAPE: (Pretape)　(1:00)　(Backstage) Mike Tenay w/ Scott Steiner Interview

Audio Note: *Track Pretape Audio & Track Announcer's Mic's & MUST HAVE CROWD CHEERING UNDER SHOT*

Tape Note: *Show Full Screen & Fades To Black*

Content Note: **Steiner Needs To Address What Just Happened To Midajah**
Scott Cuts Promo On Goldberg
From Behind, Goldberg Attacks Steiner
Goldberg Gets Some On Steiner
Security Breaks It Up—Off Hot

Producer: Darryl Marshall

38a. INFINITI:　(:03)WCW Nitro Logo I.D. Over Pretape

Audio Note: *Needs WCW Monday Nitro Music*

Infiniti Note: *Needs WCW Monday Nitro I.D.*

CM Position #6　(2:33)　DJ Ran Performs- House Only
Send Disqo To The Ring Here

09:06:35

Document Created 09/25/00 @ 5:01 PM
This Information Is Subject To Change!

415

TNT 343   Page #13   Uniondale, NY   Monday, September 25, 2000   Air Time & Program Length: 8:00:00-10:00:00 PM Eastern Time

Segment #7

39. RING: **Shot Of The Disqo Already In Ring To Introduce** 09:09:08

Audio Note: **New Partner**

Track Wireless Mic & Track Announcer's Mic's

40. ENTRANCE: **Scott Steiner**

Audio Note: *Track Announcer's Mic's @ Announce Position*

Content Note: Scott Shit Cans Disqo

   Scott Calls Out Goldberg

41. ENTRANCE: **Goldberg**   2-M Goldberg Music

Audio Note: *Track Announcer's Mic's @ Announce Position*

Pyro Note: Needs Goldberg Pyro Here

Content Note: From The Stage....Goldberg Accepts Challenge—Only If Cage Is Lowered—One-On-One, No

   Referee—First Man Out Wins

   Steiner Accepts

42. RING: (8:00)   **Scott Steiner**   v.   **Goldberg**   1-M Scott Steiner Music

Match Note: **Caged Heat Match**

Match Begins And Ends In This Segment....

Content Note: Goldberg Walks Out Of Cage

Production Note: *Hit Goldberg Music — Keep Playing Under Entire Time*

   After Goldberg Walks Out He Gets Ring Mic And Says, "Russo—You're Next!"

   Off Hot

43. BACKSTAGE: (Live)   (:10)   **(Hallway) Jeff Jarrett On His Way TO The Arena**

Audio Note: *Track Camera Mic & Track Announcer's Mic's & Needs Nitro Music Under & NEEDS LOW CROWD CHEERING UNDER*

Content Note: On His Way To Arena—Jarrett Bumps Into Beetlejuice. Beetlejuice Has Words With Jarrett.

   Jarrett Takes Out Beetlejuice With Guitar.

Producer: Woody Kearce

Document Created 09/25/00 @ 5:01 PM
This Information Is Subject To Change!

416

TNT 343   Page #14   Uniondale, NY   Monday, September 25, 2000   Air Time & Program Length: 8:00:00-10:00:00 PM Eastern Time

Segment #7   Continued

43a. INFINIT!:   **(:03)WCW Nitro Logo I.D. Over Live Shot**

Audio Note: *Needs WCW Monday Nitro Music*

Infiniti Note: *Needs WCW Monday Nitro I.D.*   09:17:18

CM Position #7   (2:33)   Nitro Girls- STAGE- "Last Resort" Music From DJ

Document Created 09/25/00 @ 5:01 PM
This Information Is Subject To Change!

417

Segment #8

43b. ARENA/PROFILE: (:18) **Closed Captioned PC- Meineke**   09:19:51
Audio Note:
Tape Note: Track Op Reel & Track Nitro Music Under & Track Announcer's Mic's @ Announce Position
Announcer Copy: Fades Up From Black & Show Full Screen & Fades To Black/Tied To Pretape
"Closed Captioning Where Available Sponsored By Meineke Discount Muffler Shops."

44. TAPE: (Pretape) (:30) **(Backstage Interview Pos.) Pamela w/ Booker T.**
Audio Note: Track Pretape Audio & MUST HAVE CROWD CHEERING UNDER SHOT
Tape Note: Show Full Screen
Content Note: Pamela Interviews Booker T. About Upcoming Title Match Tonight. (Pam Still In Bikini)
Producer: Darryl Marshall

45. ENTRANCE:
Audio Note: Track Announcer's Mic's @ Announce Position
1--M Misfits In Action Music
General Rection

46. TAPE: (:18) **(B-Roll) Clips From MIA/Team Canada Story**
Audio Note: Track Tape., Nat's Only & Track Announcer's Mic's
Tape Note: Needs Nitro Transition For In & Out & Show Full Screen During Entrance
Content Note: B-Roll MIA/Team Canada Story--Since Hacksaw Turn

47. ENTRANCE:
Audio Note: Track Announcer's Mic's @ Announce Position
2--M Jeff Jarrett Music
Jeff Jarrett
Needs Jeff Jarrett Pyro Here

48. RING: (7:00) **General Rection   v.   Jeff Jarrett**
Match Note: *Match Begins And Ends In This Segment ...*
Pyro Note:
Content Note: **Team Canada To Ring- Distracts Rection**
Jarrett Over
Jeff Jarrett Music On Out
Production Note: **Jarrett Keeps Getting Heat On Reaction**
MIA To Ring--Big Schmazz
Heels Get Heat
Jarrett Puts Rection In Figure 4

Document Created 09/25/00 @ 5:01 PM
This Information Is Subject To Change!

TNT 343   Page #16   Uniondale, NY   Monday, September 25, 2000   Air Time & Program Length: 8:00:00-10:00:00 PM Eastern Time

Segment #8   Continued

49. ENTRANCE:

Audio Note: **Sting Music & Entrance**

Content Note: *Track Sting Music For Intro & Track Wireless Mic(s) & Track Announcer's Mic's @ Announce Position*

Sting Clears The Ring BabyFaces Comeback

Sting Helps Up Rection

Production Note: *Sting Music On Out*

50. STAGE:

Audio Note: **Lance Storm Short Promo**

Content Note: *Track Wireless Mic*

From Stage Lance Storm Cuts Promo

"Hey Sting, You Want To Stick Your Nose In My Business? How About If I Send Back My Soldiers—And You Send Back Yours And You Try Me One—On—One In A NON- Title Match"

Sting Answers—"It's ShowTime—Let's Do It!"

Hot To Break

50a. INFINITI:

Audio Note: **(:03)WCW Monday Nitro Logo I.D. Over Hot Action**

Infiniti Note: *Needs WCW Monday Nitro Music*   09:27:39

Needs WCW Monday Nitro I.D.

CM Position #8   (2:33)   Lance & Sting In Ring Ready For Match In Next Seg.

419

TNT 343   Page #17   Uniondale, NY   Monday, September 25, 2000   Air Time & Program Length: 8:00:00-10:00:00 PM Eastern Time

Segment #9

51. RING: (8:00)   Non –Title Match

Lance Storm   v.   Sting   09:30:12

Match Note:
Match Begins And Ends In This Segment....

Content Note:
Match Already In Progress
Helluva Match—Sting Over

Production Note:
Sting Music On Out

Off Hot

51a. GRAPHICS: "Bull Contest" Promo (Graphic)

Audio Note:
Track Announcer's Mic's

Graphics Note:
Show Full Screen When Producer Calls For It During Match

52. TAPE: (Pretape)   (:17)   (Shot 9/24/00) Vignette #3- David Flair Looking For House

Audio Note:
Track Pretape Audio & Track Announcer's Mic's & NEEDS LOW CROWD CHEERING UNDER

Tape Note:
Show Full Screen & Fades To Black

Content Note:
David Flair Vignette #3—David Approaches House He's Been Looking For All Night

52a. TAPE: (Op Reel)   (:30)   WCW Magazine Spot

Audio Note:
Track Op Reel..Self Contained

Tape Note:
Fades Up From Black & Show Full Screen & Fades To Black

52B. INFINITI!:   (:03)WCW Monday Nitro Logo I.D. Over Tape

Audio Note:
Needs WCW Monday Nitro Music

Infinit! Note:
Needs WCW Monday Nitro I.D.

CM Position #9   (2:30)   Nitro Girls- STAGE- "Rollin" Music From DJ   09:38:59

Document Created 09/25/00 @ 5:01 PM
This Information Is Subject To Change!

420

TNT 343   Page #18   Uniondale, NY   Monday, September 25, 2000   Air Time & Program Length: 8:00:00-10:00:00 PM Eastern Time

Segment #10

53. TAPE: (Pretape) (1:34) **(Shot 9/24/00) Vignette #4- David Flair Finds House** 09:41:29

Audio Note: Track Pretape Audio & Track Announcer's Mic's & Needs Nitro Music Under & NEEDS LOW CROWD CHEERING UNDER

Tape Note: Fades Up From Black & Show Full Screen

Content Note: David Enters Wrong House—David Then Goes To Right House—Next Door—Nobody Home.

54. BACKSTAGE: (Live) (:30) **(Backstage Interview Pos.) Gene Okerlund w/ Vince Russo Interview**

Audio Note: Track Stick Mic & MUST HAVE CROWD CHEERING UNDER SHOT

Producer: Darryl Marshall

55. ARENA/RING: (Live) (:30) **Cage Lowering Over The Ring**

Audio Note: Track Announcer's Mic's & Needs Nitro Music Under & NEEDS LOW CROWD CHEERING UNDER

56. Has Been Deleted

57. ENTRANCE: (:30) **Vince Russo Music & Entrance**

Audio Note: Track Vince Russo Music For Intro & Track Announcer's Mic's @ Announce Position

Content Note: Vince Russo w/ Towel Over His Head, Lights Down In Arena, Spotlight On Russo, Entire Security Force With Him—Off To Break)

57a. INFINITI!: (:03)WCW Monday Nitro Logo I.D. Over Live Shot

Audio Note: Needs WCW Monday Nitro Music

Infiniti Note: Needs WCW Monday Nitro I.D.

57b. TAPE: (Op Reel) (:30) **1-800- CALL ATT Road Report Spot**

Audio Note: Track Op Reel, Self Contained

Tape Note: Fades Up From Black & Show Full Screen & Fades To Black

CM Position #10 (2:30) **DJ Ran Performs- House Only** 09:45:03

B-truck- Play Credit Card Spot To House Here

Document Created 09/25/00 @ 5:01 PM
This Information Is Subject To Change!

421

TNT 343   Page #19   Uniondale, NY   Monday, September 25, 2000   Air Time & Program Length: 8:00:00-10:00:00 PM Eastern Time

Segment #11

57c. TAPE: (Op Reel) (:30)   **WCW Halloween Havoc Spot**   09:47:33

Audio Note: Track Op Reel...Self Contained
Tape Note: Fades Up From Black & Show Full Screen & Fades To Black

57d. GRAPHICS: WCW World Heavyweight (Title Page)

Audio Note: Track Announcer's Mic's
Graphics Note: Show Full Screen Before Entrances

58. ENTRANCE: 1-M Booker T. Music

Booker T.

Audio Note: Track Announcer's Mic's @ Announce Position
Pyro Note: Needs Booker T. Pyro Here

59. RING: (10:00)   WCW World Heavyweight title Match- Caged Heat

Vince Russo   v.   Booker T.

Match Note: Match Begins And Ends In This Segment...

Announcer Note: Have To Leave The Cage To Win The Match

Content Note: Prior To Bell—Entire Babyface Locker Room Comes To Ring And Surrounds Cage
Before Bell Russo Attacks Booker T. With Bat
It's All Russo—He Goes For Door—Blocked By Baby's
Russo Gets Back On Booker
Russo Pulls Ladder From Underneath—Sets Up Ladder—Starts To Climb To Top Of Cage—Baby
Faces Start Climbing Cage
Once Russo Goes To Pull Himself Through–

Segment #11 Continued On Next Page...

Document Created 09/25/00 @ 5:01 PM
This Information Is Subject To Change!

422

Segment #11   Continued

60. ENTRANCE:

Audio Note:

Content Note:

Sting Music & Entrance

Track Sting Music For Intro & Track Wireless Mic(s) & Track Announcer's Mic's @ Announce Position

Sting Steps On Ramp Hands—Russo Bumps Down

Jarrett Hits The Cage—Climbs To Top—Jarrett/Sting Go

Back In Ring—Booker Comeback

Lex Luger Sneaks Down To Cage From Other Side And Hands Russo A Steel Pipe Through Cage

Russo Nails Booker With Pipe

Russo Goes To Leave Cage—Cameraman In His Way

Russo Nails Cameraman—But Door Is Still Blocked By Babies

Russo Tries Ladder Again

Paramedics To The Ring To Help Cameraman—Paramedics Open Door And Get In Ring

Russo Sees His Advantage

Russo Goes For Door—Is Cut Off By Paramedic Who Nails Russo

Reveal

Paramedic Gets Heat On Russo Than Leaves

Russo Dead In Cage

Nash Sends Thrillers To Ring—Thrillers Lay Out Babies With Weapons

Booker Is Getting Heat On Russo

Steiner To Cage—Booker Slams Steel Door In Steiner's Face—Steiner Goes Down—He's Out

Booker Goes To Leave—

Luger

61. ENTRANCE:

Audio Note:

Content Note:

Goldberg Music & Entrance

Track Goldberg Music For Intro & Track Wireless Mic(s) & Track Announcer's Mic's @ Announce Position

Booker Lets Goldberg In Cage

Goldberg Stalks Russo

Goldberg Spears Russo Through Cage As Booker Walks Out Door—At Exact Same Time

Go Hot Off—

Announcer Note: Who's The WCW Champion?!!!– We Will Find Out On Thunder!

62. INFINIT!:

Audio Note: (:05)Copyright-Over Hot Action

Infinit Note: Need WCW Monday Nitro Music

Need Copyright Chyron

Terminal Break   (:10)   09:58:03

WCW Halloween Havoc   Confidential Format

Las Vegas, NV
Sunday, October 29, 2000
Page 1 of 11
As Of: 10/29/00 @ 5:30 PM Eastern Time

a. INFINIT!:	(:15)	**FBI Warning**
Infint! Note:		This FBI Warning Still Will Come From Infinit! When Director Calls For It
1. TAPE (Op Reel):	(:10)	**WCW Logo Identification**
Audio Note:		Track Op Reel ...Self Contained
Tape Note:		Fades Up From Black & Show Full Screen & Fades To Black/Tied To Pretape
2. TAPE (Pretape):	(:30)	**(Outside) Exterior Shots Of MGM Grand, Las Vegas, NV/Fans Filing Into The Arena**
Audio Note:		Track Pretape Audio & Track Announcer's Mic's & Needs Halloween Havoc Music Under & NEEDS LOW CROWD CHEERING UNDER
Tape Note:		Show Full Screen & Tied To Pretape
Content Note:		**Shots Of Exterior Of Las Vegas MGM Grand/Fans Filing Into Arena**
3. TAPE (Pretape):		**(Outside) Soundbytes From Fans With Their Picks For Tonight**
Audio Note:		Track Pretape Audio & NEEDS LOW CROWD CHEERING UNDER
Tape Note:		Show Full Screen & Fades To Black/Tied To Havoc Open
Content Note:		**Soundbytes From Fans Re: Their Picks For Tonight**
4. TAPE (Op Reel):	(:47)	**(Package) WCW Halloween Havoc (Road To Halloween Havoc)/ Open**
Audio Note:		Track Op Reel ...Self Contained
Tape Note:		Fades Up From Black & Show Full Screen & Fades To Black
5. LIVE:	(:30)	**Arena Wide Shot w/Pyrotechnics**
Audio Note:		Track Announcer's Mic's @ Announce Position & Track Pyro Mic & Needs Live WCW Halloween Havoc Theme Music Under
Infint! Note:		Needs Live Chyron w/Las Vegas, NV
Pyro Note:		Go Pyro w/ WCW Halloween Havoc Open Look
6. GRAPHICS:		**WCW World Tag Team Title Match (Title Page)**
Audio Note:		Track Announcers Mic's @ Announce Position
Infint! Note:		Show Full Screen When Director Calls For It Before Entrances
7. RING:		1-M Boogie Knights Music
		Boogie Knights
Audio Note:		Track Announcers Mic's @ Announce Position & Ring Announce Off Line
8. TAPE: (Op Reel)		**(:15) (B-Roll) Clips Of Boogie Knights Defeating Jindrak/O'Haire-Then Sander's Reverses The Decision**
Audio Note:		Track Op Reel ... Nat's Only & Track Announcer's Mic's
Tape Note:		Needs Havoc Transition On In & Out & Show Full Screen During Entrances
9. RING:		2-M Natural Born Thrillers Music
		Mark Jindrak
		Sean O'Haire
Audio Note:		Track Announcers Mic's @ Announce Position & Ring Announce Off Line

WCW Halloween Havoc   Confidential Format

10. RING:		**3-M** Filthy Animals Music
		Filthy Animals
Audio Note:		Track Announcers Mic's @ Announce Position & Ring Announce Off Line
Content Note:		Filthy Animals (Rey, Kidman, Konnan, Tygress)
		Konnan/Tygress To Announce Position

11. RING:	**(15:00)**	**3 Way Dance For The WCW World Tag Team Titles Match**
		Boogie Knights v. Mark Jindrak v. Rey Mysterio, Jr.
		Sean O'Haire Kidman
Audio Note:		Track Announcers Mic's @ Announce Position
Content Note:		Konnan/Tygress Talk About Upcoming Mixed-Tag Match Vs. Franchise/Torrie
		Helluva Match
		Boogie Knights Have Match All But Won – Get Screwed Out Of Win By Rey/ Kidman
		Jindrak/O'Haire Over
Production Note:		*Jindrak/O'Haire Music On Out*
		Boogie Knights Go After Rey/Kidman
		Konnan Runs In For Save – Gets Cut Off By Jindrak/O'Haire
		Jindrak/O'Haire Get Heat On Konnan
		Heels Getting Heat On Baby's

12. RING:		**Misfits In Action Music**
Audio Note:		Track Misfits In Action Music For Intro & Track Announcers Mic's @ Announce Position
Content Note:		Sergeant A-Wall Out For Save – Clears Ring Of Heels
		Referees Out To Help Filthy Animals – Konnan Hurt
		Konnan Refuses Help – Animals Walk To Back
		A-Wall Remains In Ring

12a. GRAPHICS:		**WCW Hardcore Match (Title Page)**
Audio Note:		Track Announcers Mic's @ Announce Position
Infinti! Note:		Show Full Screen When Director Calls For It Before Entrance

13. RING:		**1-M** Natural Born Thrillers Music
		Reno
Audio Note:		Track Announcers Mic's @ Announce Position & Ring Announce Off Line

14. TAPE: (Op Reel)		**(:15) (B-Roll) Clips Of A-WALL Defeating Reno For The Hardcore Belt-Then Sander's Reverses The Decision**
Audio Note:		Track Op Reel ... Nat's Only & Track Announcer's Mic's
Tape Note:		Needs Havoc Transition On In & Out & Show Full Screen During Entrance

15. RING:	**(15:00)**	**WCW Hardcore Title Match**
		Sergeant A-WALL v. Reno
Audio Note:		Track Announcers Mic's @ Announce Position
Announcer Note:		Inform Us That, Apparently Against The Wishes Of Mike Sanders, The WCW Executive
		Board Has Re-Instated Old-School Hardcore Rules – No DQ, Falls Count Anywhere
Note:		As A Result, This Match Must Go To The Back For Several Near-Falls
Content Note:		Reno/A-Wall Work Their Way Back Out Into The Arena For The Finish
		Reno Manages To Steal This One
Production Note:		*Reno Music On Out*

WCW Halloween Havoc   Confidential Format
Page 3 of 11

17. TAPE (Pretape): (:45)	(Backstage) Natural Born Thrillers With The Franchise
Audio Note: Tape Note:	Track Pretape Audio & NEEDS LOW CROWD CHEERING UNDER Show Full Screen
Content Note:	Franchise Thanks Jindrak And O'Haire For Putting The Boots To Konnan For Him Earlier (We Find Out It Was A Pre-Meditated Attack) Franchise Lets Us Know That He Heard From Coach Nash, Who Had Asked Him To Keep An Eye On The Thrillers Tonight – Sanders And Franchise Share A Wink – "This Is Going To Work Out Great For All Of Us..."

18. Announce Pos.: (2:00)	Stevie Ray, Tony Schiavone, & Mark Madden
Audio Note: Infiniti Note:	Track Announcer's Mic's @ Announce Position Needs Live Chyron w/Announcers Name Bar When Director Calls For It
Content Note:	Welcome Us (Officially) To WCW Halloween Havoc 2000 Update Goldberg Story -- We've Received Word Re: Goldberg's Injury From Thunder Goldberg Has Not Yet Arrived – No One Has Heard From Him Since Thunder

19. TAPE: (Op Reel)	(:15) (B-Roll) Clips From Thunder TBS 147- Goldberg Posting Himself
Audio Note: Tape Note:	Track Op Reel ... Nat's Only & Track Announcer's Mic's Needs Havoc Transition On In & Out & Show Full Screen During Announce Position
Content Note:	B-Roll Footage From Thunder Of Goldberg Posting Himself – Several Angles, If We Have Them

20. TAPE (Pretape): (:45)	(Backstage) Kronik Speaking With The Nevada Athletic Commission Representatives
Audio Note: Tape Note:	Track Pretape Audio & Track Announcer's Mic's & NEEDS LOW CROWD CHEERING UNDER Show Full Screen
Content Note:	They Tip Them Off That Goldberg – If He Arrives – May Not Be In Any Condition To Wrestle Tonight Kronik Needs To Play This Very Smooth

20a. RING: (10:00)	Lt. Loco v. The Perfect Event Corp. Cajun
Audio Note:	Track Announcers Mic's @ Announce Position

16. BACKSTAGE: (Live) (:45)	(Backstage) Konnan & Filthy Animals With Coach
Audio Note:	Track Camera Mic & Track Announcer's Mic & NEEDS CROWD CHEERING UNDER
Content Note:	Konnan Is Hurt From Earlier Konnan Walks Away From Danny Before He Can Finish Examining Him Animals Are Worried For Konnan – He Wants Franchise Bad, And Isn't Willing To Let Anything Get In His Way

21. RING:	1-M The Franchise Music The Franchise Torrie Wilson
Audio Note:	Track Announcers Mic's @ Announce Position & Ring Announce Off Line

22. RING:	The Franchise Short Promo
Audio Note:	Track Wireless Mic
Content Note:	Re: Tonight's Match, Konnan's Condition Calls Out Konnan Now

WCW Halloween Havoc   Confidential Format
Page 4 of 11

23. RING: **2-M** Filthy Animals Music
Filthy Animals
Audio Note: Track Announcers Mic's @ Announce Position & Ring Announce Off Line

Content Note:	Tygress Only
	Tygress Gets In Franchise's Face – Konnan's Hurt (As Are Billy And Rey), But She's Here,
	So Let's Do This!
	Franchise And Torrie Bully Tygress Around
	Konnan Hits Ring From Crowd (Behind Franchise's Back) (Still Selling)

24. RING: **(12:00)**   **Mixed Tag Team Match**
Franchise   v.   Konnan
Torrie Wilson   Tygress
Audio Note: Track Announcers Mic's @ Announce Position

Content Note:	Konnan Over Franchise 1-2-3
Production Note:	*Konnan (Filthy Animals) Music On Out*

25. TAPE (Pretape):   **(1:00)**   **(Backstage Interview Pos.) Gene Okerlund w/ David Flair**
Audio Note: Track Pretape Audio & NEEDS LOW CROWD CHEERING UNDER
Tape Note: Show Full Screen

Content Note:	Mean Gene In The Back With David Flair (With Gentlemen In Lab Coats)
	Re: DNA Match Vs. Buff Bagwell – As Soon As Flair Gets His Sample He's Going To Bring
	It Back To These Men, Who Will Rush It Off To Their Exclusive Testing Facilities – "….And
	Then We'll All Find Out What I Already Know!"

26. RING: **1-M** Buff Bagwell Music
Buff Bagwell
Audio Note: Track Announcers Mic's @ Announce Position & Ring Announce Off Line

27. RING: **Buff Bagwell Short Promo**
Audio Note: Track Wireless Mic

Content Note:	"Tonight, David Flair Wants To Find Out If Buff Daddy Is The Real Daddy. Well, Little
	Flair – If You Think You're Rough Enough To Take Some Of Buff's Stuff, Come On And
	Give It Your Best Shot. Just Know That, While You're Just Looking For A Sample, Buff Is
	Gonna Go For Your Jugular – Because I'm Buff, I'm The Stuff… And You Ain't Nothing But
	A Powder Puff."

28. RING: **2-M** David Flair Music
David Flair
Audio Note: Track Announcers Mic's @ Announce Position & Ring Announce Off Line

Content Note:	Carrying Slides/Test Tubes

WCW Halloween Havoc   Confidential Format

29. RING:	(10:00)	DNA Match

Buff Bagwell   v.   **David Flair**

Audio Note: Track Announcers Mic's @ Announce Position

Content Note:	Buff In Control Throughout
	Buff Opens David Up – Buff Over
Production Note:	Buff Music Plays
	During Celebration, Lex Luger Hits The Ring
	Luger Brutalizes Buff – Opens Him Up
	David Gets His Sample
	David Staggers To The Back
Production Note:	Lex Luger Music On Out

---

30. BACKSTAGE: (Live) (:45) (Backstage) David Flair Running To The Medical Techs Backstage

Audio Note: Track Camera Mic & Track Announcer's Mic's & NEEDS CROWD CHEERING UNDER

Content Note:	David Runs Up To Medical Technicians In The Back
	David Hands Them The Sample – They Take It And Run Out
	David Collapses – Smile On His Face
	Camera Pans Up – Reveal Goldberg Arriving/Entering Building (Shaking His Head Clearing Cobwebs)

---

31. TAPE (Pretape): (1:30) (Backstage Interview Pos.) Gene Okerlund w/ Scott Steiner & Midajah

Audio Note: Track Pretape Audio & NEEDS LOW CROWD CHEERING UNDER
Tape Note: Show Full Screen

Content Note:	Steiner Takes Issue With This -- We're Not Here To Talk About Goldberg – We're Here To Talk About The Next WCW Champion
	Scotty Cuts Promo On Booker T. – Needs To Mention How He's Got All Night To Think About All The Different Ways He's Going To Punish Booker

---

32. RING: 1-M The Cat Music
The Cat
w/ Ms. Jones

Audio Note: Track Announcers Mic's @ Announce Position & Ring Announce Off Line

Content Note:	Carrying Corner Stool, Spit Bucket, Water Bottle, Gloves, Etc.

---

33. RING: **The Cat Short Promo**

Audio Note: Track Wireless Mic

Content Note:	Calls Out Sanders

---

34. RING: 2-M Natural Born Thrillers Music
"Above Average" Mike Sanders

Audio Note: Track Announcers Mic's @ Announce Position & Ring Announce Off Line

Content Note:	"Above Average" Mike Sanders (W/Palumbo & Stasiak)
	Also Carrying Corner Stool, Spit Bucket, Water Bottle, Etc.
	Sanders Wearing Pads, Headgear, Etc.

428

WCW Halloween Havoc Confidential Format

35. RING:	(10:00)	3 Round Kickboxing Match For The Sole-Commissionership Of WCW
		The Cat v. "Above Average" Mike Sanders
Audio Note:		Track Announcers Mic's @ Announce Position
Note:		Three 2-Minute Rounds, After A Knockdown You Have A Ten-Count To Regain Your Feet – Match Over When Participant Cannot Answer 10-Count
Content Note:		Sanders Barely Survives Round One
		Between Rounds One And Two, Cat Doesn't Even Need To Sit
		Sanders Gets Worked On His Corner By Stasiak/Palumbo... Who Begin To Bicker With Each Other
		Round Two – Cat All Over Sanders Again
		Stasiak Wants To Throw In Towel – Palumbo Won't Let Him
		Between Rounds Two And Three, Palumbo/Stasiak Bickering So Much They Aren't Tending To A Beat-Up Sanders
		Franchise Comes Out To The Ring – Asks Ref To Send Palumbo/Stasiak To Back
		As Ref Sends Palumbo/Stasiak To Back, Franchise Cuts Open Sanders' Glove And Slips Horseshoe Inside – Tapes It Back Up
Note –		Sanders Needs Oversized Gloves So Horseshoe Will Fit
		Round Three, Cat Has Sanders Beat – Until Sanders Connects With A Wild Haymaker With Loaded Glove – Cat Out
		Cat Cannot Answer 10-Count: Sanders Over
Production Note:		Sanders Music On Out

36. BACKSTAGE: (Live) (:45)	(Backstage) Nevada Athletic Reps Examine Goldberg
Audio Note:	Track Camera Mic & Track Announcer's Mic's & NEEDS LOW CROWD CHEERING UNDER
Content Note:	They Are Skeptical As To His Ability To Participate Tonight
	Goldberg Is Hot

37. TAPE (Pretape): (1:30)	(Backstage Interview Pos.) Gene Okerlund w/ Kronik
Audio Note:	Track Pretape Audio & NEEDS LOW CROWD CHEERING UNDER
Tape Note:	Show Full Screen
Content Note:	Kronik Gloats – Tells Goldberg He Has Until The End Of The Show To Get Cleared To Wrestle – If Not, "...You Forfeit... And That's A Loss... And That's Your Ass Going Out The Door For Good!"

38. RING:	1-M Mike Awesome Music
	That 70's Guy Mike Awesome
Audio Note:	Track Announcers Mic's @ Announce Position & Ring Announce Off Line

39. TAPE: (Op Reel)	(:13) (B-Roll) Clips Of Mike Awesome Putting Vampiro Through Table
Audio Note:	Track Op Reel ... Nat's Only & Track Announcer's Mic's
Tape Note:	Needs Havoc Transition On In & Out & Show Full Screen During Entrances

429

WCW Halloween Havoc   Confidential Format

40. RING:

Audio Note:

2-M Vampiro Music

Vampiro

Track Announcers Mic's @ Announce Position & Ring Announce Off Line

40a. TAPE: (Op Reel)

Audio Note:
Tape Note:

(:15) (B-Roll) Clips Of Vampiro Brutalizing Crowbar On Nitro TNT 347

Track Op Reel ... Nat's Only & Track Announcer's Mic's
Needs Havoc Transition On In & Out & Show Full Screen During Entrances

40b. RING:

Audio Note:

Content Note:

Vampiro Short Promo

Track Wireless Mic

Vampiro Will Challenge Mike Awesome That If Vampiro Wins, He Will Get The WCW
World Title Shot Tomorrow Night On Nitro.
Mike Awesome Accepts

41. RING: (15:00)

Audio Note:

Content Note:

That 70's Guy Mike Awesome   v.   **Vampiro**

Track Announcers Mic's @ Announce Position

Wild, Brutal Match
At Different Point, Ref Goes To Disqualify Each Man – Opponent Appeals To Referee To
Not DQ Opponent – Match Allowed To Continue
Crowbar Down To Ring (Still Selling From Monday)
Awesome Over 1-2-3

Production Note: *Awesome Music On Out*

42. BACKSTAGE: (Live) (1:30)(Backstage Interview Pos.) Gene Okerlund w/ General Rection & Misfits In Action

Audio Note:

Content Note:

Track Camera Mic & Track Stick Mic & NEEDS LOW CROWD CHEERING UNDER

Heartfelt Promo Where Rection Tells Us What This Match Means To Him – Going To Bring
Home The United States Title... As Well As Major Gunns
This Is A Matter Of Pride... And He'll Do It On His Own

42a. ARENA: (:30) Ringside Shot Of Halloween Havoc Contest Winners & Then Arena Live Shot For Cover Pitch

Audio Note:

Announcer Copy:

Track Announcer's Mic's & Track Halloween Havoc Music Under & NEEDS LOW CROWD CHEERING
UNDER

With Us Here Tonight Is The Lucky Winner Of The WCW MasterCard "Play With Power"
Sweepstakes.
Leonard Bullock Is Here With His Wife Tammy And Two Friends As Guests Of WCW And
Capital One. Leonard Received Four Tickets To Tonight's Show And A Backstage, Hotel
Accommodations And Flights Were Also Part Of The Prize Package.
I Hear It's Easy To Apply. You Can Call 1-800-WCW-CARD And Fill Out An Application
Over The Phone. Apply Today!

43. Has Been Deleted

43a. GRAPHICS:
Audio Note:
Infini! Note:

WCW Canadian/US Heavyweight Match (Title Page)
Track Announcers Mic's @ Announce Position
Show Full Screen When Director Calls For It Before Entrances

WCW Halloween Havoc   Confidential Format

44. RING: (17:00)	**1-M** Team Canada Music
	Team Canada
Audio Note:	Track Announcers Mic's @ Announce Position & Ring Announce Off Line

45. RING:	**Lance Storm Short Promo**
Audio Note:	Track Wireless Mic
Content Note:	Call For Playing Of Canadian National Anthem
Production Note:	*Anthem Plays- Long Version*

46. RING:	**2-M** Misfits In Action Music
	General Rection
Audio Note:	Track Announcers Mic's @ Announce Position & Ring Announce Off Line

47. RING: (14:00)	**WCW Canadian/United States Heavyweight Title Handicap Match**
	Lance Storm v. **General Rection**
	Hacksaw Jim Duggan
Audio Note:	Track Announcers Mic's @ Announce Position
Content Note:	Rection Fighting Against All Odds
	Major Gunns Stops "Primetime" From Interfering From Outside Ring
	Rection Goes Over Duggan
Production Note:	*MIA Music On Out*
	MIA's To Ring – Huge Celebration As Team Canada (Storm, Duggan, Skipper) Exits

47a. Announce Pos.: (1:00)	**Stevie Ray, Tony Schiavone, & Mark Madden**
Audio Note:	Track Announcer's Mic's @ Announce Position

47b. TAPE: (Op Reel): (:30)	**WCW Mayhem 2000 Spot**
Audio Note:	Track Op Reel … Self Contained
Tape Note:	Fades Up From Black & Show Full Screen & Fades To Black

48. TAPE (Pretape): (1:00)	**(Backstage Interview Pos.) Pamela w/ Jeff Jarrett**
Audio Note:	Track Pretape Audio & NEEDS LOW CROWD CHEERING UNDER
Tape Note:	Show Full Screen & Tied To Package
Content Note:	Jarrett Promises To Show Us The Metamorphosis Of Sting, All Right – From "Nobody" To
	"Also-Ran," Straight Through "Has-Been" And Right Up To "Never-Was!"
	"Trick Or Treat, Slap-Nuts!"

49. TAPE (Op Reel): (:38)	**(Package) "The Chosen One" Jeff Jarrett v. Sting**
Audio Note:	Track Op Reel …Self Contained
Tape Note:	Fades Up From Black & Show Full Screen & Fades To Black

50. RING:	**1-M** Jeff Jarrett Music
	"The Chosen One" Jeff Jarrett
Audio Note:	Track Announcers Mic's @ Announce Position & Ring Announce Off Line
Pyro Note:	Needs Jeff Jarrett Pyro Here

50a. ARENA: (LIVE)	**Arena Black Out Thunder Lighting & Sound Effects**
Audio Note:	Track Wireless Mic & Track Announcers Mic's @ Announce Position
Special Audio Note:	Needs Sting Music Playing Under

51. RING:	**2-M** Sting Music
	Sting
Audio Note:	Track Announcers Mic's @ Announce Position & Ring Announce Off Line

431

WCW Halloween Havoc   Confidential Format

52. RING:	(17:00)	Jeff Jarrett	v.	Sting
Audio Note:		Track Announcers Mic's @ Announce Position		
Content Note:		Fight Goes All Through Arena With Sting In Control		
		Along The Way, One After Another, Several Fake Stings (All Appropriately Made Up As		
		Sting During Various Stages In His Career) Appear And Attack Sting		
		Fight Makes Its Way Back To The Ring – Final Fake Sting Emerges From Beneath Ring		
		Wearing A Referee's Shirt—Takes Out Ref		
		Sting Lays Out Referee Sting		
		Jarrett Lays Out Sting With Guitar		
		Real Referee Barely Makes Three-Count		
		Jarrett Over		
Production Note:		Jarrett Music On Out		

53. TAPE (Pretape):	(1:00)	(Backstage Interview Pos.) Pamela w/ Booker T.
Audio Note:		Track Pretape Audio & Track Announcer's Mic's & NEEDS LOW CROWD CHEERING UNDER
Tape Note:		Show Full Screen
Content Note:		Booker Cuts Promo On Scott Steiner
		Booker Mentions Goldberg's Problems – Tells Us That To Give Goldberg More Time To Get
		Cleared, He Has Volunteered His Title Match To Go Up Next

54. TAPE (Op Reel):	(:49)	(Package) Booker T. v. Scott Steiner
Audio Note:		Track Op Reel ...Self Contained
Tape Note:		Fades Up From Black & Show Full Screen & Fades To Black

54a. GRAPHICS:		WCW World Heavyweight Title Match (Title Page)
Audio Note:		Track Announcers Mic's @ Announce Position
Infin! Note:		Show Full Screen When Director Calls For It Before Entrances

54a. RING:		Michael Buffer With Talent Intros
Audio Note:		Track Wireless Mic On Line

55. RING:		1-M Booker T. Music
		Booker T.
Audio Note:		Track Announcers Mic's @ Announce Position & Ring Announce Off Line
Pyro Note:		Needs Booker T. Pyro Here

56. RING:		2-M Scott Steiner Music
		Scott Steiner
		W/ Midajah
Audio Note:		Track Announcers Mic's @ Announce Position & Ring Announce Off Line
Content Note:		No Scott

57. BACKSTAGE: (Live)		(Go Position) Scott Steiner Waiting For Match
Audio Note:		Track Camera Mic & Track Announcer's Mic's & NEEDS LOW CROWD CHEERING UNDER
Content Note:		We Hear Steiner's Music Playing In Arena As Scott Chews Out Backstage Personnel At Go
		Position – His Match Was Supposed To Be Last! What The Hell Is This Crap?!
		Midajah Tries To Calm Scott Down
		Scott Exits, Ballistic

58. RING: (Cont.)		2-M Scott Steiner Music
		Scott Steiner
		W/ Midajah
Audio Note:		Track Announcers Mic's @ Announce Position & Ring Announce Off Line

WCW Halloween Havoc   Confidential Format

59. RING:	(20:00)	**WCW World Heavyweight Title Match**
		Booker T. v. **Scott Steiner**

Audio Note: Track Announcers Mic's @ Announce Position

Content Note:	Scott Is Berserk/Out Of Control
	Helluva Match – Every Time Booker Counters Steiner, Scott Loses More Of His Temper
	Scott Finally Goes Off The Deep End
	Referee Tries To Stop Steiner From Punishing Booker – Scott Bumps Ref
	Another Ref Comes In To Stop The Carnage – Scott Lays Him Out, Too
	Remaining Refs To Ring
	Steiner DQ'd
	Agents To Ring
	Jarrett To Ring – Attempts To Calm Scotty Down
	Jarrett And Midajah Manage To Bring Scotty To Back
	Booker Hurt Badly
Production Note:	*Booker Music On Out*

60. TAPE (Op Reel): (:58)   (Package) Goldberg v. Kronik
Audio Note: Track Op Reel ...Self Contained
Tape Note: Fades Up From Black & Show Full Screen & Fades To Black

61. RING: **1-M** Kronik Music
Kronik
Audio Note: Track Announcers Mic's @ Announce Position & Ring Announce Off Line

62. RING: **Kronik Short Promo**
Audio Note: Track Wireless Mic

Content Note:	Tells Us That This Is The End Of The Line For Goldberg – He Can't Work Tonight, And That
	Means A Forfeit – So Ring The Bell, Play Our Music Pay Us Our Money For Doing What We
	Said We'd Do All Along!
Production Note:	*Hit Kronik Music After Promo*

63. BACKSTAGE: (Live)   (Backstage) Nevada Commission Approaches Doug Dillenger
Audio Note: Track Camera Mic & Track Announcer's Mic's & NEEDS LOW CROWD CHEERING UNDER
Audio Note: Play Kronik Music Under This Shot Too!!
Producer Note: DO NOT SHOW TO HOUSE!!!!

Content Note:	They Tell Doug "He's Cleared To Wrestle."
	Doug Tells Them "Took Your Damn Time Deciding That, Didn't You?"
	Doug Walks Off

64. RING: Goldberg Music Plays
Audio Note: CUT TO GOLDBERG MUSIC HERE!!!
Audio Note: Track Goldberg Music For Intro & Track Announcers Mic's @ Announce Position

Content Note:	Kronik Reacts In Ring

65. BACKSTAGE: (Live)   (Backstage) Goldberg MSG Entrance From Locker Room
Audio Note: Track Goldberg Music Under & Track Announcer's Mic's & Track Camera Mic & & NEEDS LOW CROWD CHEERING UNDER

Content Note:	Dillenger Knocks On Goldberg's Door – MSG Entrance

WCW Halloween Havoc   Confidential Format

66. RING:	**2-M** Goldberg Music
	Goldberg
Audio Note:	Track Announcers Mic's @ Announce Position & Ring Announce Off Line
Pyro Note:	**Needs Goldberg Pyro Here**

67. RING:	**(8:00)**	**Kronik**	**v.**	**Goldberg**
Audio Note:		Track Announcers Mic's @ Announce Position		
Content Note:		Helluva Match		
		Goldberg Over		
Production Note:		*Goldberg Music On Out*		
		Off Hot		

68. Infinit!:	**(:05) Copyright Info**
Producer Note:	Copyright Needs To Be Shown During The Last 5 Seconds Of Spot

434

Confidential Format

Thunder TBS 148

Irvine, CA

Monday October 30, 2000   (To Air On Wednesday, November 1, 2000)

7:00 PM Pacific Time   Ring & Set Changes
                                        David Penzer Introduces Pamela
                                        Nitro Girl Performance During Set Change
7:15 PM Pacific Time   Thunder TAPED Starts!
9:00 PM Pacific Time   Thunder TAPED- Ends!

435

TBS 148   Page #1   Irvine, CA   Wednesday, November 1, 2000   Air Time & Program Length: 9:05:00-11:04 :45 Eastern Time

09:05:00

SEGMENT #1

1. TAPE: (Op Reel)   (:10)   **WCW Logo Identification**
Audio Note: Track Op Reel, Self Contained
Tape N te: Fades Up From Black & Show Full Screen & Fades To Blac /The/To Package

2. TAPE: (Op Reel)   (:30)   **(Package) Highlights From Nitro TNT 348- Irvine, CA**
Audio Note: Track Op Reel, Self Contained
Tape Note: Fades Up From Black & Show Full Screen & Fades To Black

3. BACKSTAGE: (Live)(:30)   **(Outside- Parking Lot) A Cool Looking Vintage Car Arrives At The Arena**
Audio Note: Track Camera Mic & Track Announcer's Mic's & MUST HAVE CROWD CHEERING UNDER SHOT
Content Note: A Cool-Looking Vintage Car W/New Jersey Plates Pulls Up Outside Building

4. TAPE: (Op Reel)   (:45)   **(Package) WCW Thunder Open**
Audio Note: Track Op Reel...Self Contained
Tape Note: Fades Up From Black & Show Full Screen & Fades To Black

5. LIVE: (:30)   **Pyro Arena Wide Shot**
Audio Note: Track Announcer's Mic's @ Set & Track Pyro Audio & Needs Live Thunder Music
In/null Note: Needs Live Chyron W/ Thunder Id W/ Irvine, CA
Pyro Note: Go Pyro Program Open

6. RING: **Shot Of 3 Count Already In The Ring**
Audio Note: Track Announcer's Mic's @ Announce Position & Track Wireless Mic
Content Note: 3 Count (W/Circles)

7. RING: **3 Count Promo**
Audio Note: Track Wireless Mic
Content Note: Evan Hogs The Mic During The Promo, Pissing Off Shane And Shannon Who Are Waiting Their Turn To Speak
Shane Eventually Asks Evan Why He Doesn't Give Them A Chance To Talk
Evan Tells Them They Need To Chill, Since He's The Leader Of The Group
What Makes You The Leader?
Evan Points To His Stomach, Matter-Of-Factly~ "...Because I've Got The Abs."

10/30/00 5:32 PM
This Information Is Subject To Change!!

436

TBS 148   Page #1   Irvine, CA   Wednesday, November 1, 2000   Air Time & Program Length: 9:05:00-11:04:45 Eastern Time

SEGMENT #1   Continued

8. ENTRANCE:

Audio Note:

1-M Jung Dragons Music
Jung Dragons
W/ Leia Meow
Track Announcer's Mic's @ Announce Position

9. TAPE: (Op Reel)

(:13) (B-Roll) Clips Leia Meow Getting Hot At The Jung Dragons In The Past

Audio Note: Track Op Reel & Track Announcer's Mic's & MUST HAVE CROWD CHEERING UNDER SHOT
Needs Thunder Transition On In & Out & Show Full Screen During Entrance During Entrance
Tape Note: B-Roll Past Footage Of Leia Getting Hot At Dragons (Particularly Jamie-San)
Content Note: Shane And Shannon Are Hot W/Evan – He Took So Long W/His Promo That They Ran Out Of Time To Sling
3 Count Begin To Argue With Each Other
Leia Barks At The Dragons – Don't Just Stand There Watching Them – Get In That Ring And Get 'Em!
Dragons Jump 3-Count

10/30/00 5:32 PM
This Information Is Subject To Change!!

437

SEGMENT #1   Continued

10. RING: (10:00)   **3 Count**   v.   **Jung Dragons**

Match Note: Match Begins And Ends In This Segment.

Announcers: Tell Us That The New C.E.O. Of WCW Ric Flair Is In Atlanta Today In A Series Of Meetings That Will Have Dramatic Implications On November's Mayhem PPV – We Hope To Get Some Word By Next Monday. Meanwhile, Flair Has Taken It Upon Himself To Book Tonight's Main Event – Jeff Jarrett And Vampiro Vs. Mike Awesome And Sting! Also Tonight – We Understand That Our WCW Champion Booker T Has Something He Wants To Say – We'll Get A Word With Him A Bit Later.

Content Note:
On
Hot Match
During Course Of Match, Evan Begins To Get Cocky, Hot-Dogging And Being A Glory Hound
Also During Match, Leia Continues To Chew Out Jamie-San Who Slips Up A Couple Of Times
Finish: Shane (Or Shannon) Set Up Jamie For Finish – Evan Steals A Tag And Makes The Cover Himself (Glory-Hound Spot)
Evan Over Jamie 1-2-3
3 Count Music On Out

Production Note: Shane And Shannon Get In Evan's Face – What's His Problem?
Evan Tries To Blow Them Off
They Stop Evan And Lay Him Out – Shannon And Shane Leave Evan Lying
Meanwhile, Leia Has Been Chewing Out A Selling Jamie-San As Jimmy And Kaz Look On
Leia Tells Jamie "You're Finished"
Leia Tells The Dragons To Lay Out Jamie-San "He's The Reason You Guys Aren't Going Anywhere!" – They Lay Him Out
Dragons Leave Jamie-San Lying – Leia Takes His Mask Before She Leaves
Evan And Jamie Are Left In The Ring – They Give Each Other A Look, Regarding Each Other As They Both Sell Their Way
Up
Off Hot

10a. Infiniti: (:03) **Thunder ID Logo ID Shot Over Hot Action**
Audio Note: Track Announcer's Mic & Needs Live Thunder Music
Infiniti Note: Needs Thunder ID

CM Position #1   (3:00)   **Music Performance- House Only**

438

TBS 148   Page #1   Irvine, CA   Wednesday, November 1, 2000   Air Time & Program Length: 9:05:00-11:04:45 Eastern Time

SEGMENT #2

11. BACKSTAGE: (Live) (1:00)   (Backstage Interview Pos.) Gene Okerlund w/ Coach Nash & "The Event" Chuck Palumbo

Audio Note: *Track Camera Mic & Track Stick Mic & MUST HAVE CROWD CHEERING UNDER SHOT*

Content Note: Nash Tells Us That Stasiak Made His Bed, Once And For All, On Nitro When He Left Palumbo Out To Dry Against Kronic
Palumbo Cuts A Promo On Stasiak Re: Their Match Tonight
Coach Nash Gives Palumbo A Pat On The Ass And Tells Him To Go Get His Game Face On -- Palumbo Exits As Nash Says,
" Do This All For The Kids, Y'know…"

11a. ARENA/PROFILE: (:08)   Open Sponsor BB-Castrol

Audio Note: *Needs Live WCW Thunder Music & Track Announcer's Mic @ Announce Position*

Tape Note: *Show Full Screen & Tied To Pretape*

Announcer Copy: "Brought To You By The Motor Oil That Provides Maximum Protection. Castrol GTX, Drive Hard."

12. TAPE: (Pretape)   (:45)   (Backstage) Bam Bam Bigelow Storms Into The Building

Audio Note: *Track Pretape Audio & Track Announcer's Mic's & MUST HAVE CROWD CHEERING UNDER SHOT*

Tape Note: *Show Full Screen*

Content Note: Crowbar Is Signing In
Bam Bam Walks Into The Building & Shitcans Crowbar
Bam Bam Then Walks Up To Doug Dillenger And Gets Right In His Face
"I'm Tired Of Sitting At Home I'M Back & You Better let everyone Know!

13. ENTRANCE: 1-M Elix Skipper Music   "Primetime" Elix Skipper

Audio Note: *Track Announcer's Mic's @ Announce Position*

13a. GRAPHICS: "Iwatch" Promo From Tony Schiavone

Audio Note: *Track Announcer's Mic's*

Graphics Note: *Show Full Screen When Producer Calls For It Before Entrances*

14. RING: "Primetime" Elix Skipper Promo

Audio Note: *Track Wireless Mic*

Content Note: Calls Out Lt. Loco For The Impression He Did Of Him Last Week On Nitro

TBS 148   Page #1   Irvine, CA   Wednesday, November 1, 2000   Air Time & Program Length: 9:06:00-11:04:45 Eastern Time

SEGMENT #2   Continued

15. ENTRANCE:

2-M Misfits In Action Music

Lt. Loco

W/ Major Gunns

Audio Note: *Track Announcer's Mic's @ Announce Position*

15a. TAPE: (Op Reel)

(:13) (B-Roll) Clips Of Lt. Loco Parodying "Primetime" Last Week On Thunder TBS 147

Audio Note: *Track Op Reel & Track Announcer's Mic's & MUST HAVE CROWD CHEERING UNDER SHOT*
Tape Note: *Needs Thunder Transition On In & Out & Show Full Screen During Entrance During Entrance*

16. RING: (9:00)

"Primetime" Elix Skipper   v.   Lt. Loco

Announcer Note: *Match Begins And Ends In This Segment...*

Talk About Bam Bam Bigelow's Demand For A Match With Goldberg Tonight

Content Note: With Primetime In Control, Major Gunns Jumps Up On Apron

She Attempts To Distract Primetime By Removing Her Bombs Away Shirt... But All She Does Is Distract The Referee

As The Ref Gawks At Gunns, Primetime Lays Loco Out With His Grey Cup Ring

Production Note: Primetime Over 1-2-3

"Primetime" Elix Skipper Music On Out

Gunns, Beside Herself, Tends To Loco

Off Hot

16a. Infiniti:

(:03)Thunder ID Over Hot Action

Audio Note: *Track Announcer's Mic & Needs Live Thunder Music*
Infiniti Note: *Needs Thunder ID*

CM Position #2   (3:01)

Music Performance- House Only

SEGMENT #3

16b. TAPE: (Op Reel)   (:30)   WCW Magazine Spot
Audio Note: *Track Pretape Audio...Self Contained*
Tape 1 :46: *Fades Up From Black & Show Full Screen & Fades To Blk x*

17. ENTRANCE: Coach Kevin Nash w/ Music & Entrance
Audio Note: *Track Kevin Nash (Wolfpac) Music For Intro & Track Announcer's Mic's @ Announce Position*

18. RING: (7:00)   Coach Kevin Nash Promo
Audio Note *Track Wireless Mic*
Tape Note:
Content Note: Nash Tells Us That This Has Been A Long Time Coming -- Calls Out Stasiak, Because He Can't Wait To See Palumbo -- My
Boy... A Nice Boy - Kick Stasiak's Whacked-Out Ass
Nash To Color

19. ENTRANCE: 1-M OLD PERFECT EVENT Music
Audio Note: *Track Announcer's Mic's @ Announce Position*
"PerfectShawn" Shawn Stasiak

20. TAPE: (Op Reel)   (:13) (B-Roll) Clips Of Stasiak Abandoning Palumbo on Nitro;
Kronik Laying Palumbo Out
Audio Note: *Track Op Reel & Track Announcer's Mic's & MUST HAVE CROWD CHEERING UNDER SHOT*
Tape Note: *Needs Thunder Transition on In & Out & Show Full Screen During Entrance*

21. ENTRANCE: 2-M Natural Born Thrillers Music
Audio Note: *Track Announcer's Mic's @ Announce Position*
"The Event" Chuck Palumbo
Content Note: No Chuck
Coach Nash Doesn't Know Why He Isn't Coming -- Makes Excuses -- "He's A Kid, Y'know? He Probably Got Distracted On
The Way To The Ring -- Caught A Glimpse Of Himself In A Shiny Object And Couldn't Look Away Or Something.... He's
Coming. Don't Worry. He Wouldn't Miss This For Anything In The World."

22. ENTRANCE: 2-M Natural Born Thrillers Music
Audio Note: *Track Announcer's Mic's @ Announce Position*
"The Event" Chuck Palumbo - RESTART
Content Note: Still No Chuck
Nash Starting To Get Hot

SEGMENT #2   Continued

23. TAPE: (Pretape)   (Backstage) A Cameraman Runs Down The Hallway Toward The Locker Rooms

Audio Note:	*Track Pretape Audio & Track Announcer's Mic's & MUST HAVE CROWD CHEERING UNDER SHOT*
Tape Note:	*Show Full Screen*
Content Note:	**We Hear A Producer Say "They Said He's Down Here!"**
	Camera Looks Around A Corner – We Reveal Palumbo Laid Out – Broken Furniture Everywhere
	He's Not Moving

24. ARENA: Coach Kevin Nash Leaves The Announce Position

Audio Note:	*Track Wireless Mic*
Content Note"	**Coach Nash Runs To The Back From Announce Position**
	Stasiak Smugly Watches Him Go
	They Make Eye Contact Before Kevin Leaves – Stasiak Shrugs "Innocently"
	With Kevin Gone, Stasiak Indicates For The Ref To Raise His Hand
	"Your Winner Via Forfeit – Shawn "PerfectShawn" Stasiak!"
Production Note"	*Stasiak Music On Out*
	Off Hot

24a. Infiniti: (:03)Thunder ID Over Hot Action

Audio Note:	*Track Announcer's Mic & Needs Live Thunder Music*
Infiniti Note:	*Needs Thunder ID*

CM Position #3   (2:30)   Music Performance- House Only

10/30/00 5:32 PM
This Information Is Subject To Change!!

TBS 148   Page #1   Irvine, CA   Wednesday, November 1, 2000   Air Time & Program Length: 9:05:00-11:04:45 Eastern Time

SEGMENT #4

25. TAPE: (Pretape)   (1:00)   (Backstage) Coach Nash & The Natural Born Thrillers With Palumbo Backstage

Audio Note:	Track Pretape Audio & Track Announcers Mic's & MUST HAVE CROWD CHEERING UNDER SHOT
Tape Note:	Fades Up From Black & Show Full Screen & Tied To Pretape
Content Note:	Coach Working On Palumbo
	Nash Asks If Chuck Remembers Who Did This To Him
	Chuck – Still Groggy And Selling – Tells Nash He Heard His Music Playing, And Next Thing He Knew He Got Jumped From Behind
	Nash And The Thrillers Feel Stasiak Is Behind It
	"Dat Stasiak – He One Rotten Kid…"
	It Won't Be Long Before Stasiak Finds Himself S.O.L. – Thriller -Style!

26. TAPE: (Pretape)   (1:00)   (Backstage Interview Pos.) Gene Okerlund w/ Bam Bam Bigelow

Audio Note:	Track Pretape Audio & MUST HAVE CROWD/CHEERING UNDER SHOT
Tape Note:	Show Full Screen & Tied To Package
Content Note:	Bam Bam Tells His Side Of The Story – He's Sat At Home For Months – Got Injured In A Fire, And Did Anyone From This Company Do Anything For Me? No – They Wrote Me Off!
	"Sorry Lex – I Know You've Got Big Plans For Goldberg At Mayhem, But He's Gotta Get Through Me First t. And I Don't Care When! And If They Don't Give Me A Match, I Will Just take it!"
	Bam Bam Feels (Like Lex) That A Victory Over Goldberg (Retiring Him) Is All He Needs To Be A Player Again
	Crowbar Attacks Bam Bam Bigelow During The Middle Of The Interview
	Crowbar & Bam Bam Go At It A Little
	Security In To Break It Up

27. TAPE: (Op Reel)   (2:30)   (Package) Bam Bam Bigelow Arrival At WCW

Audio Note:	Track Op Reel, Self Contained
Tape Note:	Fades Up From Black & Show Full Screen & Fades To Black
Content Note:	Bam Bam Bigelow Arrives On The Scene With His Sites Set On Goldberg
	We Need To Use This Package To Remind Everyone Of The Threat That Bigelow Was To Goldberg When He First Entered WCW

TBS 148   Page #1   Irvine, CA   Wednesday, November 1, 2000   Air Time & Program Length: 9:05:00-11:04:45 Eastern Time

SEGMENT #4   Continued

27a. Infiniti: (:03)Thunder ID Over Package
Audio Note: Track Announcers Mic & Needs Live Thunder Music!
Infiniti Note: Needs Thunder ID

27b. TAPE: (Op Reel)   (:30)   WCW Mayhem Spot
Audio Note: Track Package Audio - Self Contained
Tape Note: Fades Up From Black & Show Full Screen & Fades To Black

CM Position #4   (2:30)   Music Performance- House Only

TBS 148   Page #1   Irvine, CA   Wednesday, November 1, 2000   Air Time & Program Length: 9:05:00-11:04:45 Eastern Time

SEGMENT #5

28. ENTRANCE:

Audio Note:
1-M Filthy Animals Music
Filt'ry Animals
Track Announcer's Mic's @ Announce Position

28a. GRAPHICS:

Audio Note:
Graphics Note:
"New Time 9:00 PM Eastern" For Thunder On Wednesday
Track Announcer's Mic's
Show Full Screen When Producer Calls For It Before Entrances

29. RING:

Audio Note:
Content Note:
Filthy Animals Promo
Track Wireless Mic
Konnan Does His Shtick
Rey And Kidman Challenge Boogie Knights To A Match For Costing Them The Tag Belts On Nitro

30. ENTRANCE:

Audio Note:
2-M Boogie Knights Music
Boogie Knights
Track Announcer's Mic's @ Announce Position

31. RING: (9:00)

Match Note:
Content Note:

Production Note:
Rey Mysterio Jr.   v.   Boogie Knights
Kidman
Match Begins And Ends In This Segment..
Helluva Match
Rey And Billy Over
Filthy Animals Music On Out
Off Hot
Rey/Billy Indicate To Camera On Out "Jindrak And O'Haire – We're Coming After You."

31a. Infiniti!:   (:03)

Audio Note:
Infiniti Note:
Thunder ID Over Hot Action
Track Announcer's Mic & Needs Live Thunder Music
Needs Thunder ID

CM Position #5   (3:00)
Music Performance- House Only

TBS 148   Page #1   Irvine, CA   Wednesday, November 1, 2000   Air Time & Program Length: 9:05:00-11:04:45 Eastern Time

SEGMENT #6

31b. TAPE: (Pretape)   (:30)   (Backstage Interview Pos.) Gene Okerlund w/ Crowbar
Audio Note: Track Pretape Audio & MUST HAVE CROWD CHEERING UNDER SHOT
Graphics Note: Fades up from Black & Show Full Screen
Content Note: Crowbar Steps Up And Challenges Bam Bam For A Match Tonight

32. GRAPHICS: WCW United States Heavyweight Match(Title Page)
Audio Note: Track Announcer's Mic's
Graphics Note: Show Full Screen When Producer Calls For It Before Entrances

33. ENTRANCE: 1-M   Misfits In Action Music
                    Sergeant A-WALL
Audio Note: Track Announcer's Mic's @ Announce Position

36. ENTRANCE: 2-M   Lance Storm Music
                    Lance Storm
Audio Note: Track Announcer's Mic's @ Announce Position

36a. STAGE: Lance Storm Short Promo
Audio Note: Track Wireless Mic
Content Note: Lance Stops On The Ramp With A Mic
                Storm Intros A-Wall's Opponent

36b. ENTRANCE: 3-M   Meng Music
                    Meng
Audio Note: Track Announcer's Mic's @ Announce Position

TBS 148   Page #1   Irvine, CA   Wednesday, November 1, 2000   Air Time & Program Length: 9:05:00-11:04:45 Eastern Time

SEGMENT #6 Continued

37. RING: (8:00)   Sergeant A-WALL   v.   Meng

Match Note:	*Match Begins And Ends In This Segment!*
Content Note:	Lance Storm To Color
	A-WALL Over
	Misfits In Action Music On out
Production Note:	A-WALL Leaves
	lance Gets In the Ring
	Kill MIA Music
Production Note:	Lance Chastises Meng In The Ring
	Meng Goozles Storm
	Off Hot

37a. TAPE: (Op Reel)   (B-Roll) Slo-Mo Replay- Castrol GTX

Audio Note:	*Track Op Reel & Track Announcer's Mic's & MUST HAVE CROWD CHEERING UNDER SHOT*
Tape Note:	*Show Full Screen & Fades To Black*
Announcer Copy:	"Brought To You By Th Motor Oil That Provides Maximum Protection, Castrol GTX, Drive Hard."

37b. Infiniti: (:03)Thunder ID Over Hot Action

Audio Note:	*Track Announcer's Mic & Needs Live Thunder Music*
Infiniti Note:	*Needs Thunder ID*
CM Position #6 (2:30)	Music Performance- House Only

TBS 148   Page #1   Irvine, CA   Wednesday, November 1, 2000   Air Time & Program Length: 9:05:00-11:04:45 Eastern Time

SEGMENT #7

37c. TAPE: (Op Reel)   (:10)   Closed Caption PC- Wizards Trading Cards

Audio Note: Needs Live Thunder Music & Track Announcer's Mic's @ Set
Profile Note: Needs Closed Captioning Graphics Over Arena Wide Shot
Announcer Note: "Closed Captioning Where Available Sponsored By Wizards Of The Coast WCW Trading Card Game."

38. TAPE: (Pretape)   (1:00)   (Backstage Interview Pos.) Gene Okerlund w/ Jeff Jarrett & Vampiro

Audio Note: Track Pretape Audio & MUST HAVE CROWD CHEERING UNDER SHOT
Tape Note: Fades Up from Black & Show Full Screen
Content Note: Re: Tonight's Main Event.

Jarrett Claims That He And Vampiro Are The Two Guys In WCW Who Have Both Taken Care Of Sting – So He Doesn't Even
Know What Flair Had in Mind When He Booked This Thing.
Jarrett Knocks Awesome ("That 70s Guy – Is That A Reference To His I.Q.?")
Vampiro Cuts Quick Promo On Sting, Then Devotes His Attention To Vampiro – It's Not Over Between Us, My Friend – I've
Got All Sorts Of Sick, Twisted Demented Stuff For You, Awesome, Just Ask Your Partner Sting What I'm Capable Of..."

39. ARENA: (Live)   (:15)   Arena Wide Shot For Cover Pitch

Audio Note: Track Announcer's Mic's
Announcer Note: Announcers Throw To...

40. TAPE: (Pretape)   (5:00)   Mark Madden Sit Down Interview w/"PerfectShawn" Stasiak

Audio Note: Track Pretape Audio- Self Contained
Tape Note: Fades Up From Black & Show Full Screen & Fades To Black
Infinit! Note: Needs Chyron With Tuesday 10/31/00
Content Note: Re: His Tenure With The Thrillers ("...A Bunch Of Moronic Frat Boys...")

The Potential He Sees Within Himself – Now Able To Run Free Without Being Held Back By The NBTs
His Relationship W/Coach Nash
His Friggin' Gorilla
His Former Partnership W/Palumbo – Mention Kronik Match From Nitro, And Reference Upcoming Match Vs. Stasiak – "
Guess By Now, Everyone In WCW Will Have Seen My Little Surprise For Chuckles First-Hand. And I've Got A Whole Lot
More Where That Came From..."
Go Off Promising To Be The First Thriller (Or Former Thriller) To Capture The WCW Title

40a. Infinit!:   (:03)Thunder ID Over Pretape

Audio Note: Track Announcer's Mic & Needs Live Thunder Music
Infinit! Note: Needs Thunder ID

CM Position #7   (2:31)   Music Performance- House Only

10/30/00 5:32 PM
This Information Is Subject To Change!!

448

TBS 148   Page #1   Irvine, CA   Wednesday, November 1, 2000   Air Time & Program Length: 9:05:00-11:04:45 Eastern Time

SEGMENT #8

40b. TAPE: (Op Reel)   (:30)   **WCW Magazine Spot**
Audio Note: Track Pretape Audio - Self Contained
Tape Note: Fades Up From B :34 & Show Full Screen & Fades To Black

41. ENTRANCE: **1-M** Team Canada Music
   Lance Storm
Audio Note: Track Announcer's Mic's @ Announce Position

42. RING: **Lance Storm Short Promo**
Audio Note: Track Wireless Mic
Content Note: Storm Goes To Talk, But Can't Because Of Goozle
   Calls For Canadian National Anthem
Production Note: Anthem Plays

43a. GRAPHICS: **2-M** Norman Smiley Music
   Screamin' Norman Smiley
Audio Note: Track Announcer's Mic's @ Announce Position
Graphics Note:

43. ENTRANCE: **"Iwatch" Promo From Tony Schiavone**
Audio Note: Track Announcer's Mic's
   Show Full Screen When Producer Calls For It Before Entrances

44. RING: (8:00)   **Lance Storm**   v.   **"Screamin'" Norman Smiley**
Content Note: Match Begins And Ends In This Segment...
   Helluva Match
   Be Sure To Have Norman Give Storm The Big Wiggle
   Storm Over With Canadian Maple Leaf
   Lance Storm Music On Out
Production Note: Storm Won't Release The Hold
   Meng Out TO Ring
   Storm Gets Up & SuperKicks Meng
   Meng No Sells Kick
   Lance, In Shock, Powders
   Meng Music On Out
   Off Hot

10/30/00 5:32 PM
This Information Is Subject To Change!!

TBS 148   Page #1   Irvine, CA   Wednesday, November 1, 2000   Air Time & Program Length: 9:05:00-11:04:45 Eastern Time

SEGMENT #8   Continued

44a. Infiniti: (:03)Thunder ID Logo ID Shot Over Hot Action

Audio Note: *Track Announcer's Mic & Needs Live Thunder Music*
Infiniti Note   *Needs Thunder ♪*

CM Position #8   (2:45)   Music Performance- House Only

450

TBS 148   Page #1   Irvine, CA   Wednesday, November 1, 2000   Air Time & Program Length: 9:05:00-11:04:45 Eastern Time

SEGMENT #9

44b. TAPE: (Op Reel)   (:44)   Promotional Considerations #1
Audio Note: Needs Live Thunder Music & Track Op Reel
Tape Note: Fades Up from Black & Show Full Screen & Fades T ; Black

45. ENTRANCE: 1-M Bam Bam Bigelow Music   **Bam Bam Bigelow**
Audio Note: Track Announcer's Mic's @ Announce Position

46. Has Been Deleted

47. ENTRANCE: 2-M Crowbar Music   **Crowbar**
Audio Note: Track Announcer's Mic's @ Announce Position

48. RING: (6:00)   **Bam Bam Bigelow   v.   Crowbar**
Match Note: Match Begins And Ends In This Segment...
Content Note: Bam Bam Bigelow Over
Production Note: Bam Bam Bigelow Music On Out
Off Hot

48a. Infiniti!:   (:03) **Thunder ID Logo ID Shot Over Hot Action**
Audio Note: Track Announcer's Mic & Needs Live Thunder Music
Infiniti Note: Needs Thunder ID

CM Position #9   (2:15)   **Music Performance- House Only**

| TBS 148 | Page #1 | Irvine, CA | Wednesday, November 1, 2000 | Air Time & Program Length: 9:05:00-11:04:45 Eastern Time |

SEGMENT #10

48b. TAPE: (Op Reel) (:44) Promotional Considerations #2
Audio Note: Needs Live Thunder Music & Track Op Reel
Tape Note: Fades Up From Black & Show Full Size :3 & Fades To Black/Tied To Pretape

49. TAPE: (Pretape) (1:00) (Backstage Interview Pos.) Gene Okerlund w/ Booker T.
Audio Note: Track Pretape Audio & MUST HAVE CROWD CHEERING UNDER SHOT
Tape Note: Show Full Screen
Content Note: Booker T. Talks About His Match At Havoc W/Steiner/ And The 3-Way Monday Night -- Both Times, He Failed To Get The
Job Done "I Failed To Beat Scott Steiner"
Booker Doesn't Like The Way That Feels -- All Of A Sudden, This Belt Is Real Heavy To Me, A Constant Reminder That Until
I Beat Scott Steiner In The Middle Of That Ring, I'm Not The Champion That I've Always Said I Would Be
Issues A Challenge For A Re-Match Against Steiner At Mayhem -- "...Name Your Stips, And I'll Be There."

50. ENTRANCE: (3:00) 1-M Jeff Jarrett Music
"The Chosen One" Jeff Jarrett
Audio Note: Track Announcer's Mic's @ Announce Position
Pyro Note: Needs Jeff Jarrett Pyro here

51. TAPE: (Op Reel) (:13) (B-Roll) Stills Of Jarrett Beating Sting At Havoc
Audio Note: Track Op Reel & Track Announcer's Mic's & MUST HAVE CROWD CHEERING UNDER SHOT
Tape Note: Show Full Screen During Entrance

52. RING: "The Chosen One" Jeff Jarrett Short Promo
Audio Note: Track Wireless Mic
Content Note: Needs To Again Take Issue With Flair Booking This Match
Calls For His Freak Of A Partner To Come Out...

53. ENTRANCE: 2-M Vampiro Music
Vampiro
Audio Note: Track Announcer's Mic's @ Announce Position

54. Has Been Deleted

TBS 148   Page #1   Irvine, CA   Wednesday, November 1, 2000   Air Time & Program Length   9:05:00-11:04:45 Eastern Time

SEGMENT #10   Continued

55. ENTRANCE: **3-M** Mike Awesome Music
Audio Note: **That 70's Guy: Mike Awesome**
Content Note: *Track Announcer's Mic's @ Announce Position*
    To Bottom Of Ramp

55a. TAPE: (Op Reel)   **(:13) (B-Roll) Stills From Halloween Havoc- Awesome With**
    Powerbomb On Vampiro
Audio Note: *Track Op. Reel & Track Announcer's Mic's & MUST HAVE CROWD CHEERING UNDER SHOT*
Tape Note: *Needs Thunder Transition On in & Out & Show Full Screen During Entrance During Entrance*

56. ARENA: (Live)   **Blackout/Thunder & Lightening For Sting Intro**
Audio Note: *Track Camera Mic & Track Announcer's Mic's & Needs Sting Music Under & MUST HAVE CROWD CH[EERING] UNDER SHOT*
Announcer Note: *"That Can Only Mean One Thing – Sting's Up Next!"*

56a. Infinit!:   **(:03)Thunder ID Over Live Shot**
Audio Note: *Track Announcer's Mic & Needs Live Thunder Music*
Infinit! Note: *Needs Thunder ID*

CM Position #10   (3:16)   **Music Performance- House Only**

TBS 148   Page #1   Irvine, CA   Wednesday, November 1, 2000   Air Time & Program Length: 9:05:00-11:04:45 Eastern Time

SEGMENT #11

56b. TAPE: (Op Reel)   (:30)   WCW Mayhem Spot

Audio Note: *Track Op Reel; Self Contained*
Tape Note: *Fades Up Fro ; Black & Show Full Screen & Fades To Back*

57. ENTRANCE:

Audio Note: **4–M** Sting Music
Sting
Track Announcer's Mic's @ Announce Position

57a. GRAPHICS: **"New Time 9:00 PM Eastern" For Thunder On Wednesday**

Audio Note   *Track Announcer's Mic's*
Graphics Note: *Show Full Screen When Producer Calls For It Before Entrances*

58. RING: (10:00)   Jeff Jarrett   v.   Mike Awesome
Vampiro   Sting

Match Note: *Match Begins And Ends In This Segment...*
Content Note: Sting Gets Vampiro In Scorpion Death Lock
Vampiro Won't Tap Out- He Looks Like He Is Enjoying It
Finally, With A Smile On His Face, Vampiro Passes Out
Sting & Awesome Over

Production Note: *Sting Music On Out*

59. Infiniti: Copyright- Shown Over Hot Action
Audio Note: *Needs Thunder Music*
Terminal Break: Hard Out @ 11:04:45

WCW Weekly: In Your Face Newsletter

Here's the latest from World Championship
Wrestling.

<<-------------------------------MAYHEM---------
----------------------------->>

THE DATE

Sunday, Nov. 26 at 6:30 p.m. ET from the U.S.
Cellular Arena in Milwaukee,WI. It's live and only
on Pay-Per-View!

THE CARD

Caged Heat Match For The World Heavyweight Title -
Scott Steiner vs. Booker T.

*There Will Be A Straightjacket Suspended Above
The Cage.*

Lex Luger vs. Goldberg

For The U.S. Heavyweight Title - Lance Storm vs.
General Rection

Jarrett vs. Buff Bagwell

<<----------------------------NEWS-&-VIEWS----
--------------------------->>

FULL DISCLOSURE

Every Thursday, WCW.com editor Chad Damiani
examines the stories behind the matches, and gives
you the skinny on backstage politics, injuries and

real-life squabbles.

This week: The new twist surrounding Steiner and
Booker T., General

Rection's not-so-secret pain and injury updates.

http://www.wcw.com/2000/news/

WCW DAILY

Hardcore champ Crowbar talked about using his
title as a springboard to becoming a bigger star,
his scariest bump and how great the fans in
Englandwere. Head to the Friday, Nov. 17 WCW Daily
to find out more about WCW's new Hardcore
champion.

http://www.wcw.com/2000/news/

That's just the beginning. Get all the WCW Hot
News!

http://www.wcw.com/2000/news/

<<-------------------------------WCW-LIVE!------
---------------------------->>

WCW LIVE!

Tune in to WCW LIVE!, WCW.com's free, live
webcasts hosted by Bob Ryder

and Jeremy Borash. Then check out the Nitro pre-
show, Monday at 7 p.m., and the post show,
immediately after Nitro.

http://www.wcw.com/2000/wcwlive/

```
<<------------------------------APPEARANCES------
----------------------------->>
```

Friday, Nov. 17

Bill Goldberg will make an appearance on "Live with Regis" Friday, Nov. 17. The phenom will discuss his book and WCW Mayhem. Check your local listings for stations and times.

Atlanta - Buff Bagwell will be at the 3 Dollar Cafe in Kennesaw, GA., from 6-8 p.m. Come meet Buff and have him sign your stuff.

Washington - Diamond Dallas Page will hold an autograph session, from 10a.m. to noon, at the MCI Center in Washington, D.C.

Memphis, TN - Come meet Sid Vicious as he signs autographs and poses for pictures with fans from 9-11 p.m. at the following location:

Banana Joes

3684 Ridgeway Road

Memphis, TN

Saturday, Nov. 18

Memphis, TN - Sid Vicious will again meet fans, from 10 a.m. to noon at Memphis' Mid South Coliseum. The WCW superstar will be on hand to promote ticket sales for the Dec. 22 Nitro and Thunder tapings.

Philadelphia - Come meet WCW superstars Mike Awesome and KroniK at the TempleUniversity football game. The guys will be there prior to the game to sign autographs and meet fans, so get there early.

Sunday, Nov. 19

Atlanta - Fans in Atlanta can meet Crowbar, Chuck Palumbo, Shawn Stasiak, Cpl. Cajun and Big Vito at The Lodge, a Buckhead restaurant. Look for the superstars from 7-9 p.m.

Monday, Nov. 20

Augusta, GA - WCW superstars Goldberg and Chiquita will be on hand to meet fans when the doors open for Monday Nitro at the Richmond County Civic Center. Look for the phenom and Nitro Girl Chiquita at an arena merchandising booth.

Also, former Harlem Heaters, Booker T. and Stevie Ray will sign autographs for Nitro ticket holders at a merchandising booth when doors open for the show.

Check back often for new appearances information on your favorite WCW

superstars.

http://www.wcw.com/2000/appearances/

<<----------------------------iWATCH-WEDNESDAY-- --------------------------->>

INTERACT WITH WCW THUNDER ON iWATCH WEDNESDAY

TBS is body-slamming your PC with a new enhanced TV application that lets you join in the WCW action. Live chats, contests, trivia and polls put you in the ring and give you a chance to win great prizes! Log on to TBSsuperstation.com every Wednesday during WCW Thunder and bash heads with the big boys!

http://www.superstation.com/iwatch/index.htm

Fusient Media Ventures To Acquire World Championship Wrestling

Classic Sports Network Founders Re-Enter Cable Ring

Eric Bischoff Named President, WCW Entertainment

NEW YORK - January 11, 2001 - Fusient Media Ventures, an integrated media company that invests in high-potential, branded media properties, has entered into an agreement with Turner Broadcasting System, Inc. (TBS, Inc) to acquire the business of World Championship Wrestling (WCW), an industry leader in live action-based entertainment. Following the acquisition, TBS, Inc. will retain a minority interest in the WCW business and long-term programming rights.

The proposed acquisition marks the return of Classic Sports Network founders Brian Bedol and Stephen Greenberg to the cable arena and the return of former WCW president Eric Bischoff to the world of professional wrestling. Celebrated for successfully building an entrepreneurial-based cable network, which they later sold to ESPN, Bedol and Greenberg went on to found Fusient Media Ventures. Fusient will take over all day-to-day operations of WCW, with Bedol as the new CEO. Bischoff, who helped build the WCW franchise into a ratings powerhouse during the mid-90s, will assume the role of president. The partnership of Bedol, Greenberg and Bischoff brings together more than 50 years of combined experience in the entertainment, television and sports industries.

"We're going to reestablish the WCW as the champion of professional wrestling entertainment," said Brian Bedol, chief executive officer of WCW Incorporated. "There is huge untapped potential for the franchise and with Eric Bischoff on board we will crank everything up to make the WCW franchise even bigger, better, stronger and more entertaining than anything wrestling fans have ever experienced before."

"We are pleased to have reached an agreement with Fusient Media Ventures that truly represents a win for all parties," said Bradley J.

459

Siegel, president of general entertainment networks, TBS, Inc. "The Fusient management team's experience in programming, production and marketing at Classic Sports Network lends itself perfectly to the WCW business. Their entrepreneurial business-building expertise, combined with the powerhouse brands and distribution that TBS Superstation and TNT provide, will be a winning combination."

The broad-based WCW franchise includes WCW Monday Nitro Live (TNT), one of the most popular programs on cable television; WCW Thunder (TBS Superstation), one of the network's most watched programs; WCW Worldwide, seen in syndication in 94% of the country; and 12 monthly pay-per-view specials that consistently are among the industry's top sellers.

"Wrestling fans can rest assured that we will give the WCW the adrenaline shot it needs to once again become the most exciting brand of wrestling in the world," said Eric Bischoff.

Bischoff began his career with the WCW in the early 1990s as an on-air announcer and rose through the ranks to become president of the company. Under his leadership, WCW became the top-rated wrestling franchise on television, an accomplishment that lasted for 96 weeks.

The complete ownership group will be announced at closing.

About WCW: World Championship Wrestling (WCW), a division of Turner Broadcasting System, Inc., is an industry leader in creating live action-based entertainment for millions of enthusiastic fans each week.

About Fusient Media Ventures: Fusient Media Ventures is focused on identifying, funding, developing and distributing next generation content and converged media brands. The company is headquartered in New York, with offices in Los Angeles.

GENERAL Format
WCW Monday Nitro (TNT 368) Gainesville, FL
Order Of Events
Monday, March 19, 2001

Time	Duration	Event
6:29:30 PM Eastern Time	(0:30)	WCW MasterCard Spot- CALL 1 800 # Spot
6:30:00 PM Eastern Time	(3:00)	DJ Ran Crowd Welcome & Music Plays
6:33:00 PM Eastern Time	(10:00)	Nitro Girls Entrance One-By-One
		Nitro Girls Throw Out Shirts To Crowd
6:43:00 PM Eastern Time	(1:00)	DJ Ran Introduces David Penzer
6:44:00 PM Eastern Time	(2:00)	David Penzer W/ Crowd Warm Up &
		Announcements- & Announcer Introductions
6:46:00 PM Eastern Time	(3:00)	Nitro Girls Performance
		PLEASE TAPE THIS DARK MATCH!!
6:49:00 PM Eastern Time	(6:00)	1-M 2-M
		Adam Windsor v. Bret Dail
		Production Note:
6:55:00 PM Eastern Time	(5:00)	DJ Ran Plays Till...
7:00:00 PM Eastern Time		Tape Delay-Monday Nitro Begins!
9:00:00 PM Eastern Time		Tape Delay-Monday Nitro Off Air!

Document Created 03/19/01 @ 5:28 PM
This Information Is Subject To Change!

461

TNT 368	Page #1	Gainesville, FL	Monday, March 19, 2001	Air Time & Program Length:	8:00:00-10:00:00 PM Eastern Time

Segment #1　　　　　　　　　　　　　　　　　　　　　　　　　　　　　　08:00:00 Eastern

1. TAPE: (:30) **(B-Roll) Diamond Dallas Page "Tribute"**
Audio Note:　　*Track Tape... Nat's Only & Track Announcer's Mic's & Track ALL Music*
Tape Note:　　*Fades Up From Black & Show Full Screen & Tied To B-Roll*

3. TAPE: (:30) **(B-Roll) Clips From Greed- Scott Steiner Over DDP**
Audio Note:　　*Track Tape... Nat's Only & Track Announcer's Mic's*
Tape Note:　　*Show Full Screen*
Infinit! Note:　　*Needs Live Chyron W/ "Exclusive Footage From Greed"*

2. ENTRANCE: **Scott Steiner w/ Midajah & Ric Flair & Animal Music & Entrance**
Audio Note:　　*Track Scott Steiner Music Under Track Announcer's Mic's @ Announce*

4. RING: (10:00) **Scott Steiner Promo**
Audio Note:　　*Track Wireless Mic(s)*
Agents:　　Terry Taylor/Johnny Ace

4a. ENTRANCE: **Dusty Rhodes Music**
Audio Note:　　*Track DUSTY Rhodes Music Under & Track Wireless Mic From Arena*

7. BACKSTAGE: (Live) **(Backstage) Dusty Rhodes & Dustin Rhodes On NitroVision**
Audio Note:　　*Track Stick Mic & Track Camera Mic & Track Wireless Mic's & Track Announcer's Mic's*

5. ENTRANCE: **Booker T. Music & Entrance**
Audio Note:　　*Track Booker T. Music Under & Track Wireless Mic From Arena & Track Announcer's Mic's @ Announce*

6. RING: **Booker T. Promo**
Audio Note:　　*Track Wireless Mic(s)*

CM Position #1 (2:34)

Document Created 03/19/01 @ 5:26 PM
This Information Is Subject To Change!

462

TNT 368   Page #5   Gainesville, FL   Monday, March 19, 2001   Air Time & Program Length: 8:00:00-10:00:00 PM Eastern Time

Segment #2

6a. TAPE: (Op Reel)   (1:06)   **Promotional Considerations #1**   08:13:34
Audio Note: Needs Live WCW Monday Nitro Music & Track Op Reel... Self Contained
Tape Note: Fades Up From Black & Show Full Screen & Fades To Black/ Tied To Pretape

8. TAPE: (Pretape)   (1:00)   **(CAMCORDER SHOT) Buff Bagwell & Animal Watching A Monitor**
Audio Note: Track Pretape Audio & NEEDS LOW CROWD CHEERING UNDER
Tape Note: Fades Up From Black & Show Full Screen

9. ENTRANCE: **1-M** Jason Jett Music
Audio Note: **Jason Jett**
            Track Announcer's Mic's @ Announcer Position

10. TAPE: **(:15)(B-Roll) Clips From TBS 167 & Greed**
Audio Note: Track Tape... Nat's Only & Track Announcer's Mic's
Tape Note: Show Full Screen During Entrance

11. ENTRANCE: **2-M** Disqo Music
Audio Note: **Disqo**
            Track Announcer's Mic's @ Announce Position

12. RING: **Disqo Promo**
Audio Note: Track Wireless Mic

13. RING: (7:00)   **1 Fall- 10 Minute Time Limit**
            Jason Jett   v.   **Disqo**
Match Note: Match Begins And Ends In This Segment ...
Agent: **Ricky Santana**
Referee: **Scott James**

13a. TAPE: (:15)   **(Bumper) "Tonight" Huge Announcement From Eric Bischoff**
Audio Note: Track Nitro Music Under & Track Tape... Nat's Only & Track Announcer's Mic's
Tape Note: Show Full Screen & Fades To Black

CM Position #2   (3:00)   08:22:55

Document Created 03/19/01 @ 5:28 PM
This Information Is Subject To Change!

463

TNT 368   Page #7   Gainesville, FL, Monday, March 19, 2001   Air Time & Program Length: 8:00:00-10:00:00 PM Eastern Time

Segment #3

13b. TAPE: (Op Reel)   (:15)   (BILLBOARDS) WCW Road To Spring Breakout 08:25:55
Audio Note: Track Op Reel...Self Contained
Tape Note: :   Fades Up From Black & Show Full Screen & Fa..les To Black/Tied To Pretape

14. TAPE: (Pretape)   (1:00)   (CAMCORDER SHOT) Ric Flair Tracking With Jeff Jarrett In His Office
Audio Note: Track Pretape Audio & NEEDS LOW CROWD CHEERING UNDER
Tape Note: Show Full Screen

15. ENTRANCE: 1-M NEW SHANE HELMS Music "Sugar" Shane Helms w/ SugarBabies
Audio Note: Track Announcer's Mic's @ Announce Position

16. TAPE: (:15)(B-Roll) Clips From Greed- Helms v. Guerrero
Audio Note: Track Tape...Net's Only & Track Announcer's Mic's
Tape Note: Show Full Screen During Entrance

17. RING: "Sugar" Shane Helms Promo
Audio Note: Track Wireless Mic

18. ENTRANCE: 2-M Kidman Music
Audio Note: Track Announcer's Mic's @ Announce Position
Kidman
Witchblade On TNT Bug
Track Announcer's Mic's
Show Lower 3rd When Producer Calls For It

18a. GRAPHICS:
Audio Note:
Infinit Note: Track Announcer's Mic's

19. RING: (8:00)   NON-Title Match-1 Fall- 10 Minute Time Limit
"Sugar" Shane Helms   v.   Kidman
Match Note: Match Begins And Ends In This Segment ...
Agent: Ricky Santana
Referee: Billy Silverman

20. TAPE: (:15)   (Bumper) "Tonight" Huge Announcement From Eric Bischoff + Next Week On Nitro- "Season Final"
Audio Note: Track Nitro Music Under & Track Tape...Net's Only & Track Announcer's Mic's
Tape Note: Show Full Screen & Fades To Black

CM Position #3   (2:34)   08:35:25

Document Created 03/19/01 @ 5:28 PM
This Information Is Subject To Change!

TNT 368   Page #10   Gainesville, FL, Monday, March 19, 2001   Air Time & Program Length: 8:00:00-10:00:00 PM Eastern Time

Segment #4

20a. TAPE: (Op Reel) (:20) **Announcer VO- WCW Road To Spring Break Out Over B-Roll Of University Of Florida (wcw.com)** 08:37:59
Track Announcer's Mic's & Track B-Roll Net's & Track Music Under
Fades Up From Black & Show Full Screen & Tied To Tape

Audio Note:
Graphics Note:

20b. TAPE: (Op Reel) (1:00) **(Spot) WCW Vignette #1- Festivities From U of FL**
Track Op Reel...Self Contained
Fades Up From Black & Show Full Screen & Fades To Black/Tied To Tape

Audio Note:
Tape Note:

21. TAPE: (Pretape) (:30) **(Camcorder) Lex Luger's Locker Room**
Track Pretape Audio & Track Announcer's Mic's & NEEDS CROWD CHEERING UNDER
Show Full Screen & Tied To Pretape

Audio Note:
Tape Note:

23. TAPE: (Pretape) (:45) **(Backstage) Bam Bam Bigelow**
Track Pretape Audio & NEEDS CROWD CHEERING UNDER
Show Full Screen

Audio Note:
Tape Note:

22. ANNOUNCE POS.: (:30) **Tony Schiavone & Scott Hudson**
Track Op Reel & Track Announcer's Mic's @ Announce Position
Needs Lower 3rd Chyron With Announcer ID

Audio Note:
Infinet Note:

23a. TAPE: (Pretape) (1:00) **(Camcorder) Lex Luger's Locker Room**
Track Pretape Audio & Track Announcer's Mic's & NEEDS CROWD CHEERING UNDER
Show Full Screen & Fades To Black/Tied To Bumper

Audio Note:
Tape Note:

24. TAPE: (:15) **(Bumper) "Tonight" Huge Announcement From Eric Bischoff + Next Week On Nitro- "Season Final"**
Track Nitro Music Under & Track Tape...Net's Only & Track Announcer's Mic's
Show Full Screen & Fades To Black

Audio Note:
Tape Note:

CM Position #4 (3:04) WCW MasterCard Spot Played In Arena 08:42:19

Document Created 03/19/01 @ 5:28 PM
This Information is Subject To Change!

465

TNT 368   Page #12   Gainesville, FL, Monday, March 19, 2001   Air Time & Program Length: 8:00:00-10:00:00 PM Eastern Time

Segment #5

24a. ENTRANCE: 1-M Stacy Music
Stacy
Audio Note: Track Announcer's Mic's @ Announce Position

08:45:23

24b. RING: Stacy Introduces Shawn Stasiak
Audio Note: Track Wireless Mic(s)

25. ENTRANCE: 2-M Shawn Stasiak Music
"The Mecca Of Manhood" Shawn "The Star" Stasiak
Audio Note: Track Announcer's Mic's @ Announce Position

26. TAPE: (:15)(B-Roll) Clips From Greed- BBB v. Stasiak
Audio Note: Track Tape... Nat's Only & Track Announcer's Mic's
Tape Note: Show Full Screen During Entrance

27. RING: Shawn Stasiak & Stacy Promo
Audio Note: Track Wireless Mic(s)

27a. GRAPHICS: WCW Spring Breakout Ticket Sales Lower 3rd
Audio Note: Track Announcer's Mic's
Initiate Note: Show Lower 3rd When Producer Calls For It

28. ENTRANCE: 2-M Bam Bam Bigelow Music
Bam Bam Bigelow
Audio Note: Track ALL WIRELESS Mic's & Track Announcer's Mic's @ Announce Position

29. RING: (7:00) 1 Fall- 10 Minute Time Limit
Shawn Stasiak   v.   **Bam Bam Bigelow**
Match Note: Match Begins And Ends In This Segment ...
Agents: Johnny Ace/Terry Taylor
Referee: Mickie 3

30. TAPE: (:15) (Bumper) "Tonight" Huge Announcement From Eric
Bischoff
Audio Note: Track Nitro Music Under & Track Tape... Nat's Only & Track Announcer's Mic's
Tape Note: Show Full Screen & Fades To Black

08:52:38

CM Position #5 (2:30) Set Up Table, Chairs, Contracts, Pens In Ring
Send Terry Taylor To Ring Here

466

TNT 368   Page #15   Gainesville, FL, Monday, March 19, 2001   Air Time & Program Length: 8:00:00-10:00:00 PM Eastern Time

Segment #6

30a. TAPE: (Op Reel)   (:55)   Promotional Considerations #2   08:55:08
Audio Note: *Needs Live WCW Monday Nitro Music & Track Op Reel... Self Contained*
Tape Note: *Fades Up From Black & Show Full Screen & Fades To Black*

33. ENTRANCE: 1-M Scott Steiner Music
Audio Note: **Scott Steiner**
Tape Note: **W/ Midajah & Ric Flair & Animal**
Infiniti Note: *Track Announcer's Mic's @ Announce Position*
WCW World Heavyweight Champ

33a. GRAPHICS: **Witchblade On TNT**
Audio Note: *Track Announcer's Mic's*
Infiniti Note: *Show Lower 3rd When Producer Calls For It*

32. ENTRANCE: 2-M Booker T. Music
Audio Note: **Booker T.**
Pyro Note: *Track Announcer's Mic's @ Announce Position*
Infiniti Note: **Needs Booker T. Pyro Here**
WCW United States Heavyweight Champ

33a. RING: (12:00)   **Booker T. Promo**
Audio Note: *Track Wireless Mic's*

33b. TAPE/AUDIO: (:55)   **(Via Telephone) On Nitro Vision- Still Picture Of Eric Bischoff**
Audio Note: *Track Op Reel & Track Announcer's Mic's If Necessary*
Show Full Screen
Needs Live Chyron In Lower 3rd "Live Via Telephone"

34. RING: **Contract Signing**
Audio Note: *Track Announcer's Mic's @ Announce Position*
Agent: **Johnny Ace**

CM Position #6   (2:34)

Document Created 03/19/01 @ 5:28 PM
This Information Is Subject To Change!

467

TNT 368   Page #17   Gainesville, FL Monday, March 19, 2001   Air Time & Program Length: 8:00:00-10:00:00 PM Eastern Time

Segment #7

34a. ARENA/PROFILE: (:18)   **Closed Captioned PC- Meineke**   09:10:37

Audio Note: Track Op Reel & Track Nitro Music Under & Track Announcer's Mic's @ Announce Position

Tape Note: Fade's Up From Black & Show Full Screen & Fades To Black√Tied To Spot

Announcer Copy: "Closed Captioning Where Available Sponsored By Meineke Discount Mufflers."

34b. TAPE: (Op Reel) (:30)   **(Spot) WCW Road To Spring Breakout Tuned In Sponsored Spot For Next Week- Panama City**

Audio Note: Track Op Reel...Self Contained

Tape Note: Fades Up From Black & Show Full Screen & Fades To Black

34c. TAPE: (:30)   **(Replay) Slo-Mo Replay From Seg #6**

Audio Note: Track Tape... Nat's Only & Track Announcer's Mic's

Tape Note: Show Full Screen

35. TAPE: (Pretape) (:30)   **(Camcorder) Animal & Buff Talking Backstage w/ Ric Flair In His Office**

Audio Note: Track Pretape Audio & NEEDS CROWD CHEERING UNDER

Tape Note: Show Full Screen

36. ENTRANCE: **1-M** Kanyon

Kanyon

Audio Note: Track Announcer's Mic's @ Announce Position

37. TAPE: **(:15)(B-Roll) Clips Greed- Cat v. Kanyon & TNT 367- Kanyon v. Smooth**

Audio Note: Track Tape... Nat's Only & Track Announcer's Mic's

Tape Note: Show Full Screen During Entrance

39. ENTRANCE: **2-M** M.I. Smooth **Music**

M.I. Smooth

Audio Note: Track Announcer's Mic's @ Announce Position

39a. GRAPHICS: **WCW Spring Breakout Ticket Sales Lower 3rd**

Audio Note: Track Announcer's Mic's

Initialit Note: Show Lower 3rd When Producer Calls For It

Document Created 03/19/01 @ 5:28 PM
This Information Is Subject To Change!

468

TNT 368 Page #11 Gainesville, FL Monday, March 19, 2001 Air Time & Program Length: 8:00:00-10:00:00 PM Eastern Time

Segment #7 Continued

40. RING: (6:00) **1 Fall- 10 Minute Time Limit**
Kanyon v. M.I. Smooth

Match Note: Match Begins And Ends In This Segment ...
Agent: Fit Finlay
Referee: Charles Robinson

40a. TAPE: (:15) **(Bumper) "Tonight" Will Ric Flair Kiss Ass??**

Audio Note: Track Nitro Music Under & Track Tape... Nat's Only & Track Announcer's Mic's
Tape Note: Show Full Screen & Fades To Black

CM Position #7 (2:34) **WCW MasterCard Spot Played In Arena**

091:8:40

Document Created 03/19/01 @ 5:28 PM
This Information Is Subject To Change!

469

TNT 368   Page #20/Gainesville, FL, Monday, March 19, 2001   Air Time & Program Length: 8:00:00-10:00:00 PM Eastern Time

Segment #8

40b. TAPE: (Op Reel)   **(1:00)**   **(Spot) WCW Vignette #2- From U Of FL**   09:21:14
Audio Note:
Tape Note: Track Op Reel, Self Contained
Fades Up From Black & Show Full Screen & Fades To Black/Tied To Graphics

40c. GRAPHICS: **(:20)**   **WCW Road To Spring Break Out Graphics W/ Lower 3rd Graphics- Panama City Beach, FL**
Audio Note:
Graphics Note: *Track Announcer's Mic's & Track Music Under*
Tape Note: *Show Full Screen & Tied To Pretape*
Infinit! Note: *(Accompanied By The Panama City Beach Lower Third)*

40d. TAPE: (Pretape)   **(1:00)**   **(Backstage) Dusty & Dustin Rhodes Interview**
Audio Note: *Track Pretape Audio & NEEDS CROWD CHEERING UNDER*
Tape Note: *Show Full Screen*

41. ENTRANCE: **1-M** Rick Steiner Music
Rick Steiner
Audio Note: *Track Announcer's Mic's @ Announce Position*

42. TAPE: **(:15)(B-Roll) Clips From Greed- Rick Steiner v. Booker T.**
Audio Note:
Tape Note: *Track Tape... Mic's Only & Track Announcer's Mic's*
Show Full Screen During Entrance

43. ENTRANCE: **2-M** Konnan Music
Konnan
Audio Note: *Track Announcer's Mic's @ Announce Position*

43a. GRAPHICS: **Witchblade On TNT Bug**
Audio Note: *Track Announcer's Mic's*
Infinit! Note: *Show Lower 3rd When Producer Calls For It*

44. RING: **(6:00)**   **1 Fall- 10 Minute Time Limit**
Konnan   v.   Rick Steiner
Match Note: *Match Begins And Ends In This Segment ...*
Agent: Fit Finlay
Referee: Billy Silverman

CM Position #8   **(2:34)**

Document Created 03/19/01 @ 5:28 PM
This Information Is Subject To Change!

470

TNT 368   Page #22   Gainesville, FL, Monday, March 19, 2001   Air Time & Program Length: 8:00:00-10:00:00 PM Eastern Time

Segment #9

45a. TAPE: (Op Reel)   (:15)   **(Spot) WCW Road To Spring Breakout Tease For** 09:32:08
Audio Note: **Next Week- Panama City**
Tape Note: *Track Op Reel...Self Contained*
Fades Up From Black & Show Full Screen & Fades To Black/Tied To Pretape

46. TAPE: (Pretape)   (1:00)   **(Camcorder) Rick Steiner's Locker Room**
Audio Note: *Track Pretape Audio & NEEDS CROWD CHEERING UNDER*
Tape Note: *Show Full Screen & Tied To Pretape*

47. TAPE: (Pretape)   (:45)   **(Backstage) Lance Storm & Mike Awesome Interview**
Audio Note: *Track Pretape Audio & NEEDS CROWD CHEERING UNDER*
Tape Note: *Show Full Screen & Fades TO Black/Tied To Bumper*

47a. TAPE: (:15)   **(Bumper) "Tonight" Will Ric Flair Kiss Ass??**   09:34:53
Audio Note: *Track Nitro Music Under & Track Tape... Nat's Only & Track Announcer's Mic's*
Tape Note: *Show Full Screen & Fades To Black*

CM Position #9   (3:00)

471

| TNT 368 | Page #23 | Gainesville, FL, Monday, March 19, 2001 | Air Time & Program Length: | 8:00:00-10:00:00 PM Eastern Time |

Segment #10

48. TAPE: (Pretape) (:30) (Camcorder) Ric Flair Talking To Jeff Jarrett 09:37:53
Audio Note: Track... *Pretape Audio & NEEDS CROWD CHEERING UNDER*
Tape Note: *Fades Up From Black & Show Full Screen*

49. ENTRANCE: 1-M Lance Storm Music
"Canadian Killer" Mike Awesome
Lance Storm
Audio Note: *Track Announcer's Mic's @ Announce Position*

50. TAPE: (:15)(B-Roll) Clips From Greed- Awesome/Storm v.
Konnan/Hugh
Audio Note: *Track Tape... Nat's Only & Track Announcer's Mic's*
Tape Note: *Show Full Screen During Entrance*

51. RING: **Lance Storm Promo**
Audio Note: *Track Wireless Mic*

52. ENTRANCE: 2-M O'Haire/Palumbo Music
Sean O'Haire
Chuck Palumbo
Audio Note: *Track Announcer's Mic's @ Announce Position*
Infiniti Note: *WCW World Tag Team Champs*

53. TAPE: (:15)(B-Roll) Clips From Greed-O'Haire/Palumbo v.
Luger/Bagwell
Audio Note: *Track Tape... Nat's Only & Track Announcer's Mic's*
Tape Note: *Show Full Screen During Entrance*

54. RING: (8:00) NON-Title Match- 1 Fall- 10 Minute Time Limit
Lance Storm v. **Sean O'Haire**
Mike Awesome **Chuck Palumbo**
Match Note: *Match Begins And Ends In This Segment...*
Agent: Ricky Santana
Referee: Nick Patrick

55. TAPE: (:15) (Bumper) "Up Next" Will Ric Flair Kiss Ass??
Audio Note: *Track Nitro Music Under & Track Tape... Nat's Only & Track Announcer's Mic's*
Tape Note: *Show Full Screen & Fades To Black* 09:47:08

CM Position #10 (2:30) DJ Ran Performs- House Only

Document Created 03/19/01 @ 5:28 PM
This Information Is Subject To Change!

Segment #11

55a. ARENA/PROFILE: (:08)   **Closing Billboard- Castrol GTX Over Arena Wide** 09:48:38

Audio Note: *Track Op Reel & Track Nitro Music Under & Track Announcer's Mic's @ Announce Position*

Tape Note: *Fades Up From Black & Show Full Screen*

Announcer Copy: "Brought To You By The Motor Oil That Provides Maximum Protection. Castrol GTX, Drive Hard.

56. ENTRANCE: **Ric Flair Music & Entrance**

Audio Note: *Track Ric Flair Music Under & Track Wireless Mic From Arena & Track Announcer's Mic's @ Announce*

57. TAPE: **(:15)(B-Roll) Clips From Greed- Flair/Jarrett v. Rhodes'**

Audio Note: *Track Tape... Nat's Only & Track Announcer's Mic's*

Tape Note: *Show Full Screen During Entrance*

57a. GRAPHICS: **WCW Spring Breakout Ticket Sales Lower 3rd**

Audio Note: *Track Announcer's Mic's*

Infiniti Note: Show Lower 3rd When Producer Calls For It

57b. ENTRANCE: **Jeff Jarrett Music & Entrance**

Audio Note: *Track Jeff Jarrett Music Under & Track Wireless Mic From Arena & Track Announcer's Mic's @ Announce*

58. RING: (8:00)   **Ric Flair Promo**

Audio Note: *Track Wireless Mic*

Agent: *Terry Taylor*

59. ENTRANCE: **Dustin Rhodes Music & Entrance**

Audio Note: *Track DUSTIN Rhodes Music Under & Track Wireless Mic & Track Announcer's Mic's @ Announce*

60. ENTRANCE: **Dusty Rhodes Music & Entrance**

Audio Note: *Track DUSTY RHODES Music Under & Track Wireless Mic & Track Announcer's Mic's @ Announce*

61. INFINITI: **(:05)Copyright-Over Hot Action**

Audio Note: *Need WCW Monday Nitro Music*

Infiniti Note: Need Copyright Chyron

Terminal Break   (:10)   09:57:46

GENERAL Format
TBS 168
Gainesville, FL
Order Of Events
Monday, March 19, 2001   (To Air On Wednesday, March 21, 2001)

9:05 PM Eastern Time   (2:00)   Nitro Girls
1-M   2-M
Disorderly Conduct   v.   Shane Twins
9:10 PM Eastern Time   TAPED- Thunder Starts!
11:00 PM Eastern Time   TAPED- Thunder Ends!

474

TBS 168   Page #1   Gainesville, FL   Wednesday, March 21, 2001   Air Time & Program Length: 9:00-11:00 Eastern Time

00:00:00

SEGMENT #1

101. TAPE: (Op Reel)   (:10)   **WCW Logo Identification**
Audio Note: Track Op. Reel- Self Contained
Tape Note: Fades O/S From Black & Show Full Scr. and & Fades To Black/Tied To Package

102. TAPE: (Op Reel)   (:30)   **(Package) WCW Thunder Open- Highlights From TNT 368**
Audio Note: Track Op. Reel- Self Contained
Tape Note: Fades Up F/ In Black & Show Full Screen & Fades To Black

103. TAPE: (Op Reel)   (:28)   **(Package) WCW Thunder Open**
Audio Note: Track Op. Reel- Self Contained
Tape Note: Fades Up From Black & Show Full Screen & Fades To Black

104. LIVE: (:30)   **Pyro Arena Wide Shot**
Audio Note: Track Announcer's Mic's @ Set & Track Pyro Audio & Needs Live Thunder Music
Int'l/Int' Note: Needs Live Chyron Hit/ Thunder Id
Pyro Note: Go Pyro Program Open

105. ENTRANCE: **1-M** Jung Dragons Music
Audio Note: **Jung Dragons**
   Track Announcer's Mic' s @ Announcer Position

105a. GRAPHICS: **"Enhanced TBS" Promo From Tony Schiavone**
Audio Note: Track Announcer's Mic's

106. ENTRANCE: **2-M** Air Raid Music
   Air Raid
Audio Note: Track Announcer's Mic' s @ Announcer Position

107. RING: (10:00)   **1 Fall- 10 Minute Time Limit**
   Jung Dragons   v.   **Air Raid**
Match Note: Match Begins And Ends In This Segment...
Agent: Ricky Santana
Referee: Scott James

CM Position #1   (3:00)

TBS 168   Page #2   Gainesville, FL, Wednesday, March 21, 2001   Air Time & Program Length: 9:00-11:00 Eastern Time

SEGMENT #2

108. TAPE: (Op Reel)   (:30)   **(B-Roll) Clips From Greed- Rhodes' v. Flair/Jarrett**   09:14:38
Audio Note: Track Op. Reel & Track Announcer's Mic's & MUST HAVE CROWD CHEERING UNDER SHOT
Tape Note: Fades Up From Black & N´ads Thunder Transition On In & Out & Show Full Screen

109. ENTRANCE: **Dustin Rhodes Music & Entrance**
Audio Note: Track Dustin Rhodes Music For Intro & Track Announcer's Mic's @ Announce Position

110. RING: (8:00)   **Dustin Rhodes Promo**
Audio Note: Track Wireless Mic
Agent: Terry Taylor

111. BACKSTAGE: (Live)   **(CAMCORDER) Ric Flair On The ThunderVision**
Audio Note: Track Camera Mic & Track Stick Mic & Track Wireless Mic In Arena

CM Position #2   (3:01)

03/19/01 5:43 PM
This Information Is Subject To Change!!

476

SEGMENT #3

112. ENTRANCE: 1-M Jason Jett Music

Track Announcer's Mic's @ Announce Position

09:26:09

Jason Jett

Audio Note:

113. TAPE: (Op Reel) (:10) (B-Roll) Clips Of Jett Over Alex Wright/Kwee-Wee & Disqo

Track Op Reel & Track Announcer's Mic's... & MUST HAVE CROWD CHEERING UNDER SHOT

Needs Thunder Transition On In & Out & Show Full Screen During Entrance

Audio Note:
Tape Note:

114. ENTRANCE: 2-M Cash Music

Cash

Track Announcer's Mic's @ Announce Position

Audio Note:

114a. GRAPHICS: WCW Spring Break Out Ticket Sales In Lower 3rd Graphics

Track Announcer's Mic's

Audio Note:

115. RING: (10:00) 1 Fall- 10 Minute Time Limit

Jason Jett   v.   Cash

Match Begins And Ends In This Segment...

Match Note:
Agent:
Referee: Fit Finlay, Billy Silverman

116. TAPE: (:15) (Bumper) Tonight- Dustin Rhodes v. Jeff Jarrett & Scott Steiner + "Next Week On Monday Nitro- Season Final!"

Track Tape, Not's Clip & Track Announcer's Mic's & Needs Thunder Asset Xfade
Show Full Screen & Fade To Black

09:36:34

CM Position #3   (2:30)

TBS 168   Page #4   Gainesville, FL   Wednesday, March 21, 2001   Air Time & Program Length: 9:00-11:00 Eastern Time

SEGMENT #4

116a. ARENA/PROFILE: (:08)   **Arena Wide Shot: Closed Caption PC- Meineke**   09:38:54
Audio Note:
Profile Nb x:
Announcer Note: "Closed Captioning Where Available Sponsored By Meineke Discount Mufflers"
Track Op Reel & Track Thunder Music Under & Track Announcer's Mic's @ Announcer Position
Fades Up From Black & Needs Closed Captioning Graphics C'sr Arena Wide Shot

116b. TAPE: (Op Reel) (:10)   **TAPE: Closed Caption PC- Meineke**
Audio Note:
Tape Note:
Track Op Reel
Fades Up From Black & Show Full Screen & Fades To Black/Ted To Pretape

117. TAPE: (Pretape) (1:00)   **(CAMCORDER) Ric Flair Having A Talk With Rick Steiner**
Audio Note:
Tape Note:
Track Pretape Audio & MUST HAVE CROWD CHEERING UNDER SHOT
Fades Up From Black & Show /ul Screen & Ted To Pretape

118. TAPE: (Pretape) (:45)   **(Backstage) The Cat w/ M.I. Smooth & Ms. Jones**
Audio Note:
Tape Note:
Track Pretape Audio & MUST HAVE CROWD, CHEERING UNDER SHOT
Show Full Screen & Fades To Black

119. ARENA: (Live) (:10)   **Arena Wide Shot For Cover Pitch**
Audio Note: Track Announcer's Mic's

120. TAPE: (Op Reel) (2:00)   **(Package) WCW Greed Highlights**
Audio Note:
Page Note:
Track Op Reel
Fade Up From Black & Show Full Screen & Fades To Black

CM Position #4   (2:30)

TBS 168   Page #5   Gainesville, FL Wednesday, March 21, 2001   Air Time & Program Length: 9:00-11:00 Eastern Time

SEGMENT #5

121. ENTRANCE: **1-M** Kanyon Music
Kanyon
Audio Note: Track Announcer's Mic's @ Announce Position

09:46:07

122. TAPE: (Op Reel)   **(:10) (B-Roll) Clips From TNT 368- Kanyon Over Smooth**
Audio Note: Track Op Reel & Track Announcer's Mic's & MUST HAVE CROWD CHEERING UNDER SHOT
Agent:
Tape Note: Needs Thunder Transition On In & Out & Show Full Screen

123. ENTRANCE: **2-M** Animal Music
Road Warrior Animal
Audio Note: Track Announcer's Mic's @ Announce Position

124. ENTRANCE: **3-M** M.I. Smooth Music
M.I. Smooth
Audio Note: Track Announcer's Mic's @ Announce Position

125. ENTRANCE: **4-M** The Cat Music
The Cat
W/ Ms. Jones
Audio Note: Track Announcer's Mic's @ Announce Position

126. RING: **(12:00)** 1 Fall- 10 Minute Time Limit
Kanyon   v.   **The Cat**
Road Warrior Animal   **M.I. Smooth**
Match Note: Match Begins And Ends In This Segment...
Agent: Fit Finlay
Referee: Charles Robinson

127. TAPE: **(:15)** **(Bumper) Tonight- Dustin Rhodes v. Jeff Jarrett & Scott Steiner**
Audio Note: Track Tape, Nat's Only & Track Announcer's Mic's & Needs Thunder Music Under
Tape Note: Slow Full Screen & Fades To Black

CM Break #5 **(3:00)**

09:58:52

TBS 168   Page #6   Gainesville, FL, Wednesday, March 21, 2001   Air Time & Program Length: 9:00-11:00 Eastern Time

SEGMENT #6

128. ENTRANCE:

1-M Rick Steiner Music

Rick Steiner

Audio Note: Track Announcer's Mic's @ Announce Position

10:01:52

129. TAPE: (Op Reel)   **(:10) (B-Roll) Clips From TNT 368- Rick Steiner v. Konnan**

Audio Note: Track Op Reel & Track Announcer's Mic's & MUST HAVE CROWD CHEERING UNDER SHOT

Tape Note: Needs Thunder Transition On In & Out & Show Full Screen

130. ENTRANCE: **2-M** Hugh Morrus Music

Hugh Morrus

Audio Note: Track Announcer's Mic's @ Announce Position

130a. GRAPHICS: **"Enhanced TBS" Promo From Tony Schiavone**

Audio Note: Track Announcer's Mic's

131. RING: (8:00)   **1 Fall- 10 Minute Time Limit**

Rick Steiner   v.   Hugh Morrus

Match Note: Match Begins And Ends In This Segment...

Agent: Fit Finlay

Referee: Mickie J

CM Position #6   (2:30)

TBS 168   Page #7   Gainesville, FL   Wednesday, March 21, 2001   Air Time & Program Length: 9:00-11:00 Eastern Time

SEGMENT #7   Promotional Considerations #1   10:12:22

131a. TAPE: (Op Reel)   (1:06)
Audio Note: Need 2 Live 'Thunder' Music 2 Track Op Reel
Tape Note: Fades Op From Black & Show Full Screen & Fades To Black

132. ARENA: (Live)   (:10)   Arena Wide Shot For Cover Pitch
Audio Note: Track Announcer's Mic's

133. TAPE: (Op Reel)   (:30)   (B-Roll) Clips From Segment #6- Rick Steiner Showing A Fit
Audio Note: Track Op Reel & Track Announcer's Mic's & MUST HAVE CROWD CHEERING UNDER SHOT
Tape Note: Needs 'Thunder' Transition On In & Out & Show Full Screen
Infiniti Note: Needs Live Chyron W/ "During The Break"

134. TAPE: (Pretape)   (1:37)   (CAMCORDER) Shane Douglas Self-Promo
Audio Note: Track Pretape Audio & MUST HAVE CROWD CHEERING UNDER SHOT
Tape Note: Show Full Screen

Backstage

135. ENTRANCE:
1-M ??? Music
"Prime Time"
Kid Romeo
Audio Note: Track Announcer's Mic's @ Announce Position
Infiniti Note: WCW Cruiserweight Tag Team Champs

136. TAPE: (Op Reel)   (:10) (B-Roll) Clips From Greed- "Prime Time" & Kid Romeo
Win The Cruiserweight Tag Titles
Audio Note: Track Op Reel & Track Announcer's Mic's & MUST HAVE CROWD CHEERING UNDER SHOT
Tape Note: Needs 'Thunder' Transition On In & Out & Show Full Screen During Entrance
Content Note: Highlights From Greed – "Prime Time" & Romeo Win CW Tag Title

137. ENTRANCE:
2-M Chavo Guerrero, Jr. Music
Chavo Guerrero, Jr.
Audio Note: Track Announcer's Mic's @ Announce Position

SEGMENT #7   Continued

138. ENTRANCE: **3-M** Filthy Animals Music
Rey Mysterio, Jr.
Kidman

Audio Note: Track Announcer's Mic's @ Announce Position

139. TAPE: (Op Reel)   (:10)   (B-Roll) Clips From Nitro TNT 368- Helms v. Kidman

Audio Note: Track Op Reel & Track Announcer's Mic's & MUST HAVE CROWD CHEERING UNDER SHOT
Tape Note: Needs Thunder Transition On to & Out & Show Full Screen During Entrance

140. ENTRANCE: **4-M** Shane Helms Music
**"Sugar" Shane Helms
w/ SugarBabies**

Audio Note: Track Announcer's Mic's @ Announce Position
Infield/B Note: WCW Cruiserweight Champ

141. RING: (12:00)   Six Man Tag Team Match-1 Fall- 10 Minute Time Limit

"Prime Time"   v.   **Rey Mysterio, Jr.**
Kid Romeo   **Kidman**
Chavo Guerrero, Jr.   **Shane Helms**

Match Note: Match Begins And Ends In This Segment.
Agent: Ricky Santana
Referee: Scott James

142. TAPE: (:15)   (Bumper) Tonight-Dustin Rhodes v. Jeff Jarrett & Scott Steiner

Audio Note: Track Tape... Yank Obey & Track Announcer's Mic's & Needs Thunder Music Under
Tape Note: Show Full Screen & Fades To Black

CM Position #7   (2:31)   16:77:23

482

TBS 168   Page #9   Gainesville, FL   Wednesday, March 21, 2001   Air Time & Program Length: 9:00-11:00 Eastern Time

SEGMENT #8

142a. TAPE: (Op Reel) (:30)   **WCW MasterCard Spot**
Audio Note: Track Prepaid Audio ... Self Contained
Tape N te: Fades Up/Preset Blank & SHOW Full Screen & Fade To Blac; /Tied To Pretape

16:39:54

143. TAPE: (Pretape) (:30)   **(CAMCORDER) Camera Picks Up Rick Steiner Still Throwing A Fit**
Audio Note: Track Prepaid Audio & Track Announcer's MICS & MUST HAVE CROWD CHEERING UNDER SHOT
Tape Note: Show Full Screen & Tied To Pretape

144. TAPE: (Pretape) (:45)   **(Backstage) Chuck Palumbo w/ Sean O'Haire Interview**
Audio Note: Track Pretape Audio & MUST HAVE CROWD CHEERING UNDER SHOT
Tape Note: Show Full Screen & Fades TO Black

CM Position #8 (2:45)

483

TBS 168   Page #10   Gainesville, FL Wednesday, March 21, 2001   Air Time & Program Length: 9:00-11:00 Eastern Time

SEGMENT #9

144a. ARENA/PROFILE: (:08)   **Closing Billboard- Castrol GTX Over Arena Wide Shot** 10:34:34
Audio Note: *Track Op. Reel & Track Thunder Music Under & Track Announcer's Mic's @ Announce Position*
Tape Note: *Fades Up From Black & Show Full Screen*
Announcer Copy: *"Brought To You By The Motor Oil That provides Maximum Protection, Castrol GTX, Drive Hard."*

145. ENTRANCE: **1-M** Lance Storm Music
Audio Note: *Track Announcer's Mic's @ Announce Position*

146. TAPE: (Op Reel)   (:10) (B-Roll) Clips From TNT 368- Awesome/Storm Over O'Haire/Palumbo
Audio Note: *Track Op. Reel & Track Announcer's Mic's & MUST HAVE CROWD CHEERING UNDER SHOT*
Tape Note: *Needs Thunder Transition On In & Out & Show Full Screen*

"Canadian Killer" **Mike Awesome**

147. ENTRANCE: **2-M** Chuck Palumbo Music
Audio Note: *Track Announcer's Mic's @ Announce Position*

Chuck Palumbo

147a. GRAPHICS: **WCW Spring Break Out Ticket Sales In Lower 3rd Graphics**
Audio Note: *Track Announcer's Mic's*

148. RING: (10:00)   **1 Fall- 10 Minute Time Limit**
Mike Awesome   v.   **Chuck Palumbo**
Match Note: *Match Begins And Ends In This Segment...*
Agent: *Johnny Ace*
Referee: *Billy Silverman*

149. TAPE: (:15)   (Bumper) Tonight- Dustin Rhodes v. Jeff Jarrett & Scott **Steiner**
Audio Note: *Track Tape - Nat's Only & Track Announcer's Mic's & Needs Thunder Music Under*
Tape Note: *Show Full Screen & Fades To Back*

CM Position #9 (2:15)   10-66:17

SEGMENT #10

149a. TAPE: (Op Reel) (:55)   Promotional Considerations #2

Audio Note:
Tape Note: Music Like Thunder Music & 7Track Op Reel
Fades Up From Black & Show "Full" Screen & Fades To Black   10:47:32

150. TAPE: (Op Reel)   (:30)   (B-Roll) Clips From Seg #2- Earlier Tonight- Dustin Rhodes &
Ric Flair Setting Up This Match

Audio Note: Track Op Reel & Track Announcer's Mic's & MUST HAVE CROWD CHEERING UNDER SHOT
Tape Note: Needs Thunder Transition On In & Out & Show Full Screen

Content Note: Replay From Earlier (Seg #2) - Soundbites Setting Up This Match

151. ENTRANCE: **2-M** Scott Steiner Music
                                          Scott Steiner
Audio Note: **W/ Midajah**
                                          Track Announcer's Mic's @ Announce Position
                                          WCW World Heavyweight Champ

150a. ENTRANCE: **1-M** Jeff Jarrett Music
                                          Jeff Jarrett
Audio Note: Track Announcer's Mic's @ Announce Position

153. RING: (2:00)   **Scott Steiner Promo**

Audio Note: Track Wireless Mic
Infinitil Note:

155. TAPE: (Pretape)   (:30)   (CAMCORDER) Animal Leading The Camera Down The Hall
                                          To Flair's Office
Audio Note: Track Pretape Audio & Track Announcers Mic's & MUST HAVE CROWD CHEERING UNDER SHOT
Tape Note: Show Full Screen & Fades To Black

CM Position #10   (3:16)   Music Performance- House Only

485

TBS 169   Page #12   Gainesville, FL   Wednesday, March 21, 2001   Air Time & Program Length: 9:00-11:00 Eastern Time

SEGMENT #11

156. ENTRANCE:

3-M Dustin Rhodes Music

Dustin Rhodes
Track Announcer's Mic's @ Announce Position

Audio Note:

10:54:43

156a. GRAPHICS:

WCW Spring Break Out Ticket Sales In Lower 3rd Graphics
Track Announcer's Mic's

Audio Note:

157. RING: (8:00)

Handicap Match~ 1 Fall, 15 Minute Time Limit
Track Announcer's Mic's

Scott Steiner v.   **Dustin Rhodes**

Jeff Jarrett
Match Begins And Ends In This Segment...

Match Note:
Agent: Terry Taylor
Referee: Nick Patrick

158. Infiniti:

Copyright- Shown Over Hot Action
Needs Thunder Music

Audio Note:

11:02:43

Terminal Break:

Hard Out @ 11:04:45

-----Original Message-----

From: Snyder, Tracey

Sent: Friday, March 23, 2001 3:34 PM

To: *WCW (TBS)

Subject: Announcement

March 23, 2001

To: WCW Staff

From: Brad Siegel

RE: WWF announcement

Today, World Wrestling Federation Entertainment, Inc. is announcing that we have reached an agreement for the sale of WCW. This agreement with WWF holds tremendous potential for the WCW brand and assets. The press release announcing the news is attached.

As we told you last week, WCW programming will not appear on TNT and TBS Superstation after March 27. We will share more information with you about the WWF's immediate plans for WCW in the all-staff meeting scheduled for Wednesday, March 28, at 10 a.m. at the Power Plant.

Thank you.

DAVID PENZER

THANK YOU FOR READING!

Made in the USA
Middletown, DE
30 August 2024

60078696R00278